Microsoft Dynamics CRM 2016 Customization

Second Edition

Use a no-code approach to create powerful business solutions using Dynamics CRM 2016

Nicolae Tarla

BIRMINGHAM - MUMBAI

Microsoft Dynamics CRM 2016 Customization

Second Edition

Copyright © 2016 Packt Publishing

All rights reserved. No part of this book may be reproduced, stored in a retrieval system, or transmitted in any form or by any means, without the prior written permission of the publisher, except in the case of brief quotations embedded in critical articles or reviews.

Every effort has been made in the preparation of this book to ensure the accuracy of the information presented. However, the information contained in this book is sold without warranty, either express or implied. Neither the author, nor Packt Publishing, and its dealers and distributors will be held liable for any damages caused or alleged to be caused directly or indirectly by this book.

Packt Publishing has endeavored to provide trademark information about all of the companies and products mentioned in this book by the appropriate use of capitals. However, Packt Publishing cannot guarantee the accuracy of this information.

First published: December 2014

Second edition: May 2016

Production reference: 1230516

Published by Packt Publishing Ltd.
Livery Place
35 Livery Street
Birmingham B3 2PB, UK.

ISBN 978-1-78588-151-0

www.packtpub.com

Credits

Author
Nicolae Tarla

Reviewer
Ian Grieve

Commissioning Editor
Veena Pagare

Acquisition Editor
Ruchita Bhansali

Content Development Editor
Sanjeet Rao

Technical Editor
Deepti Tuscano

Copy Editor
Merilyn Pereira

Project Coordinator
Judie Jose

Proofreader
Safis Editing

Indexer
Mariammal Chettiyar

Graphics
Disha Haria

Production Coordinator
Conidon Miranda

Cover Work
Conidon Miranda

About the Author

Nicolae Tarla is a Microsoft Dynamics CRM consultant involved in solution architecture and technical presales. He has worked on various mid-size to enterprise-level Dynamics CRM and SharePoint implementations for both the private and public sectors. He has been delivering Microsoft Dynamics CRM solutions since version 3.0 of the product.

Nicolae was a technical reviewer on the book *Microsoft Dynamics CRM 2011: Dashboards Cookbook, Packt Publishing,* wrote *Microsoft Dynamics CRM 2011: Scripting Cookbook* as well as the previous edition of *Microsoft Dynamics CRM Customization Essentials, Packt Publishing,* and is an active blogger at `http://www.thecrmwiz.com`. He has also presented at various public events, including eXtreme CRM in 2014.

In 2014, Nicolae was awarded the Business Solutions MVP title for his Dynamics CRM contributions.

I would like to thank my family for the ongoing support provided during this project.

Also a big thumbs up to the community for being there, being active, and driving me to engage in yet another book project. You rock!

About the Reviewer

Ian Grieve is a Microsoft® Most Valuable Professional for Microsoft Dynamics GP and is also a certified Dynamics CRM consultant specializing in the delivery of Microsoft Dynamics GP and CRM projects. He is the ERP Practice Manager at Perfect Image Ltd. and a Microsoft Partner and VAR in the North East of England.

Ian has worked with Microsoft Dynamics GP since 2003 and, since then, has dealt with all aspects of the product life cycle from presales to implementation, to technical and functional training, to post go-live support, and subsequent upgrades and process reviews.

Alongside his work with Microsoft Dynamics GP, he has fulfilled a similar role since joining Perfect Image, dealing with Microsoft Dynamics CRM with special emphasis on project delivery and the training of end users on the management of sales, marketing, and service.

Ian is the author of *Microsoft Dynamics GP 2013 Financial Management*, *Implementing the Microsoft Dynamics GP Web Client and Microsoft Dynamics GP Workflow 2.0*, coauthor of *Microsoft Dynamics GP 2013 Cookbook*, produced the *Microsoft Dynamics GP Techniques* online learning course, and was the technical reviewer for several Microsoft Dynamics CRM books published by *Packt Publishing* including *Microsoft Dynamics CRM 2011 Cookbook*.

In his spare time, Ian runs the azurecurve – Ramblings of a Dynamics GP Consultant (`http://www.azurecurve.co.uk`) blog dedicated to Microsoft Dynamics GP and related products.

The most recent offshoot of running his blog is that Ian started writing plugins to extend the functionality of the blogging platform, WordPress. A new site, azurecurve WordPress Development (`http://wordpress.azurecurve.co.uk`), contains information on his plugins, and so does the new blog, where he discusses how development of plugins is done.

www.PacktPub.com

eBooks, discount offers, and more

Did you know that Packt offers eBook versions of every book published, with PDF and ePub files available? You can upgrade to the eBook version at www.PacktPub.com and as a print book customer, you are entitled to a discount on the eBook copy. Get in touch with us at customercare@packtpub.com for more details.

At www.PacktPub.com, you can also read a collection of free technical articles, sign up for a range of free newsletters and receive exclusive discounts and offers on Packt books and eBooks.

https://www2.packtpub.com/books/subscription/packtlib

Do you need instant solutions to your IT questions? PacktLib is Packt's online digital book library. Here, you can search, access, and read Packt's entire library of books.

Why subscribe?

- Fully searchable across every book published by Packt
- Copy and paste, print, and bookmark content
- On demand and accessible via a web browser

Instant updates on new Packt books

Get notified! Find out when new books are published by following @PacktEnterprise on Twitter or the *Packt Enterprise* Facebook page.

Table of Contents

Preface

Microsoft Dynamics CRM 2016 Customization covers the structure and configuration and customization options available to a Dynamics CRM power user. The book takes the reader on a journey through the basics of the platform, then delves into the customization options available and finishes with a high level overview of various administrative options.

What this book covers

Chapter 1, Getting Started, walks you through an introduction of the platform, and guides you through setting up the trial environment used through the book. No prior knowledge of Dynamics CRM or other skills is assumed. Upon completion of this chapter, the reader will have a free trial sandbox environment valid for 30 days, as well as the client-side configuration for certain scenarios.

Chapter 2, The Dynamics CRM Application Structure, delves into the Dynamics CRM application's structure and describes the standard modules, the elements available for customization, and their relationships to each module, as well as the available options to extend the platform further. In this chapter, you will understand how to manage the existing application structure, how to extend and/or modify the modules, and how to update the navigation accordingly.

Chapter 3, Dynamics CRM Customization, builds on the knowledge gained in the previous chapter, and goes one step further by showing the reader how to work with entities within the existing modules, how to customize and extend these entities, and how to create logical relationships between them. In addition, this chapter will loop back and reference the previous chapter by describing how these new customizations fit within the application modules, and how they can live across various modules. This chapter will also analyze the various document storage options, and the impact of choosing one model versus another.

Chapter 4, Building Better Business Functionality, takes you into the meat of the application by looking at how business affects the behavior of the platform. The reader will look at how to enforce the business rules on the platform, and how to create customizations that will guide and correct the user, thus making sure the platform works with the user. Specific features and enhancements of the platform make it easy for businesses to map their current processes on this platform. Integration with the Microsoft Office suite of products makes Dynamics CRM an even stronger platform, giving users the ability to experience a familiar interface.

Chapter 5, Dynamics CRM – Additional Features, gives you a glimpse inside and outside the platform by diving first into the internal aspects of the platform that have received great enhancements over the last few versions of the product, and then tapping into external data from the market, as well as customers and prospects. You will get an introduction to some of the new features introduced into Dynamics CRM, and you will also get some pointers for the integration with platforms around social and marketing, as well as an overview of analytics options available with the platform and the complementary products.

Chapter 6, Dynamics CRM Administration, guides you through generic administration options available on the platform. While this is by no means an exhaustive guide to the application of administration, this chapter aims to give you enough knowledge about the administration options to provide a base of knowledge. In addition, references to Microsoft documentation will point the readers to available sources to enhance their knowledge.

What you need for this book

Following the instructions provided in *Chapter 1, Getting Started*, you will be able to create a 30-day trial of Dynamics CRM Online. This environment can be used to experiment with the configurations described in this book.

In addition, Microsoft Office Outlook can be used to integrate with this environment. *Chapter 1, Getting Started*, also described how to configure this integration.

No other software or hardware is required.

Who this book is for

This book is the basic guide for both new and seasoned Microsoft Dynamics CRM end users. It takes a gradual approach to presenting the platform, starting with the basic structure, looking at customization options, and ending with basic administration concepts.

A new user will be slowly guided through the basic concepts of the platform, the structure, and the customization options, so that he/she can become a power user.

An advanced user will find coverage of certain platform aspects that he/she has not yet worked with, or will find specific gems about the differences between versions of the platform, and new features introduced with the latest version.

A power user will find details and concepts that will help him/her become better, faster, more efficient, and proficient at customizing the platform. In addition, he/she will get an overview of the platform administration's options, helping to close the communication gap between users and administrators.

This book takes a no-code approach to basic configuration and customization concepts, and is aimed at non-developers. It is intended as a guide for someone evaluating the platform features, starting new on the platform, or as reference material during the platform's life.

Due to the relatively small book size, this is by no means a comprehensive encyclopedia, but rather a reference guide to be used to quickly and efficiently ramp up on Dynamics CRM's basic concepts.

Conventions

In this book, you will find a number of text styles that distinguish between different kinds of information. Here are some examples of these styles and an explanation of their meaning.

Code words in text, database table names, folder names, filenames, file extensions, pathnames, dummy URLs, user input, and Twitter handles are shown as follows: "`OrganizationName` is the name you have selected for your online organization."

New terms and **important words** are shown in bold. Words that you see on the screen, for example, in menus or dialog boxes, appear in the text like this: "A user with necessary permission can navigate to **Settings** | **Dynamics Marketplace**."

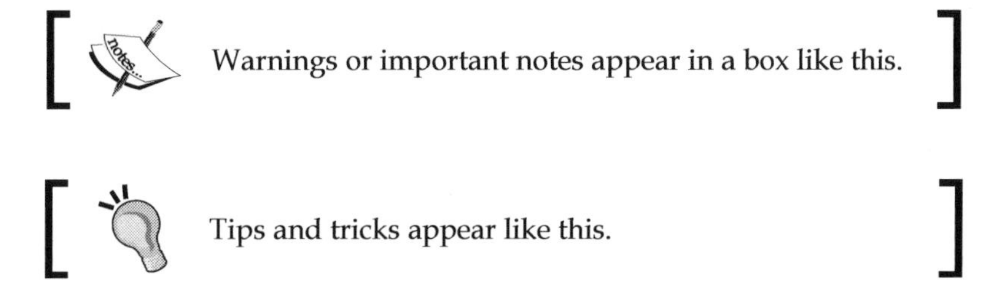

Warnings or important notes appear in a box like this.
Tips and tricks appear like this.

Reader feedback

Feedback from our readers is always welcome. Let us know what you think about this book—what you liked or disliked. Reader feedback is important for us as it helps us develop titles that you will really get the most out of.

To send us general feedback, simply e-mail `feedback@packtpub.com`, and mention the book's title in the subject of your message.

If there is a topic that you have expertise in and you are interested in either writing or contributing to a book, see our author guide at `www.packtpub.com/authors`.

Customer support

Now that you are the proud owner of a Packt book, we have a number of things to help you to get the most from your purchase.

Downloading the color images of this book

We also provide you with a PDF file that has color images of the screenshots/diagrams used in this book. The color images will help you better understand the changes in the output. You can download this file from `http://www.packtpub.com/sites/default/files/downloads/MicrosoftDynamicsCRM2016Customization_ColorImages.pdf`.

Errata

Although we have taken every care to ensure the accuracy of our content, mistakes do happen. If you find a mistake in one of our books—maybe a mistake in the text or the code—we would be grateful if you could report this to us. By doing so, you can save other readers from frustration and help us improve subsequent versions of this book. If you find any errata, please report them by visiting `http://www.packtpub.com/submit-errata`, selecting your book, clicking on the **Errata Submission Form** link, and entering the details of your errata. Once your errata are verified, your submission will be accepted and the errata will be uploaded to our website or added to any list of existing errata under the Errata section of that title.

To view the previously submitted errata, go to `https://www.packtpub.com/books/content/support` and enter the name of the book in the search field. The required information will appear under the **Errata** section.

Piracy

Piracy of copyrighted material on the Internet is an ongoing problem across all media. At Packt, we take the protection of our copyright and licenses very seriously. If you come across any illegal copies of our works in any form on the Internet, please provide us with the location address or website name immediately so that we can pursue a remedy.

Please contact us at `copyright@packtpub.com` with a link to the suspected pirated material.

We appreciate your help in protecting our authors and our ability to bring you valuable content.

Questions

If you have a problem with any aspect of this book, you can contact us at `questions@packtpub.com`, and we will do our best to address the problem.

1
Getting Started

The **Customer Relationship Management** (**CRM**) market has seen a huge uptake in the last few years. Some of the drivers for this market are the need to enhance customer experience, provide faster and better services, and adapting to the customer's growing digital presence. CRM systems, in general, are taking a central place in the new organizational initiatives.

Dynamics CRM is Microsoft's response to a growing trend. The newest version is Dynamics CRM 2016. It is being offered in a variety of deployment scenarios. From the standard on-premise deployment to a private cloud, or an online cloud offering from Microsoft, the choice depends on each customer, their type of project, and a large number of requirements, policies, and legal restrictions.

In this chapter, we'll first look at the environment we need to complete the examples presented in the book. We will create a new environment, based on a Microsoft Dynamics CRM Online trial. This approach will give us 30-day trial to experiment with an environment for free.

The following topics will be covered in this chapter:

- Introducing Dynamics CRM
- Dynamics CRM's features
- Deployment models
- Global datacenter locations
- Customization requirements
- Getting setup

Introducing Dynamics CRM

Dynamics CRM 2016 is the current version of the popular Customer Relationship Management platform offered by Microsoft. This platform offers users the ability to integrate and connect data across their sales, marketing, and customer service activities, and to give staff an overall 360-degree view of all interactions and activities as they relate to a specific customer.

Along with the standard platform functionality provided, we have a wide range of customization options, allowing us to extend and further customize solutions to solve a majority of other business requirements. In addition, we can integrate this platform with other applications to create a seamless solution.

Being the only available CRM platform on the market today, Microsoft Dynamics CRM 2016 is one of the fastest growing, gaining large acceptance at all levels, from small to mid-size and enterprise-level organizations. This is due to a multitude of reasons, some of which include the variety of deployment options, the scalability, the extensibility, the ease of integration with other systems, and the ease of use.

Microsoft Dynamics CRM can be deployed in a variety of options. Starting with the offering from Microsoft, you can get CRM Online. Once we have a 30-day trial active, this can be easily turned into a full production environment by providing payment information and keeping the environment active. The data will live in the cloud, on one of the data centers provided by Microsoft.

Alternatively, you can obtain hosting with a third-party provider. The whole environment can be hosted by a third party, and the service can be offered either as a SaaS solution or a fully hosted environment. Usually, there is a difference in the way payment is processed, with a SaaS solution, in most cases, being offered in a monthly subscription model.

Another option is to have the environment hosted in-house. This option is called on-premise deployment and carries the highest up-front cost but gives you the ability to customize the system extensively. In addition to the higher up-front cost, the cost to maintain the environment, the hardware, and the skilled people required to constantly administer the environment can easily add-up.

As of recently, we now have the ability to host a virtual CRM environment in **Azure**. This offloads the cost of maintaining the local infrastructure in a fashion similar to a third-party-hosted solution but takes advantage of the scalability and performance of a large cloud solution maintained and supported fully by Microsoft. The following white paper released by Microsoft describes the deployment model using Azure Virtual Machines:

`http://www.microsoft.com/en-us/download/details.aspx?id=49193`

Features of Dynamics CRM

Some of the most notable features of the Dynamics CRM platform include:

- Scalability
- Extensibility
- Ability to integrate with other systems
- Ease of use

Let's look at each of the features in more detail.

Scalability

Dynamics CRM can scale over a wide range of deployment options. From a single-box deployment, used mostly for development, all the way to a cloud offering that can span over a large number of servers, and can host a large number of environments, the same base solution can handle all the scenarios in between with ease.

Extensibility

Dynamics CRM is a platform in which the base offering comes with prepackaged functionality for sales, service, and marketing; and a large variety of solutions can be built on top of Dynamics CRM. The extensibility model is called xRM and allows power users, non-developers, and developers alike to build custom solutions to handle various other business scenarios or integrate with other third-party platforms.

The Dynamics CRM Marketplace is a great example of such solutions built to extend the core platform, and offered for sale by various companies. These companies are called **Independent Software Vendors (ISVs)** and play a very important role in the ecosystem created by Microsoft. In time and with enough experience, some of them become the go-to partners for various implementations.

If nothing else, the Dynamics Marketplace is a cool place to look at some of the solutions created and search for specific applications. The idea of the marketplace became public sometime around 2010 and was integrated into Dynamics CRM 2011. At launch, it was designed as a searchable repository of solutions. It is a win-win for both solution providers and customers alike. Solutions can also be rated, thus giving customers better community feedback before committing to purchasing and implementing a foreign solution into their organization.

The Dynamics Marketplace is hosted on Pinpoint, Microsoft's online directory of software applications and professional services. On this platform, independent companies, and certified partners offer their products and services. At the time of this writing, Pinpoint hosts a few marketplaces, including Office, Azure, Dynamics, and Cloud, and is available at the following location:

`https://pinpoint.microsoft.com/en-CA/Home/Dynamics`

Navigating to the Dynamics page you are presented with a search option as seen in the following screenshot:

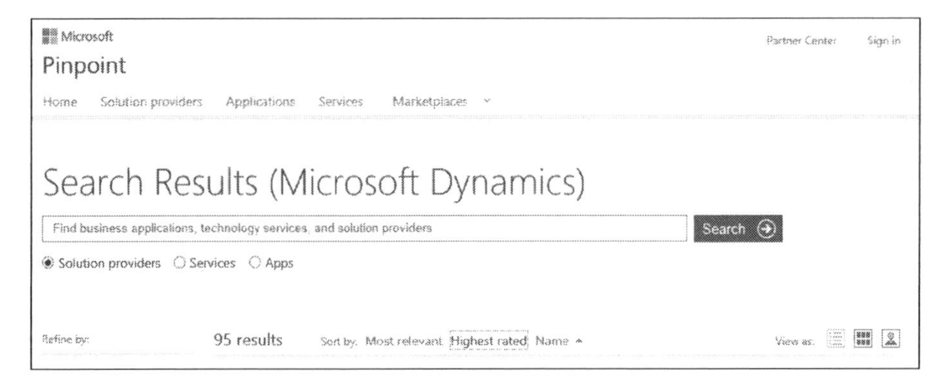

You now have the option to filter your results by **Solution providers**, **Services**, or **Apps** (applications).

In addition, you can further filter your results by distance to a geo-location derived from an address or postal code, as well as other categories as illustrated in the following screenshot:

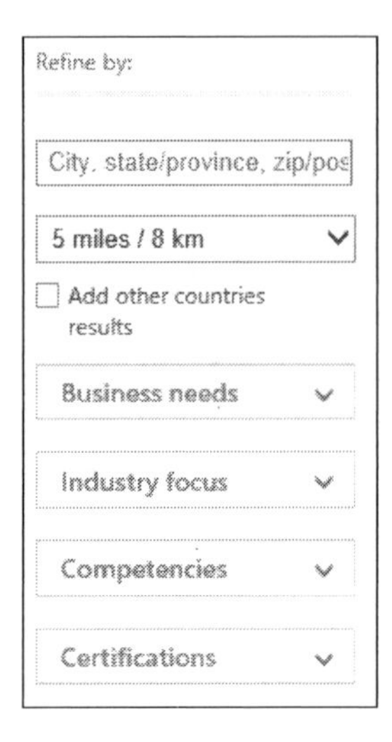

When searching for a solution provider, the results provide a high-level view of the organization, with a logo and a high-level description. The ratings and competencies count are displayed for easy visibility as shown here:

Drilling down into the partner profile page, you can find additional details on the organization, the industry's focus, details on the competencies, as well as a way to connect with the organization. Navigation to additional details, including **Reviews** and **Locations**, is available on the profile page.

The Dynamics Marketplace is also available, starting with Dynamics CRM 2011, as a part of the organization. A user with necessary permission can navigate to **Settings** | **Dynamics Marketplace**.

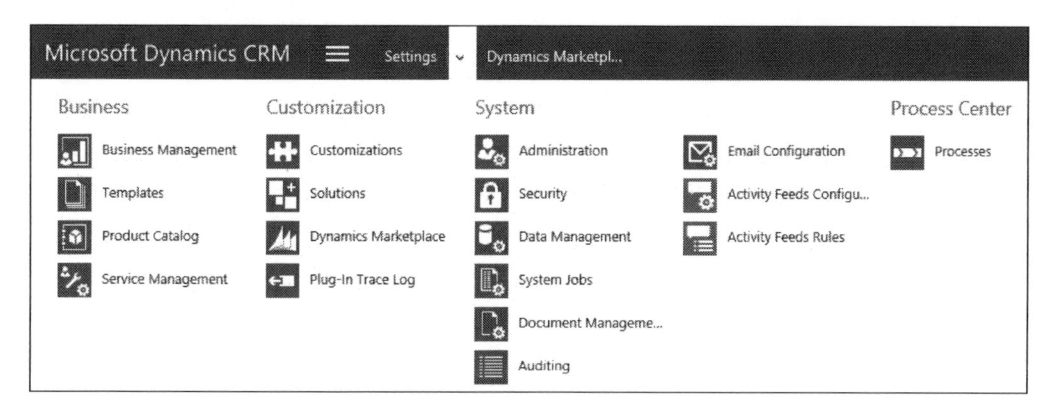

This presents the user with a view by solutions available. Options for sorting and filtering include **Popular**, **Newest**, and **Featured**. Community rating is clearly visible and provides the necessary feedback to consider when evaluating new solutions.

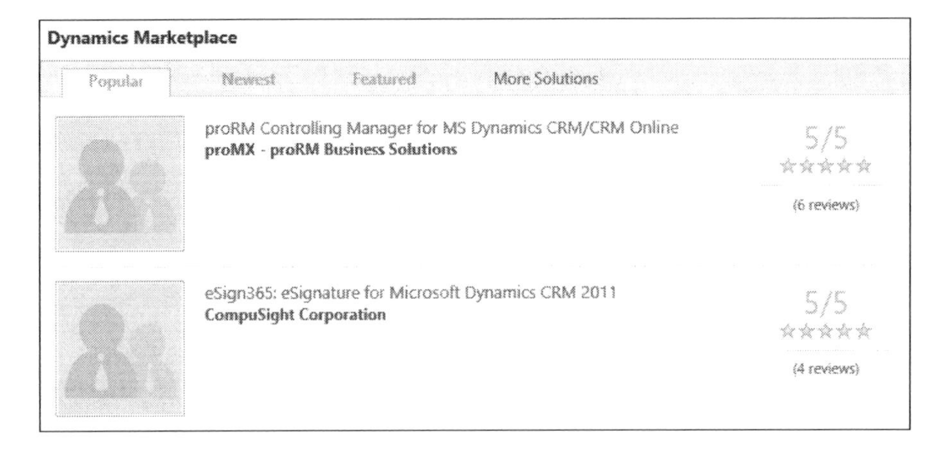

Ability to integrate with other systems

There is a large variety of integration options available when working with Dynamics CRM. In addition, various deployment options offer more or fewer integration features. With CRM Online, you tend to get more integration options into cloud services, whereas the on-premise solution has a limited number of configurable integration options, but can provide more integration using various third-party tools. The base solution comes with the ability to configure integration with the following common services:

- SharePoint for document management
- Yammer for social features

In addition, you can use specific connectors provided by either Microsoft or other third-party providers for integration with specific solutions.

When the preceding options are not available, you can still integrate with other solutions using a third-party integration tool. This allows real-time integration into legacy systems. Some of the most popular tools used for integration include, but are not limited to:

- Kingsway Software (`https://www.kingswaysoft.com/`)
- Scribe (`http://www.scribesoft.com/`)
- BizTalk (`http://www.microsoft.com/en-us/server-cloud/products/biztalk/`)

Ease of use

Dynamics CRM offers users a variety of options to interact with the system. You can access Dynamics CRM through a browser, with support for all recent versions of the major browsers now. The following browsers and versions are supported:

- Internet Explorer versions 10 and above
- Edge latest version
- Chrome latest version on Windows 7 and above
- Firefox latest version on Windows 7 and above
- Safari on Mac using the latest publicly released version on OS X 10.8 and above

In addition, a user can interact with the system directly from the very familiar interface of Outlook. The Dynamics CRM connector for Outlook allows users to get access to all the system data and features from within Outlook. In addition, a set of functions built specifically for Outlook allows users to track and interact through e-mails, tasks, and events from within Outlook.

Further to the features provided through the Outlook integration, users of CRM for Outlook have the ability to work offline. Data can be taken offline, work can be done while disconnected, and can be synchronized back into the system when connectivity resumes.

For mobile users, Dynamics CRM can be accessed from mobile devices and tablets. Dynamics CRM provides a standard web-based interface for most mobile devices, as well as specific applications for various platforms including Windows-based tablets, iPads, and Android tablets. With these apps, you can also take a limited sub-set of cached data offline, as well have the ability to create new records and synchronize them back to CRM next time you go online. The quality of these mobile offerings has increased exponentially over the last few versions, and new features are being added with each new release.

In addition, third-party providers have also built mobile solutions for Dynamics CRM. A quick search in the application markets for each platform will reveal several options for each platform.

Global Data Center Locations for Dynamics CRM Online

Dynamics CRM Online is hosted at various locations in the world. Preview organizations can be created in all available locations, but features are sometimes rolled out on a schedule, in some locations faster than others.

The format of the Dynamics CRM Online Organization URL describes the data center location. As such, the standard format is as follows:

```
https://OrganizationName.crm[x].dynamics.com
```

The `OrganizationName` is the name you have selected for your online organization. This is customizable and is validated for uniqueness within the respective data center.

`[x]` represents a number. As of this writing, this number can be anywhere between 2, 4, 5, 6, 7, 9, or no number at all. This describes the global data center used to host your organization. The following table maps the data center to the URL format:

URLformat: crm[x].dynamics.com	Global data centre location
`crm.dynamics.com`	NAM
`crm2.dynamics.com`	SAM
`crm4.dynamics.com`	EMEA
`crm5.dynamics.com`	APAC
`crm6.dynamics.com`	OCE
`crm7.dynamics.com`	JPN
`crm9.dynamics.com`	GCC

Out of these global locations, usually the following get a preview and the new features first:

Organization	Global location
`crm.dynamics.com`	North America
`crm4.dynamics.com`	Europe, the Middle East, and Africa
`crm5.dynamics.com`	Asia-Pacific

New data centers are being added on a regular basis. At the time of writing, new data centers are being added in Europe and Canada, with others to follow as needed.

Some of the drivers behind adding these new data centers revolve around not only performance improvements, as a data center located closer to a customer will provide theoretically better performance, but also a need for privacy and localization of data. Strict legislation around data residency has a great impact on the selection of the deployment model by customers who are bound to store all data local to the country of operation.

In total, by the end of 2016, the plan is to have Dynamics CRM Online available in 105 markets. These markets (countries) will be served by data centers spread across five generic global regions.

These data centers share services between Dynamics CRM Online and other services such as Azure and Office 365.

Advantages of Choosing Dynamics CRM Online

Choosing one of the available hosting models for Dynamics CRM is now not only a matter of preference. The decision can be driven by multiple factors.

During the last few years, there has been a huge push for the cloud. Microsoft has been very focused on enhancing their Online offering, and has continued to push more functionality and more resources in supporting the cloud model. As such, Dynamics CRM Online has become a force to reckon with. It is hosted on a very modern and high performing infrastructure. Microsoft has pushed literally billions of dollars into new data centers and infrastructure. This allows new customers to forego the necessary expenses on infrastructure associated with an on-premise deployment.

Along with investments on infrastructure, the **Service Level Agreement** (**SLA**) offered by Dynamics CRM Online is financially backed by Microsoft. Depending on the service selected, the uptime is guaranteed and backed financially. Application and infrastructure are automatically handled by Microsoft so you don't have to. This translates into much lower upfront costs, as well as reduced costs around ongoing maintenance and upgrades.

The Dynamics CRM Online offering is also compliant with various regulatory requirements, and is backed and verified through various third-party tests. Various rules, regulations, and policies in various locales are validated and certified by various organizations. Some of the various compliance policies evaluated include but are not limited to:

- Data Privacy and Confidentiality Policies
- Data Classification
- Information Security
- Privacy
- Data Stewardship
- Secure Infrastructure
- Identity and Access Control

All these compliance requirements are in conformance with regulations stipulated by the International Standard Organization and other international and local standards. Independent auditors validate standards compliance rules. Microsoft is ISO 27001 certified.

The Microsoft Trust Center website located at `http://www.microsoft.com/en-us/trustcenter/CloudServices/Dynamics` provides additional information on compliance, responsibilities, and warranties.

Further to the aforementioned benefits, choosing cloud over a standard on-premise deployment offers other advantages around scalability, faster time to market, and higher value proposition.

In addition to the standard benefits of an online deployment, one other great advantage is the ability to spin-up a 30-day trial instance of Dynamics CRM Online and convert it to a paid instance only when ready to go to production. This allows customizers and companies to get started and customize their solution in a free environment, with no additional costs attached. The 30-day trial instance gives us a 25-license instance, which allows us to not only customize the organization, but also test various roles and restrictions.

What do you need to customize Dynamics CRM?

First and foremost, in order to follow through with the information presented in this book, you will need an instance of Dynamics CRM Online. The following sections will describe in detail how to obtain a 30-day trial instance.

In addition, in order to subscribe to a 30-day trial, you will need a Microsoft account (formerly called Live account). You can obtain one by going to `https://signup.live.com/`.

The `Create an account` page presents you with a signup form. In the **User name** area, make sure to click on the **Get a new email address** link to have a new address created, as shown in the following screenshot:

User name

someone@example.com

Get a new email address

At the time of writing, you have a choice to select between `www.outlook.com` and `www.hotmail.com` for your newly created e-mail address. The selected username is validated, as it must be unique.

Once your account is created, you are logged into your new account and can see the welcome e-mail. At this point, you can use this account to create your 30-day trial for Dynamics CRM Online.

If you do have an existing Microsoft account, you do not need to create a new one. You can create multiple trials for both Dynamics CRM Online and Office 365.

Steps to Setting up an Environment

While this book will provide step-by-step instructions to be followed, it is strongly recommended to have an environment available to supplement the material you will be reading, and to become familiar with the platform. In order to minimize the footprint and to allow everybody to start quickly, I have opted to present all the topics based on a Dynamics CRM Online 30-day trial organization.

Opening a free 30-day trial of Dynamics CRM Online

In order to open your 30-day trial of Microsoft Dynamics CRM Online, you will need to go through a wizard-driven process.

First of all, navigate to `http://go.microsoft.com/fwlink/?LinkId=252780`

You are presented with a three-step wizard process that allows you, in a very simple manner, to sign up and provision a brand new organization.

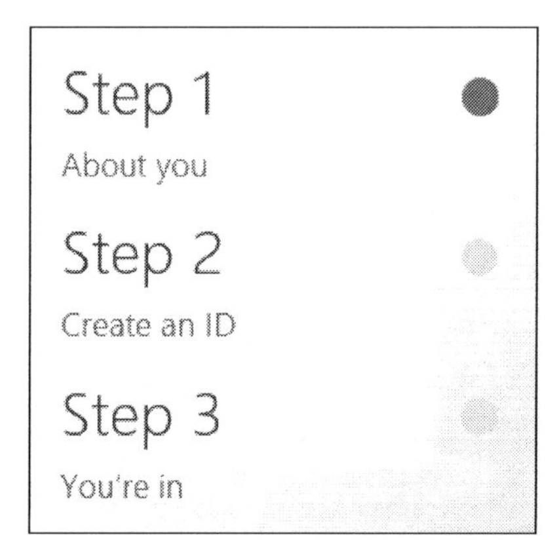

At the top-right side of the page, you will find an option to add this to an existing subscription. If you start by creating your Office 365 subscription first, you can proceed here to add Dynamics CRM Online to your existing subscription. Follow the **Sign in** link to authenticate to your existing Office 365 subscription, as seen in the following screenshot:

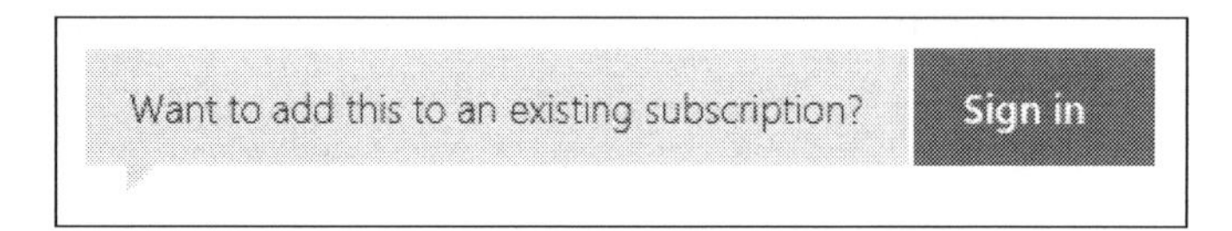

Because we are creating our Dynamics CRM Online organization first, we will ignore this option and move on to filling in the required form fields. The first option you need to select is the Country. Pay close attention to the note underneath, this is one of the options that cannot be changed afterwards.

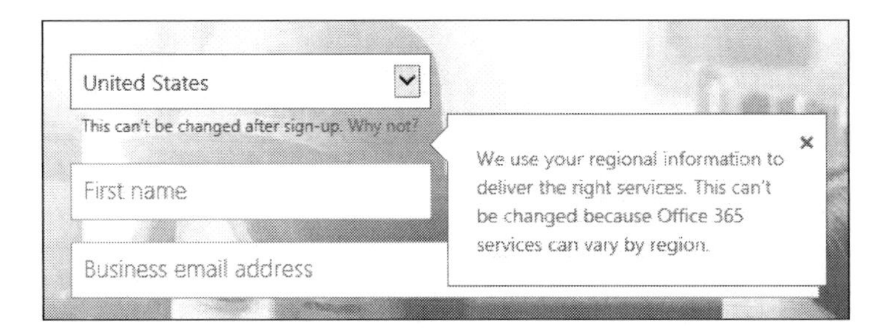

As stated in the description, this selection defines the region and implicitly the data center used for hosting your organization.

Fill in the rest of the information on the form and click on **Next** when ready.

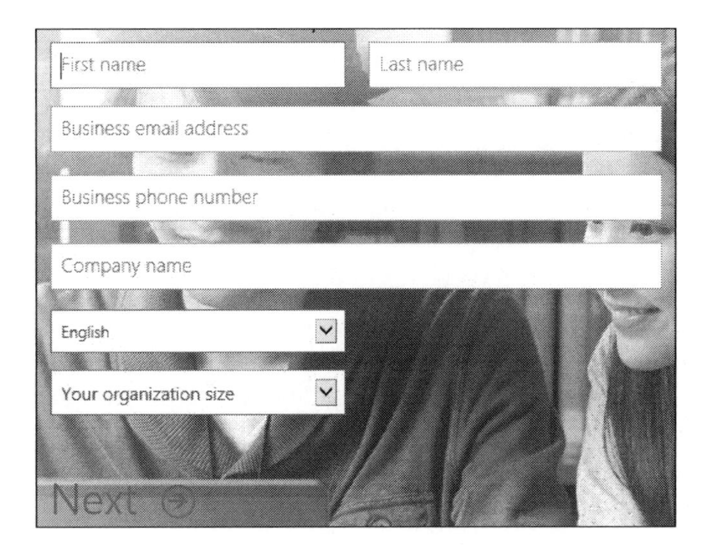

Company name on this form does not define the organization URL, you will be prompted for this information in the following step.

Step two of the wizard collects information about the username and organization URL you want to use. It also collects your initial password. Enter the desired username, organization name, and password, as seen in the following screenshot:

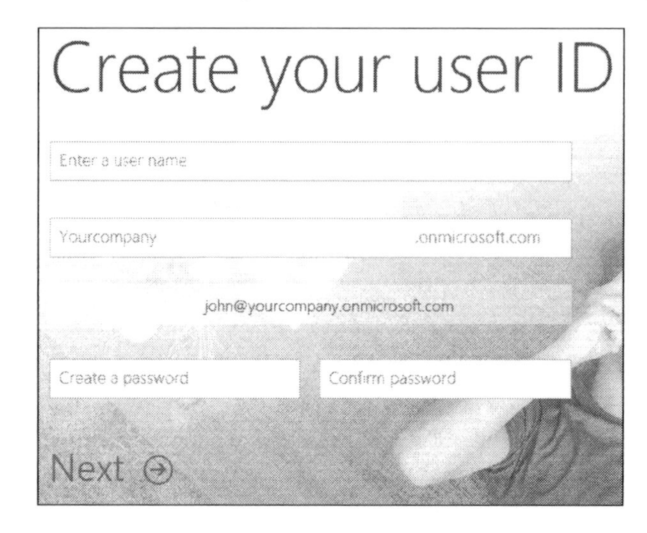

Click on **Next** once you are done filling in this section.

When defining the organization name for the URL, validation is performed to make sure this URL is unique. If the URL is not unique, you will be asked to provide a different organization name. Select a name that is not as common, until you find a unique one. The following screenshot shows the validation message you will receive if a non-unique value is entered.

Once a unique organization name is selected, your login user name is presented with a green check mark, as seen in the following screenshot:

Moving on to the last step of the wizard, you are asked to provide a phone number for verification. You will receive a text message with a code to be used to continue the signup process. Alternatively, you could select the **Call me** option and wait for a representative to validate your signup process. The selection screen looks like this:

The next screen requires you to enter the code provided by text message. Make sure you provided the correct phone number.

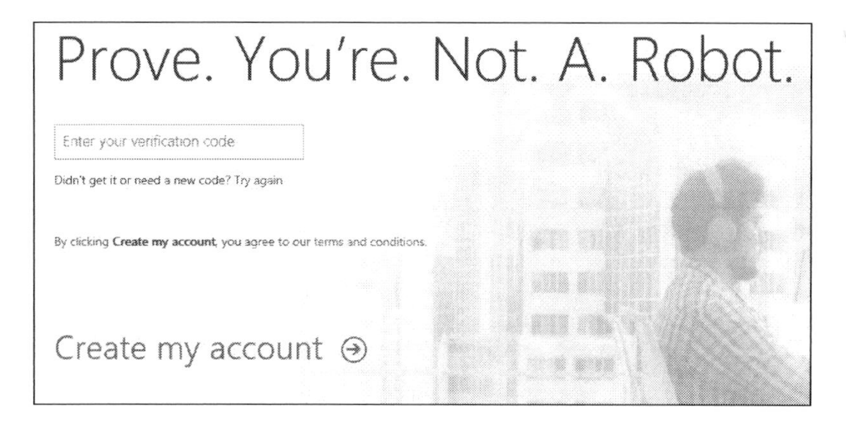

If you provided the incorrect phone number or did not receive the code by text message, click on **Try again** to have another code sent to your correct phone number.

When done, click on **Create my account**.

The following screen provides you with the user name you have selected, the URL of the Office 365 sign-in portal, and a status message. It's probably a good idea to take a screenshot of this for future reference.

When the process completes, the page is refreshed with the option to bookmark the sign-in page and a ready status message, as seen in the following screenshot:

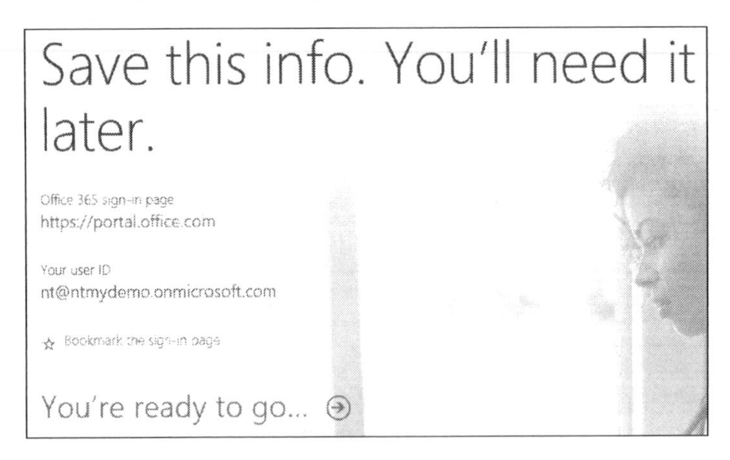

Click on the **You're ready to go...** link to proceed.

By the time this book is published, the account and organization created for these screenshots will be long expired.

The next step takes you to the initial preconfiguration of your new organization. There are a few additional details required before you can start playing with your new organization.

This new screen asks for the default **Language**, **Country/Region**, and **Currency**. This information is very important, as it will define the default configuration values for your organization. The currency will become the default currency. While additional currencies can be later added to the organization, the default will always remain the one you selected during this configuration step.

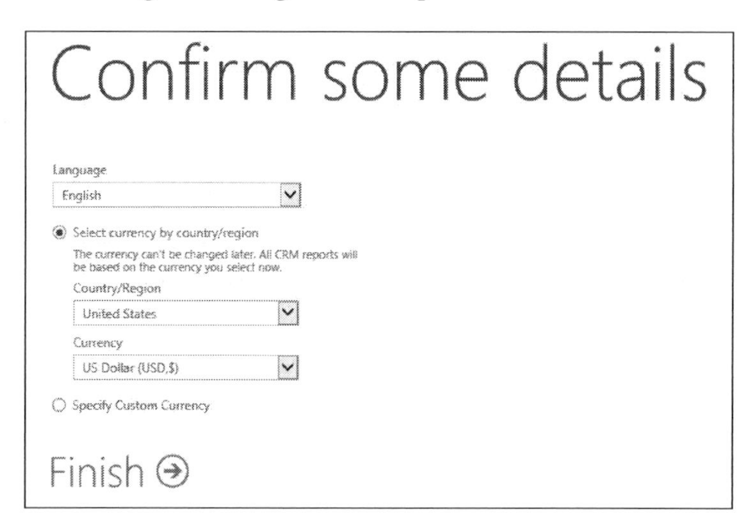

Click on **Finish** when complete.

The **Getting set up...** screen is presented while the backend provisions your organization based on the configuration values you have provided.

While waiting for this to process, you can turn your attention to your e-mail. You would have received an e-mail from Microsoft Online Services Team giving you details on the organization that is being provisioned for you, your account details and additional information about the service and expiration of the trial period. The e-mail is shown as follows:

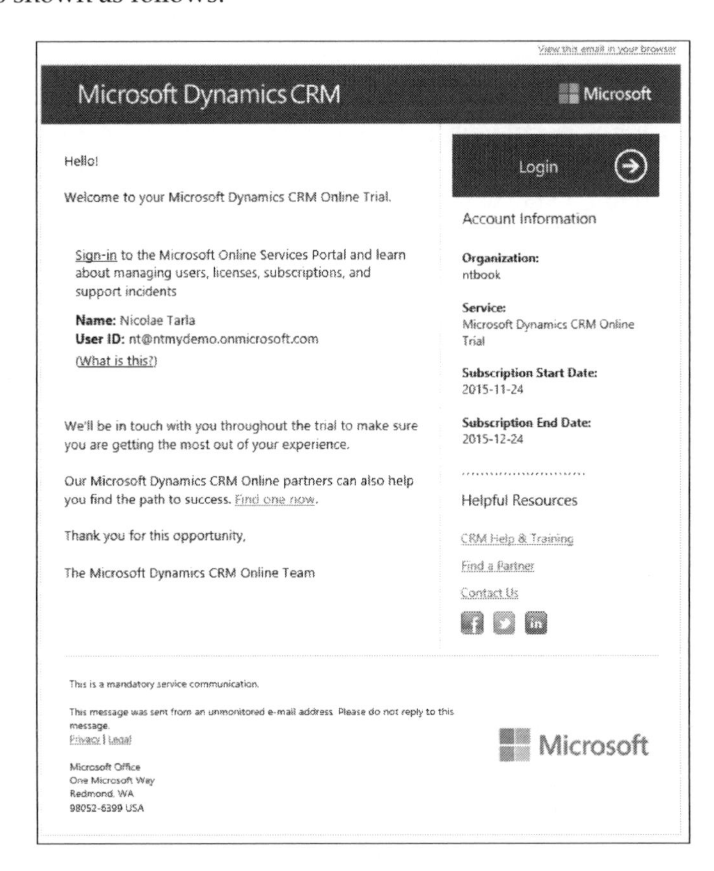

Going back to our sign-up page, the process has completed and we are presented with a final page including an option to bookmark the sign-in page in case you haven't done it before, as well as the URL of our newly created organization.

You're in!

Sign in here: https://ntmydemo.crm.dynamics.com/

Click here to bookmark sign-in page

Clicking on the provided link takes you directly to your Dynamics CRM Online instance. On the first load, you are presented with an Explore CRM wizard. If this is your first time seeing Dynamics CRM, it is a good idea to follow through to the provided links and read some more details about this version.

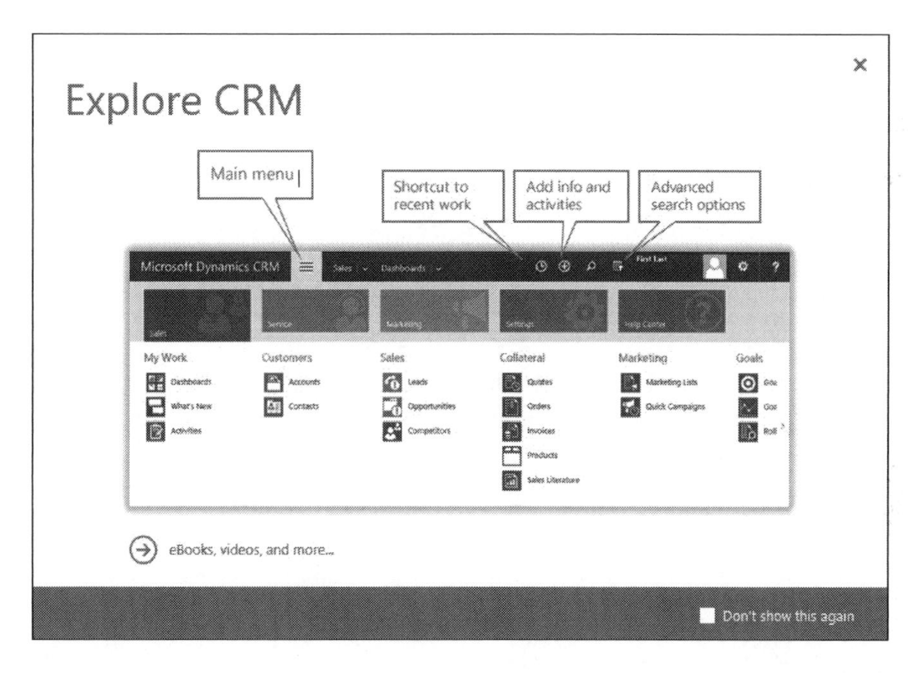

If this is not your first time, then select the **Don't show this again** check box and close this wizard.

Once you go past the initial wizard, you are dropped onto the starting dashboard of the application. By default, **Sales Activity Social Dashboard** is presented as a starting place into your new organization:

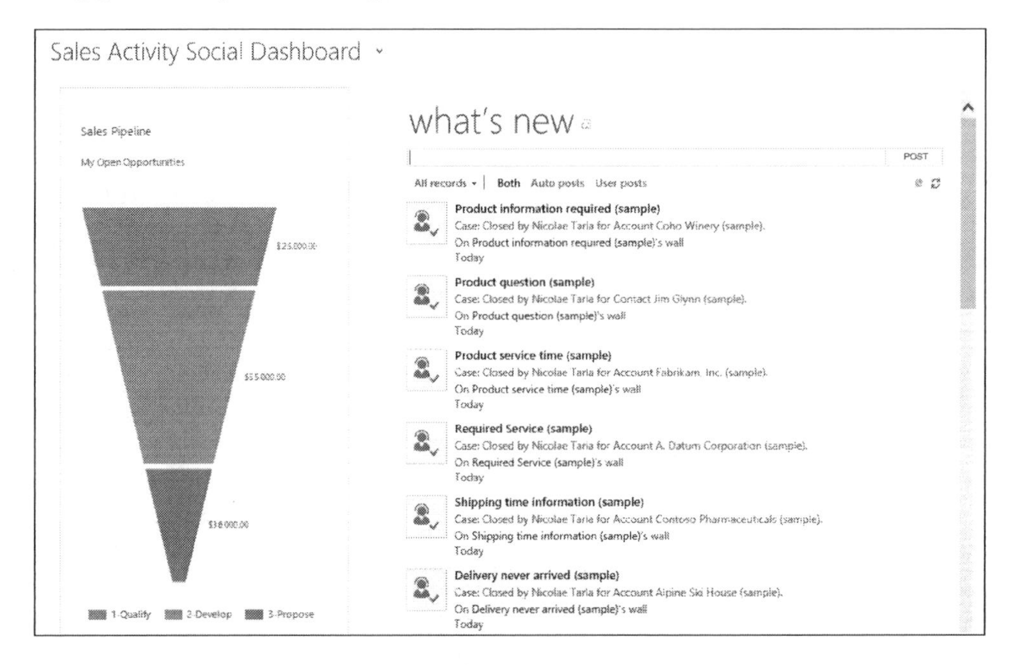

You will observe a yellow bar towards the top of the page, which offers additional configuration options. We will be looking at these later in this chapter, but do not close this bar just yet.

And with this, now we have a functional Dynamics CRM Online organization created.

But let's look at another way to get to it. Whether we've forgotten the default URL, or we need to access other features and account management options, we need to log in to the Office 365 admin center portal for the instance we are managing. The URL for this is `https://portal.office.com/`.

Log in using the previously created account and password. Once in, you will be presented with an administration console. A detailed look at additional configuration options for the Office 365 instance will be provided in *Chapter 6, Dynamics CRM Administration*.

For now, let's navigate to **Admin** | **CRM**

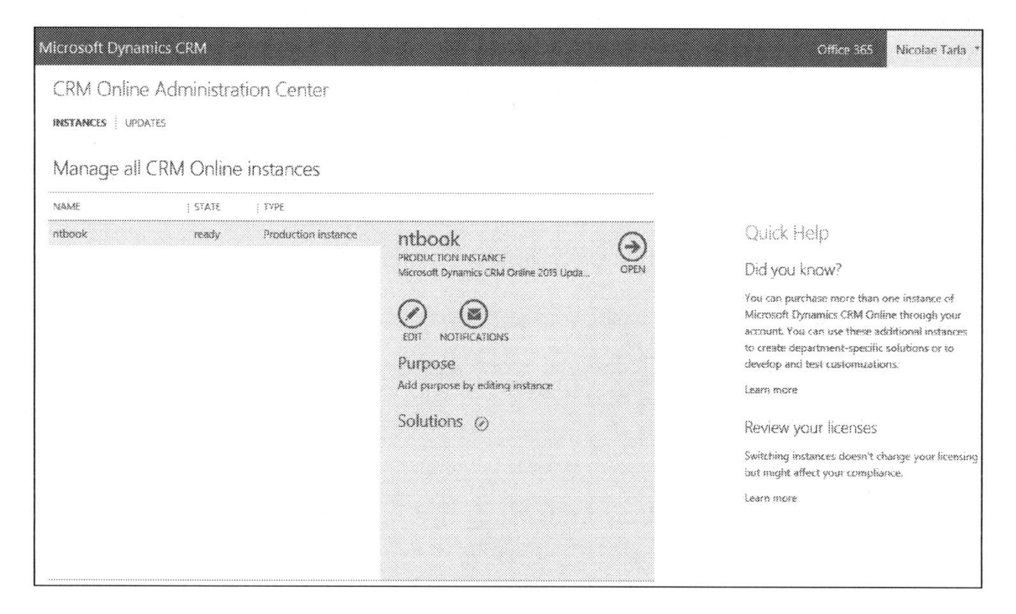

This opens up the CRM Online Administration Center. Here, you will find your current trial organization. If it is a paid subscription, you will get the opportunity to manage multiple paid production instances, as well as various nonproduction instances.

All the way at the top, you can change the view from a listing of instances for management to a listing of instances and available updates, if any. Since we've just created our instance, we will not have an option for updates, but in the following screen we can determine the current organization version:

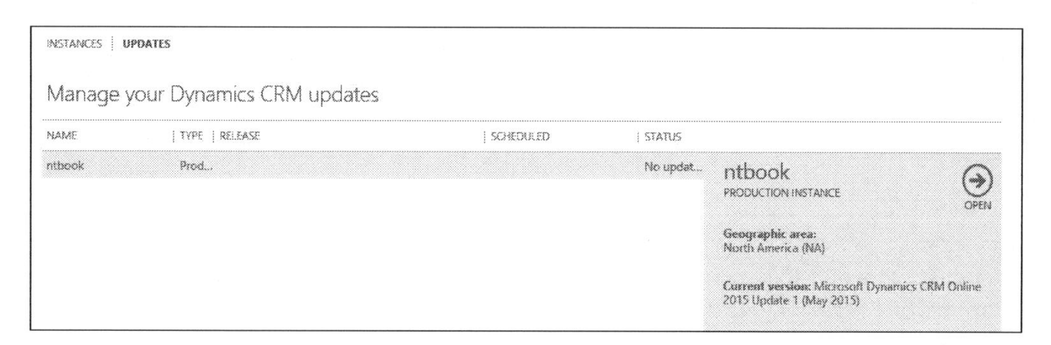

Back on the instances screen, we have the option to edit our instance properties. Selecting this option takes us to a form that allows us to change the name and URL of our organization, as well as provide a detailed message on the purpose of this organization. We can also change the instance type, from a production instance to a sandbox instance.

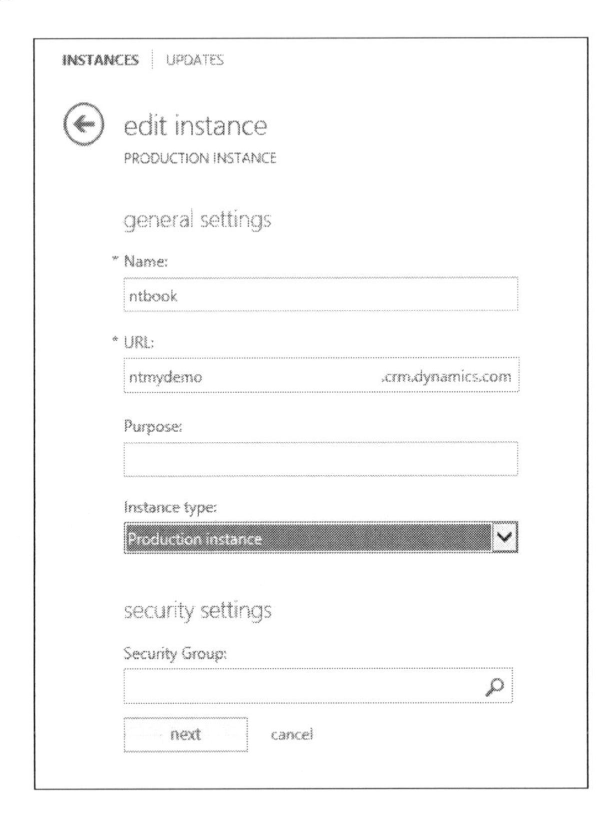

A sandbox instance is more of a nomenclature change. The former free and paid test instances have been unified under the name of sandbox instances. Visually, the sandbox instances will have the standard navigation bar background color changed to orange.

No functional changes are made to a sandbox instance. They offer the same functionality as a production instance. One very important aspect of sandbox instances is the fact that, while functionality is maintained on par with production instances, the database is completely isolated from production. A sandbox instance can contain a full set or a sub-set of production data, users, and customizations. From a support point of view, the same level of resource and support are provided to both production and sandbox instances.

As such, sandbox instances can be used for development, QA, and UAT environments.

The **Security Groups** option on this page can be used to restrict which Office 365 users can be added to your organization. If no option is specified here, all users in your Office 365 organization with a Dynamics CRM license associated will be added to your Dynamics CRM Online instance.

Managing instances is a set of features that allow an administrator to perform various operations on the Dynamics CRM Online instances managed through this portal. You can always turn a production instance into a sandbox instance, since no license changes are required to perform this action. On the other hand, you can only turn a sandbox instance into a production instance if you have an available production license.

Further down on the CRM Online Administration Center, you have an option to add various solutions to your current instance. Clicking on the solutions link takes you to the **Manage your solutions** page. Here, you can select from the available solutions. At the time of this writing, three solutions are made available with your 30-day trial organization. As seen in the following screenshot, they are:

- **Insights for Microsoft Dynamics CRM**
- **FieldOne Sky**
- **Office 365 Groups Preview**

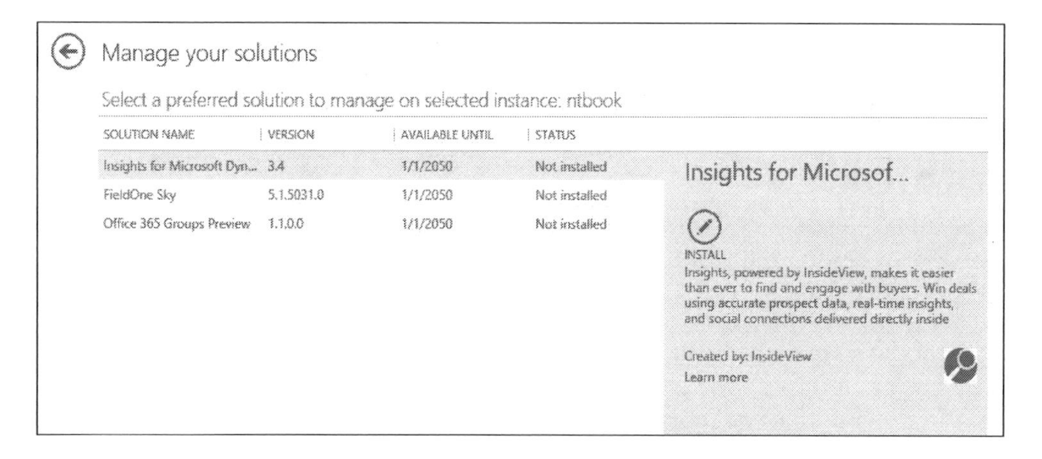

Select the solution that you are interested in installing and click on the **Install** button. Once installed, you can go ahead and configure it into your organization.

More solutions will be provided as add-ons in this manner in the future.
The platform allows for great modularity and provides an extensive solution model that allows new solutions to be made available in this manner.

This is an option available to Microsoft only.

When done installing the additional solutions, navigate back to the listing of organizations available.

On **Manage all CRM Online instances**, select the instance in the list and click on **Open**. This will take you to the same organization you were able to access directly from the URL provided during the initial trial wizard.

The Outlook connector's configuration will be covered in the next section of this chapter, while the SharePoint integration configuration and the Office Groups setup and other features will be covered in detail in a later chapter.

The trial instance of Dynamics CRM Online comes preloaded with some sample data. This makes it easy for a first-time user to see some of the visual representations on the dashboards, as well as giving a new user the opportunity to track some of the data relationships and see, on certain records, how related data is presented.

In the next few chapters, we will start investigating all the available features of the Dynamics CRM platform.

Integrating Dynamics CRM Online with Outlook

While not necessarily a requirement of this book, Dynamics CRM Online and On-Premise can integrate with Microsoft Outlook in order to provide the user with an interface already familiar to them.

Once you have your new instance of Dynamics CRM Online up and running, you can go ahead and install the Outlook client. This client is available either directly from the web interface of Dynamics CRM, presented as an option for download, or it can be downloaded from `http://www.microsoft.com/en-us/dynamics/crm-customer-center/set-up-crm-for-outlook.aspx`.

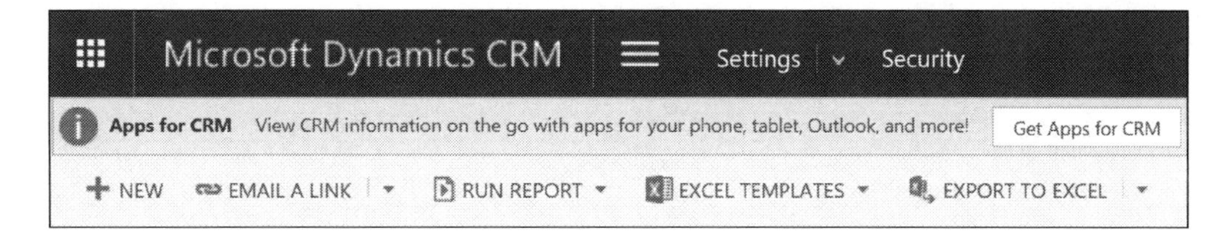

You can either download the file locally, or run it directly.

> Microsoft presents you with the option to download two files for the Outlook client. Make sure you select the one that matches the version of Office you have installed. For 32-bit Office, select `CRM2016-Client-ENU-i386.exe`, while for 64-bit versions of Office, select `CRM2016-Client-ENU-amd64.exe`.

> The following are requirements for Dynamics CRM for Outlook installation:
>
> - Must be logged in as a user with local administrator privileges
> - Must be on a machine with Windows Vista SP2 or newer
> - Must have Office 2007 or newer installed
> - Must have Internet Explorer 9 or newer
>
> The following are minimum system requirements for Dynamics CRM for Outlook:
>
> - Processor—x86 or x64 and 1.9GHz or faster dual core with SSE2 (most modern processors qualify)
> - Memory—minimum 2 GB RAM for online only, 4 GB RAM for support of offline capabilities
> - Hard Disk—1.5 GB available disk space, 2 GB for offline mode
> - Display—SVGA minimum resolution of 1024x768

Installing Dynamics CRM for Outlook

Once the file is executed, all necessary components are extracted, and you are guided through a wizard-based installation. Do make sure your Outlook application is closed, otherwise you will be prompted to close it for the installation to proceed.

If you are running the wrong version of the installer, the installation process checks and prompts you about the version mismatch, as shown in the following screenshot.

Once the install process starts, you are guided through a few screens, starting with the setup preparation.

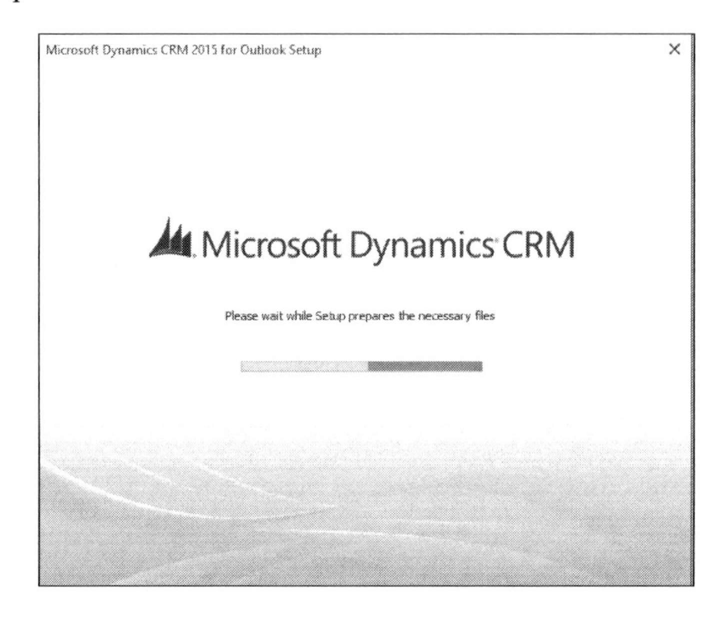

In the next step, you are prompted to accept the **License Agreement**. Tick the check box and click on **Next**.

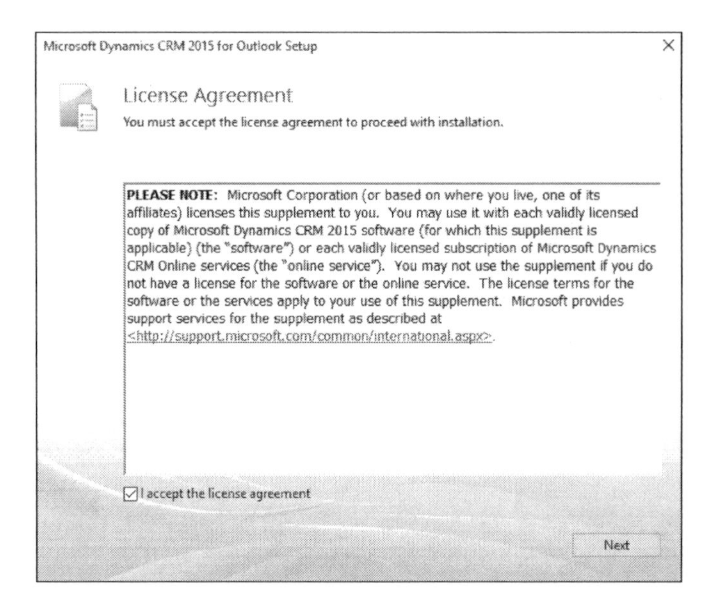

Once the acceptance is completed, we are presented with a screen in which we can directly start the installation process, or modify the installation options. Choosing to modify the default option presents a new screen where we can define whether we want to install the Dynamics CRM for Outlook with offline support or not. For the purpose of a 30-day trial, unless there is a specific need for offline support, we can leave this option unselected.

The second configuration option presented on this screen is the location where we want the files installed. We can also leave the default selection in place.

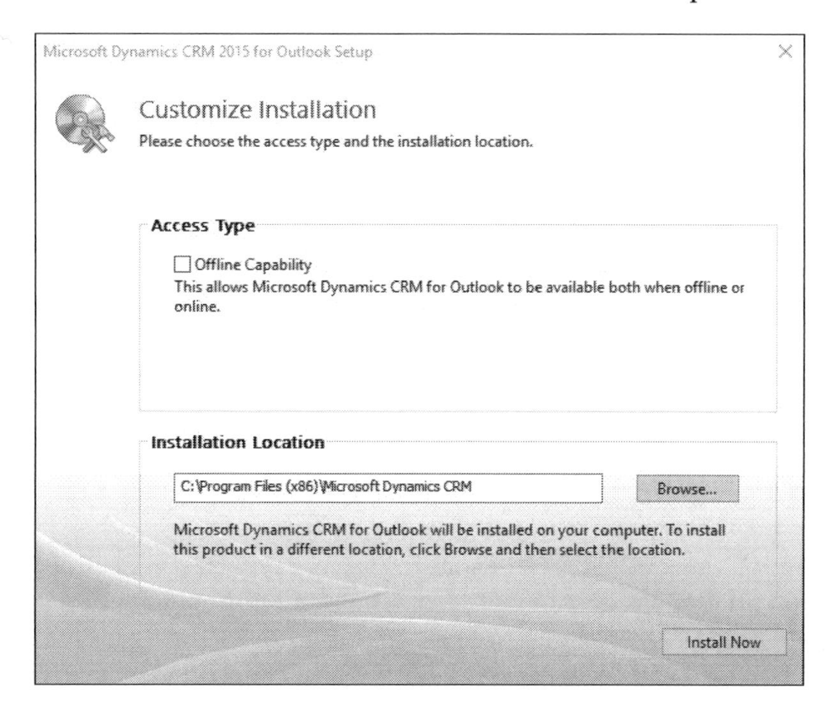

Next, let's click on **Install Now** and get started on the installation process. From here on out, the installation wizard proceeds to completion with no more questions or interruptions. On completion, click on **Close**.

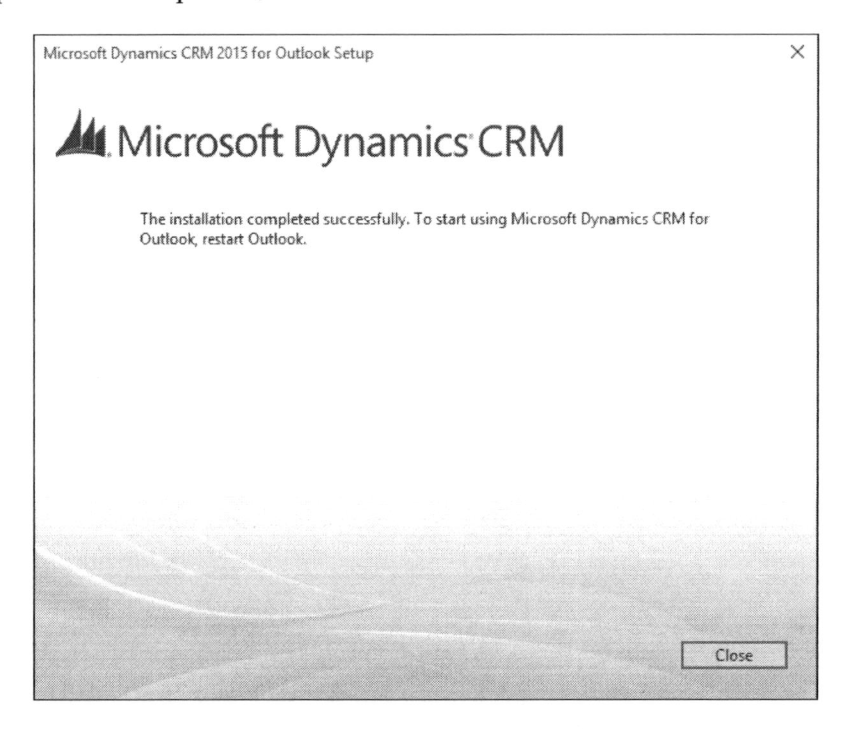

At this point, we have Microsoft Dynamics CRM for Outlook installed, and we are ready to start Outlook and configure our client to connect to our trial instance. Once we launch Outlook, we are prompted to configure the newly installed plugin. As the following screenshot shows, we have to provide the login details for our online instance:

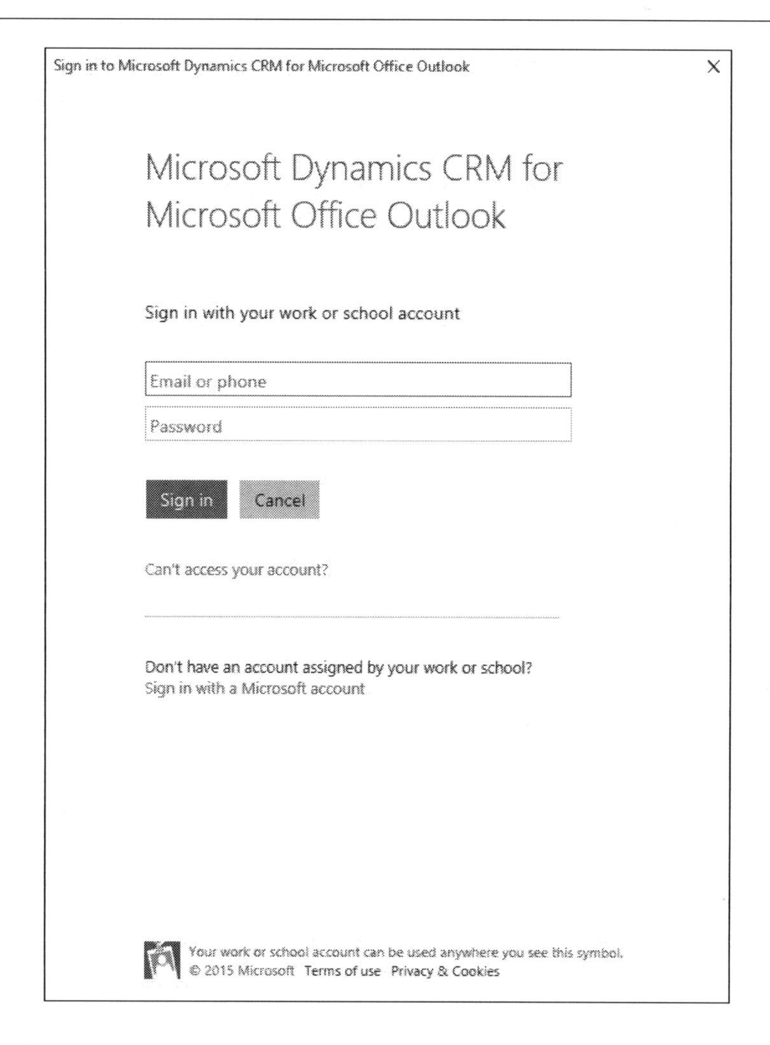

If you have forgotten your selected user name, retrieve it from the confirmation e-mail you received from Microsoft when creating your free 30-day trial.

Once authenticated, you are defaulted to CRM Online. When done, make sure that the **Connect automatically with my current credentials** check box is selected, and click on the **Connect** button, as shown in the following screenshot:

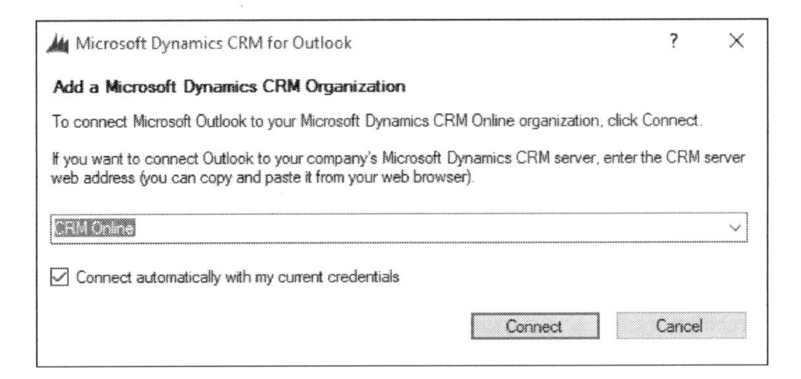

This completes the configuration of the Dynamics CRM for Outlook plugin, and you are presented with a final view of all configured connections. In here, you will see your currently configured connection, possibly along with other connections configured previously. You can also get to this window post-installation by relaunching the configuration wizard. Close this window.

Now, your Outlook is connected to your instance of Dynamics CRM. You can navigate to your Dynamics CRM environment the same way you navigate within Outlook to any other e-mail already configured. Your new Dynamics CRM environment shows in the listing of e-mails, the same as a new mailbox. Expanding this list gives us access to all the sections and entities from our CRM environment.

Configure a domain name for your environment

One of the setup steps available with an Office 365 instance is the ability to configure a domain name associated with the instance. While you can continue working with Dynamics CRM Online without setting up a domain, it is a good idea to do it now. With the domain setup, you have one less configuration step to perform before turning your trial into a production instance.

If you want to proceed to setting up a domain, you can either use an existing domain you own, or you can purchase a domain from various registrars. For the purpose of this book, I have purchased a `.info` domain from GoDaddy at `https://godaddy.com/`.

You access the Office 365 admin center by navigating to `https://portal.office.com/`.

You will be prompted to log in. Use the previously created account, which will get you to the main admin center console.

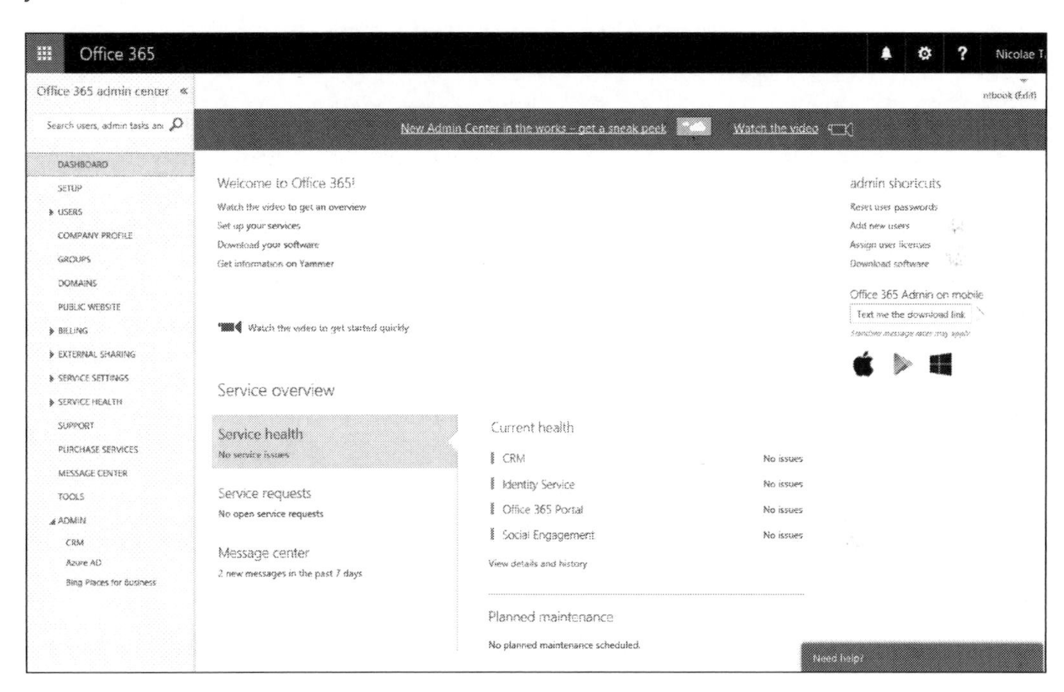

Navigate on the left navigation area and click on **DOMAINS**. This will get you to the **Manage domains** page.

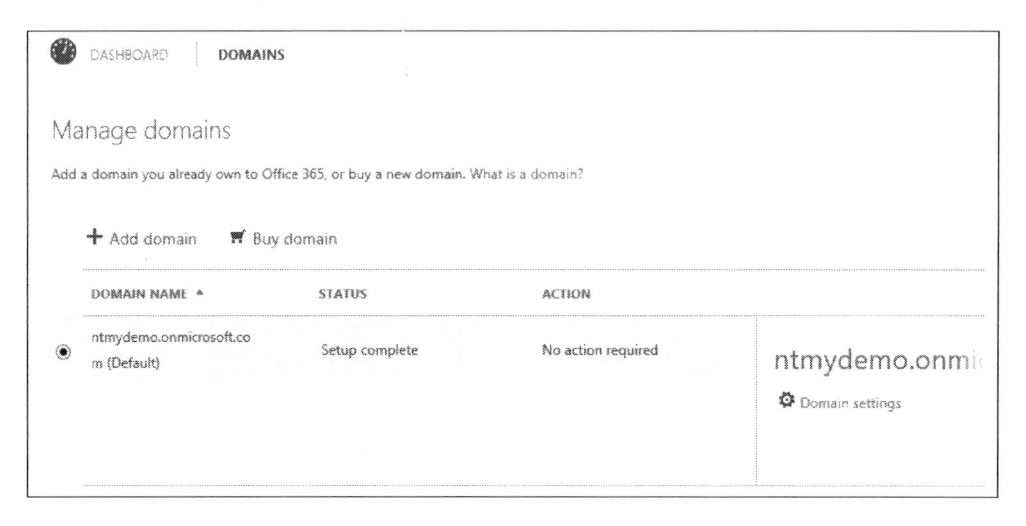

Here, you have the option to purchase a domain if you haven't already done so, or just to add a new domain. Unfortunately, you can't purchase a new domain using the **Buy domain** unless you have a paid subscription. For the purpose of this trial, I am assuming you have already purchased a domain, and you are just configuring it.

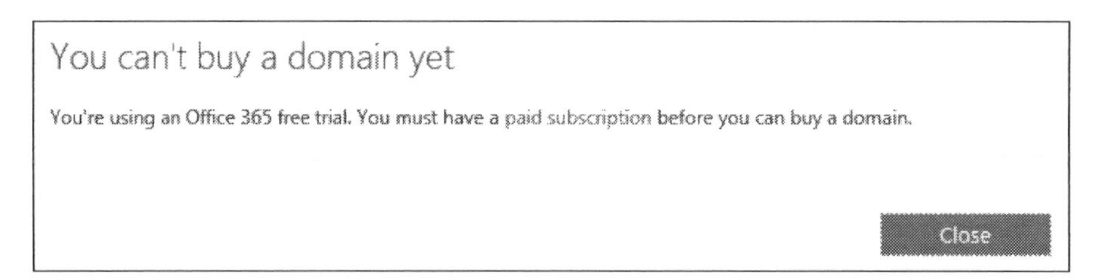

Go to **Add domain**. This takes you to the first page of the domain configuration wizard. This first page is informational in nature, describing the purpose of a domain and providing you with a link to an educational video on DNS.

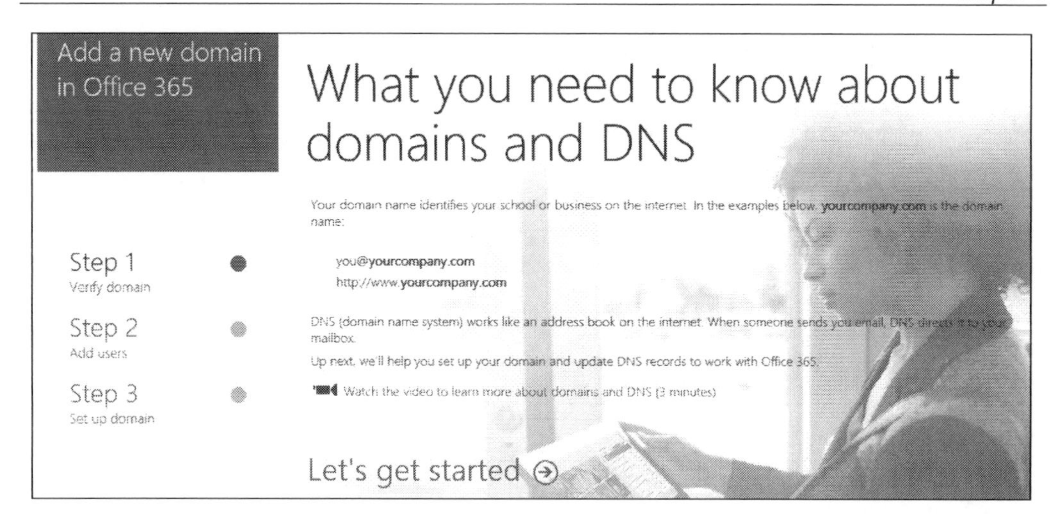

Click on **Let's get started** to continue. On the next page, enter the domain you have purchased and now own.

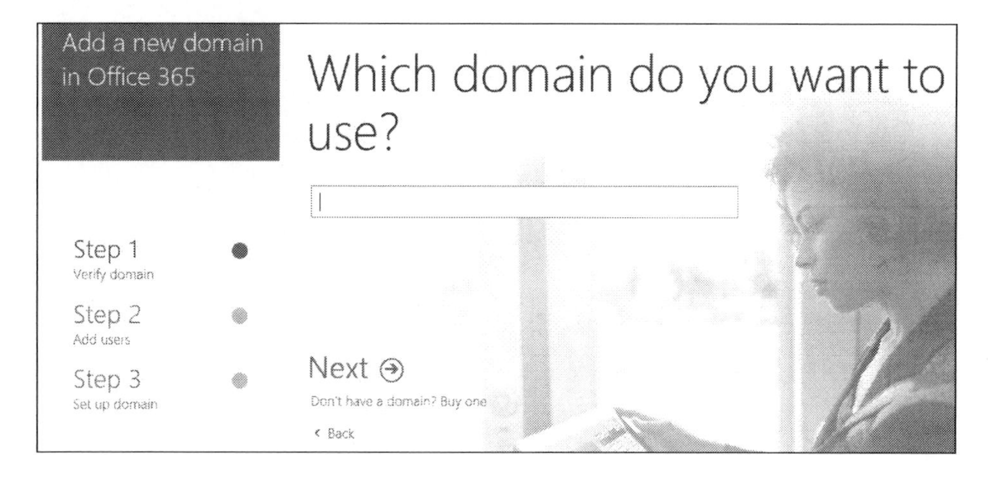

The system recognizes that the registrar is GoDaddy, and the next screen prompts you to log in to the administration console for the domain.

Alternatively, you have the option to use a TXT record to validate that you own the domain. For simplicity, I will click on **Sign in to GoDaddy**. This brings up the GoDaddy account login page.

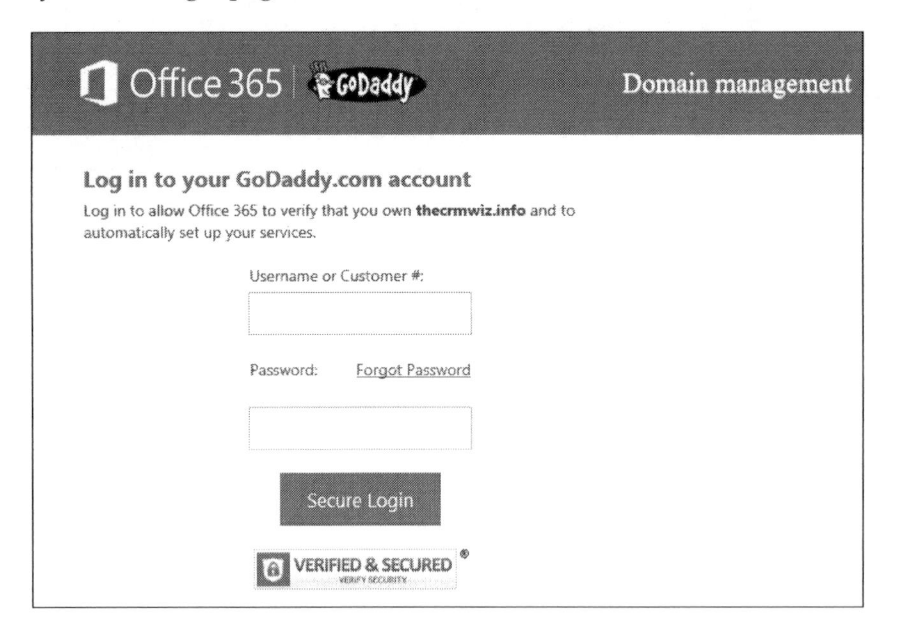

Once logged in, confirm that you accept Office 365 to make changes to your domain.

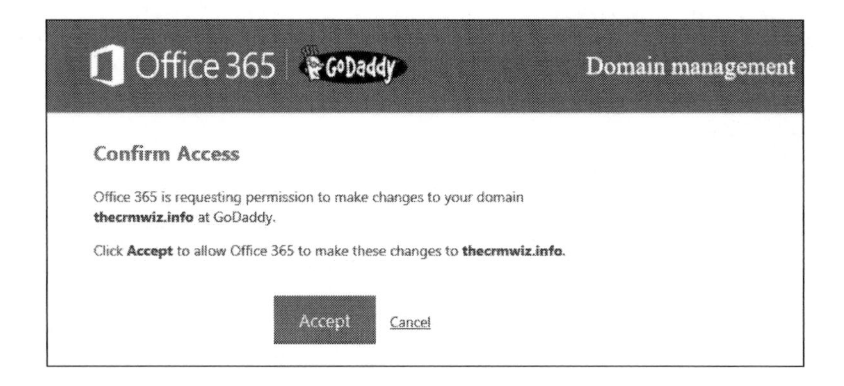

This performs the validation and completes the first step of the wizard.

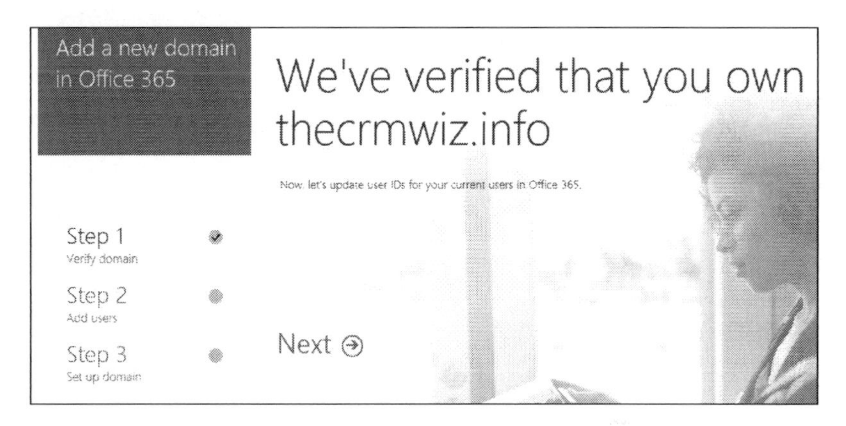

Click on **Next** to update the user accounts in your instance to use the newly configured domain name. The following screen allows you to select which users should be updated.

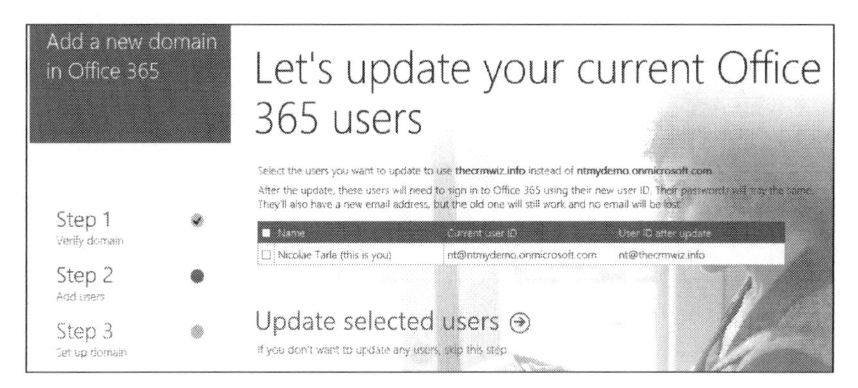

Select the users and click on **Update selected users**. Once complete, a confirmation screen displays all the updated users.

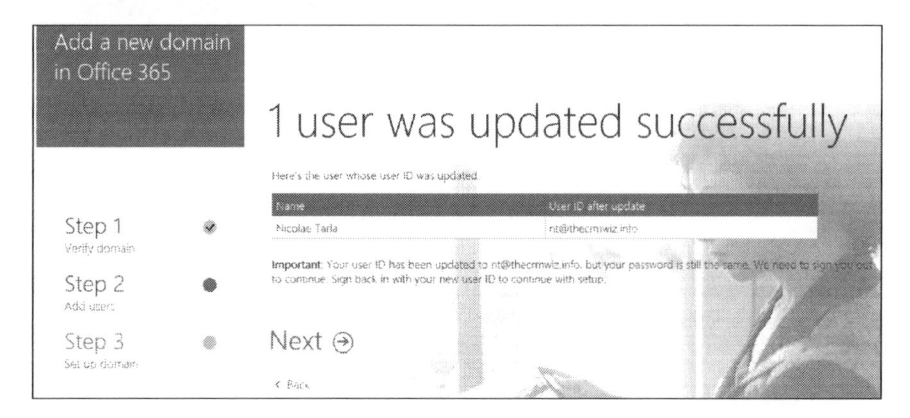

Click on **Next** to continue. If you have updated the current user you are logged in with, you will be prompted to log out and log back in with the updated username.

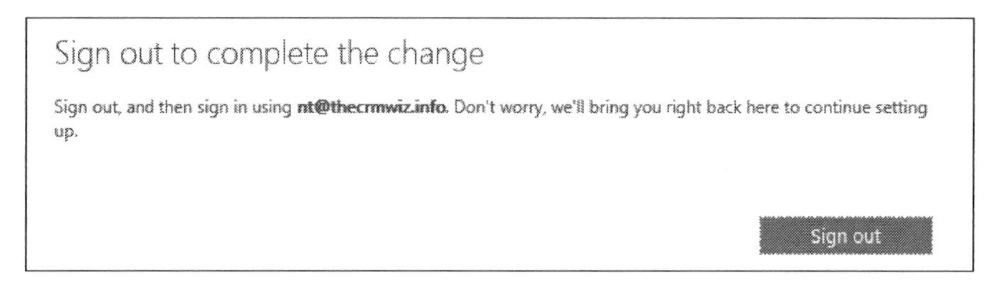

Click on **Sign out** and you are forwarded back to the login page. Here, enter the new login information and log back into the Office 365 admin center.

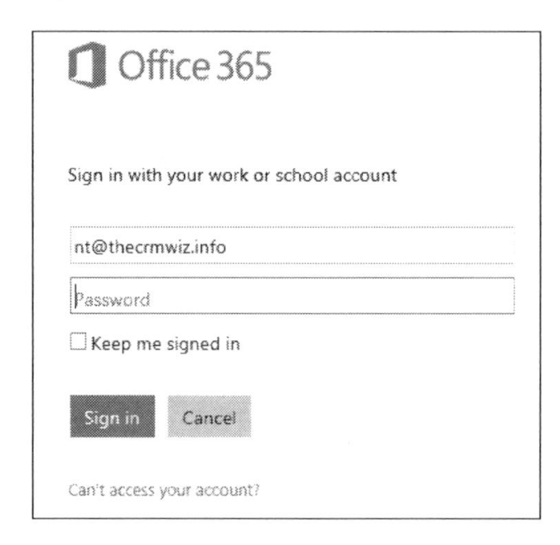

Once you log back in, you are given the option to add new users. For the purpose of this demo I will not add any more users right now, but in a standard trial you can have up to 25 users created. It will make sense to start adding new users once you have some customizations in the system and you are ready to present your solution to a customer or stakeholder.

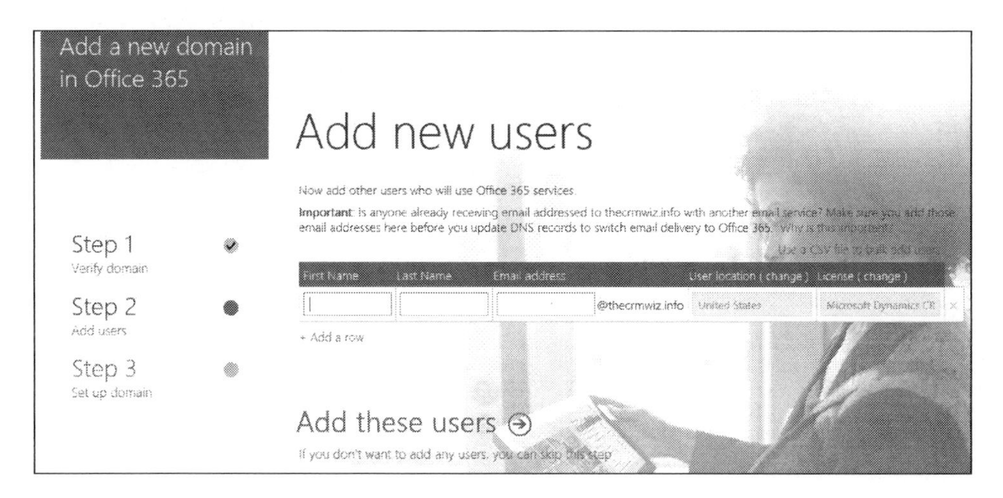

For now, let's click on **skip this step**. That moves us to the third and last step of the wizard, setting up the domain.

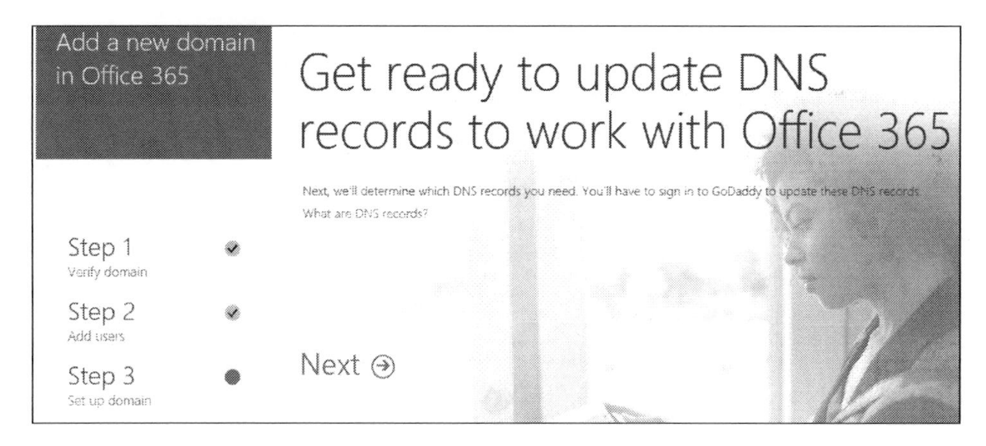

Let's click on **Next** to start this process. On a supported registrar the changes can be pushed automatically, otherwise you will have to log in to the domain administration and implement the settings provided manually. Not to worry, the process is pretty simple and self-explanatory.

The next step lets you select the services you want configured on your domain for the current Office 365 instance.

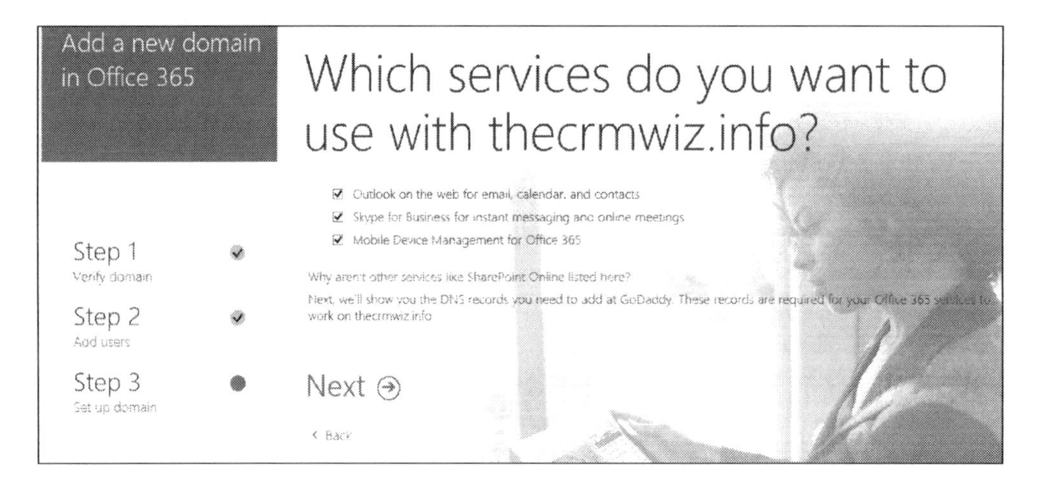

You can choose any one of the available options or all of them. Once you've made your selection, click on **Next**.

The next page gives us the option to see the necessary changes to be made to your domain configuration. The **Add records** option automatically configures your domain. Alternatively, you can enter all configuration manually.

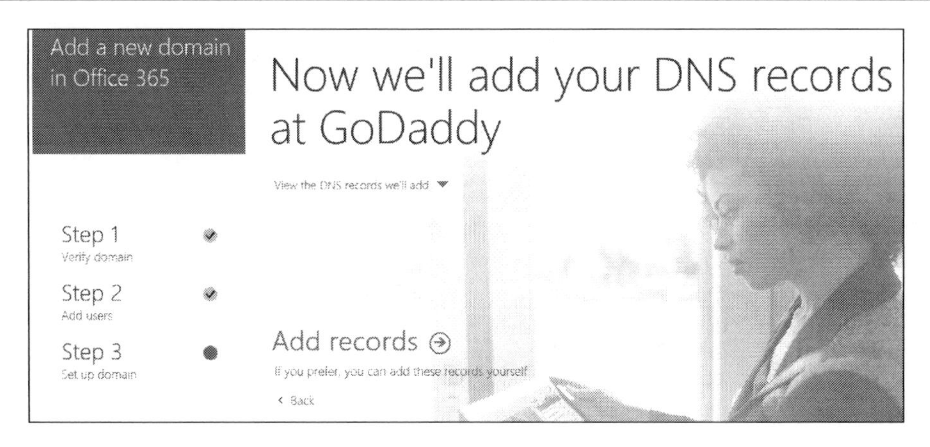

Click on **View the DNS records we'll add** to see details about the changes that will be configured on your domain.

Click on **Add records** to continue. You are again prompted to log in to your domain registrar for the changes to be pushed.

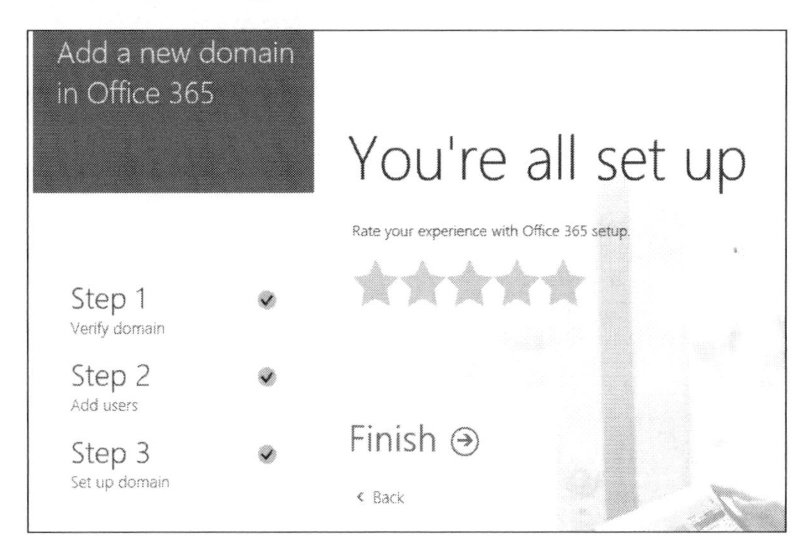

The final screen shows the completed status and provides you with an option to rate the experience.

Click on **Finish** to complete. This returns you to the **Manage domains** page in the Office 365 admin center and displays the original domain as well as the newly configured domain name.

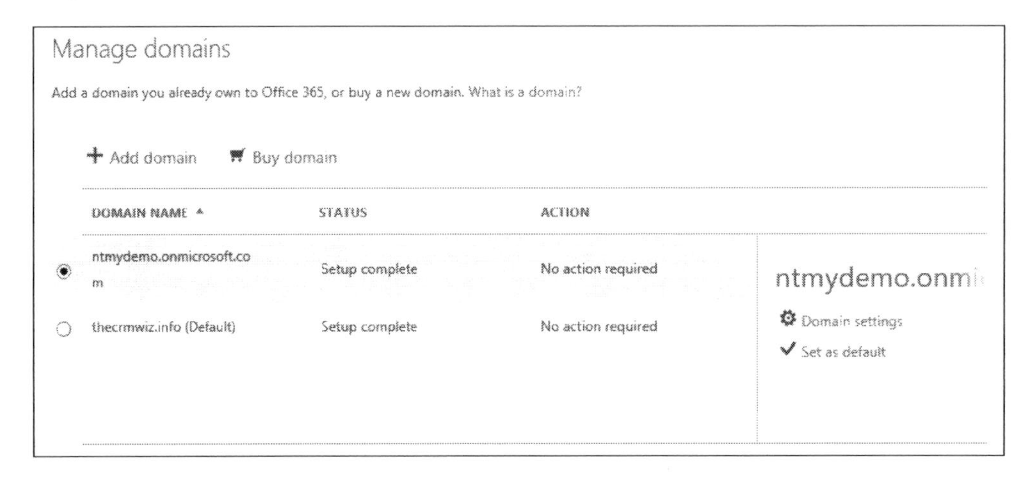

The newly added domain is marked as the default domain.

You can also navigate to **USERS** | **Active users** on the left navigation and make sure that your configured users are all using the newly configured domain name.

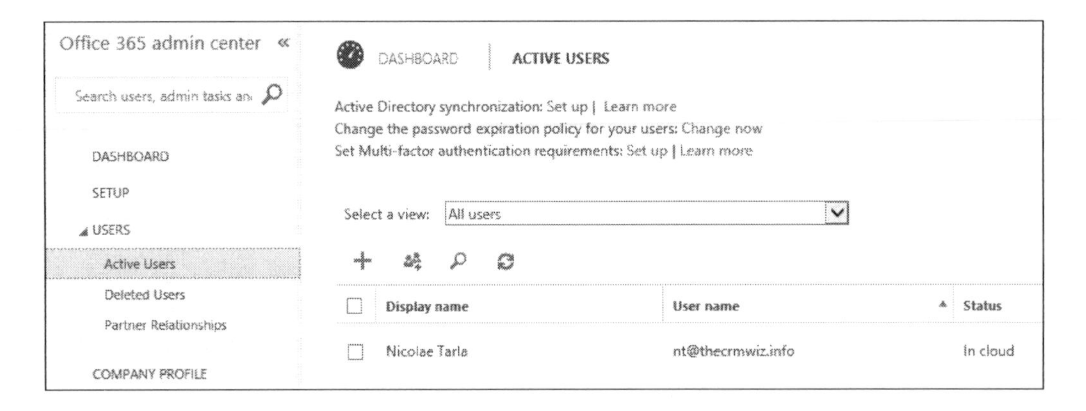

And this completes the domain configuration steps necessary for your Office 365 instance. Next, we'll be looking at adding additional trial services to your existing instance.

Integrating with Office 365 E3 trial services

Office 365 is offered in a variety of flavors, each including a different set of services. One of the common tiers offered as a trial is the E3. It includes services such as the Office suite, e-mail, document and file management, conferencing and Skype, team sites, Yammer, and so on. For additional details on what is included in Office 365 E3, see the following page:

`https://products.office.com/en-us/business/office-365-enterprise-e3-business-software`

From your existing Office 365 instance where you created your Dynamics CRM Online trial, you can add this additional trial service. Start by navigating on the left navigation area to **BILLING | Subscriptions**.

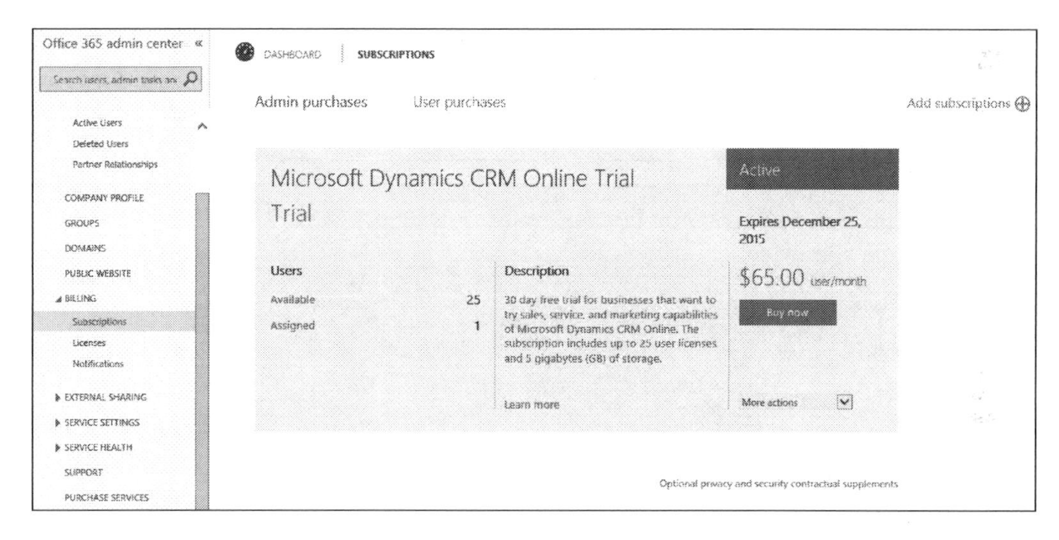

Select **Add subscription** on the top-right side of the screen. You are now presented with a listing of available subscriptions you can add to your existing instance. Scroll until you find the **Enterprise Suite** area and find **Office 365 Enterprise E3**.

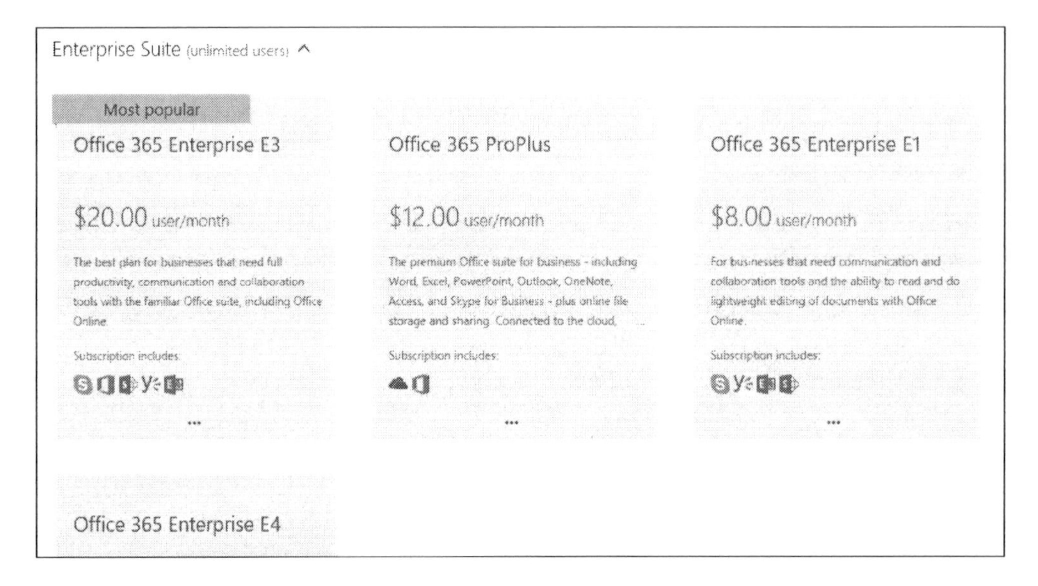

Hover over the ellipsis (...) at the bottom of the subscription, and from the popup, select **Start free trial**.

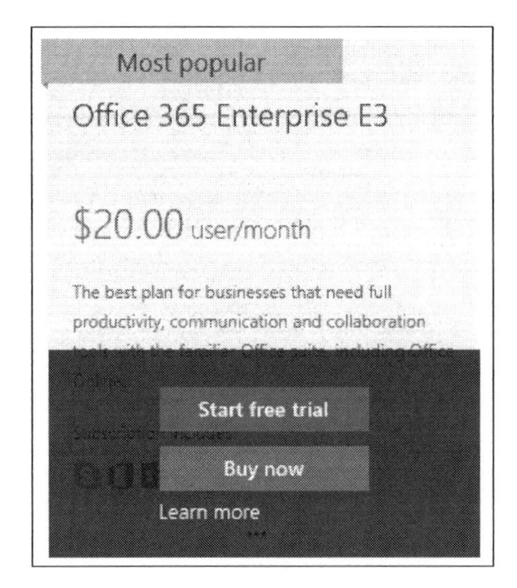

The **Check out** page confirms your selection. Click on the **try now** button.

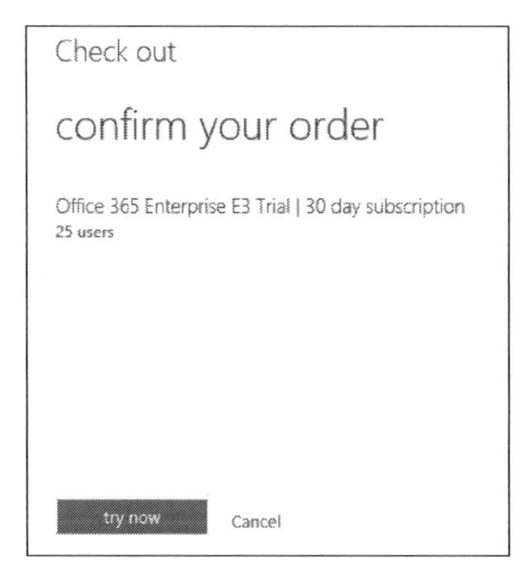

A confirmation number and the option to print a receipt is presented. Click on the **continue** button.

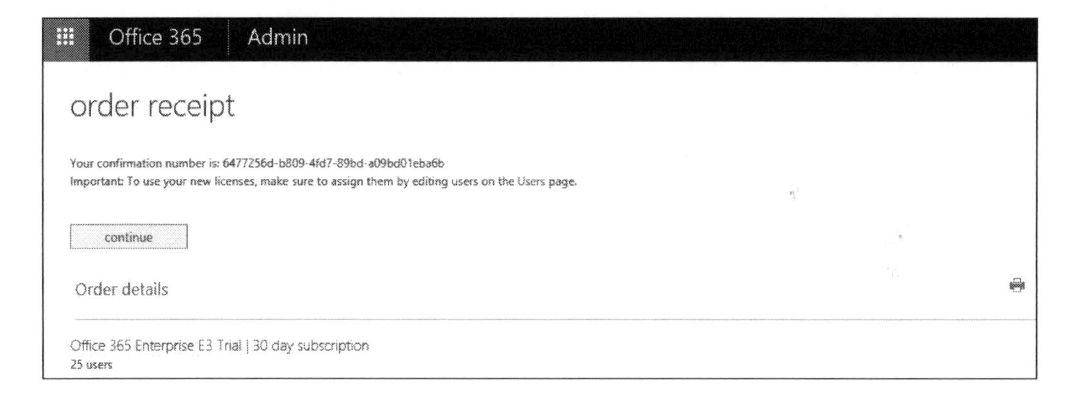

With that last step completed, all the additional services associated with the Office 365 Enterprise E3 services are now enabled and associated to your existing instance. To confirm, look at the landing page on your Office 365 admin center. In the **Current health** area, you will see a listing of all services now active on this instance, as shown in the following screenshot:

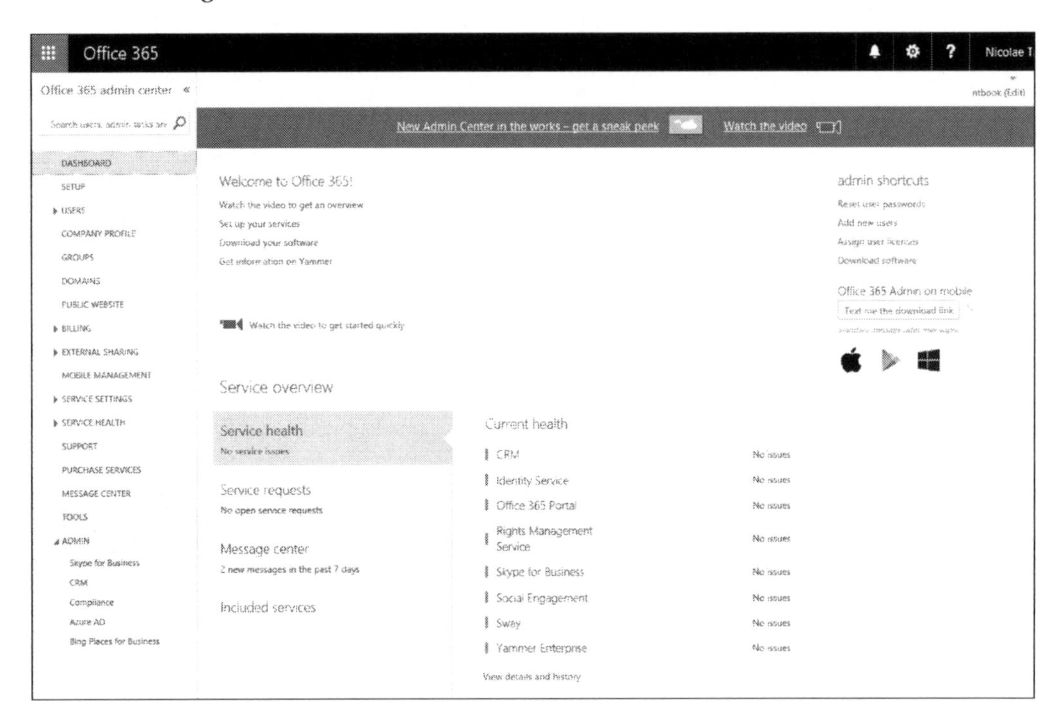

Now, we can configure all the integrations available. We will look at those tasks in some of the future chapters.

Summary

Throughout this chapter, we looked at how to create our new free trial environment for Dynamics CRM using Microsoft Dynamics CRM Online. In addition, we walked through configuring Outlook to integrate with our Dynamics CRM Online instance.

You also learned how to add to our current Dynamics CRM Online trial a trial of Office 365 Enterprise E3. This allows us to configure additional services and integration points.

The next chapter will delve into the application structure. We will look at the standard modules included with the platform, the elements available for customization and their relationship to each module and each other. We will also look at the updated navigation model used in Dynamics CRM Online, and how we can extend and modify it.

2
The Dynamics CRM Application Structure

In the previous chapter, we described how to get a Dynamics CRM Online environment up and running, configure your Outlook to integrate with this environment, and add an Office 365 E3 Trial. With this environment available now, we can start to look at some of the components of this system. We will investigate the modules that are, as default, a part of Microsoft Dynamics CRM, and the features of each of these modules.

This chapter is structured around four main categories. They are:

- The Dynamics CRM modules
- Dynamics CRM application elements
- The extensibility options
- Application Navigation

Microsoft Dynamics CRM is Microsoft's platform for Customer Relationship Management. This system allows a company to manage interactions with current and future potential customers. Usually, a CRM system is part of a bigger picture, involving customer service, customer experience, customer retention, and other aspects. The CRM platform fits into this puzzle as the software platform that provides a company with the necessary tools to perform all of these tasks.

A robust CRM system allows for both reactive and proactive actions from various staff using it. While most of the service aspects are primarily reactive, through extensive analysis and solid business processes, proactive actions can be taken to increase sales, customer retention, and quality of service, and also to create more robust marketing campaigns.

A CRM system provides a 360-degree view of a customer, with all historical interactions, purchase history, contact preferences, and survey responses, along with additional-related data as needed. This data collected by the system can be further analyzed to determine best strategies for increasing customer satisfaction and providing better quality services.

From a proactive point of view, analyzing the aforementioned customer data allows us to identify new opportunities and to prevent potential future issues.

Dynamics CRM modules

While Microsoft used to market Dynamics CRM as a platform under the **xRM** term, and is encouraging partners to extend it to cover various aspects of businesses, by default, the product includes three major modules:

- Sales
- Service
- Marketing

At the time of writing, the platform is at version 2016. It has greatly evolved over the years, and is currently one of the top players in the market.

With this evolution, all the standard modules have been enhanced, and new functionality has been added. Currently, each one of the modules can function either independently or in conjunction with the others by sharing data and providing full visibility on customers across all modules. The clear definitions between these modules are getting blurrier as the need to transfer data across practices evolves. Business processes span across these modules also, and gain a more central role in the way the user interacts with CRM, to the point where they often pass across from one module to another, blurring this segmentation even more.

CRM Sales module

The Microsoft Dynamics CRM Sales module facilitates the sales teams in managing Leads and Opportunities, as well as closing these opportunities in a shorter more orderly fashion, and increase the opportunity success rate.

Within the Sales module, the sales team has the ability to manage their own customers and contacts and get full visibility on customers, current orders, services, existing issues, and resolutions. With all this information at your fingertips, a sales person can walk into any new opportunity fully prepared, avoiding any unexpected surprises. Furthermore, they can show full knowledge of the customer and its current needs, level of satisfaction, and potential contention subjects.

The sales module is comprised of a set of entities, processes, dashboards, and reports, along with the ability to see the products and services offered as well as the associated sales literature. Within this same module, the sales team can see their progress against predefined goals. In addition, each sales staff can manage their own customer interaction through the use of some of the marketing features built in the system.

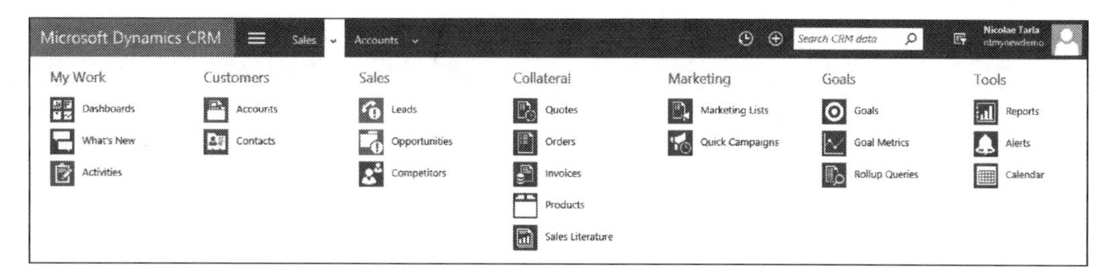

CRM Sales module Entities

The Dynamics CRM Sales module includes a set of entities that are shared across modules, as well as entities specific to sales in particular. We will be looking at these two generic categories and each of the entities included in them.

Shared Entities

Shared Entities are entities that are being used across multiple modules. While they are not specific to a certain module, they tend to be tightly integrated with the functionality of each module where they are present. Some of the most obvious ones include the **Account** and **Contact** entities, which span across the whole platform and tightly integrate with all modules.

Sales specific Entities

Sales specific entities are entities that are used mainly within the sales module. Some of these include the **Leads**, **Opportunities** and **Competitors**, as well as additional **Collateral** entities such as **Quotes**, **Orders**, **Invoices**, **Products**, and **Sales Literature**. Another set of entities directly related to the sales module include **Goals** and **Goal Metrics**, which are used in tracking sales performance.

When customizing the system, the scope of each one of the existing entities can be changed simply by modifying the navigation and associations. For example, a new entity can be made accessible only though a specific module, or an entity from one module can be surfaced in another.

The Leads entity

The Leads entity is a representation of a person or organization interested in the company's products and/or services. The lead entity is meant to track a potential customer that has not been yet qualified. It will track all communication activities through possible qualification.

The following screenshot shows a standard **New Lead** form in Dynamics CRM:

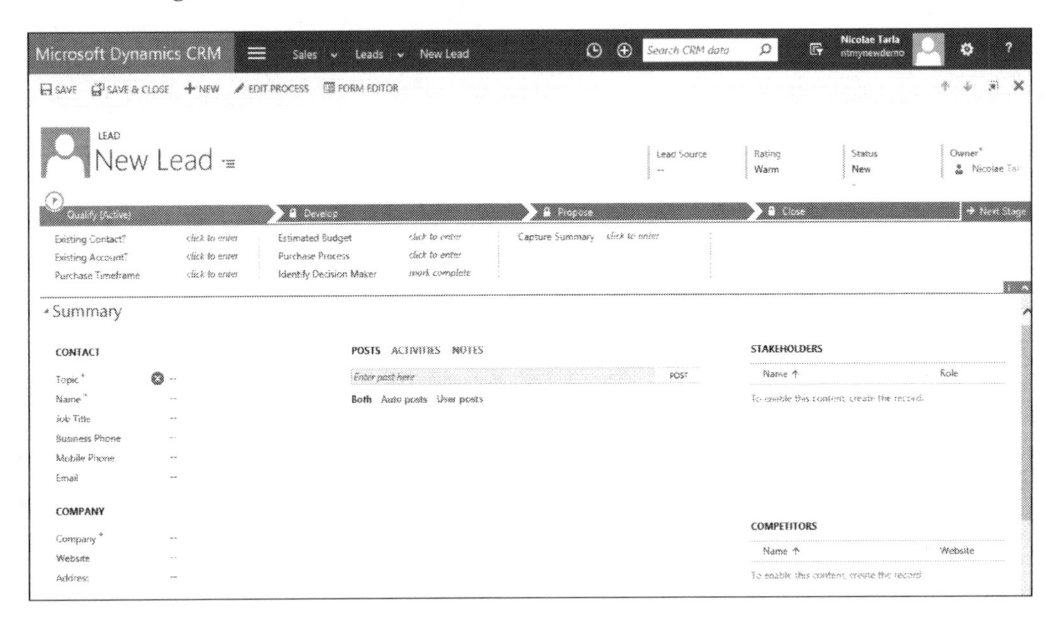

The Lead qualification process is the process of managing a possible opportunity until qualification. This process is kept separate from the opportunity management process through the use of the lead entity.

A lead record can be in one of the three default states: **Open**, **Qualified**, or **Disqualified**. Once a Lead is qualified, it can be converted into an Opportunity. From the associated data collected, **Account** and **Contact** can also be created.

The Lead record can be associated with system data, including Contacts, Accounts, Activities, and Notes. Also, documents can be attached to leads.

By default, a Lead can also be disqualified. When disqualifying a lead, the following options are available: **Lost**, **Cannot Contact**, **No Longer Interested**, or **Cancelled**. These values are customizable.

The opportunity Entity

The Opportunity entity is meant to store a potential sale to a new or existing customer. It is used by sales staff to keep track and forecast sales engagements they are working on. An opportunity can be created directly in the system, or generated as a result of qualifying a Lead.

Based on business opportunities, a company can forecast business demands for products and services, as well as sales revenues.

An opportunity in the system must be related to an Account and/or Contact. This is one of the differences between Lead and Opportunities, where the Account or Contact must be already qualified in the system for an opportunity to be able to associate with it.

Just as with leads, a sales representative can track phone calls, e-mails, and other activities against the opportunity. This gives the representative complete visibility into all steps that were performed working with each opportunity.

The following screenshot shows a standard **New Opportunity** form in Dynamics CRM:

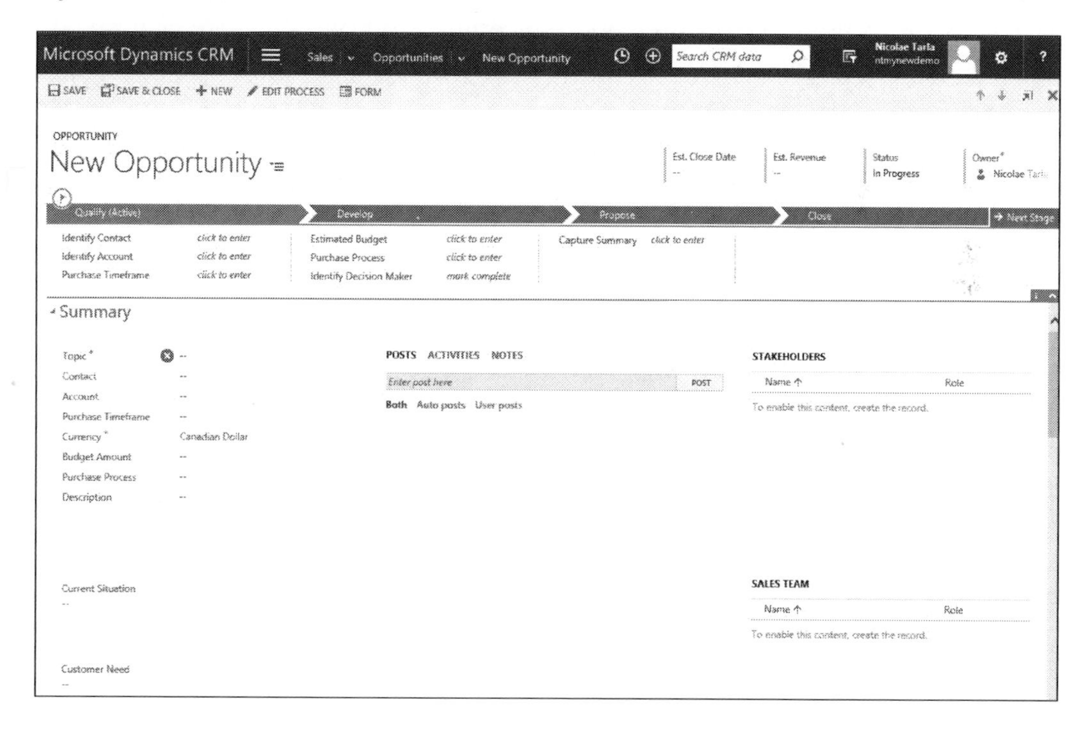

Each opportunity in the system usually has one or more products/services associated with it. This association is achieved through the use of a relational system entity called Opportunity Product. In addition, processes can be put in place to validate that only certain Products/Services are available for a specific opportunity, based on either the account/contact selected, or any other set of business rules.

Processing an Opportunity results in its closure. An opportunity can be closed either as **Won** or **Lost**. On closing of an opportunity, an opportunity close activity is generated. This activity record stores the information regarding the reason for closing, the date, and the revenue.

An Opportunity can be associated with Accounts, Contacts, Competitors, Quotes, Orders, and Activities. In addition, you can put notes and store attachments against an open Opportunity, as well as related Sales Literature.

The Quotes Entity

The Quote entity is an important part of the sales process defined within the Dynamics CRM sales force automation platform. It works in conjunction with products and orders to complete the sales cycle.

The Quote entity represents an offer of products and/or services at a predetermined price. In addition, payment terms are associated with the respective quote.

A Quote in the system can be stored as **Draft**, **Active**, or **Closed**. A Draft quote is a quote that is still being worked on. Once work is completed and it is ready to be sent to the customer, the quote becomes active. On completion, whether accepted or rejected, the quote gets closed. A completed quote that is accepted by the customer can be converted to an Order.

The following screenshot shows a standard **New Quote** form in Dynamics CRM:

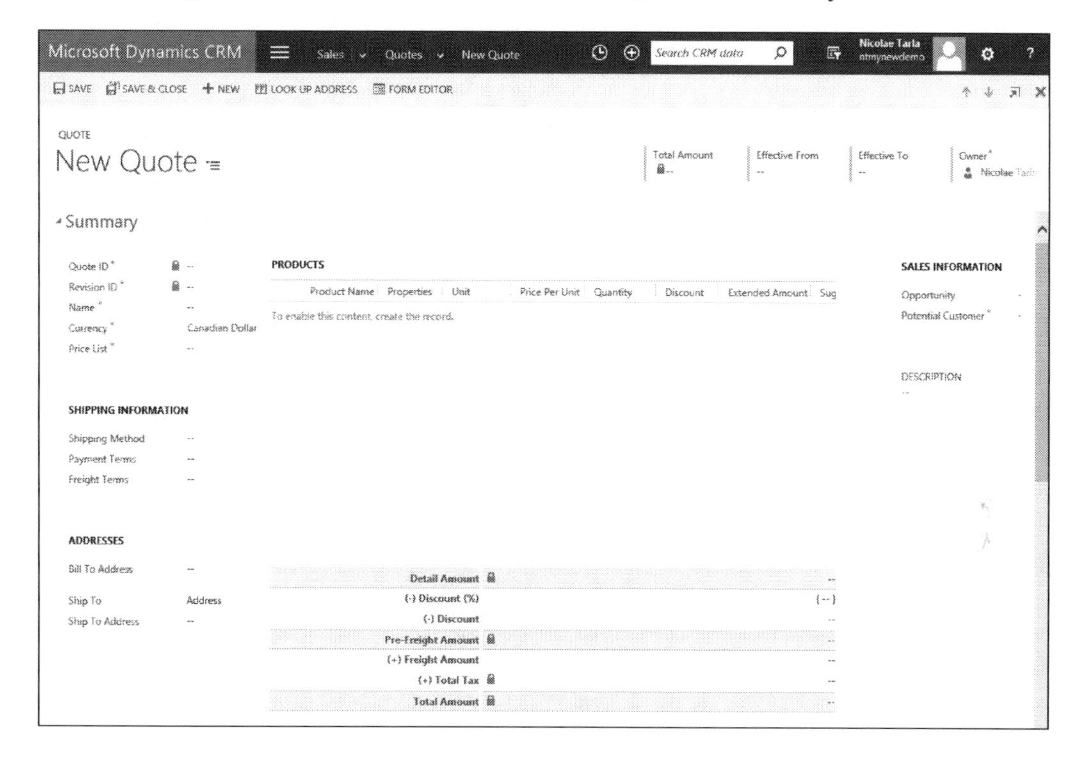

When a Quote is created from an Opportunity, the Products and Services associated with the Opportunity are automatically added to the Quote. When an Order is generated from a Quote, all products and services are also kept, and the Quote can be left open or closed.

Information stored with the Quote includes various dates as they relate to the Quote processing. These include effective from and to dates. It also stores **Bill To Address** and **Ship To Address**. **Ship to Address** can also be defined by product or service.

Other entities that can be associated to a Quote include the Customer, as Account and/or Contact, Competitors, Products and/or Services, Opportunity, as well as customer Addresses. Within a Quote, we can track Notes and associate Attachments.

The order Entity

The Order entity is in fact a Quote that has been accepted by a customer. They can be created from a Quote, or directly as a new Order.

The following screenshot presents the standard **New Order** form in Dynamics CRM:

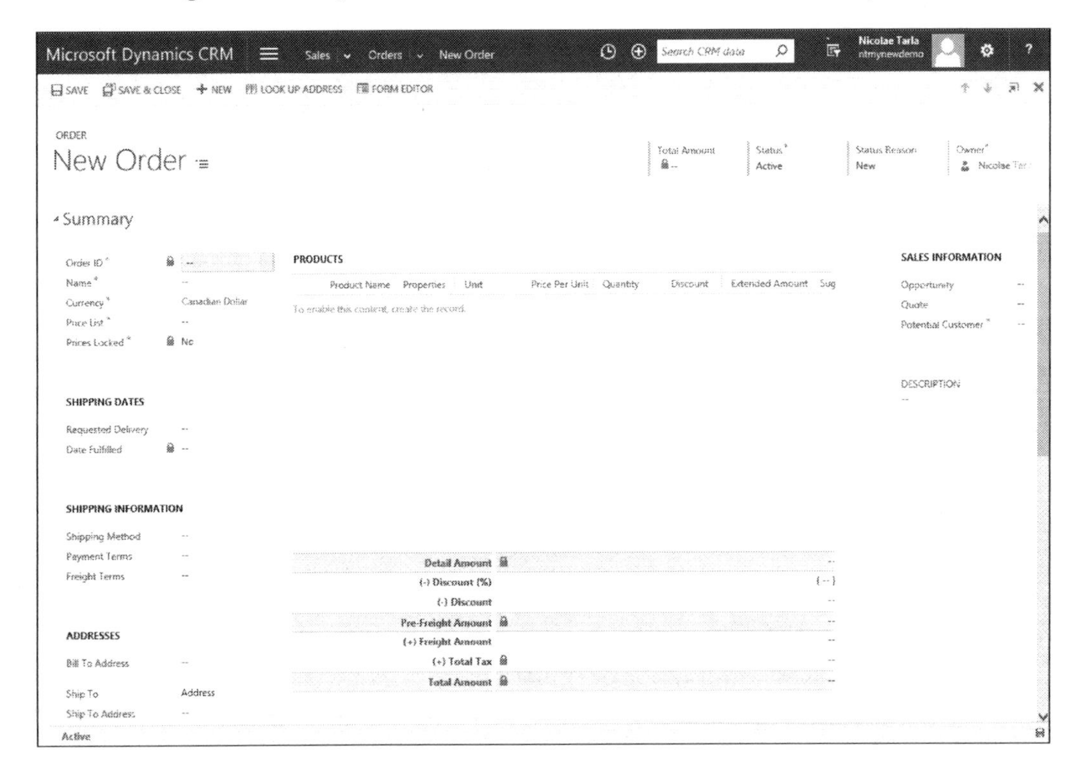

The Order form is quite similar to the Quote form, and allows us to track similar information as the Quote, as well as has the ability to associate the same related entities.

An Invoice Entity

An Invoice represents an Order that has been processed and billed. The standard **New Invoice** form in Dynamics CRM looks like this:

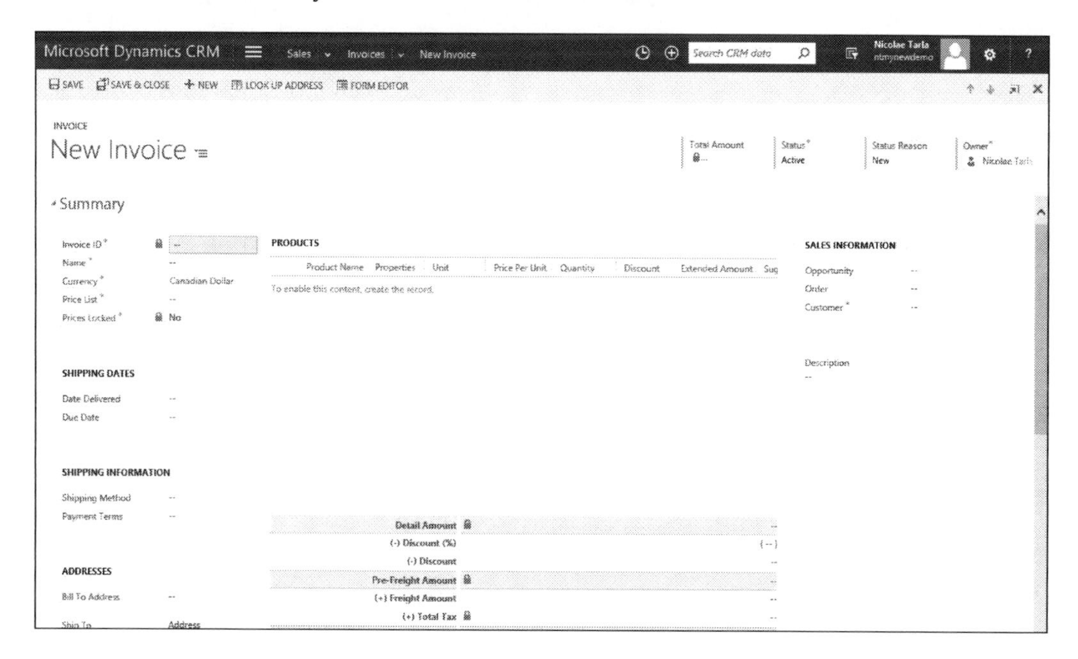

Just as Orders and Quotes, the user interface presents similar information and the ability to associate Products and/or Services. When an Invoice is generated from an Order, all the Order details are prepopulated on the Invoice. They can later be adjusted before marking the Invoice as Paid.

The Competitor Entity

The Competitor entity stores details about another organization offering similar Products and/or Services. This allows us to associate a Competitor record throughout the sales cycle. In addition, we can store details about the competitor, including listing of their products, competing directly with our products, sales literature, and any other sales materials.

The following screenshot depicts the standard **New Competitor** form in Dynamics CRM:

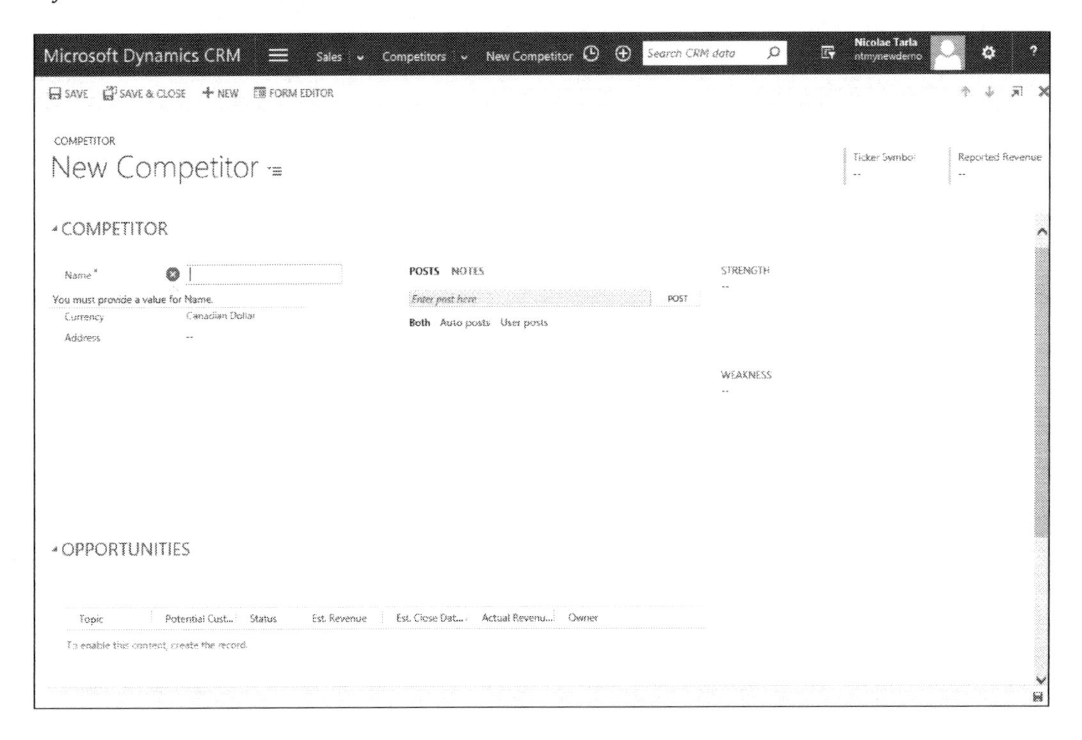

These competitors can be categorized and the details can be recorded on each competitor's strengths and weaknesses along with their profile. All this data collected allows sales representatives to make more informed decisions on each Opportunity, in order to increase its potential.

One or many Competitor records can be associated with every Opportunity.

In a way, even though it is being captured differently, a Competitor can be viewed as another Account. In fact, an organization can be both a Competitor and an Account (customer). The reason such an Account is captured as a Competitor is to provide the ability to track various other information specific to the role of a Competitor. These include strengths and weaknesses, as well as related Opportunities where this Competitor is involved in the sales process.

The Product Entity

Part of the Product Catalogue entity, the Product is a record representing an individual Product or Service offered to customers. Products can be associated with Opportunities, Quotes, Orders, and Service Cases.

A product can contain associated sales materials, as well as details about competitor offerings.

The following screenshot shows the standard **New Product** form in Dynamics CRM:

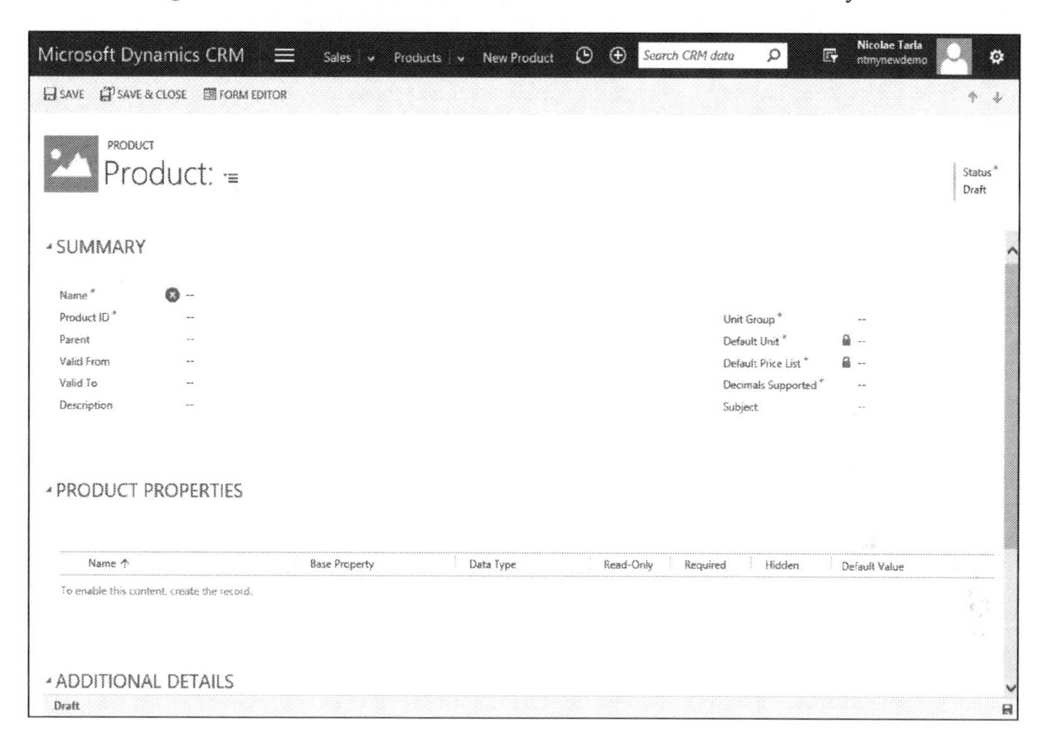

As part of the Product Catalog, a Product can have one or more pricing models and discount lists associated.

Based on user permissions, Products can be created, updated, disabled, or deleted. It is not recommended to delete any product records, because they are already associated with older Opportunities, Quotes, Orders, and Invoices, and removing them would break the integrity of the data. Always disable products rather than delete them.

Products can be configured in a hierarchical relationship. This hierarchy can be visualized, as described by the following screenshot:

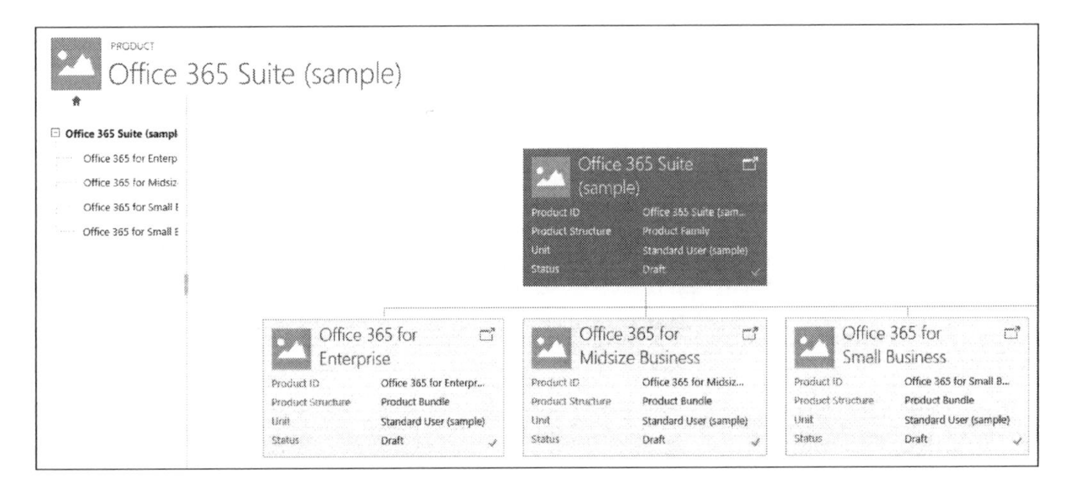

In addition to hierarchical relationships, products can also be grouped in bundles. A bundle is a grouping of products sold together, usually at a discounted price compared to the total cost of each individual product.

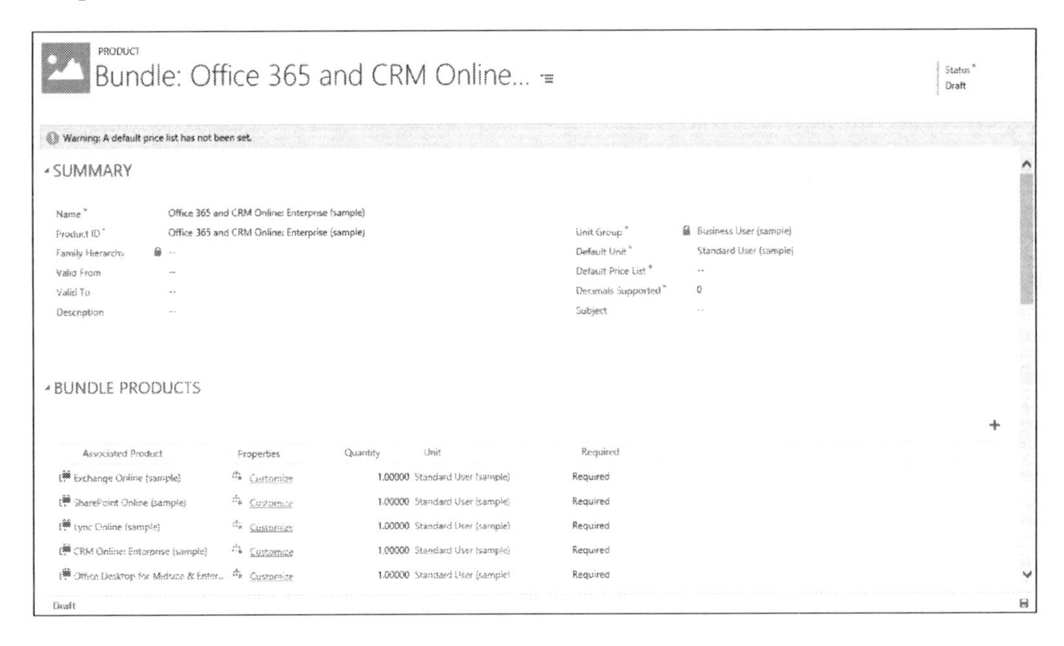

When looking at the generic view for Products, Families, and Bundles, each category is clearly represented by the icons preceding the Name.

Office 365 and CRM Online: Midsize (...	Office 365 and C...
Office 365 and CRM Online: Enterpris...	Office 365 and C...
Office 365 Service (sample)	Office 365 Servic...
Office Desktop (sample)	Office Desktop (...
CRM Service (sample)	CRM Service (sa...
Exchange Online (sample)	Exchange Online...
SharePoint Online (sample)	SharePoint Onli...

The Sales Goal Entity

The Goals configuration and tracking process allows managers to monitor progress against targets. Taking advantage of the goal management processes across Sales, and other business aspects allows for better planning and growth of the business.

Goals in Dynamics CRM can be created in a hierarchical structure, and can be rolled-up from individual users to the team and department level. This allows for greater visibility into the success of certain new initiatives and regular processes and regions.

A Goal entity interacts directly with two types of user records:

- The goal manager as the record owner, with rights to update and modify the goal properties
- The goal owner is the user that has to meet the goal targets

In addition, the Goal is set for a certain period of time, either mapped to a fiscal period or a custom arbitrary period.

The following screenshot shows the standard **New Goal** form in Dynamics CRM:

Sales Processes

Business Process Flow is a new feature introduced in Dynamics CRM 2013 and greatly enhanced in the following versions. It allows the system user to follow a predefined business process to completion, and to track progress in a visual way. On an entity form, they are represented through the visual representation at the top of the form. We have already seen these on the Lead and Opportunity entities.

The following screenshot depicts the standard Business Process Flow graphical interface, as seen on the default **New Lead** form:

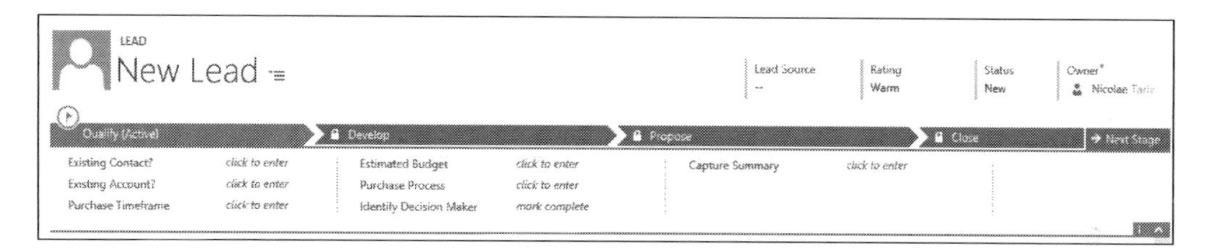

On a default base installation of Dynamics CRM, two sales processes are included as part of the sales module. They are as follows:

- Lead to opportunity sales process
- Opportunity sales process

Lead to Opportunity Sales Process

This Business Process Flow guides the user through the qualification of a new Lead into an Opportunity record.

The following screenshot shows part of the **Lead to Opportunity Sales Process** customization form:

This process defines the data needed to be captured on a Lead in order to qualify it. The preceding screenshot lists the data fields needed.

Opportunity Sales Process

This business process defines the stages to qualify an Opportunity. Just like the previous business process described, the fields required at each stage are highlighted.

The following screenshot shows part of the **Opportunity Sales Process** customization form:

BUSINESS PROCESS FLOW

Opportunity Sales Process

Details

Stage Name * **Qualify**

Entity * **Opportunity**

Stage Category **Qualify**

Step Name	Value	Required
Identify Contact	Contact	☐
Identify Account	Account	☐
Purchase Timeframe	Purchase Timeframe	☐
Estimated Budget	Budget Amount	☐
Purchase Process	Purchase Process	☐
Identify Decision Maker	Decision Maker?	☐
Capture Summary	Description	☐

+ Insert stage   Add branch

Stage Name * **Develop**

Entity * **Opportunity**

Relationship **Select relationships**

Stage Category **Develop**

Step Name	Value	Required
Customer Need	Customer Need	☐
Proposed Solution	Proposed Solution	☐
Identify Stakeholders	Identify Customer Contacts	☐
Identify Competitors	Identify Competitors	☐

+ Insert stage   Add branch

Stage Name * **Propose**

Entity * **Opportunity**

Step Name	Value	Required
Identify Sales Team	Identify Sales Team	☐
Develop Proposal	Develop Proposal	☐

MOVE

Sales Literature

In Dynamics CRM, the Sales Literature is comprised of individual sales attachments. Each attachment has one or more Keywords, an Author, and a Title. It also includes an abstract.

The **Sales Literature** is a repository driven by metadata. The **Subject** field allows you to associate each document to a specific topic defined in a taxonomy. Defining a clear, concise, and correct taxonomy from the get-go will help a lot in building a well-structured library and in providing increased value to your staff.

Each item in the **Sales Literature** repository can be associated with one or more Products and Competitors. They can then be retrieved and forwarded to Customers.

The **New Sales Literature** form looks like this:

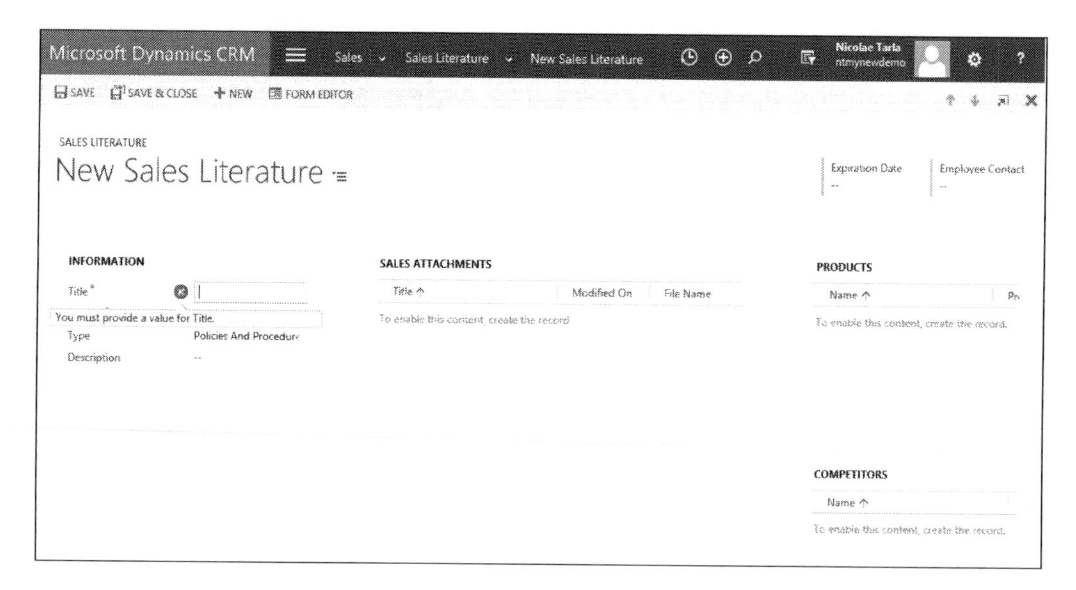

When creating **Sales Literature**, an **Expiration Date** can be defined on each record, so that the information captured becomes obsolete and unavailable to be referenced after a specified date. In addition, an owner responsible for maintaining this record is defined in the **Employee Contact** field.

The Sales Dashboards

As part of the Sales module in Dynamics CRM, Microsoft has introduced a set of Dashboards specific for Sales staff. They are as follows:

- **Sales Activity Dashboard**
- **Sales Activity Social Dashboard**
- **Sales Dashboard**
- **Sales Performance Dashboard**

Let's take a look at each dashboard and see what the difference is.

Sales Activity Dashboard

Sales Activity Dashboard consolidated the day to day data required by a sales representative to complete his regular tasks. It includes charts representing the sales pipeline, a view into open Leads, top opportunities and customers, as well as a view into pending activities.

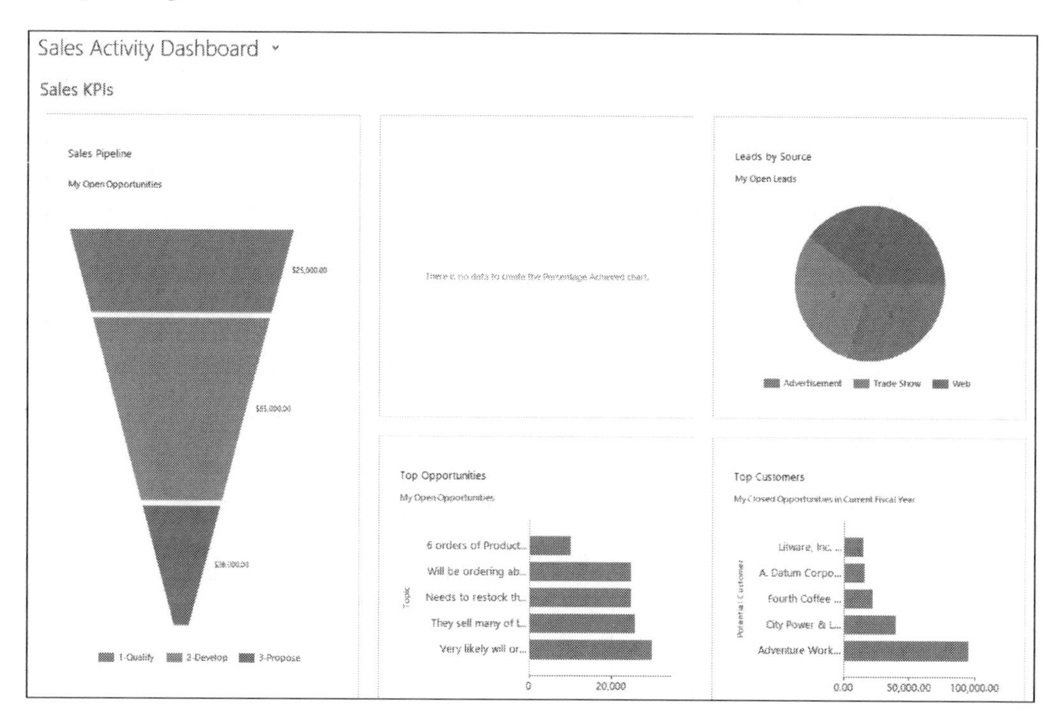

All data represented on this dashboard is data relevant to the current logged in sales representative. This is also called security filtering, and only presents dashboard information that the current logged-in user has permission to see. We will review security and ways to restrict access to only specific data in a later chapter.

This dashboard is also a good starting point for a sales representative logging into the system. Besides having visibility into graphical representations of various **Key Performance Indicators (KPIs)**, the bottom of the dashboard also presents a listing of the activities that need the user's attention. The sales representative can now start working and closing these activities.

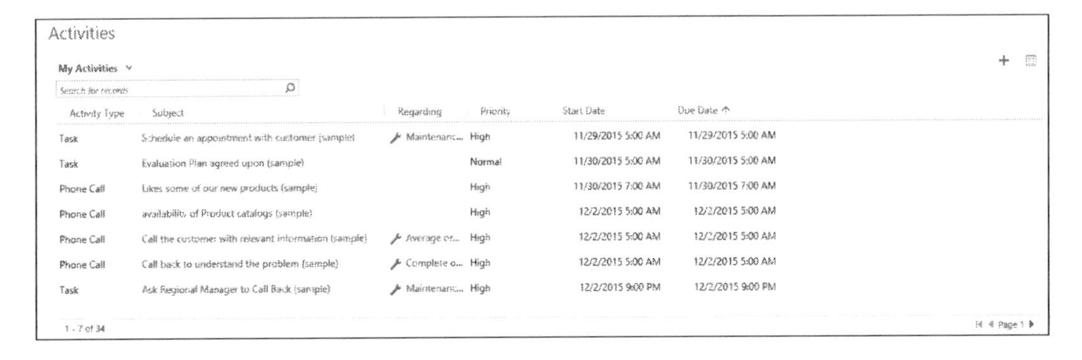

Activities

My Activities

Activity Type	Subject	Regarding	Priority	Start Date	Due Date
Task	Schedule an appointment with customer (sample)	Maintenanc...	High	11/29/2015 5:00 AM	11/29/2015 5:00 AM
Task	Evaluation Plan agreed upon (sample)		Normal	11/30/2015 5:00 AM	11/30/2015 5:00 AM
Phone Call	Likes some of our new products (sample)		High	11/30/2015 7:00 AM	11/30/2015 7:00 AM
Phone Call	availability of Product catalogs (sample)		High	12/2/2015 5:00 AM	12/2/2015 5:00 AM
Phone Call	Call the customer with relevant information (sample)	Average or...	High	12/2/2015 5:00 AM	12/2/2015 5:00 AM
Phone Call	Call back to understand the problem (sample)	Complete o...	High	12/2/2015 5:00 AM	12/2/2015 5:00 AM
Task	Ask Regional Manager to Call Back (sample)	Maintenanc...	High	12/2/2015 9:00 PM	12/2/2015 9:00 PM

1 - 7 of 34 Page 1

Sales Activity Social Dashboard

Sales Activity Social Dashboard takes from regular **Sales Activity Dashboard** most of the same data representations, but it adds the **what's new** section. Here, we can define the types of records to follow, as well as the type of posts based on who generated them.

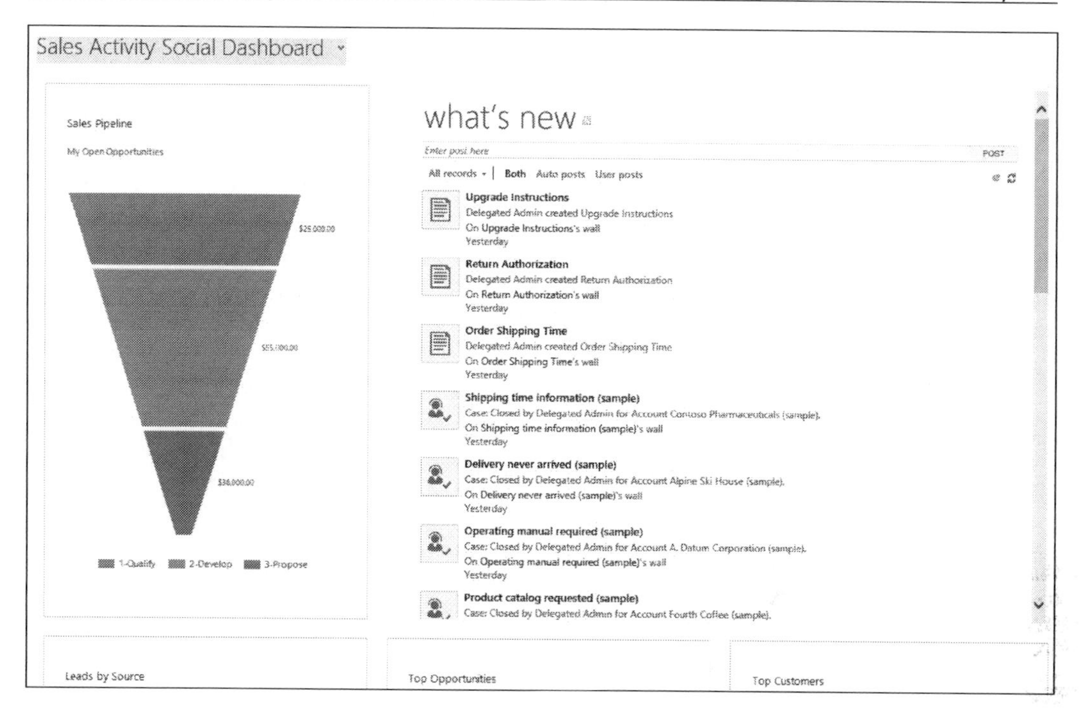

This dashboard allows greater interaction between sales representatives within the organization.

Sales Dashboard

The standard **Sales Dashboard** is less focused on charts and visual elements. Instead, it digs right into the data, and presents listings of Activities, Open Opportunities, Open Leads, and Active Accounts. We also get a look at the sales pipeline, as well as a view of the top customers by Opportunity Revenue.

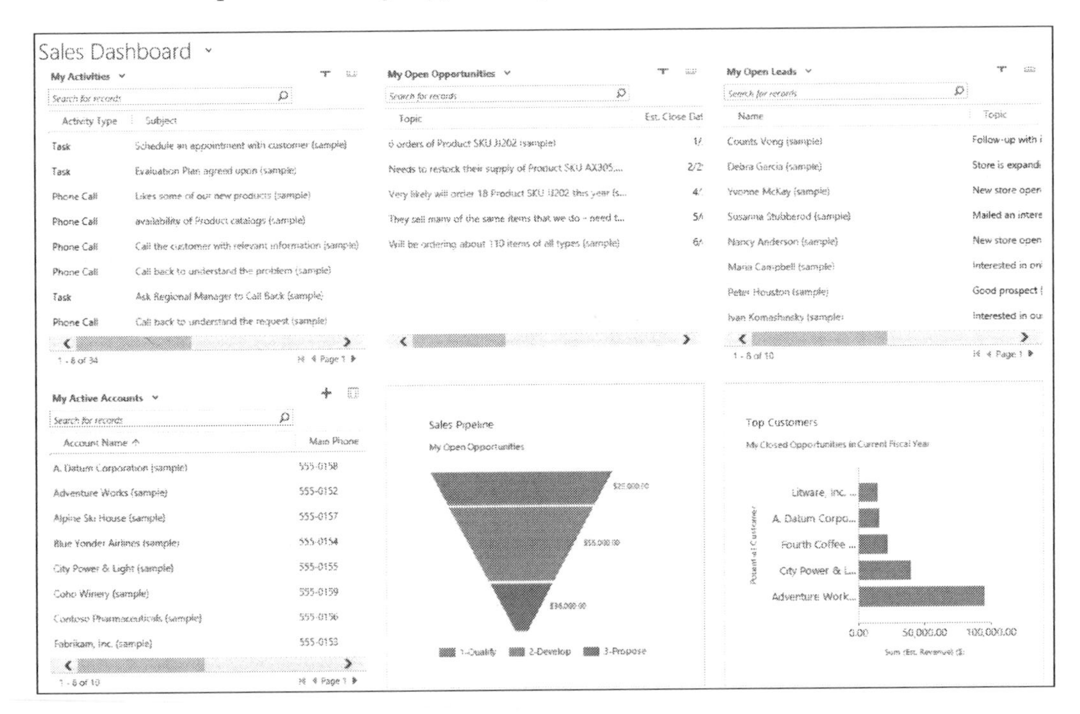

Sales Performance Dashboard

Sales Performance Dashboard focuses less on the sales data, and more on aggregating it to produce reports on Goals, total view on deals, and the progress, as well as a Sales Leaderboard.

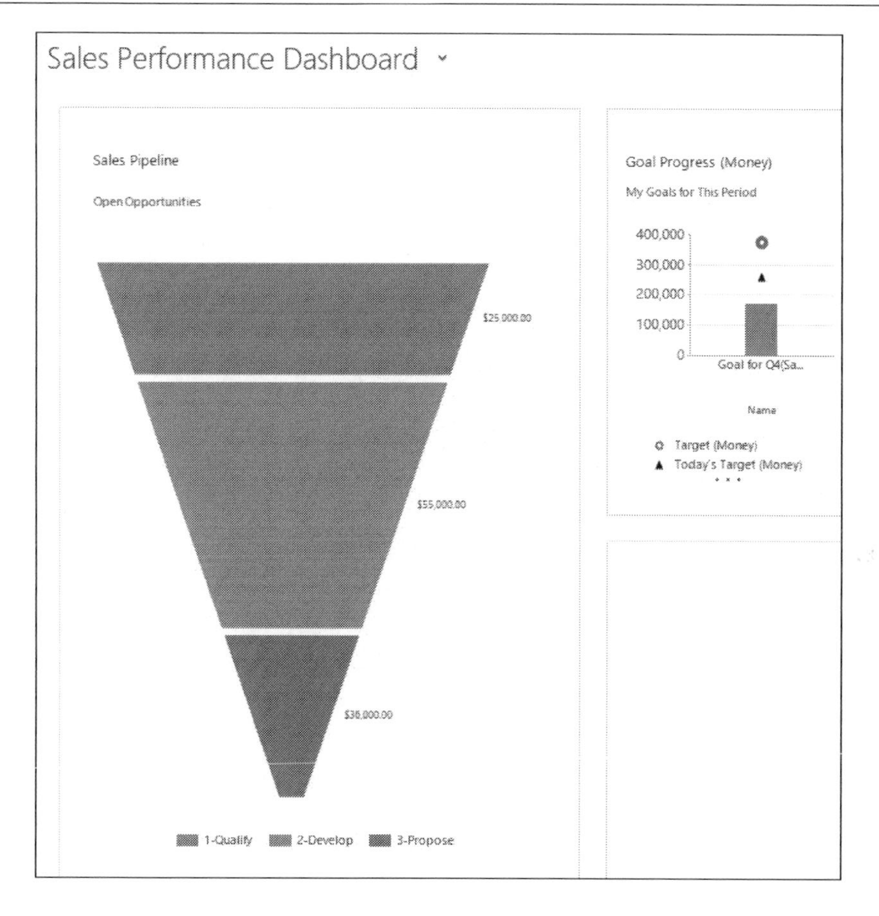

This dashboard will come in handy when comparing your sales staff performance against goals and other sales representatives or teams.

Sales Reports

A default installation of Dynamics CRM will include a set of reports to get you started. There are reports for each module of the application, as well as general reports spanning across data from multiple modules.

When working with reports, in most cases you will end up customizing your own reports. The default ones provided are presented as guidance, but they can, on certain occasions, be useful with no customization.

The standard reports revolve around Accounts and Contacts, as well as Activities, Leads, Sales History and Sales Pipeline.

The Dynamics CRM platform allows for various ways to report on data. Starting from aggregated and filtered data presented in views, and continuing with charts, the dashboard, and wizard-driven reports, the platform's capabilities are quite extensive. Add to that the ability to export to excel and perform further analysis, on using Dynamics CRM as a dataset for Power BI, and all of a sudden you can start creating some very fancy visualizations.

For special circumstances where none of the preceding options are sufficient, we still retain the ability to build specific **SQL Server Reporting Services** (**SSRS**) reports. The method varies between Dynamics CRM Online versus On-Premise, but at this point a developer should be involved in the process.

Marketing features

While the Sales module is logically separate from the Marketing one, certain features from Marketing are exposed here. As such, a sales representative has the ability to create his/her own marketing lists, and to generate quick campaigns. This is meant to allow sales staff to contact a group of customers at a time, and track this interaction within the system. This functionality is on top of the regular direct customer interaction, and is being tracked in the same way as any other customer contact.

CRM Service module

The Service module includes a set of powerful features in Microsoft Dynamics CRM, allowing service users and managers to manage and track customer complaints and service activities, as well as customer interactions within your organization.

The Service module can be looked at from the point of view of service management and service scheduling. The management aspect deals primarily with managing service tickets. They are called Cases within the context of Dynamics CRM. The other aspect, scheduling, provides the ability to schedule resources for customers.

Starting with Dynamics CRM 2016, a new feature specific to Service is the introduction of the Interactive Service Hub. This is a first kick at the can at making Dynamics CRM behave a lot more like a desktop/mobile application rather than a web application.

Interactive Service Hub

The Interactive Service Hub is an entirely new way to look at Dynamics CRM as a whole application. For those that have used the mobile application, this will look relatively familiar. The reason is because this experience is based on the **Mobile Client Application** (**MoCA**) client. This is the mobile client previously used and made available for tablets or as a modern application.

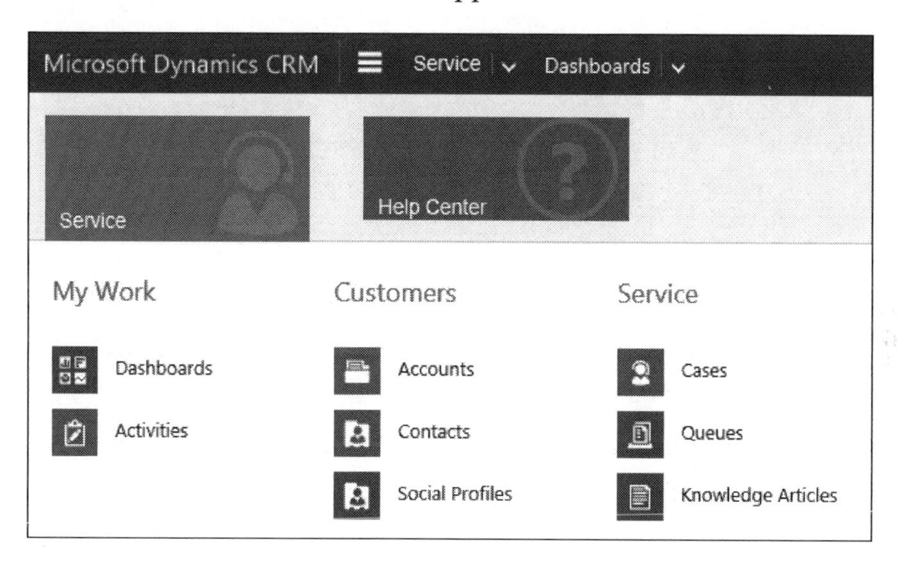

While the navigation resembles the familiar navigation of the platform, this is where the similarities end.

This being the first attempt at this, you will find that not all the features available in the standard Service module are available in the Interactive Service Hub. This is a lighter version of Service, but don't be fooled, the value of using it is there. Starting with the Dashboards, we are offered, by default, Tier 1 and Tier 2 Service dashboards, as well as Knowledge Management dashboards.

The new dashboards are now a lot more interactive and more visual than before. The information is now presented in the format of **cards**, with the ability to add global filtering and sorting and to interact easily with each card individually or in bulk. Yes, from the dashboard, you can select a few cards and perform the same action on all of them at once. Depending on the entity type behind the card, the action will vary accordingly.

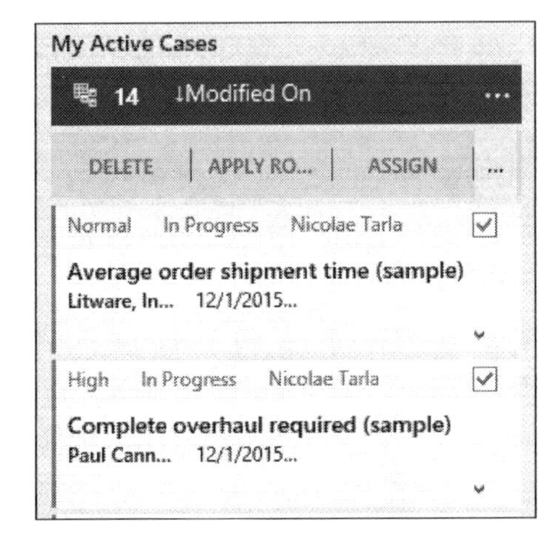

In addition, these dashboards can be switched from a card-like experience to a more visual tile-based experience.

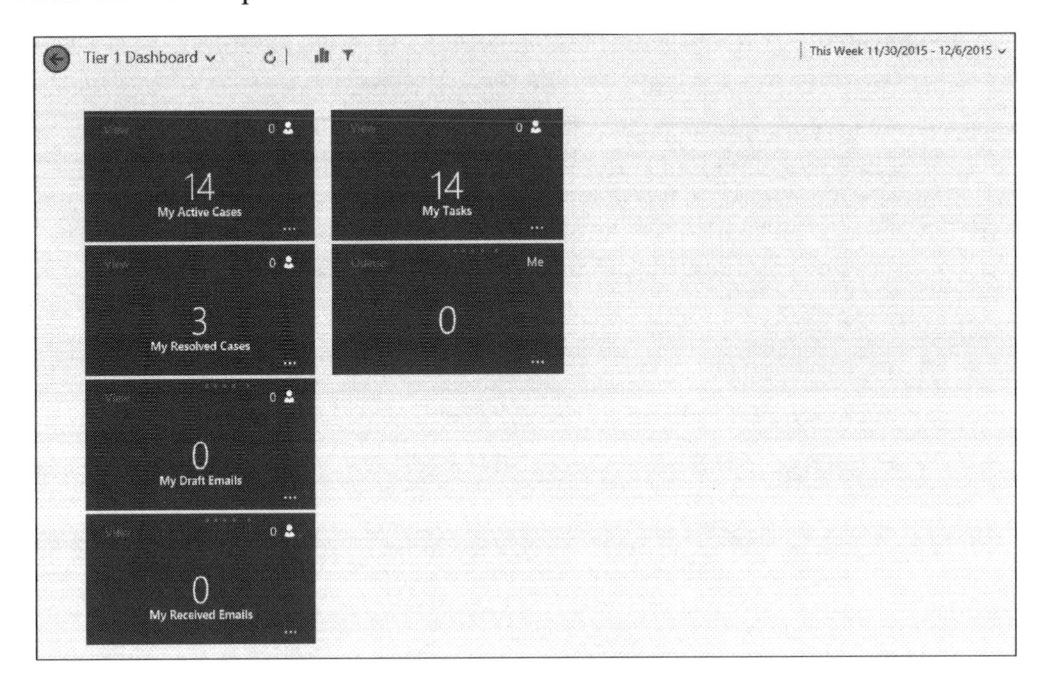

Working on a specific record, the user experience is also enhanced. Concepts such as the Timeline, which is based on the former Activity Feed, or the Related area make it a lot easier for the user working with this record to get quicker and better visibility. The tiled layout is better spaced and is also more suited to touch. Tabs are back at the top of the record, with easy access to sections such as **DETAILS**, **CASE RELATIONSHIPS**, and **SLA** (Service Level Agreement). The Business Process Flow is also visually improved, showing only as a narrow line with minimal screen real estate usage, and only expanding the selected steps when clicked on.

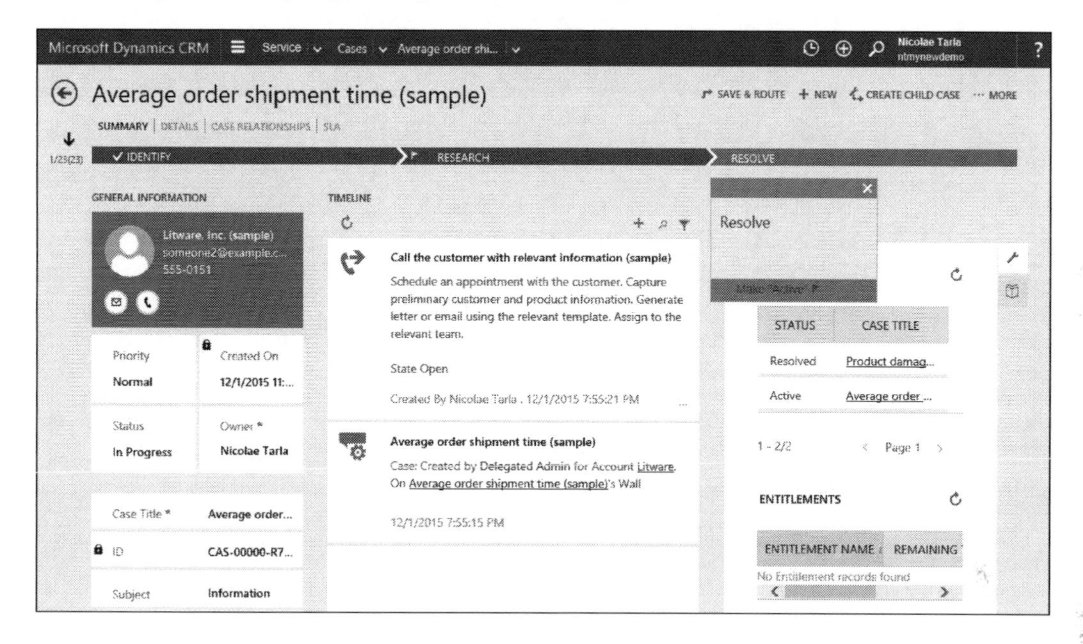

In addition to this core Service functionality, the Interactive Service Hub finally brings the ability to create and manage Knowledge Articles. This is separate from Sales Literature existing on the core platform, and brings in features such as out of the box versioning, approval processes, metadata for articles, and an enhanced editor with support for formatted articles that now can also include images. This is a very rich editor similar to that of many CMS systems.

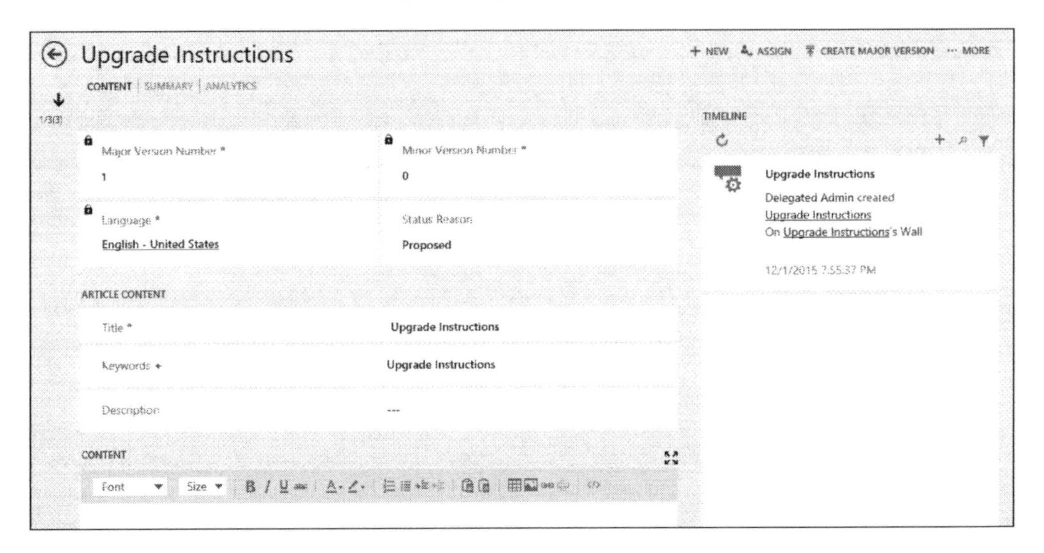

The Interactive Service Hub can be accessed at the URL of your organization followed by `engagementhub.aspx`. This translates to the following URLs depending on the type of environment you use:

For Dynamics CRM 2016 On-Premise, the URL will be:

```
http[s]://<ServerName>/<OrganizationName>/engagementhub.aspx
```

For Dynamics CRM 2016 Internet Facing Deployment (IFD), the URL will be:

```
https://<hostname>[:port]/engagementhub.aspx
```

And for Dynamics CRM 2016 Online, the URL will be:

```
https://<Name>.crm[#].dynamics.com/engagementhub.aspx
```

An important note about the Interactive hub is that, due to the fact that it is using new technologies and concepts around local client storage and caching, in order to use it, you must have a modern browser and you cannot use private browsing.

Service Entities

Just like with the Sales module, the Service module contains specific Service entities, as well as shared entities. The Service specific entities are explained in the following section.

The Case Entity

The Case entity represents an incident or a ticket logged in the system as it relates to a customer. The system users create Cases to track a request, problem, or question from an existing customer. This entity is also the central point to track all future communications and actions performed while handling the request until completion.

The Cases tracked in the system can be in one of the following states: **Active**, **Resolved**, or **Cancelled**.

The following is a screenshot of the standard **New Case** form:

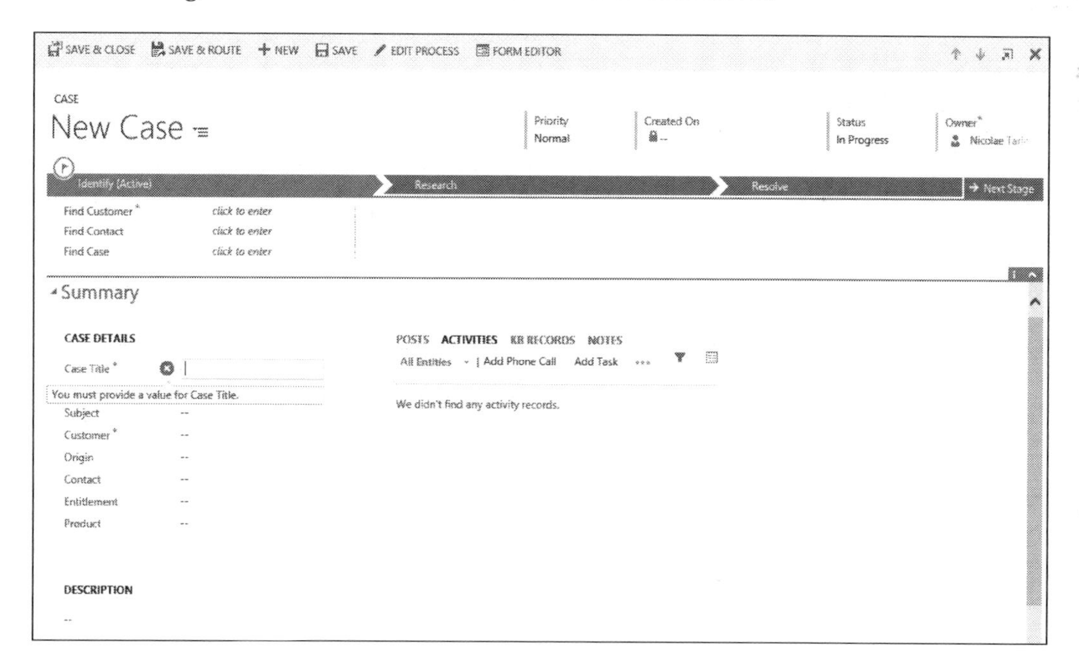

Starting with Dynamics CRM 2013 Service Pack 1, now we support the ability to relate Cases hierarchically. This allows for better organization of the data, and easier management of Cases by users.

> Only one level of hierarchy is supported. A Case cannot be associated with another Case, if in turn, it is associated with another one. On child Cases, the view into child Cases is not available.

You can associate up to 100 child Cases with a parent Case.

When closing a Case, a case resolution activity is created, which stores details about the reason for closing, the duration, and the billing status.

Contracts Entity

A Contract is an agreement with a customer to manage support services to be provided. It defines either a specific number of Cases, or a set period of time to be provided for support. Thus, the Contract defines the type and level of support a customer will receive.

Contracts can be created for existing and/or new customers. They must be related to either an Account or a Contact entity. And this is how the standard **New Contract** form looks in Dynamics CRM:

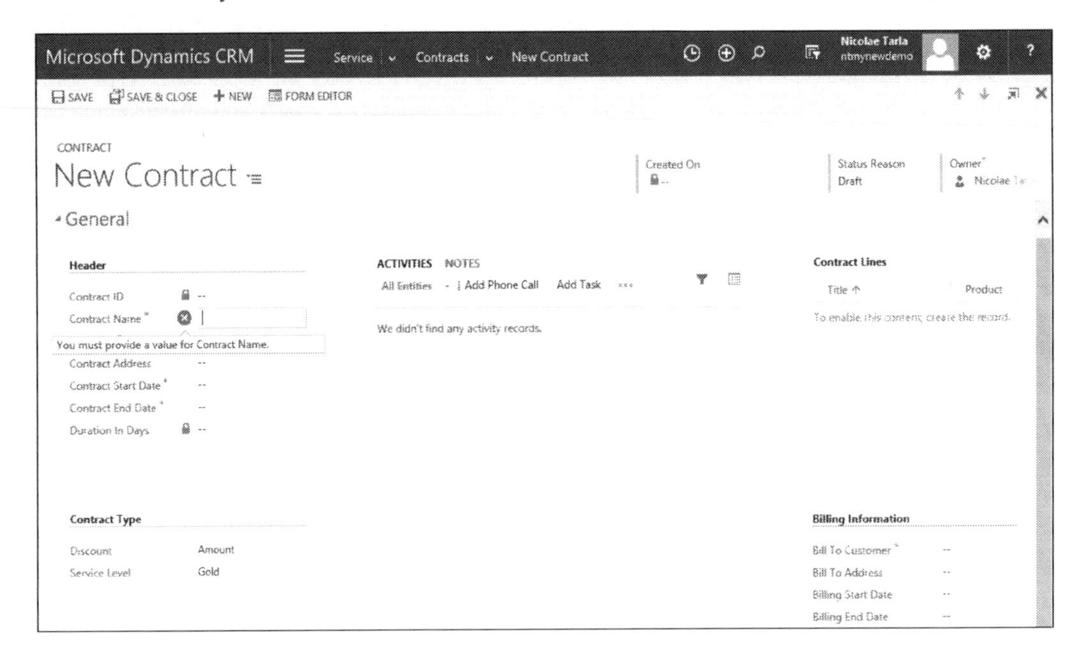

The contract is registered in the Dynamics CRM system as a Draft until it is invoiced. While a Contract is a Draft, it can be updated, and the template used can be changed.

Once **Contract** is marked as **Invoiced** or **Active**, all changes to the **Contract** are saved as **New Contract**, associated with the original **Contract**.

Queues Entity

Queues are used within Dynamics CRM to organize, prioritize, and monitor a user or a team's work. In conjunction with routing workflows, queues play an important part in automating standard business processes and improve efficiency.

From an underlying point of view, **Queues** are comprised of **Queue Items**. Each **Queue Item** is a record pointing to an existing system entity. For example, you can have a Queue holding various Cases. Each **Queue Item** would point back to an existing Case. **Queue Item** can point to a Task, Email, or Case. In addition, all new custom entities can be enabled for queues.

A queue can hold more than one entity type. Thus, a queue can hold Task and Cases together.

Each system user gets a personal Queue associated with the respective user profile. In addition, new Queues can be created, and they can be either private or public.

Services Entity

The **Service** entity represents work to be performed for a customer. It is defined by the date and time, duration, name, resource(s) assigned, and other fields as needed.

The Service appointment works in conjunction with the Service Calendar and the resource calendar, along with other factors to determine the resource ranking and availability. This entity is used in creating scheduled activities, and works in conjunction with resources, equipment, and services offered.

The following screenshot shows the **New Service** standard form in Dynamics CRM:

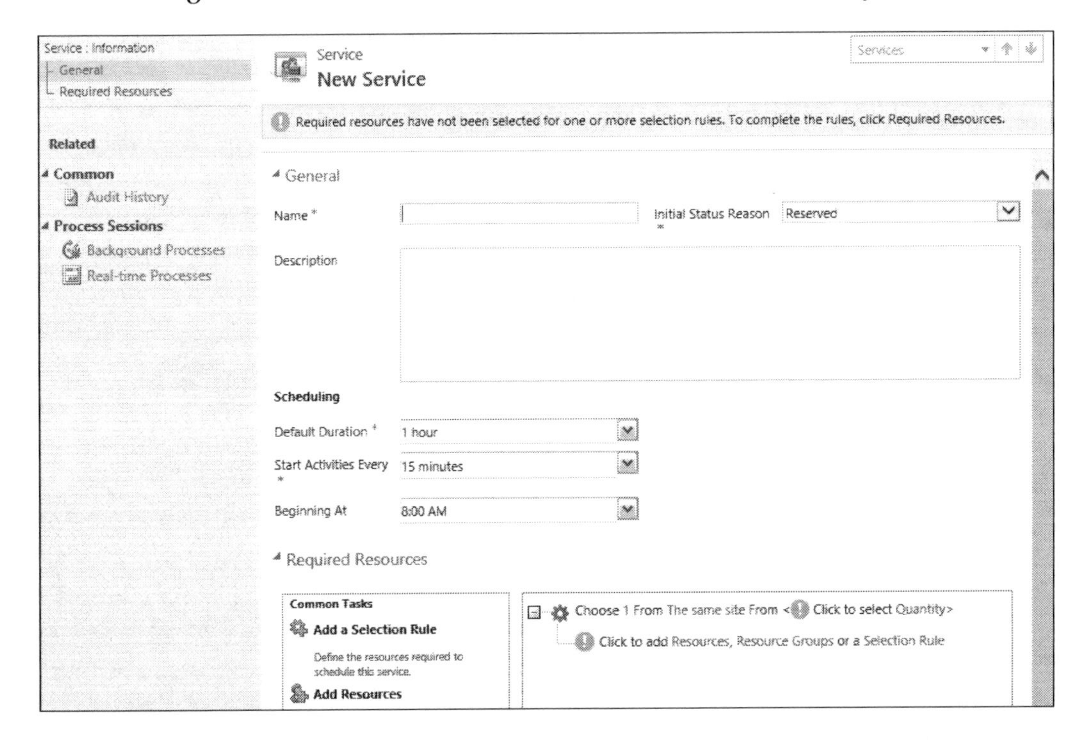

Starting with Dynamics CRM 2016, Microsoft has acquired FieldOne and has started to integrate the FieldOne Sky service as an additional offering for extensive field service functionality. The added benefits of this solution can justify the additional cost for certain customers, but for many scenarios, the out of the box functionality provided around service and scheduling calendars can be sufficient. We will take a closer look at the added functionality of FieldOne Sky in a later chapter.

The Calendar Entity

The Service Calendar is the representation of all Service records created, based on resources and equipment availability, and the duration of a service activity. The Calendar entity is aggregating the Service data with holiday schedules and business closures, and presents availability for scheduling new service activities.

Calendars are related to Calendar Rules, which define duration and availability, recurrence, and start/end times. These rules can be ordered and ranked to determine precedence. Rules can overlap.

Goals Management

Just as the Sales module, in the Service module, goals can be configured for users. While these goals will probably not deal with sales amounts, unless upsells are counted, they will most definitely deal with the scope and number of service calls handled, as well as possibly with **Service Level Agreements** (**SLAs**).

Just like before, Goals are being set up for users, rolled up at a team level, and must be configured for a specific duration.

Goals can be related as parent/child goals, and the results will be automatically rolled up.

Service Processes

With a default Dynamics CRM deployment, for the service module, we only get one predefined Business Process Flow. This is the **Phone to Case Process**.

The Business Process Flow for the **Phone to Case Process** looks like this:

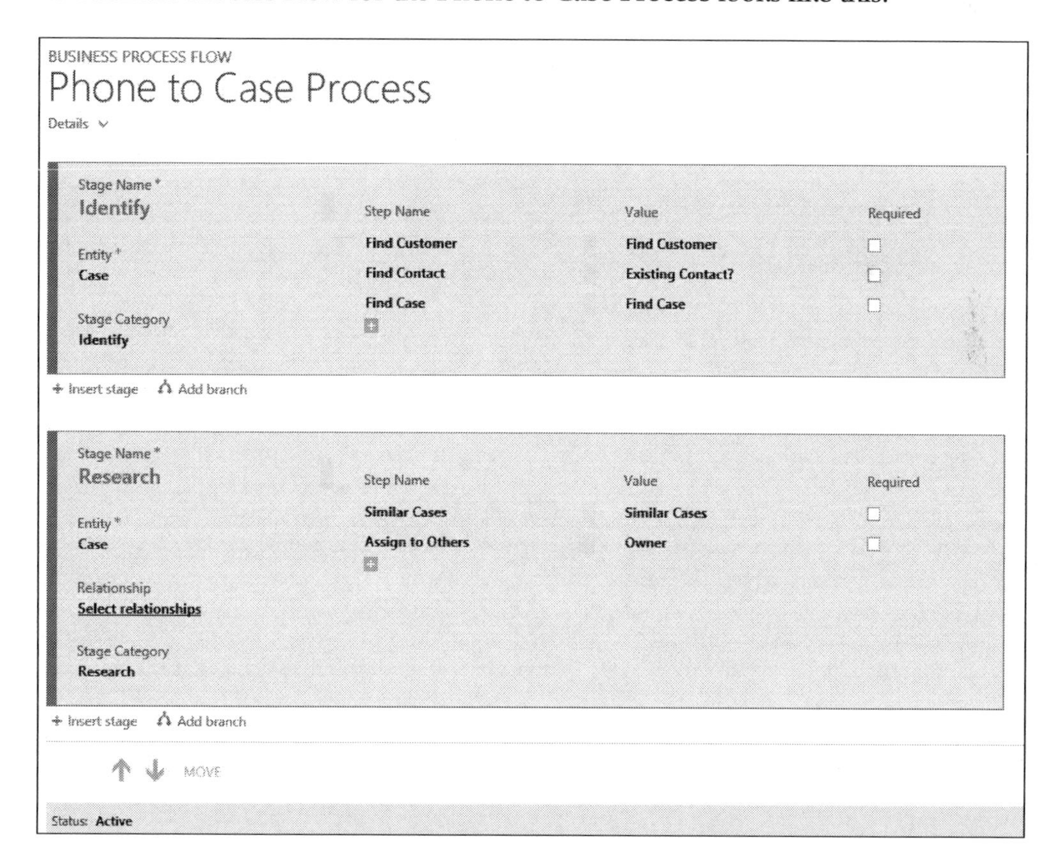

This process lives on the Case entity, and handles the standard approach to solving Cases through three standard stages.

This Business Process Flow created in the preceding wizard will be displayed on a **New Case** form as follows:

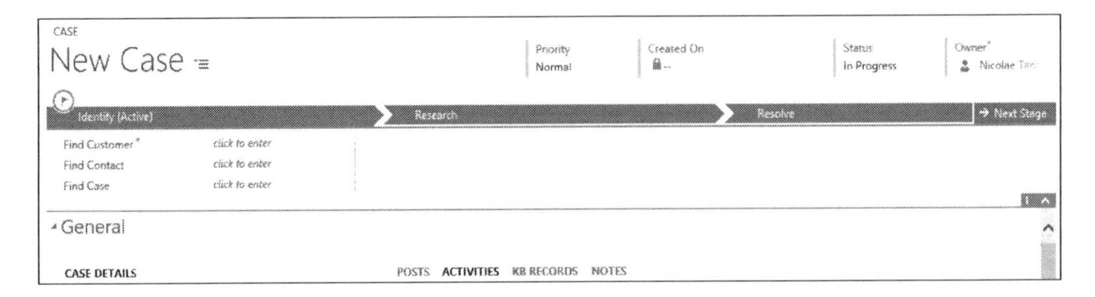

Service Dashboards

For the Service aspect of the business, just like for Sales, dashboards are an invaluable resource to present data to the system users in a variety of ways. By default, the Service module comes with five standard dashboards serving various roles.

Customer Service Representative Social Dashboard

As an aggregation of Case details, listing of activities and the social component presenting real time posts from various records, **Customer Service Representative Social Dashboard** is the default dashboard for the Service module.

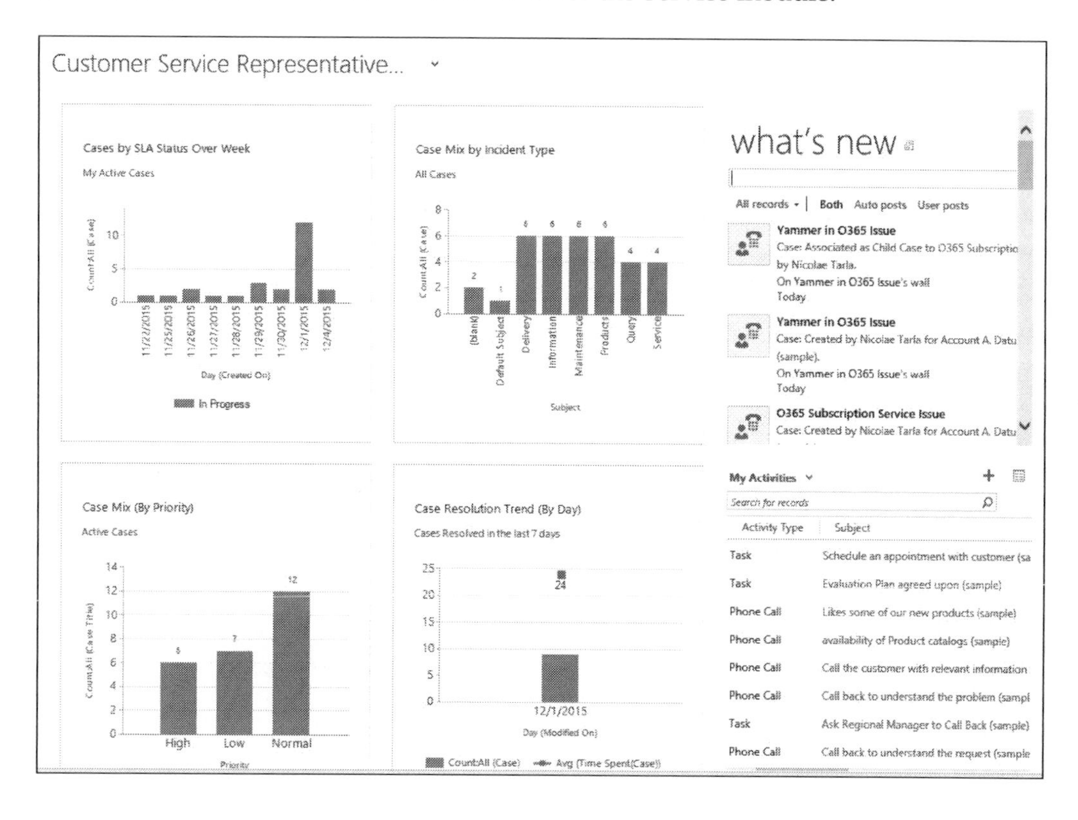

Customer Service Representative Dashboard

As a trimmed down, down to the meat and potatoes of Service, the CSR Dashboard strips out the social aspect and focuses entirely on the data a service representative will need to work with on a day-to-day schedule.

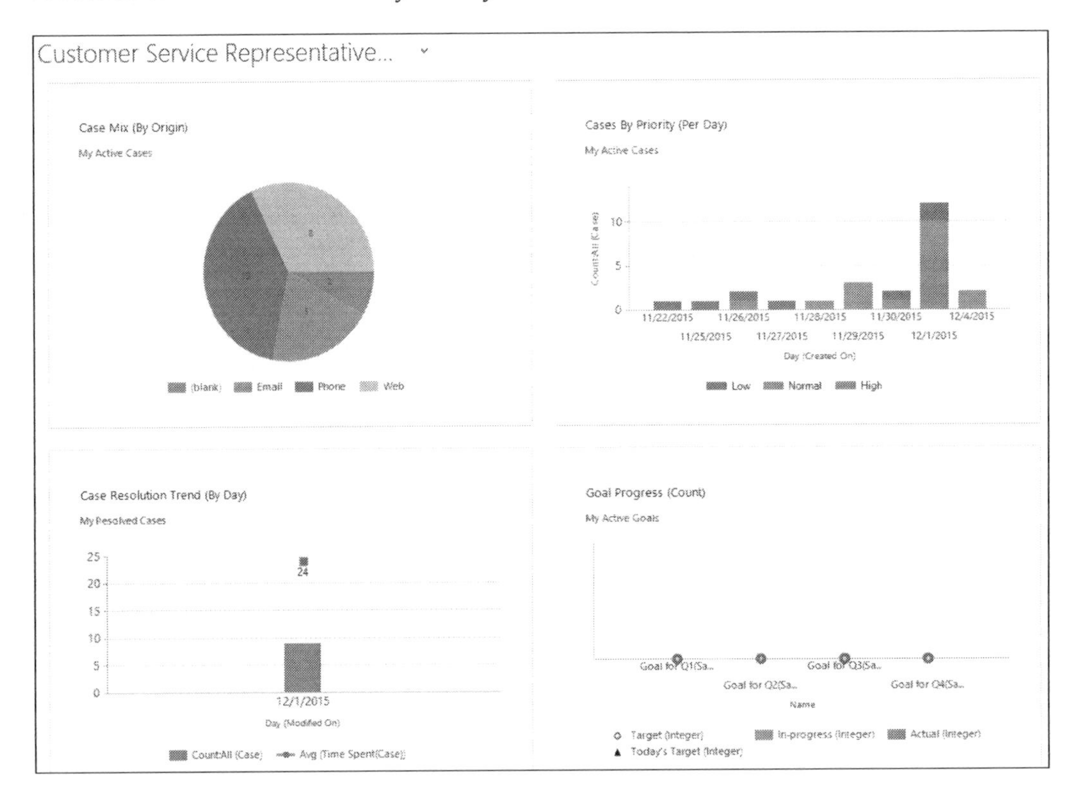

It focuses entirely on the Case types, various categories, resolution performance, and goals, as well as the activities in the service representative's queue.

Customer Service Performance Dashboard

The Performance Dashboard focuses primarily on the service representative's performance against SLAs, and looks at Case mix and trends. It is a charting dashboard giving a quick overview of the current status.

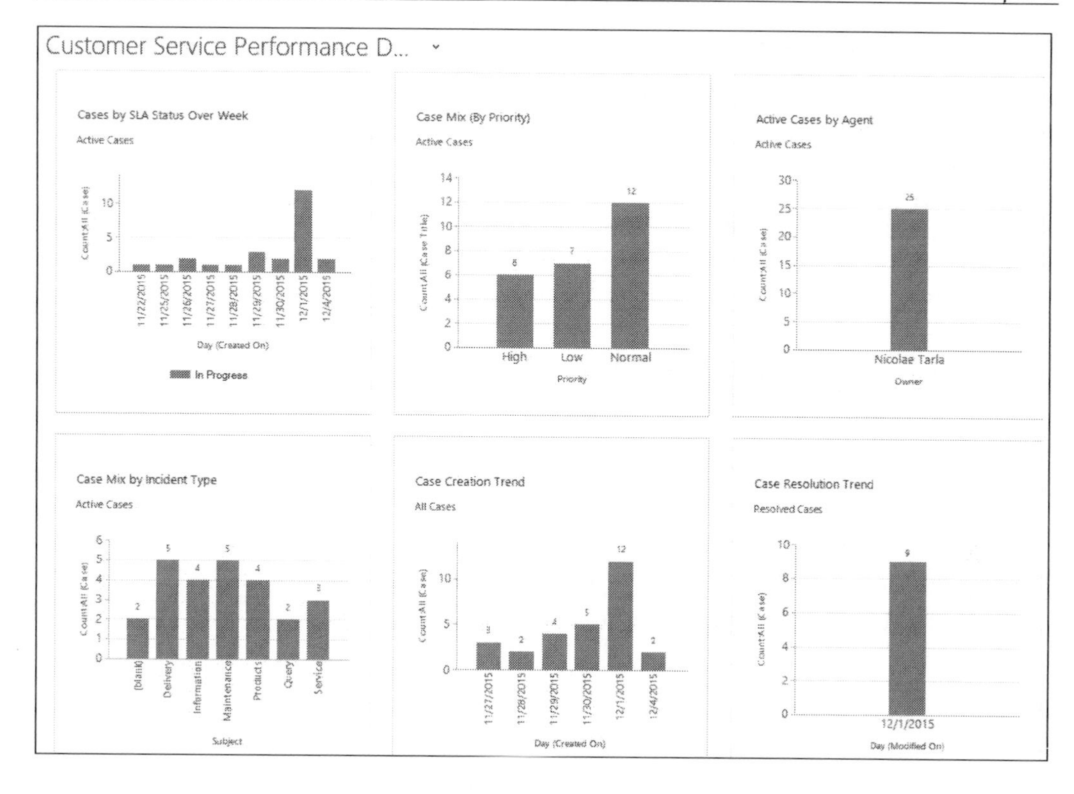

Customer Service Operations dashboard

The Operations Dashboard is analyzing Cases by origin and priority, and structures data by owner and priority. The Leaderboard section looks at Cases across the current team.

In addition to Case-specific diagrams, this Dashboard also includes information about Articles in the Knowledge Base, and their status.

Customer Service Manager dashboard

The Manager dashboard combines the social aspect of notifications with generic information across the whole team. Sections of this dashboard present views into Cases by agents, team, queues, and priority.

Service Reports

Just like the other modules, the Service module presents us with a set of standard reports. These include, but are not limited to, reports around Activities, Case Summaries, and Service Activity Volumes.

A large variety or additional reports can be customized in various ways. More information on reporting customization can be found in *Chapter 6, Dynamics CRM Administration*.

CRM Marketing Module

The Marketing module completes the set of modules provided with the Dynamics CRM platform. This module is targeted at marketing professionals, and provides them a solid set of tools for retaining existing customers, attracting new ones, and expanding the business.

This module fits in nicely with the Sales module, as it allows you to track the generation of Leads from specific campaigns.

Marketing Entities

As part of this module, the main entities revolve all around customer communication. We have management of Marketing Lists, Campaigns, and Quick Campaigns. They all work in conjunction with base system entities such as accounts, contacts, leads, and even sales literature.

Marketing Lists

The Marketing List is the foundation of any marketing campaign. It is a collection of customers grouped on specific criteria.

Marketing Lists can be created in Dynamics CRM in two ways. They can be static or dynamic. A **static** Marketing List is a list that once created, remains unchanged until a system user performs the changes manually. On the other hand, a **dynamic** Marketing List is a list that is generated based on a condition. On each refresh of the list, the condition is applied as a filter across all records, and the list is regenerated.

The standard **New Marketing List** form in Dynamics CRM looks like this:

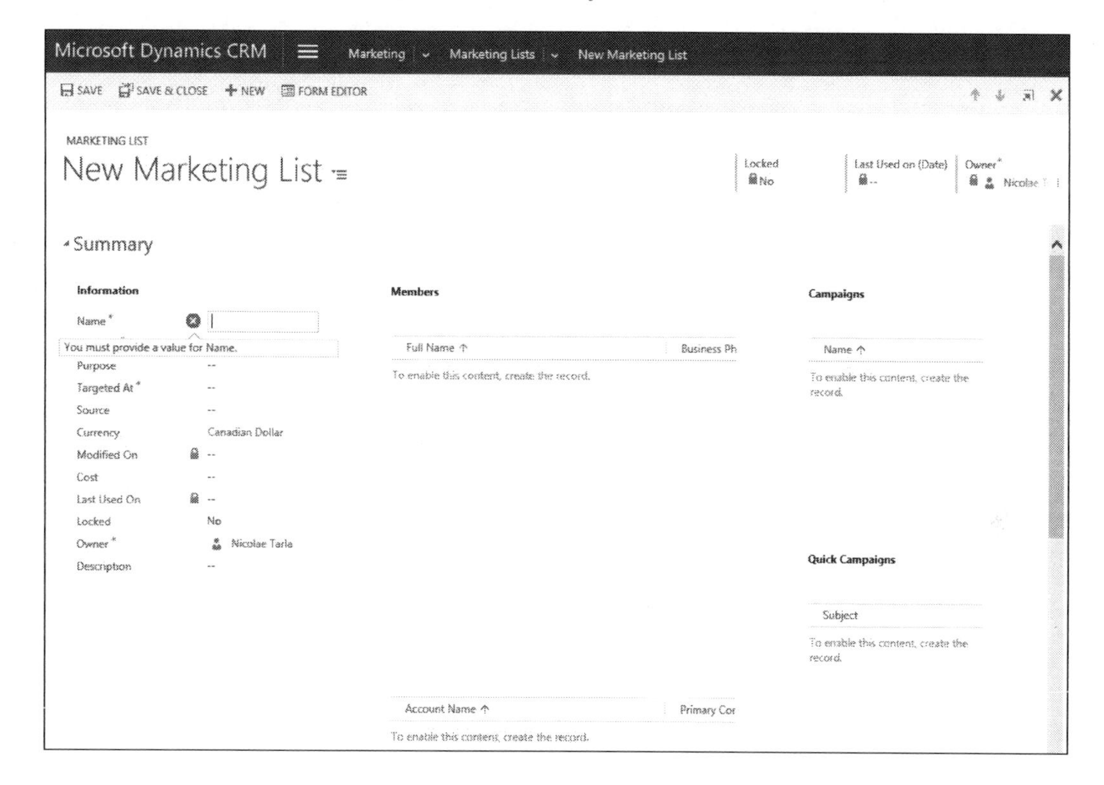

On the standard Marketing List's management form, besides the definition fields and the members associated with the list, we can see which Campaigns and Quick Campaigns our list is associated to. This is an easy way to find out whether a Marketing List is being used in the system, and where.

Campaigns

The Campaign in Dynamics CRM is the entity collecting information about promoting a product, service, or business. The medium(s) in which communication with the customer is achieved, as well as related cost information are some of the details tracked on a Campaign.

The Campaign is meant to achieve a clear result. As such, within the Campaign itself, there are **Key Performance Indicators (KPIs)** and metrics available to measure the success of a Campaign.

Within a regular Campaign, communication to customers can take place in various ways. A Campaign allows us to track, for example direct mail, e-mail, and phone communication against one or more specific Marketing Lists.

A Campaign is comprised of planning activities and tasks, campaign activities, communications, and responses from customers. A Campaign also has a list of related products and/or services as well as various sales literature elements.

A Campaign can be targeted to more than one type of entity. For example, we can target it to Accounts and Leads by creating two different Marketing Lists and associating both to the Campaigns.

In the process of organizing a Campaign, we can structure and organize all tasks and activities, just like planning any other project. As such, we can add campaign activities for research, content preparation, target marketing list creation, lead qualification, content distribution, direct initial contact, direct follow-up contact, and reminder distribution. All these activities can be assigned to the team participating in the creation and management of each Campaign.

The **New Campaign Activity** form looks like this:

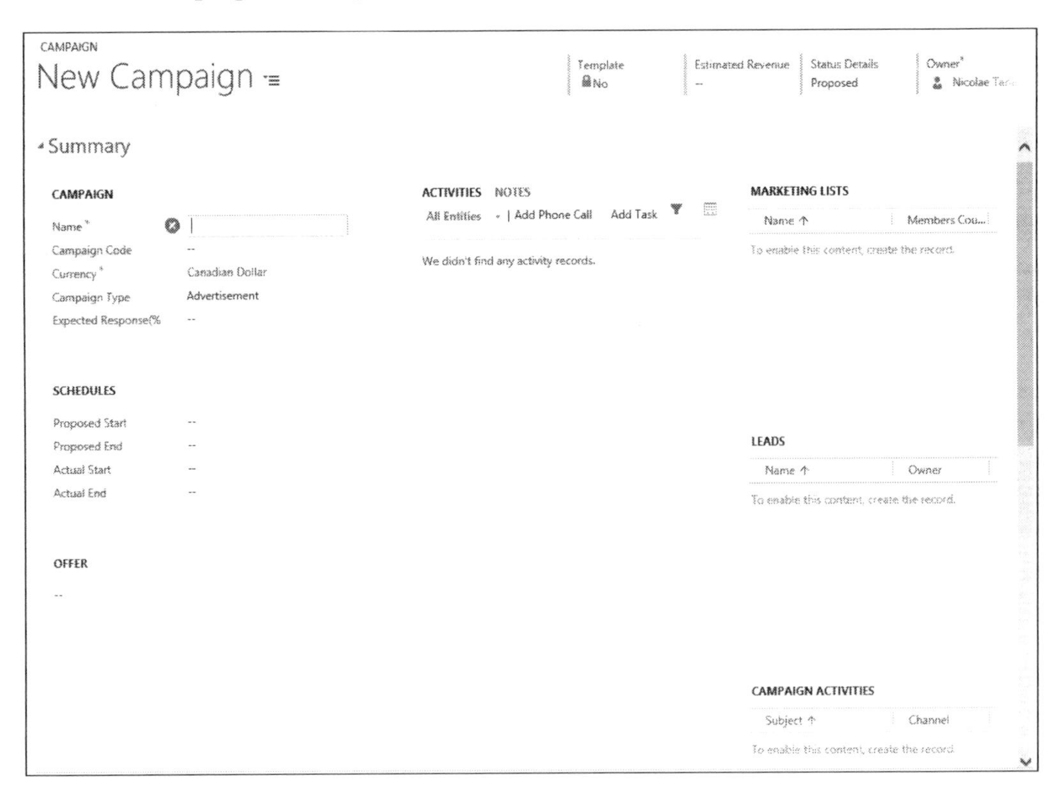

In addition, we can create a set of planning activities within the Campaign. They help with the preparation of the Campaign. These are standard Activities in the context of Dynamics CRM and are associated directly with the Campaign.

The following screenshot shows the expanded options for adding new activities in Dynamics CRM:

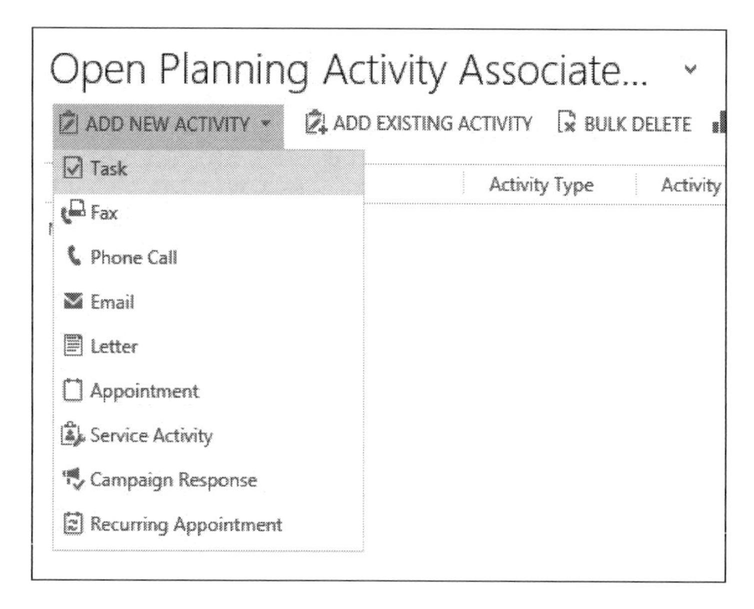

Campaign responses can also be tracked within the Campaign. They can be either directly tracked for e-mail marketing campaigns, or manually entered for other types of campaigns.

The following screenshot shows the **New Campaign Response** standard form in Dynamics CRM:

A Campaign can be comprised of all the previously mentioned elements, but it can also be a parent of another Campaign. As such, we can create a hierarchical Campaigns structure, with various subcampaigns managed independently. Reporting across all related Campaigns can then roll-up all related data to give the marketing analysts an overall view at the highest level.

Quick Campaigns

Quick Campaign is very similar in structure to a regular Campaign. The main difference is the number of channels that can be used to reach out to customers. In a Quick Campaign, we are limited to a single method of communication to our customers. As such, for an e-mail blast, the only method of communication is e-mail, and thus we can use a Quick Campaign.

As far as targeting a Quick Campaign goes, we can target only the members of a single Marketing List or to the resulting members selected through a query. This query could return entities of various types, for example, Accounts, Contacts, and Leads.

The way to create **Quick Campaign** is from within a **Marketing List**. From the navigation ribbon, select the ellipsis to expand the additional options, and select **Create Quick Campaign**.

The next screenshot shows where **Create Quick Campaign** is located on a **Marketing List** entity:

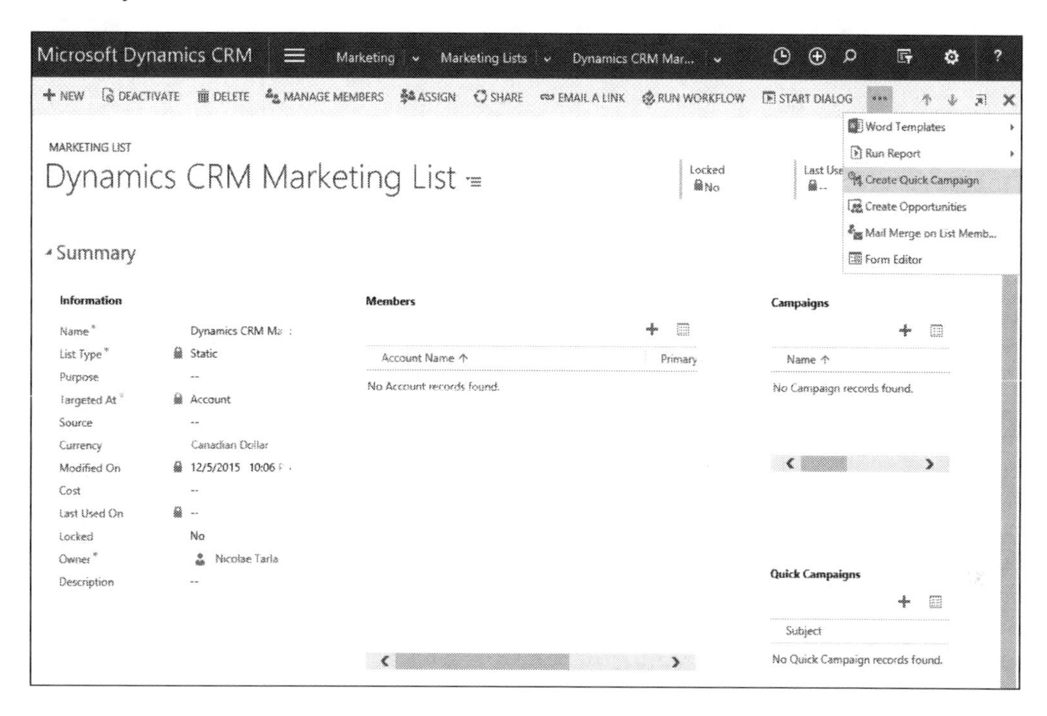

Quick Campaign Wizard will then guide you through the necessary steps to create the Campaign.

The **Quick Campaign Wizard** starts with the following screen:

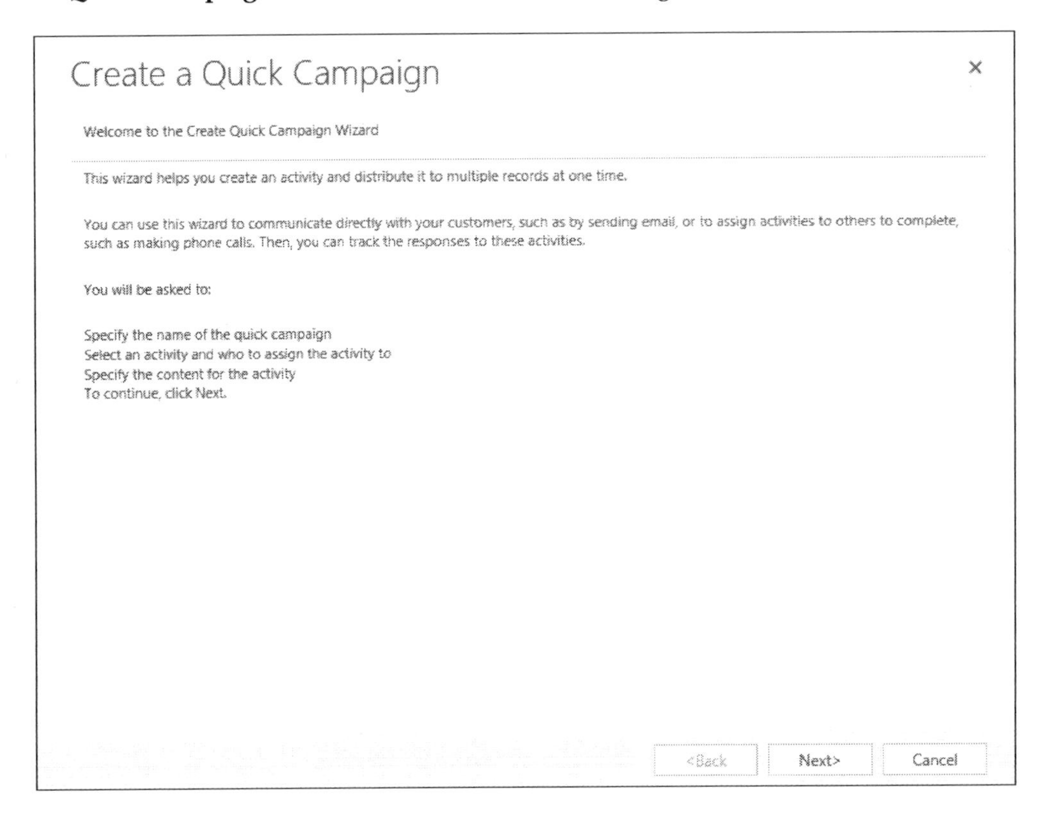

The wizard will ask you to provide a Name for the campaign, the type of activity for this campaign, the activity owner(s), and select a template or create the body of the campaign activity.

Once the wizard completes creating the Quick Campaign, and it is executed, and the Campaign is marked as **Closed**.

The default **Quick Campaign** form looks like this:

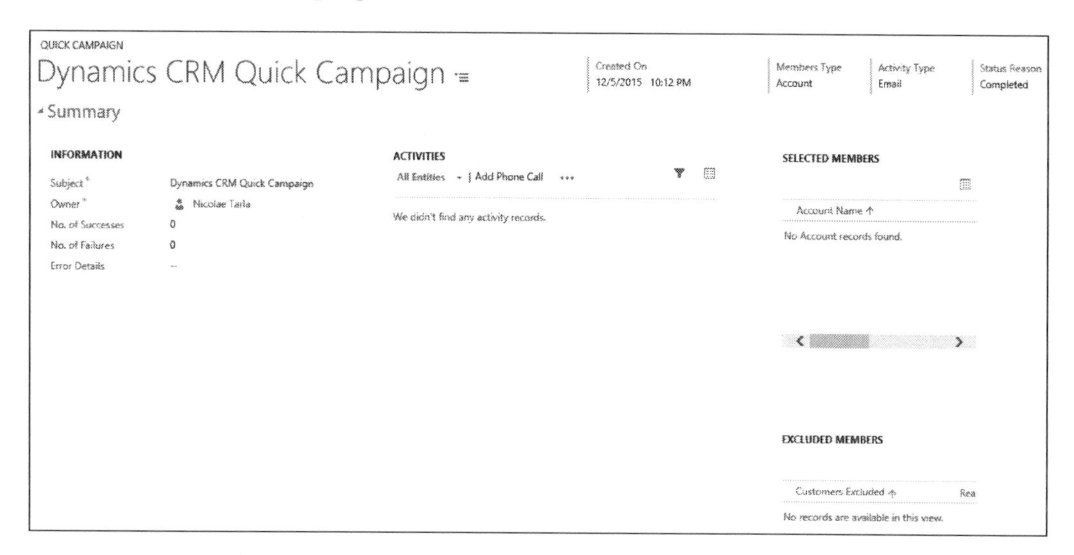

Activities are automatically created and tracked in the Campaign. Once all related activities are completed, the campaign is marked **Complete**.

Dynamics CRM Marketing Module Dashboards

With the Marketing module, Microsoft provides two default dashboards. They are:

- The Marketing Dashboard
- The Marketing Social Dashboard

Let's take a quick look at each one individually.

Marketing Dashboard

The Marketing Dashboard focuses on Campaigns, Leads generated by Campaigns, costs, and revenue. In addition, activities and Campaigns owned by the current system user are rolled up and made available from a simple interface.

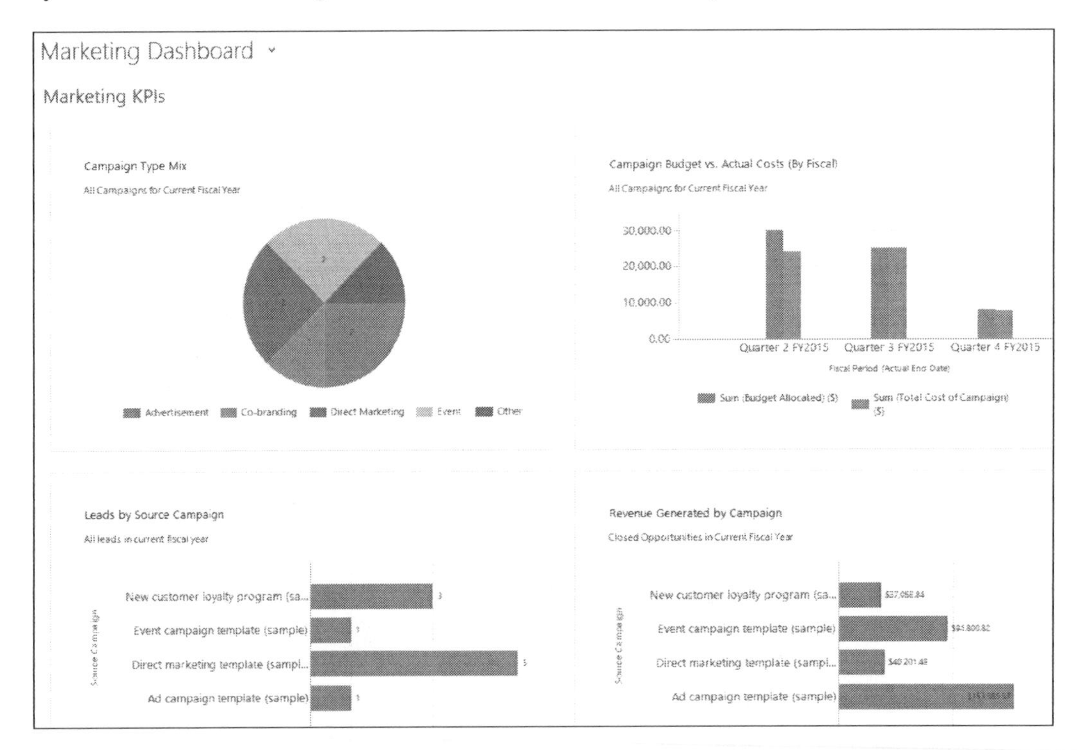

This is the main working dashboard for a marketing representative. A quick glance at this dashboard can easily show performance and activities.

Marketing Social Dashboard

Marketing Social Dashboard builds on top of the previous dashboard, adding the same social features we have seen in the other modules. A marketing representative using this dashboard can follow specific entities and receive notifications directly in the dashboard through the Social Pane displayed on the top right area of the dashboard.

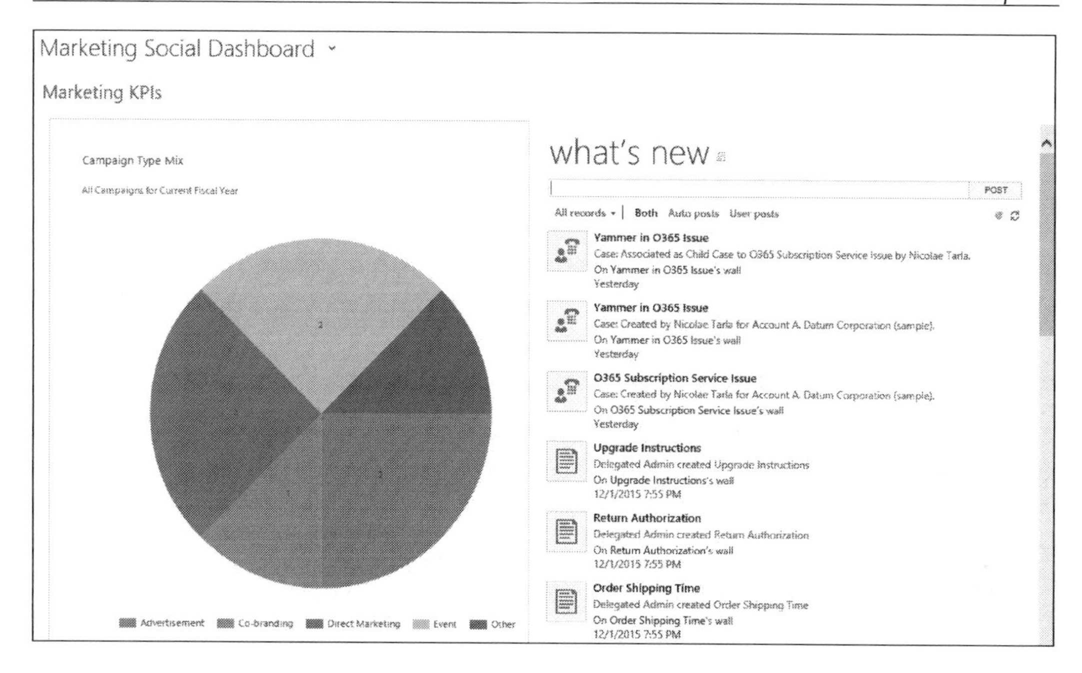

Marketing Reports

Marketing reports are also included with the Dynamics CRM platform by default. The main Marketing reports provided with the system include the ability to report on Campaigns and Campaign Performance.

Additional reports can be customized and added to the system, as described in *Chapter 6, Dynamics CRM Administration*.

Dynamics CRM application elements

Dynamics CRM in comprised of a few standard elements working together to achieve the system's functionality.

Modules

As seen earlier in this chapter, Modules are a grouping of functionalities that serve a specific business scope. The standard modules provided by Microsoft include Sales, Service, and Marketing.

The Sales module deals with all functionality needed to progress a Lead to fruition.

The Service module focuses on tracking activities related to existing customer interactions. This module focuses on caring for customers, and helps the representatives build a better relationship with existing customers.

The Marketing module deals with engaging existing and potential customers, by facilitating marketers to plan, execute, and gauge the success of campaigns engaging customers across multiple channels. This module also helps marketers quantify the success of each campaign and the impact of your marketing efforts.

Entities

Entities are containers used to model, store, and manage business data. Through the use of entities, the platform allows us to structure data, create relationships, and manage actions.

Each entity is comprised of a varying number of attributes. These attributes are in fact data items, of a particular type, stored in the database. Each one of these attributes can be displayed on an Entity form as a field. For example, **Account** will have a **Name** attribute, possibly an **ID** attribute, a **Description** attribute, and many others.

From a tabular point of view, we can think of each Entity as a table, or an Excel spreadsheet. Each column is an attribute. Each record is a line in this table. Each field is a specific record's attribute, and can be defined as one of the available data types.

Within Dynamics CRM, entities are classified in three major categories. They are system entities, business entities, and custom entities.

Business and custom entities can be configured as customizable or non-customizable. A customizable entity can be modified by modifying its attributes, renaming it or changing processes associated with it.

System Entities

System entities are used internally by the framework. They can handle workflows and asynchronous jobs.

System entities cannot be deleted and/or customized.

Business Entities

Business entities are the standard entities provided by the framework as part of the three available modules. They are present in the default user interface and are available for customization.

Custom Entities

Custom entities are entities that are created as part of extending the standard framework with new functionality. They can be made visible through the standard user interface, or can be kept hidden and participate in custom processes only.

Processes

Dynamics CRM allows business to define and enforce consistent business processes, helping users to focus more on performing their regular work and less on remembering what needs to be done at each step on the way.

The processes defined can be as complex as needed, and can be grouped and related to achieve even greater complexity. The processes on the CRM platform can be created and managed by nondevelopers. This brings ease of use, and allows managers and power users to manage them and update them as time goes by. For this reason, the system can easily stay up to date with the business as it evolves.

Within the Dynamics CRM platform, at the time of writing, there are four categories of processes available. They are Dialogs, Workflows, Actions, and Business Process Flows. We will look at each one individually, and we will identify when you should use one over another.

Dialogs

The Dialogs in Dynamics CRM are used to create a graphical interface to guide a user through a process to be followed when interacting with a customer or performing a set of actions. They are similar to a script used in a Call Center scenario. They are meant to be executed in one session from beginning to end.

Dialogs help users collect data, create new records, and guide the user through a set of actions to be performed based on various answers from a customer. A running dialog collecting user input looks like this:

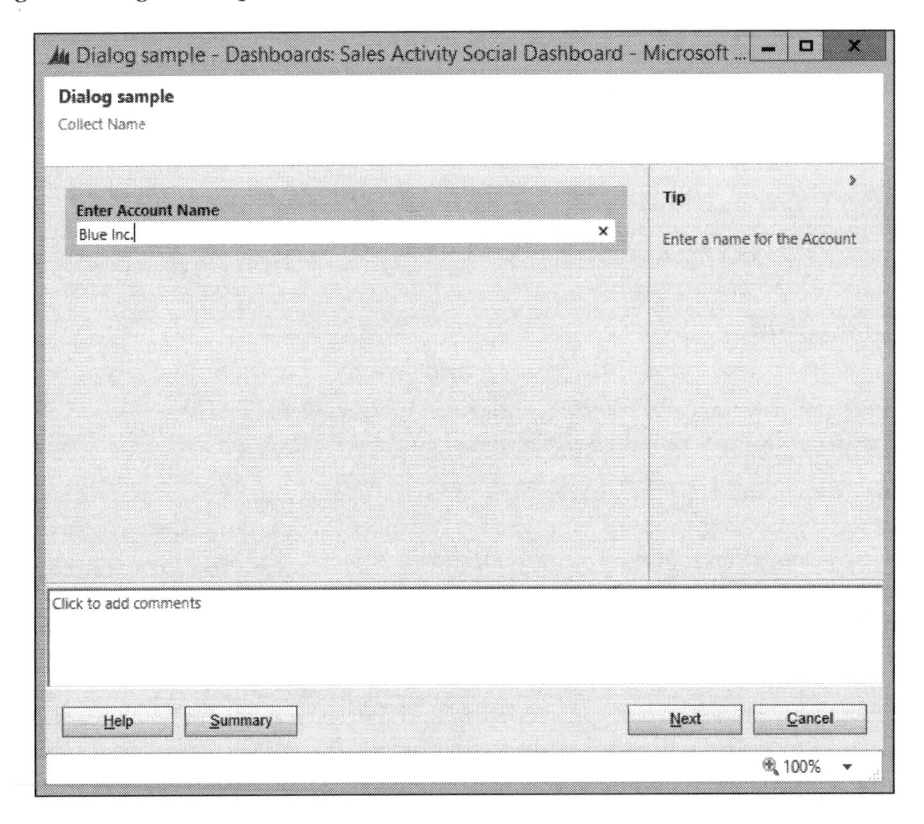

Workflows

Workflows help automate actions behind the scenes. They do not present a user interface, and are not limited to being completed in a single session. Workflows can run over a period of time to completion.

A workflow is usually initiated by a system action, but they can also be customized to be triggered by a user directly. They can work asynchronously or synchronously. The synchronous workflows are also referred to as real-time workflows, and they have been introduced with CRM version 2013. Starting with the same version, we have the ability to convert an asynchronous workflow to a real-time workflow.

Actions

An Action in Dynamics CRM is a custom process that allows us to create custom message. They are used to add new functionality to the application, or to combine multiple requests into a single one. They use the underlying web service architecture to group complex or specific action.

Creating an Action is very similar to creating a Workflow. They can be created using the wizard-driven interface or custom code. Custom code is only supported for on premise deployments.

An action is associated to a specific entity or can be defined at a global level. Through an action we can invoke plugins, which are custom components built by developers.

New actions are exposed through the standard API, and can be triggered through custom code and through integration from other applications.

One very important aspect of **Actions** is that they are not supported with offline clients.

Business Process Flows

The Business Process Flows are visual elements that allow a system user to input required data, by grouping the required fields together at the top of the screen. They can be created using the wizard-driven user interface, and show the user the progress of a process through a predetermined set of steps to completion.

The Opportunity Sales Process is a very good example of such customization. From a user perspective, they will see the following section on their screen:

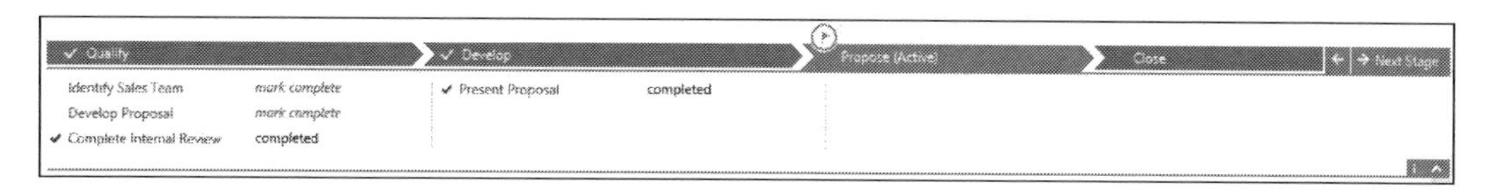

For the customizers of the system, the interface to generate this is quite simple and easy to use, and looks as such:

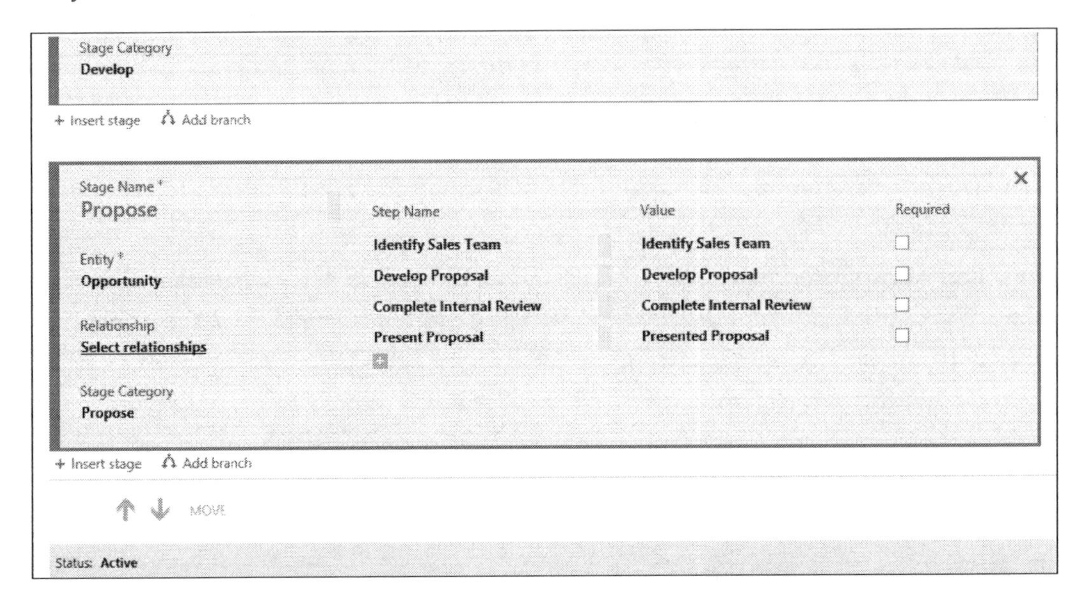

Each stage of the process is defined, and within it, each required field can be added and marked as **Required** or not. Progressing through stages requires that all fields marked as required are filled in before advancing to the next stage. The control also allows users to navigate back and forward to see what is required at each stage.

With Business Process Flows, we have the ability to create branches. This functionality was added with version 2015 to solve the if/else scenario. For example, if customer status is gold, take one path, otherwise take another path.

Dashboards

Dashboards in Dynamics CRM are visual components that allow users quick access to aggregated data in the system. They are visualization and analytics tools that enhances the value of your system by allowing users to quickly glance at aggregated data and to dig deeper into underlying data used to generate the visualization.

They act as business intelligence tools, providing snapshots of the system data presented in various forms.

Dashboards are comprised of various elements, including charts, grids, IFRAMES, and web resources. With additional customizations, reports can be incorporated into dashboards also.

Dashboards are in fact containers for these elements, and can present up to six visualizations at a time. They are comprised of tabs, sections, and components, and can be created easily through the wizard-based interface, and can be targeted to a specific module, user, or team.

From an ownership perspective, Dashboards can be organization-owned or user-owned. A user-owned dashboard can be shared with other users.

Reports

A user can report on system data in various ways. From the simple **Advanced Find**, where tabular data can be retrieved and exported to Excel for further analytics, to wizard driven report generation and all the way to custom **SQL Server Reporting Services** (**SSRS**) reports. Data can also be used as a data source in Power BI.

This large flexibility makes reporting easy to use and very powerful.

Each one of these options has its own strong points and weaknesses. For example, while custom SSRS reports are the most powerful, not only from the amount of data collected and complexity of data relationship, they do require a developer with extensive SSRS reporting and Dynamics CRM knowledge to produce them.

Power users of the system will find it easy to create wizard-driven reports. While limited in the complexity and having a standard user interface, the ease of creating them will appeal to users with no development background.

These reports support the use of custom parameters for filtering data, and allow us to save for offline use as well as export in some of the most common formats including Excel, Word, and PDF.

The Extensibility options

The Dynamics CRM is a very flexible platform, with a multitude of extensibility options. The system can be extended through various methods and components. Third-party solutions can be acquired from the Dynamics CRM Marketplace, and internal customizations can be performed, packaged, and exported from one environment to another.

The following chapter will go into details regarding the customization options available when working with Dynamics CRM.

Application navigation

User experience has evolved a lot with each new version of Dynamics CRM. This continues with the release of Dynamics CRM 2015, where the navigation was again redesigned based on user feedback. In line with the Windows 8 tiled interface, the navigation has been enhanced to present the user with options to get to data with less clicks, and to flatten the interface. As part of this process, now navigation is less obtrusive, takes less screen real estate, and is more dynamic. The sub-layers of navigation have been restructured to minimize the amount of scrolling. As such, new groups have been created and present options vertically as smaller tiles.

The default navigation is presented as such:

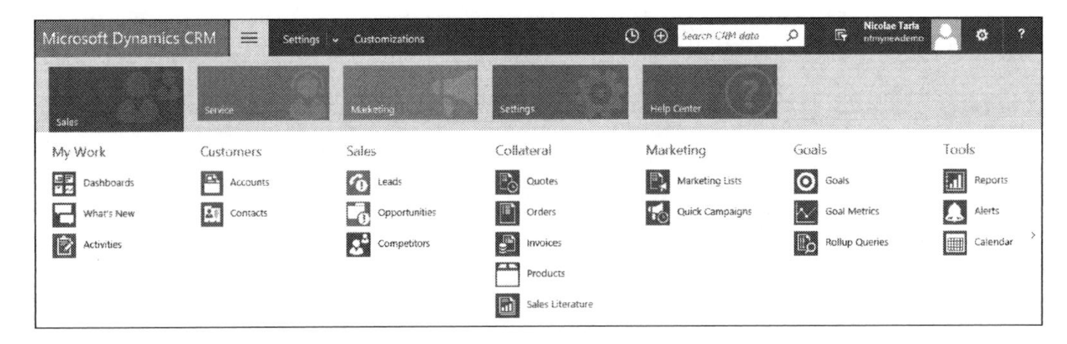

The navigation remains highly customizable, and the logical modules are clearly presented. This navigation can easily be changed to add new modules, remove existing ones, and rearrange items.

The application ribbons have also been redesigned, with a similar horizontal display at the top of the form, just below the navigation. The most common actions are left visible, with additional ribbon elements collected under a **MORE COMMANDS** menu. In addition, tabs on a form have now been added to a quick dropdown after the record name for easy access and navigation.

Summary

Throughout this chapter, we looked at some of the most important elements comprising the Microsoft Dynamics CRM platform. We have reviewed the three standard modules structuring the default Dynamics CRM platform: Sales, Service, and Marketing. We also looked at the major components of these modules, and how they relate to a specific module or work across multiple modules. We also looked at entities, what an entity is in the context of Dynamics CRM, and we reviewed Dashboards, Reports, and the default Navigation through the application. At this point, we should have an understanding of how everything ties together, and what to look for when we need to customize the system.

The next chapter will take you through some of the most common elements comprising an entity, the available customization options as well as working with existing and new entities.

3

Dynamics CRM Customization

In *Chapter 2, Dynamics CRM Application Structure*, we looked at the basic structure of Dynamics CRM, the modules comprising the application, and what each of these modules contains. Now, we'll delve deeper into the application, and look at how we can customize it.

In this chapter, we will look at the following topics:

- The Solution Package
- Entity Elements
- Business versus Custom entities
- Extending entities
- Record Images
- Entity Forms, Quick View, and Quick Create Forms
- Entity Views and Charts
- Entity Relationships
- Messages
- Composite Fields
- SLA's and the Timer Control
- Working with Documents

We'll look at how to work with each of the elements comprising the Sales, Service, and Marketing modules. We will go thought the customization options, and see how we can extend the system to fit new business requirements.

Solution Package

When talking about customizations for Microsoft Dynamics CRM, one of the most important concepts is the solution package. The solution package is a container of all customizations. This packaging method allows customizers to export customizations, and reimport them into other environments, as well as group-specific sets of customizations by business functionality or project cycle. Managing solutions is an aspect that should not be taken lightly, as down the line, a properly designed solution packaging model can help a lot or create difficulties.

As mentioned before, solutions are used to pack a set of features together. They are used to extend the core functionality of the platform through grouped sets of features.

Solutions that contain only Dynamics CRM-specific configuration or features can be imported directly into Dynamics CRM using the default solution management framework and the interface provided. For complex solutions that contain both Dynamics CRM Solution Components as well as other external components, an installer solution is required. One such example is if you provide a custom solution that includes customization of Dynamics CRM to store additional data as well as maybe a portal or any other kind of application to allow this data to be captured through the use of the standard API. For such a solution, an installer application can be created to deploy all customizations together. This type of scenario is outside the scope of this book and requires a development group or qualified partner to assist.

Solutions are created specific to a version of the Dynamics CRM platform. At the time of this writing, Dynamics CRM 2016 has just been released. There are several previous versions. Usually, a solution exported from a specific version can be imported into the same version or a newer version of the platform. As a rule of thumb, try to keep the solutions within two versions of the exported version to minimize the impact of changes introduced with newer versions.

Components of Solution

Solutions are comprised of a few core components. These components are created using the customization tools available or the APIs provided. These components are part of the following application:

- **Solution Schemes** are definitions of system entities, attributes, and relationships. They also include definition of Global Option Sets.
- **User Interface Elements** are items such as the Application Ribbon, the Site Map, Entity Ribbons, the definition of Entity Forms as well as web resources.

- **Analytics elements** include things such as Graphs, Dashboards, and Reports.
- **Templates** are definitions used for Mail-Merge, E-mails, Contracts, and Knowledge Base Articles.
- **Security Model** definitions include the various Security Roles as well as the definition of Field Level Security profiles.
- **Processes and Code** elements include the definition of Processes as well as custom code elements. We will not cover custom code elements in this book, but we will have a look at the various Process types later on.

All these solution components are available to be included in all solutions. They are defined in a solution exported as a ZIP file.

Opening such a solution file shows the following three XML files, as the following screenshot demonstrates:

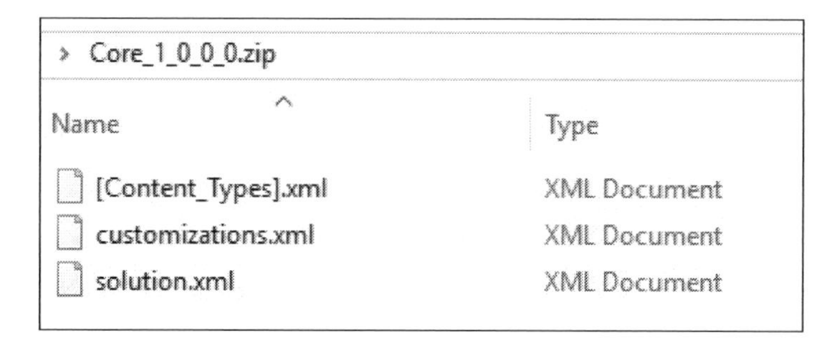

The first file lists the available customized content types, if any. The `solution.xml` file contains the following elements:

- Solution definition data
- Version
- Platform version
- Solution name and properties
- Publisher details
- Components
- Missing dependencies

With each solution created, a publisher is required. This is usually the partner or group providing the solution. This information is stored in a Publisher entity.

Multiple Publishers can exist at the same time customized on each deployment, but only one at a time can be associated to a solution.

Dependencies are related solution items. For example, a component could require elements from another entity. This other entity does not necessarily have to be included in the solution. When it is not, a missing dependency is recorded in the solution. When deploying the solution, a check is done on the target system to determine whether the missing dependency is installed on the target by another solution. If it is not found, a missing dependency error is thrown and the installation is aborted.

The last element of a solution is the `customizations.xml` file. This is the meat of the solution, and it includes all the elements added to the solution. The document is structured by entity, but also includes details about the other solution components described earlier.

Analyzing the content of these XML files is beyond the scope of this book, but additional details about working with solutions can be found in the MSDN documentation available at the following website:

`https://msdn.microsoft.com/en-us/library/gg334530.aspx`

Types of Solution

Within the context of Dynamics CRM, there are two types of Solutions:

- Unmanaged Solutions
- Managed Solutions

Each one of these solution types has its own strengths and properties, and are recommended to be used in various circumstances.

Unmanaged Solutions

An Unmanaged Solution is the default state of a solution. A solution is unmanaged for the duration while customization work is being performed in the context of the solution. An unmanaged solution is not necessarily intended to be distributed as such. It is a way for developers and system customizers to group together their customizations, while work is being performed on the system. When the work is completed, and the unmanaged solution is ready to be distributed, it can be packed as a managed solution.

On an unmanaged solution, the system customizer can perform various tasks. These include:

- Adding and removing components
- Deleting components that allow deletion
- Export and import the solution as Unmanaged Solution
- Export the solution as Managed Solutions

Changes made to components in an Unmanaged Solution are also applied to all unmanaged solutions that include those components.

Deleting an unmanaged solution results in the removal of the container alone, while the unmanaged components of the solution remain in the system.

Deleting a component in an unmanaged solution results in the deletion of that component from the system. In order to remove a component from an Unmanaged Solution, that component should be removed and not deleted from the solution.

Managed Solutions

Once work is completed in an Unmanaged Solution, and the solution is ready to be distributed, it can be exported as a Managed Solution. Packaging a solution as a Managed Solution presents the following advantages:

- Solution components cannot be added or removed from a Managed Solution
- A Managed Solution cannot be exported from the environment it was deployed in
- Deleting a Managed Solution results in uninstalling all the component customizations included with the solution

A Managed Solution cannot be installed in the same Organization that contains the Unmanaged Solution that was used to create it.

Within a Managed Solution, certain components can be configured to allow further customization. Through this mechanism, the managed solution provider can enable future customizations to modify aspects of the solution provided.

Solution Publisher

Besides the solution type, each solution contains a **Solution Publisher**. This is a set of properties that allows the solution creators to communicate different information to the solution users, including ways to contact the publisher for additional support. The solution publisher record will be created in all organizations where the solution is being deployed.

The Solution Publisher record is also important when releasing updates to an existing solution. Based on this common record, an update solution can be released and deployed on top of an existing solution.

Solution Layering

When multiple solutions are deployed in an Organization, there are two methods by which the system defines the order in which changes take priority. They are **Merge** and **Top Wins**. The user interface elements are being merged by default. Elements such as the forms, ribbons, command bars, and site map are being merged, and all base elements and new custom elements are being rendered. For all other solution components, the Top Wins approach is being taken, where the last solution bringing a customization is taking precedence.

The system checks for integrity on all solution exports, imports, and other operations. When exporting a solution, a warning is presented if dependent entities are not included. The customizer has the option to ignore this warning.

When importing a solution, if the dependent entities are missing, the import is halted and the import fails. Also, deleting a component from a solution is prevented if dependent entities require it to be present.

For additional details and recommendation in solution layering, check out the MSDN documentation available at `https://msdn.microsoft.com/en-us/library/gg334576.aspx#BKMK_UnmanagedandManagedSolutions`.

In particular, pay close attention to the layering diagram included in the MSDN documentation. This should give you a clear picture of how layering various solution types influences the behavior of the resulting environment.

The Default Solution

Dynamics CRM allows you to customize the system without taking advantage of solutions. By default, the system comes with a **Default Solution**. This is an Unmanaged Solution, and all system customizations applied outside the scope of a solution are applied to it.

The **System Solution** includes all customizations defined within Microsoft Dynamics CRM. This solution defines the default application behavior. Most of the components in this solution can be further customized.

Solution Segmentation

One of the new great features added with Microsoft Dynamics CRM 2016 is the concept of solution segmentation. For the longest time, we have struggled with situations where a small change to an entity required us to deploy the entire entity definition, and run the risk of overriding changes made by newer solutions added to the system. This is where solution layering described earlier plays an important role in how we customize the system. Segmentation does not completely avoid the issues, but greatly avoids the risk when used properly. But let's take a closer look at how this works and what it does.

Let's assume we want to make changes to the **Account** entity, and add a new text field to capture the Twitter handle, and a new form called **Account Details**. With the new solution segmentation features available, I can now define a solution to include only these items. When deploying this solution, I do not have to worry about overriding any of the other views or field definitions.

In order to add only the two items, when opening our solution and adding the **Account** entity we are presented now with a new intermediary screen:

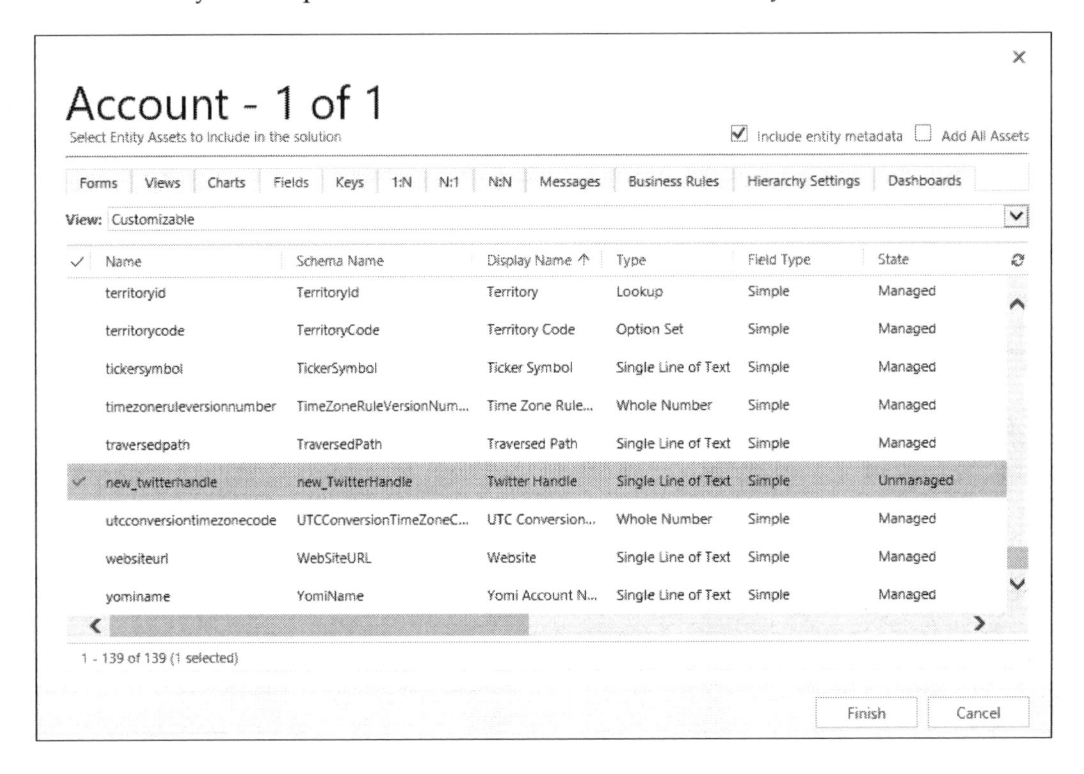

We can now clearly see how easy it is to navigate to the tab containing the type of customization we want to add, find the new field in this case, select it, and click on **Finish** when done.

Two options to observe though at the top right of this form are as follows:

- The **Add All Assets** option is unchecked. Checking this option basically puts you back to the solution options we had before Dynamics CRM 2016, where everything related to an entity was included in the solution. There are still cases when we want to select this option, for example for brand new entities that are added with our solution.
- The other is the **Include entity metadata** option. This option is checked by default, and allows us to add all the entity definitions. It is recommended to be checked, but be aware that it will make the solution file larger. For situations where no changes are made to the entity metadata, and the entity is already existing in the target system, this option can be unchecked.

Having a quick look at the entity added to the solution, we can now see the **Account** entity added, but in the fields, we only see the newly added field.

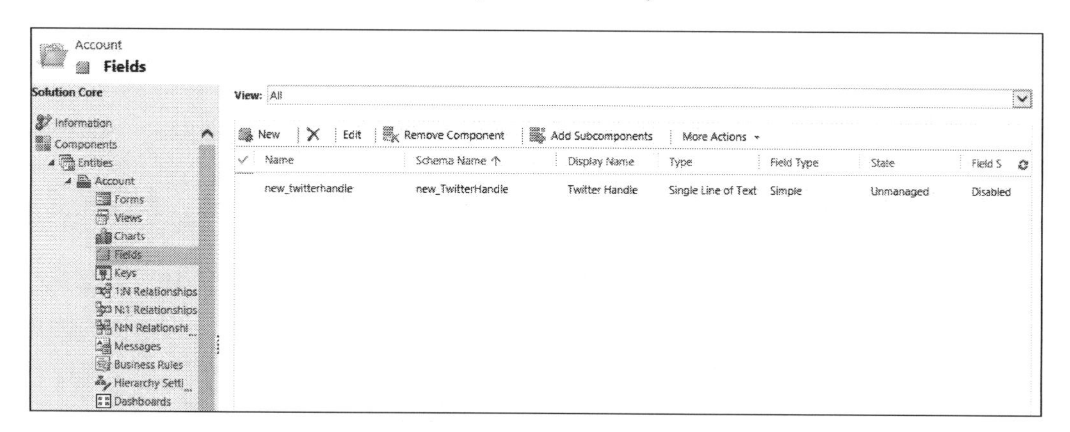

All good so far, but what if you already have an entity added to a solution, and you just need to add a new custom element? For example, you could already have the **Account** entity, and you want to add custom properties to the solution, such as Rating and Score. No problem, from the solution definition, select the **Account** entity, and on the top ribbon, you will find an **Add Subcomponents** option now. This allows you do just that, as shown in the following screenshot:

Solution Cloning and Patching

Another great feature added with Microsoft Dynamics CRM 2016 is the ability to create advanced scenarios when working with solutions. For the last few versions, Microsoft provided the ability to associate version numbers with our solutions, but the solution package model was not aligned to the capabilities of proper versioning.

Starting with Dynamics CRM 2016, we can now take advantage of proper versioning, and have a bit of checks and bounds as to which items are incremental. But before we dig into **Cloning** and **Patching**, let's look at the standard versioning model provided. We've always seen recommendations to start versioning with a format of 1.0.0.0. This is basically a set of four numeric values. During the course of time, various standards have been released for versioning. One example includes a major version, a minor version, along with an alphanumeric string denoting the release type (alpha, beta, and so on). Other models include the major and minor version, followed by another numeric field denoting the change version.

The newer model strives to cover the complexities of newer software solutions. We've moved from three to four numeric values. Depending on the school of thought followed, they can denote either:

- Major.Minor.Build.Revision
- Major.Minor.Maintenance.Build

There are other ways to create sequence-based software versioning, some of them, as combinations of the previously described approaches.

With Dynamics CRM, the onus to increment and confirm the versioning is still with the customizer creating and packaging the solution.

The solution cloning in Dynamics CRM 2016 is the ability to create a new version that increments the major and minor versions. As a process, this is done by selecting **Clone Solution** on the **All Solutions** ribbon.

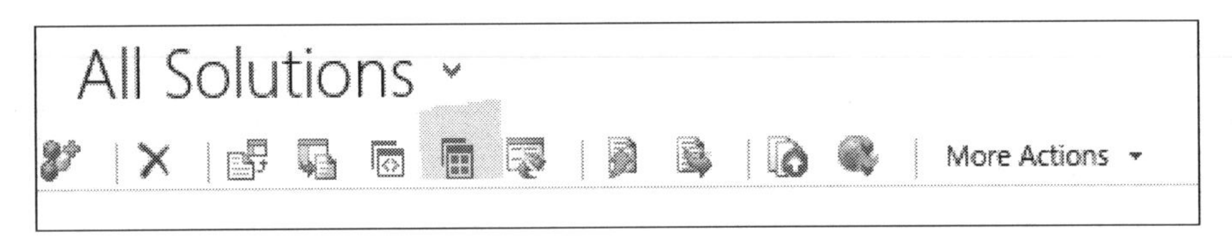

Selecting this option brings up the following **Clone To Solution** screen:

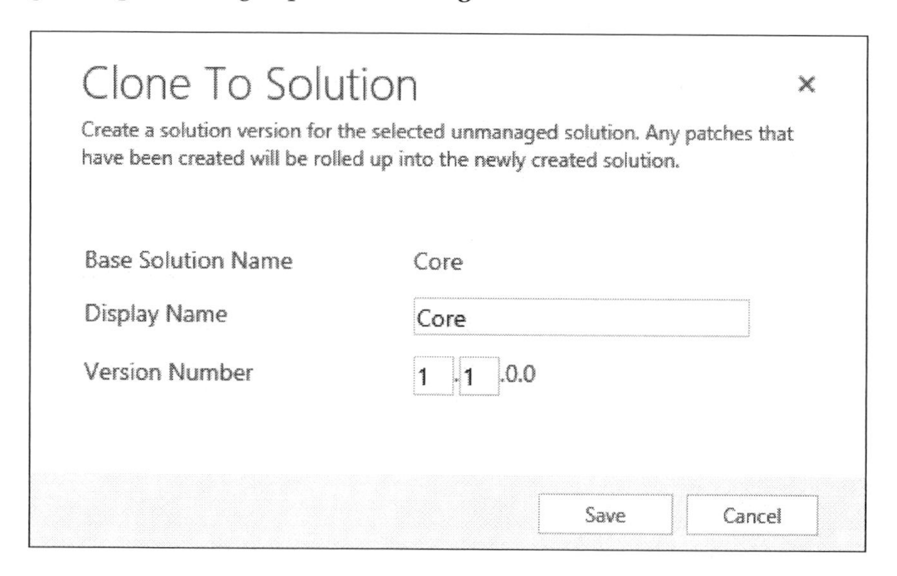

As you can see, cloning a solution called **Core**, we can modify the **Display Name** option if needed as well as only the major and minor version numbers.

One important aspect to understand is that cloning a solution basically creates a brand new solution including the original solution and all the patches applied to it. The original solution as well as the existing patches that are included are then all removed from the organization. Make sure you save the original solution and patches as needed before proceeding with cloning.

The solution patching is quite different in behavior. It is triggered by clicking on the **Clone a Patch** ribbon button.

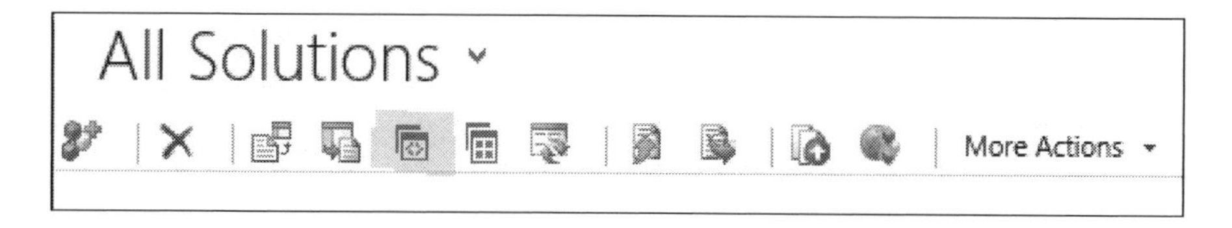

A patch is used for a small change or fix released in between regular release cycles. This, in most cases, is restricted to a small component being modified, and it is where we take advantage of solution segmentation. We can include only the definition of a field that changes properties, a view that is modified, and so on.

Once the **Clone to Patch** command is issued, the following window allows us to define the patch properties:

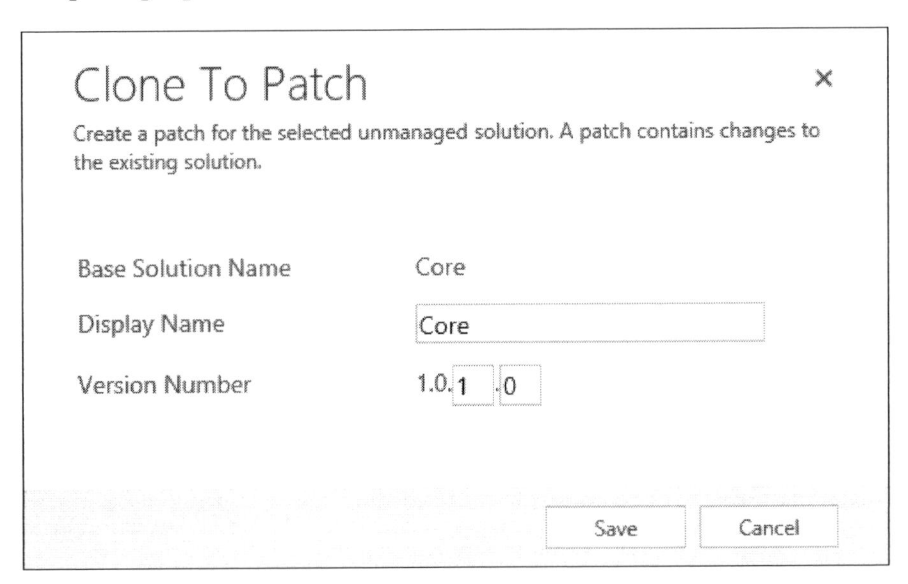

Just like before, **Display Name** can be edited as needed. In contrast with earlier though, only the last two versioning digits are editable now.

You can create and deploy as many patches as needed before moving on to the next version.

One thing you will observe, if the solution definition XML file mentioned earlier in this chapter is opened, a reference to the base solution is kept in the patch definition.

Entity Elements

Within a solution, we work with various entities. In Dynamics CRM, there are three main entity types:

- System entities
- Business entities
- Custom entities

Each entity is comprised of various attributes, while each attribute is defined as a value with a specific data type. We can think of an entity as a data table. Each row represents an entity record, while each column represents an entity attribute. As with any table, each attribute has specific properties that define its data type.

The System entities in Dynamics CRM are used internally by the application, and are not customizable. They too cannot be deleted.

As a system customizer or developer, we will work mainly with Business entities and Custom entities. The Business entities are the default entities that come with the application. They are customizable, and can be extended as needed. Custom entities are all not new entities that are created as part of our system customizations.

Aspects of customizing an entity include renaming the entity, modifying, adding, or removing entity attributes, or changing various settings and properties. Let's look at all these in detail.

Renaming an Entity

One of the options to customize an entity is by renaming it. In the **General** properties of the entity, the **Display Name** field allows us to change the name of an entity. **Plural Name** can also be updated accordingly.

> When renaming an entity, make sure all references and messages are updated to reflect the new entity name. Views, charts, messages, business rules, and even certain fields could reference the original name, and they should be updated to reflect the new name assigned to the entity.

Pay close attention when modifying the properties of the default **Name** field of an entity. This is usually a required field. While it can be marked as not-required and hidden off the form, the drawback to this approach is that this field is used in lookups to this entity. If this field is not populated, your lookup will only show a multitude of blank record references. A better approach is to either relabel this field and use it to store record-specific distinct data, or to hide it and create a process that automatically populates some specific information about each record. This way all lookups will reflect the data in this field correctly and you will not run into any other issues.

Change Entity Settings and Properties

When creating and managing entities in Dynamics CRM, there are generic entity settings that we have to pay attention to. We can easily get to these settings and properties by navigating within a solution to **Components** | **Entities** and selecting an entity from the list. We will get a screen similar to the following **Account** entity:

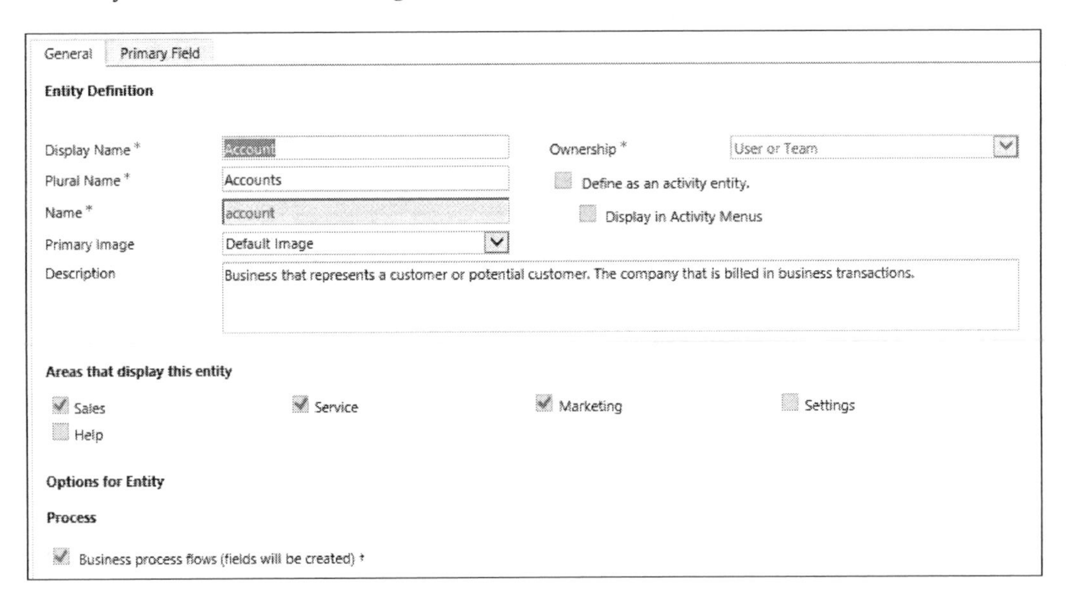

The settings are structured in two main tabs, with various categories on each. We can look at each set of settings and properties individually in the next sections.

Entity Definition

This area of the **General** tab groups together general properties and settings regarding entity naming properties, ownership, and descriptions. Once an entity is created, the **Name** value remains set and cannot be modified. If the internal **Name** value needs to be changed, a new entity with the new **Name** must be created.

Areas that display this entity

This section sets the visibility of this entity. An entity can be made available in only one or more standard modules of the application. The Account is a good example, as it is present in all three areas of the application.

Options for Entity

The **Options for Entity** section contains a subset of sections with various settings and properties for configuring the main properties for the entity. They include items such as whether the entity can be customized by adding Business Process Flows, Notes, Activities, and Auditing, as well as other settings.

Pay close attention to the settings marked with a plus, as these settings, once enabled, cannot be disabled.

One of the subsections deals with mobile access. Here, we can define whether the entity can be accessed from various mobile devices as well as Outlook, and whether it is read-only or not.

Primary Field Settings

The **Primary Field Settings** tab contains the configuration properties for the entity's primary field. Each entity in the Dynamics CRM platform is defined by a primary field. This field can only be a text field, and the size can be customized as needed. The **Display Name** section can be adjusted as needed. Also, **Requirement Level** can be selected from one of the three values: **Optional**, **Business Recommended**, or **Business Required**.

Business versus Custom Entities

As mentioned previously, there are two types of customizable entities in Dynamics CRM. They are Business entities and Custom entities. Business entities are customizable entities that are created by Microsoft and come as part of the default solution package. They are part of the three modules: Sales, Service, and Marketing. Custom entities are all the new entities that are being created as part of the customization and extending process.

Business Entities

Business entities are part of the default customization provided with the application by Microsoft. They are either grouped into one of the three modules of functionality, or spread across all three. Examples of Business entities include, but are not limited to: Account, Contact, Lead, Opportunity, Case, and so on.

Most of the properties of Business entities are customizable in Dynamics CRM. There are though certain items that are not customizable across these entities. These are in general the same type of customizations that are not changeable when creating a Custom entity. For example, the entity internal name cannot be changed once an entity has been created. In addition, the **Primary Field** properties cannot be modified once an entity is created.

The **Display Name** field of an entity can be modified for the default value. This is a very common customization. In many instances, we need to adjust the default entity name to match the business for which we are customizing the system. For instance, many customers use the term Organization instead of Account. This is a very easy customization, achieved by updating the **Display Name** and **Plural Name** fields. While implementing this change, make sure to update the entity messages also, as a lot of them use, by default use, the original name of the entity.

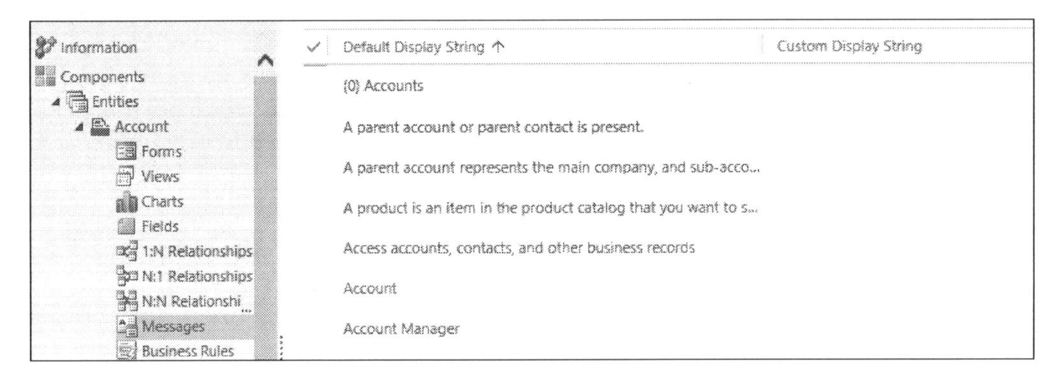

Custom Entities

All new entities created as part of a customization implemented in Dynamics CRM are Custom entities. When creating a new Custom entity, we have the freedom to configure all settings and properties as needed from the beginning. We can use a naming convention that makes sense to the user, and generate all messages from the beginning taking advantage of this name.

During creation, we must pay close attention to some properties that cannot be changed once enabled. These include enabling **Business Process Flows** on the entity, enabling **Notes**, **Activities**, and **Connections**, configuring the entity to support **Queues**, as well as defining the entity's **Primary Field** properties.

A Custom entity can be assigned, by default, to display in one of the three main modules, or be displayed in the **Settings** and/or the **Help** section.

If a new module is created, and custom entities need to be part of this new module, we can achieve this by customizing the application navigation. While customizing the application navigation might not be such a straight-forward process, tools released to the community are available that make this job a lot easier and more visual. The default method to customize the navigation is described in details in the SDK, and it involves exporting a solution with the navigation configuration, modifying the XML data, and reimporting the updated solution.

Extending Entities

Whether we are looking to extend a customizable Business entity or a Custom entity, the process is very similar. We extend entities by creating new entity forms, views, charts, relationships, and/or business rules.

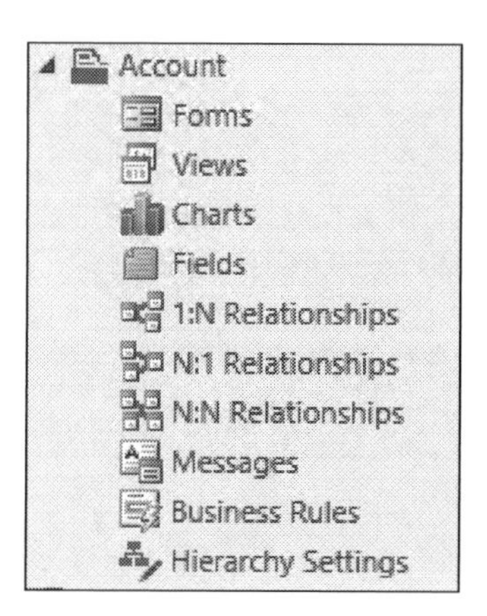

We will be looking at each of these options in detail in the upcoming sections.

Record Images

When creating a new record in Microsoft Dynamics CRM, we have the ability to define an image for the record. One example is, when storing Accounts, you can capture the company logo as an image associated with the record. You do this by clicking on the image container at the left of the title, as shown in the following screenshot:

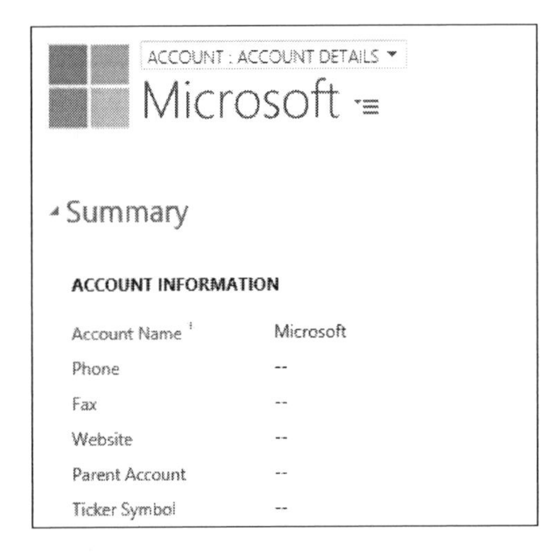

This prompts the user to select the image by either browsing on the local computer, or if an image is already selected to revert back to the default image. The following screenshot shows what is displayed on the screen:

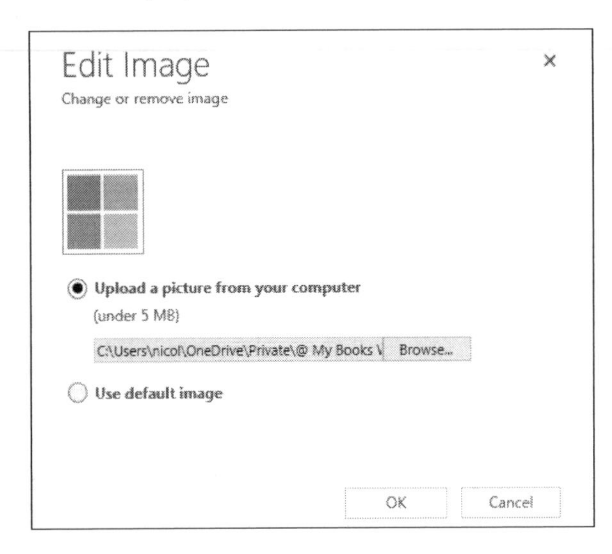

Once you click on **OK**, the image selected becomes the default record image.

Entity Forms, Quick View, and Quick Create Forms

The most common customization to the Microsoft Dynamics CRM platform is the ability to modify an entity form. We can add, remove, and hide fields and sections on the form, as well as implement logic to make the form behave in a dynamic fashion. First, let's look at a standard form, and what components are part of it.

The Entity Form

With the current version being Dynamics CRM 2016, most of the updated entities now have four different types of forms. They are as follows:

- The Main Form
- The Mobile Form
- The Quick Create Form
- The Quick View Form

Various other forms can be created on an entity, either from scratch or by opening an existing form, and saving it with a new name. When complex forms need to be created, in many circumstances, it is much easier to start from an existing entity form rather than recreating everything.

The Main Form is the default form associated with an entity. This form will be available by default when opening a record. There can be more than one main form, and they can be configured to be available to various roles. A role must have at least one form available for the role. If more than one form is available for a specific role, then they will be available to be selected by the user. Forms available for various roles are called **Role-Based Form**. As an example, HR could have a specific view into an account showing more information than a form available to a sales role.

When editing the main form of an entity, it will look like the following **Account** form:

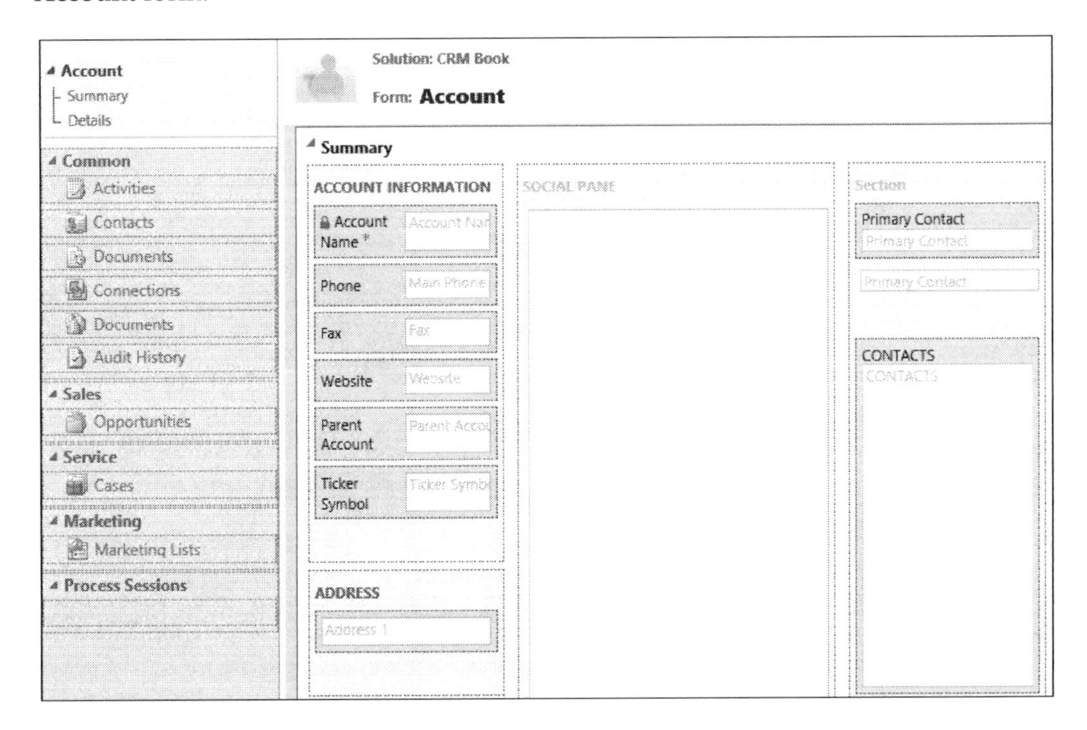

The Mobile Form is a stripped down form that is made available for mobile devices with small screens. When customizing mobile forms, attention should be paid not only to the fact that a small screen can only render so much before extensive scrolling becomes exhaustive, but also to the fact that most mobile devices transfer data wirelessly, and as such, the amount of data should be limited.

The editing window of the Mobile Form looks like the following **Account Mobile** form. This is basically just a listing of the fields made available, and the order in which they are presented to the user.

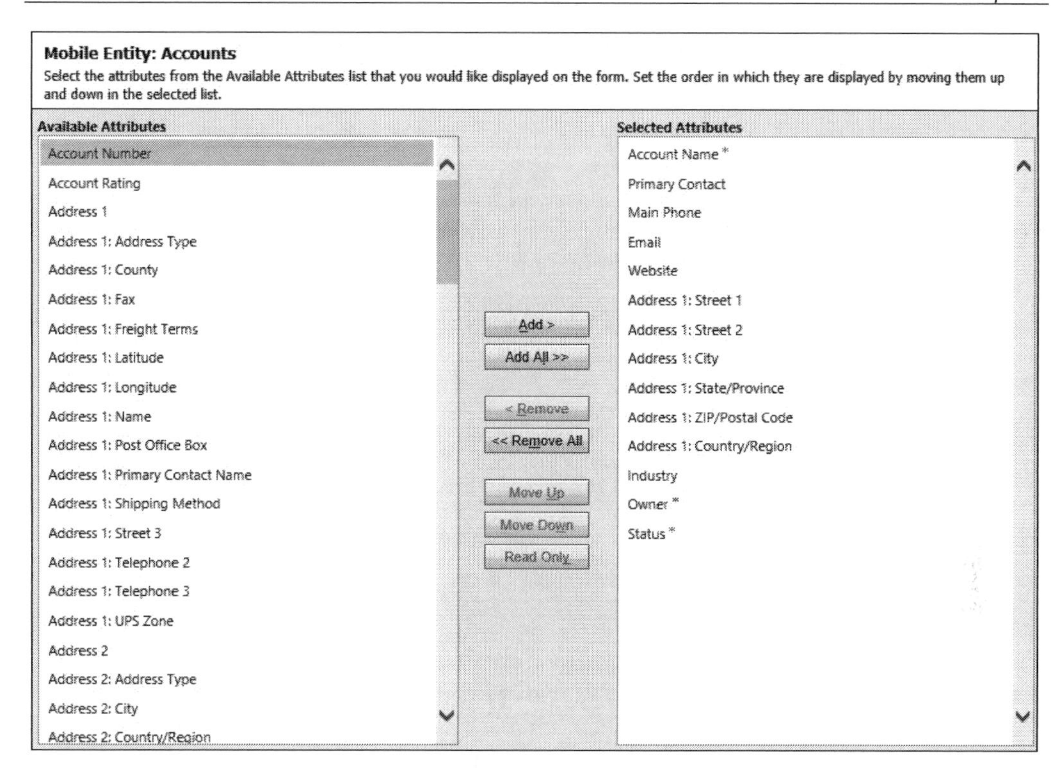

The Quick Create Form is a shortened version of the Main Form, in which only a limited number of fields is made available for the user to complete. The idea is that only a few fields are mandatory, and must be included in order to be able to open a record in the system. Later on, a user can come back and populate additional information as needed. A quick form will open over an existing form, and closing it will leave the user on the original form. Therefore, a user can quickly create new records without navigating away from the current record.

The Quick Create Form gives us more flexibility than the Mobile Form, while still presenting a trimmed down version of the Mobile Form.

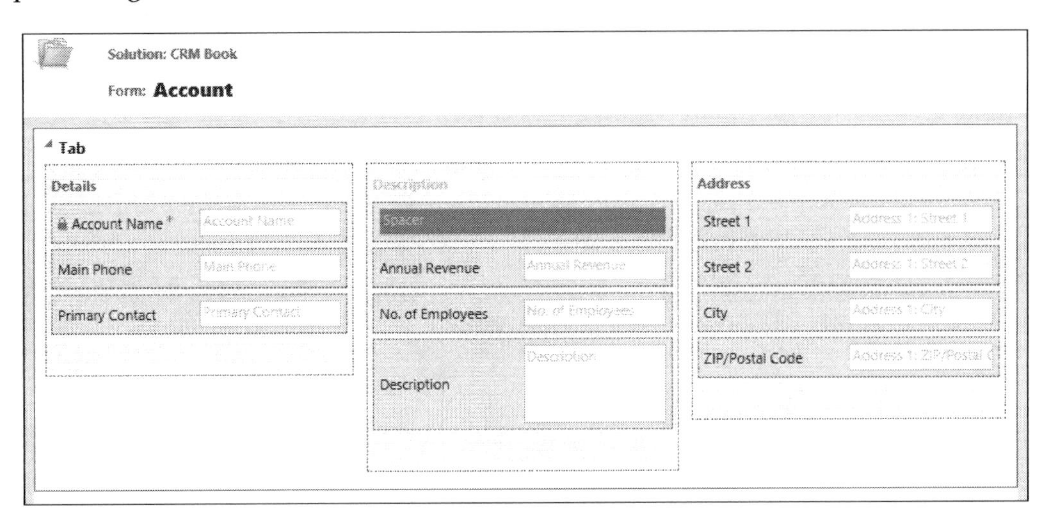

The Quick View Form is similar in functionality to the Quick Create Form, but is being used once a record has already been created. The only difference between the Quick View and Quick Create forms is when they are displayed to the user. As far as extensibility is concerned, we have the same customization options available. The reason why we have two different forms in this case is because we have the ability to display different information to the user based on when he/she is looking at the data.

Customizing Forms

In Dynamics CRM, forms are comprised of various elements. We have various layout elements, including Tabs and Sections, iFrames, Sub-Grids, and Spacers. At the lowest level, we have data fields, which can be placed within some of the previously mentioned containers. Let's look at each one of these elements in detail.

Tabs

A Tab is the highest level of grouping elements visually on the form. A Tab can be set to open by default as expanded or collapsed. Clicking on the tab name on an open form allows the user to expand or collapse it. This makes navigation on a form easier.

Tabs can be opened, closed, and hidden programmatically too, by using scripts. For example, if the value of a field is set to a certain value, then we show another tab, otherwise we keep it hidden.

The following screenshot shows us a Tab on the **Account** form:

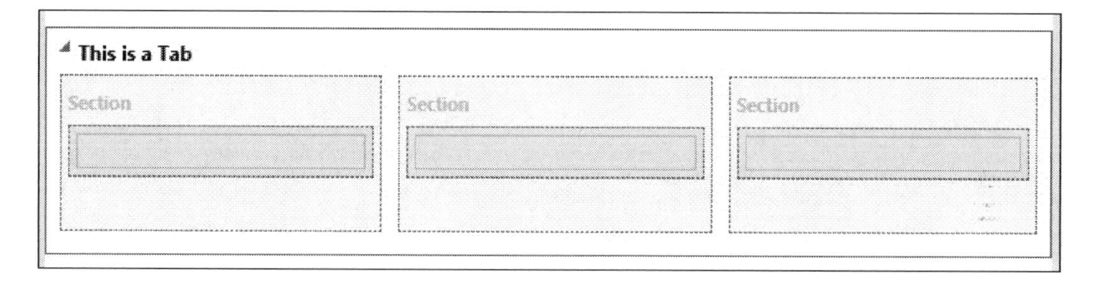

Tabs can be created with various predefined layout options. When editing the form, on the toolbar, we are presented with the following options as follows:

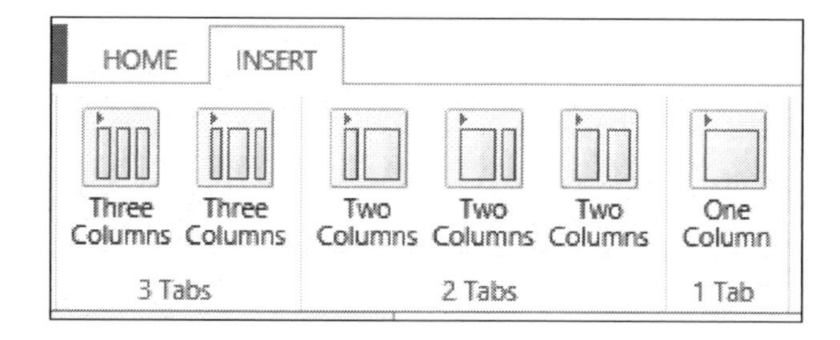

Once a tab is inserted on the form, the layout can be further customized. You can change the originally selected layout, and adjust the width of the columns as needed. This is all done by double-clicking on the Tab in the edit mode of the form. This will display a **Tab Properties** window. On the **Formatting** tab, you are presented with the following layout options:

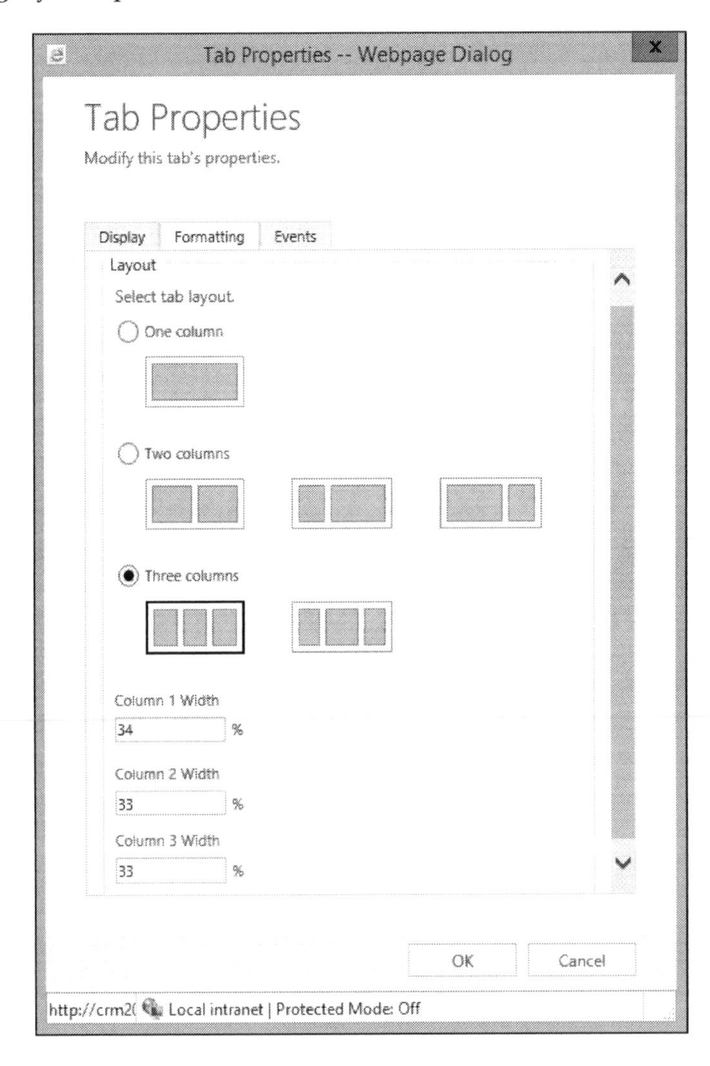

Sections

The Section is a subgrouping element that is used for further designing your forms. Creating a Tab with three columns will automatically generate three new sections aligned side by side. We can then add additional section to each of the columns from the Tab.

A section's layout can be also customized to present information in multiple columns. The **Layout** options are presented by double-clicking on the section in the edit mode. This opens up a **Section Properties** window. On the **Display** tab, the first grouping is the **Layout** settings, which allows us to customize up to four new columns.

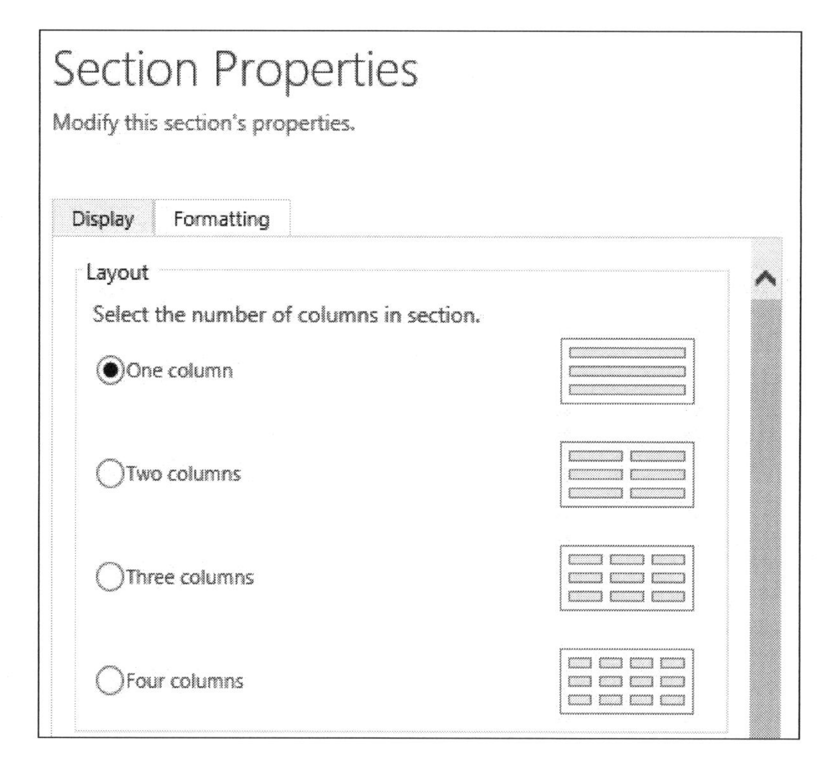

In addition, we can customize the formatting of the form fields, by settings formatting for the field label's location and alignment.

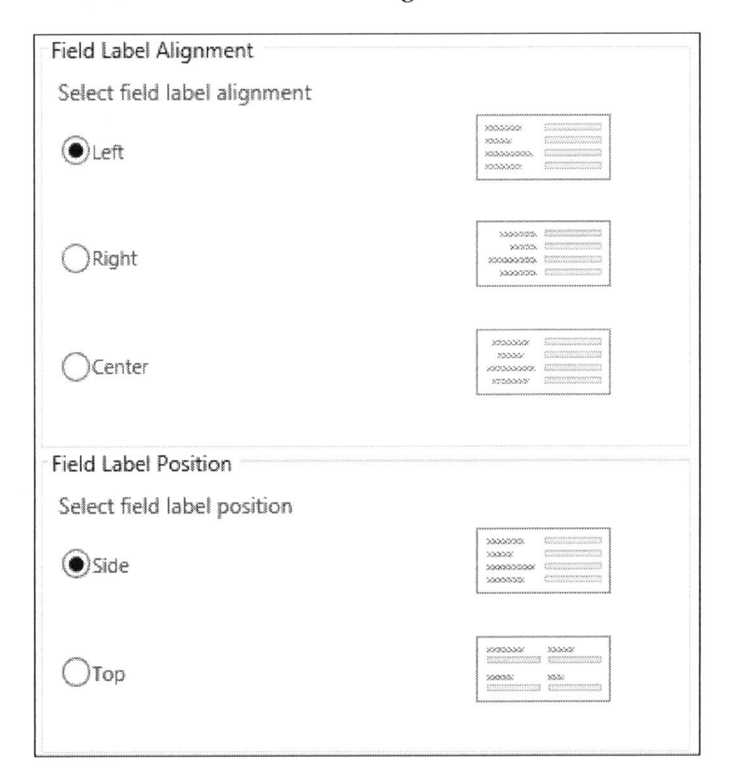

When customizing the form layouts, pay close attention to the amount of data presented horizontally, and make sure that on lower resolution, it does not result in unexpected line wrapping. Items laid out might look perfect at a higher resolution, but on lower resolution screens, the fields might get wrapped on resulting in a layout that is not ideal for the user.

iFrames

iFrames are a feature that allows us to bring in external pages or web resources into a form. Using this approach, we can introduce custom HTML elements into the entity forms. This allows us to extend the system with custom elements. A good use for this is taking advantage of custom forms formatting and dashboard elements and reports.

Pay attention to the formatting of iFrames. The risk is that bringing in forms with larger formats than the actual iFrame will result in scrolling the iFrame.

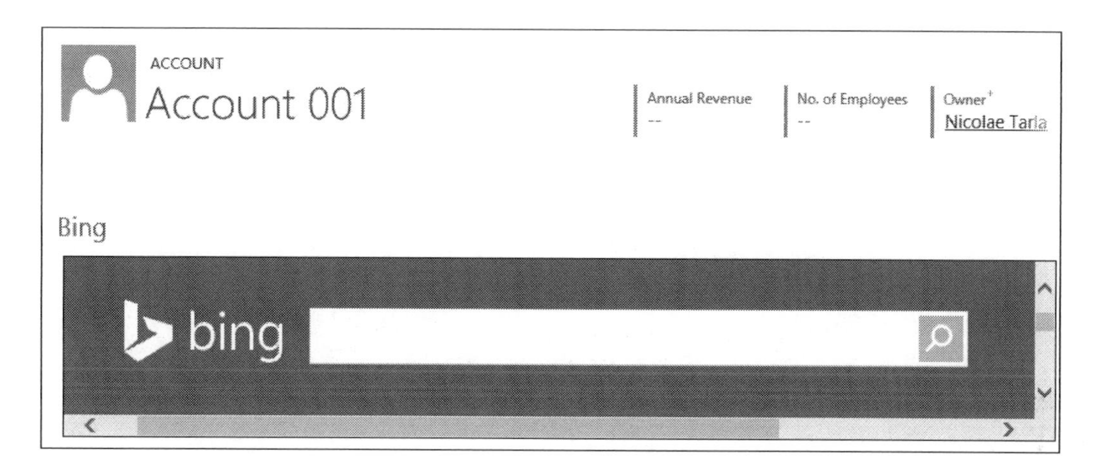

Sub-grids

In Dynamics CRM, the sub-grids allow us to display listings of related entities. They are based on existing views, with specific filters added. For example, on an Account entity, we can have a listing in a subgrid showing all the Contacts related to the current Account.

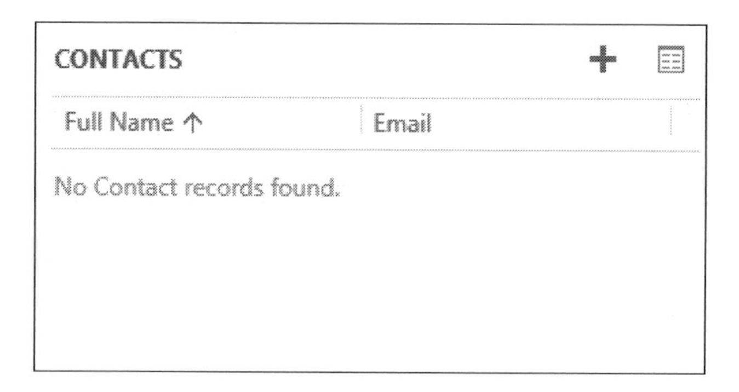

A sub-grid is bound by the same limitation as the iFrame, where if the view is larger than the allocated space on the form, we will be treated to scroll bars. This makes the user experience less friendly.

As far as options for configuration go, for subgrids, we can adjust the layout anywhere between a single column to up to four columns. We also get to adjust the height of the sub-grid, by either setting a fixed height, or allowing it to expand as needed. All these settings are available by double-clicking on the grid in the edit form. This opens up a **Set Properties** window. Going to the **Formatting** tab, we get all the layout options described in the following screenshot:

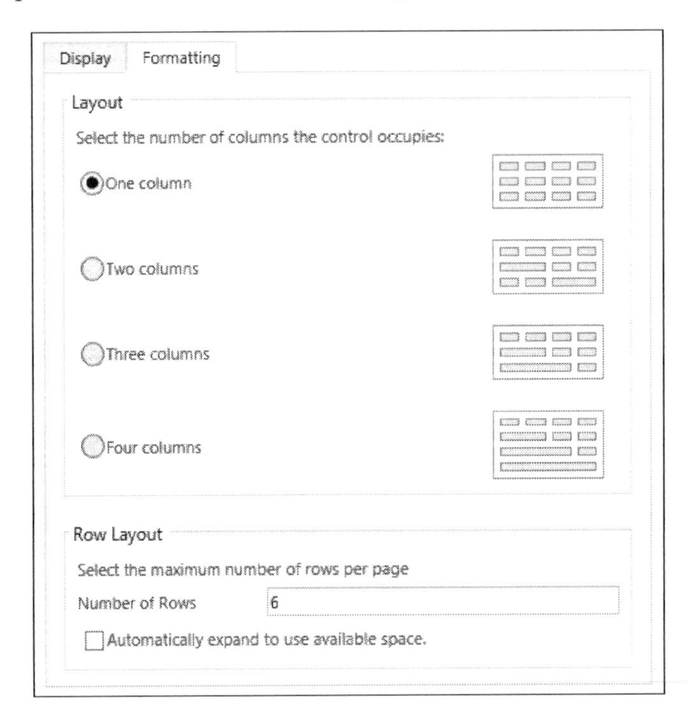

In addition to formatting, when working with sub-grids, we have some very handy ways of customizing the data to be displayed in the grid. We can select the related entity, the specific view to be used, as well as filter by related records only.

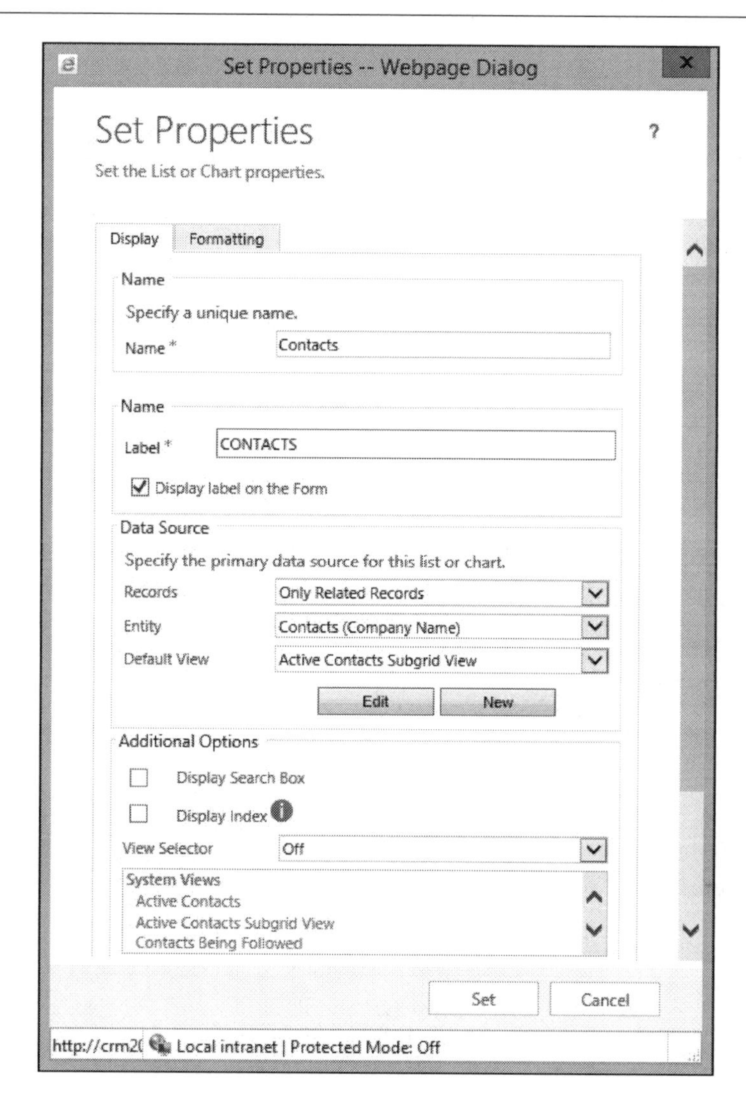

The **Additional Options** section allows us to customize whether the user can change the view used, along with a few other display options.

Fields

The fields are the building bricks of the forms. They are used to collect and display the record data. In Dynamics CRM, fields are defined with various data types. Just like the data residing in the database, each field is defined with a related data type, and some specific fields include formatting properties.

The data types used in Dynamics CRM are as follows:

- **Single Line of Text**
- **Option Set**
- **Two Options**
- **Image**
- **Whole Number**
- **Floating Point Number**
- **Decimal Number**
- **Currency**
- **Multiple Lines of Text**
- **Date and Time**
- **Lookup**

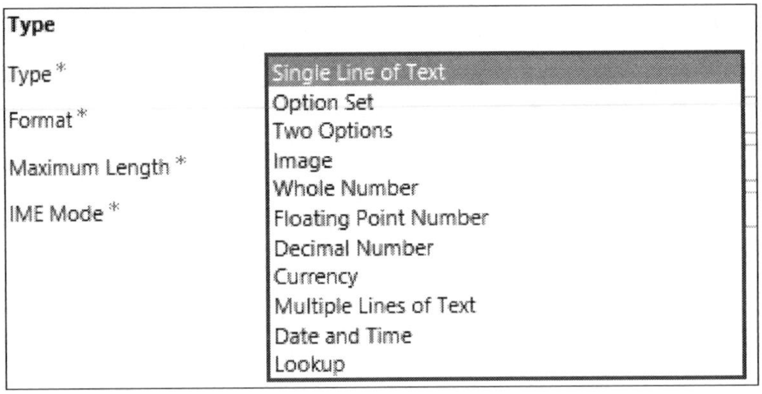

There are certain similarities between some of these data types. For example, **Single Line of Text** and **Multiple Lines of Text** capture all characters, and are differentiated only by the total number of characters allowed. **Two Options** is similar to **Option Set**, but captures only two possible options. They are also rendered differently on the form.

Under each of these data types, there are various options for formatting the data. For example, in **Single Line of Text**, the data can be left as a string of characters limited by the length of field defined, or it can be formatted as one of the following options: **Email**, **Text**, **Text Area**, **URL**, **Ticker Symbol**, and **Phone**.

The **Whole Number** data type can be formatted as a regular whole number, such as **Duration**, **Time Zone**, or **Language**.

The **Duration** value in the database is the value representing the total number of minutes. On the form, the field is represented as a drop-down menu with the suggested option from one minute all the way to three days. The field is smart enough to also interpret user input. For example, typing in this 60 (minutes) resolves automatically to one hour. The duration formats supported include the following options: x minutes, x hours, and x days. You can also enter values such as x.x hours.

The **Time Zone** field displays a list of selections in the format of (GMT-08:00) Pacific Time (US & Canada) or (GMT-12:00) International Date Line West. In the database, the values are stored as numbers.

The **Language** field displays a list of all the languages provisioned in the current organization. The values are presented as a drop-down list. At the database end, the selection is stored as a number using LCID codes. These codes are four or five digit codes, and all the values are available from the MSDN documentation.

The **Currency** data type allows us to select the currency precision. We can select from zero-to four-digit precision, as well as **Pricing Decimal Precision** and **Currency Precision**. **Pricing Decimal Precision** is a global value defined in the system settings. **Currency Precision** applies the precision defined by the currency used by the record.

The **Date and Time** data type allows us to select whether we intend to display date and time, or only the date.

The **Lookup** data type allows us to select the related entity where values are being selected. For example, a lookup field allows us on a Contact to select the parent account, by presenting a window that allows us to search for the specific Account record.

Global Option Sets

Global option sets, as the name implies, are groups of values defined at a global level. They are available to be shared on various entities and forms, and are kept in sync across all the locations where they are used. Changing the values in a global option set results in the change being applied in all locations where they are used.

Global option sets are not located and are customizable in the solution at the level of the entity where they are referred from, but in a separate category in the solution called **Option Sets**. Here, we can manage all existing and new global option sets. When referencing one of these on a form, you create a new field, just like you would create any other field. You select **Data Type** as **Option Set**, but instead of assigning custom values, you select the **Use Existing Option Set** radio button. This allows you to select, from the drop-down list, one of the existing Global Option Sets already created, or to create a new one using the **New** button. Once you select the option set to be used, you can edit it if needed, but keep in mind that any changes will be reflected in all locations where this global option set is being used. Also you can select **Default Value** for this option set. This is the value that will be automatically selected when no option is selected by the user.

Spacers

Spacer is used for formatting. Because Forms are being generated by adding fields and ordering these fields on the form, in certain instances we need to leave blank spaces for clarity. Thus, a Spacer will take the same space as a regular field, but no actual data in present.

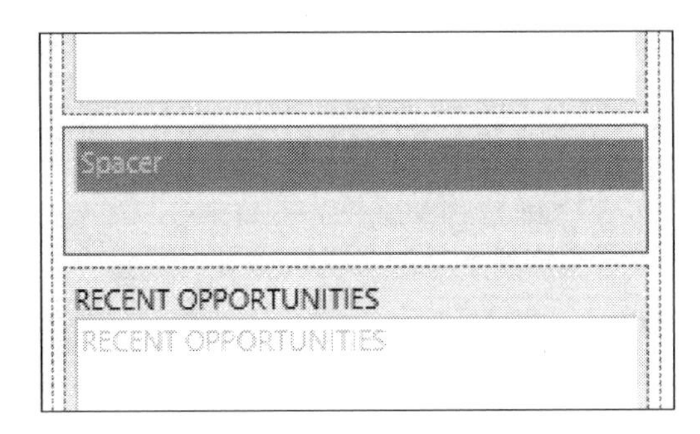

Entity Views and Charts

Entity **Views** are saved queries against system data. These queries apply filters to present subsets of data as needed. The views also contain formatting details regarding how the data will be displayed, the columns, and their order. Views can be defined programmatically or in XML. When using XML, the views can be exported, modified, and reimported into Dynamics CRM. You can export an entity using an unmanaged solution, modify the entity properties in the XML definition file and then repackage and reimport the solution into your organization.

An Entity View is a saved query available globally throughout the organization. Each entity can have multiple views, with various filter conditions and formatting.

Each entity can have various types of views. They can serve various purposes, and include the following: **Advanced Find Views**, **Associated Views**, **Lookup Views**, **Public Views**, and **Quick Find Views**. Also, each entity will have one **Default Public View**.

Just like any other record in Dynamics CRM, the Public Entity Views can be created, updated, retrieved, deleted, and deactivated.

You can start creating a new view in a solution by adding an entity to the solution, navigating to views, and clicking on **New**.

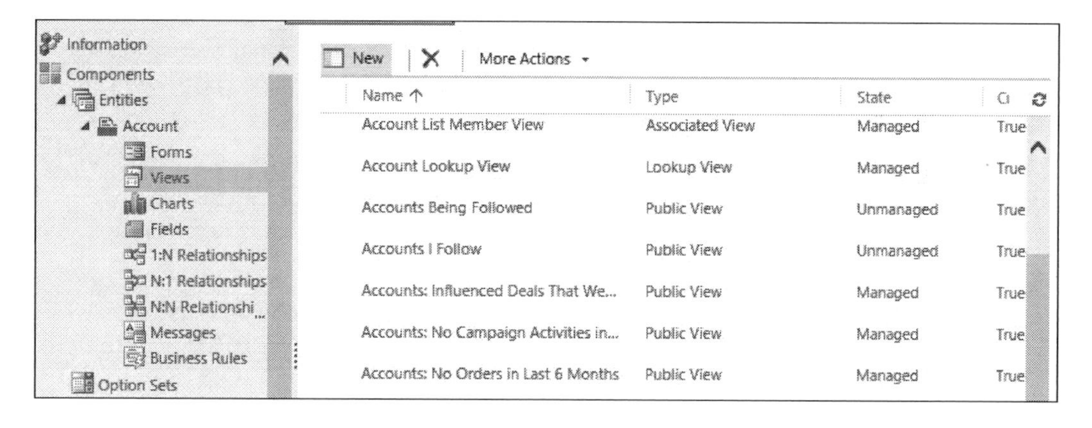

On the entity properties, define the **Name** and **Description** fields. Once done, start configuring the view.

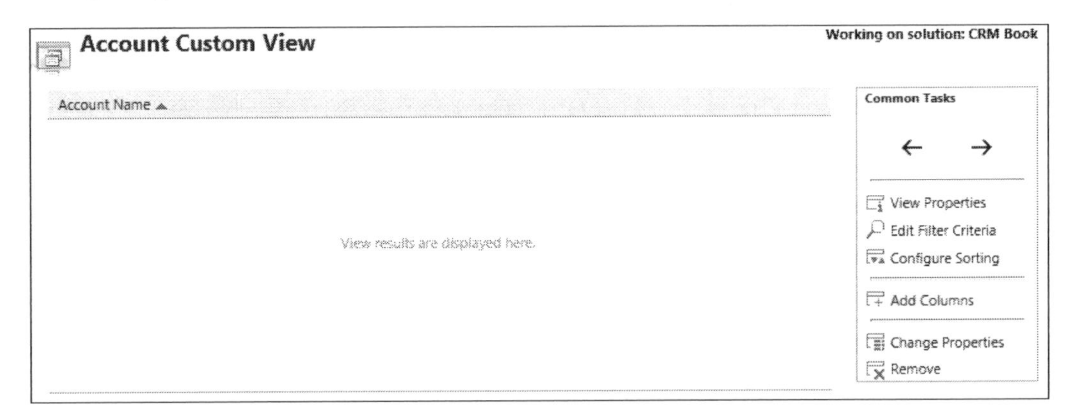

You can customize the following properties on a view:

- **View Properties**: This option allows you to change the view name and description.
- **Edit Filter Criteria**: This option allows you to define the filtering criteria for the view. Using a very simplistic wizard-based interface, a system customizer can easily create and enhance the filter applied to the view.
- **Configure Sorting**: This option allows a customizer to choose two filtering columns and the order of sorting for each. You can use one or both sorting option at the same time.
- **Add Columns**: This option allows a system customizer to bring into the view new data fields from the same entity, or form directly related entities. In a view of accounts, a system customizer can bring in information from the related **Created By** system user entity.
- **Change Properties**: This option allows a system customizer to modify each view column's properties. You can change the fixed width of the column. You also get properties in this view about the field data type and internal name.

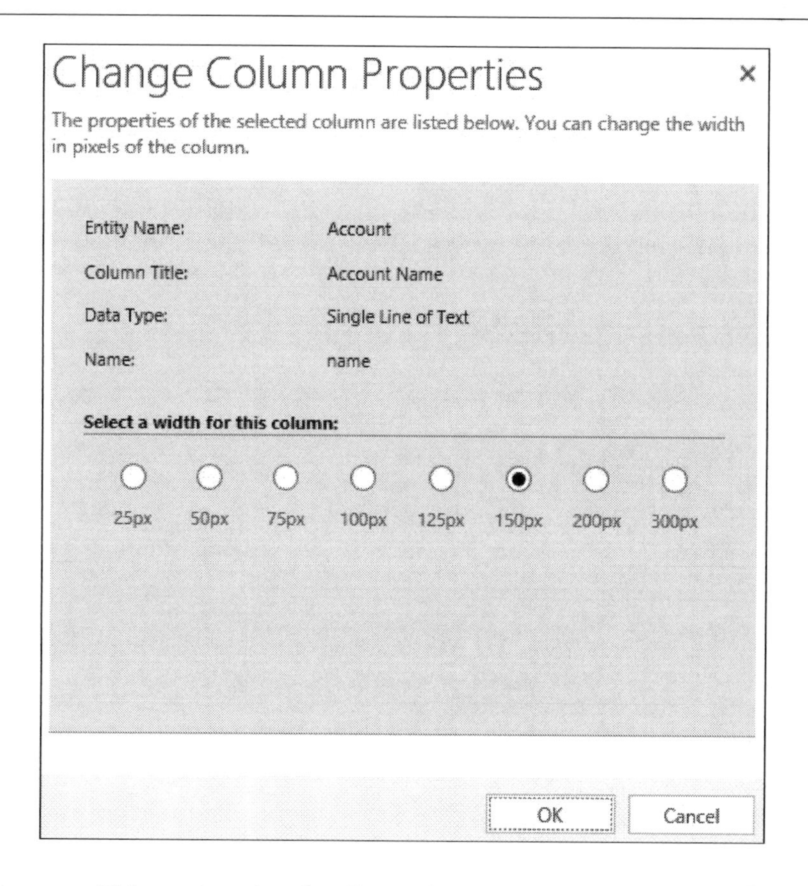

- **Remove**: This option simply allows the system customizer to remove a specific column from the view.

The left and right arrows at the top of the command area allows a system user to move and rearrange the columns in a view. Select a column you want to rearrange, and click on the arrows until you have it positioned in the correct spot.

Charts

Once we have a view customized, we can move on and create a Chart. Charts are visual representations of views created in the system.

Within the solution you use for customization, navigate to the entity to which you want to add a chart. Navigate to **Entities** | **Entity Name** (for example, **Account**) and click on **Charts**.

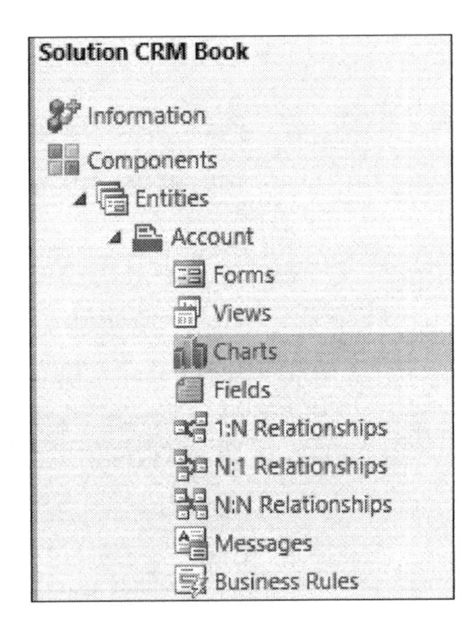

Most Business entities will have, by default, a set of Charts already created. You can modify these or create new ones.

Creating a new Chart involves the system customizer, from within the solution entity's charts section by clicking on **New**. He/she is presented with a set of options to customize the Chart as needed.

From this view, we can choose the type of Chart to be used. We have options for **Column**, **Bar**, **Area**, **Line**, **Pie**, or **Funnel** charts.

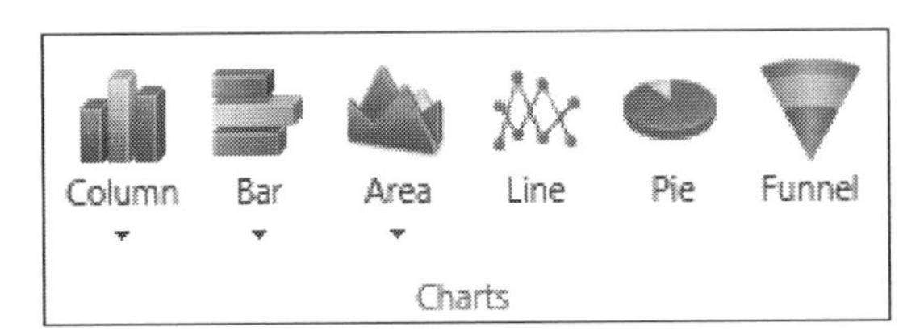

All charts are based on a View. When creating a chart, the first item to select in the definition of the chart is the view used to collect the records that will drive the chart data. The steps are as follows:

1. Select one of the entity views available from the drop-down list.
2. Next step is to name your chart, and verify the preview. You have options to adjust the series used in generating the chart, add new series, define, and add categories, as well as define a description for the chart.
3. Once we have the chart(s) created, we can see them by navigating to the view. We can also start adding these charts to Dashboards.

Dashboards

A dashboard is a special type of form in Dynamics CRM. It is comprised of up to six area. Each of these areas can present one of the following types of data: **Charts**, **Lists**, **iFrames**, and/or **Web Resources**.

In Dynamics CRM, there are two types of dashboards:

- **Organization-owned dashboards**
- **User-owned dashboards**

The difference between these two types is the behavior.

An **organization-owned dashboard**, once created, must be published to make it available to the organization. As such, it cannot be assigned or shared. It is created as part of a solution, and published with the solution.

A **user-owned dashboard** is a dashboard created by a user. Therefore, the user owns the dashboard, and he/she can assign or share it with other users.

A generic dashboard looks like this:

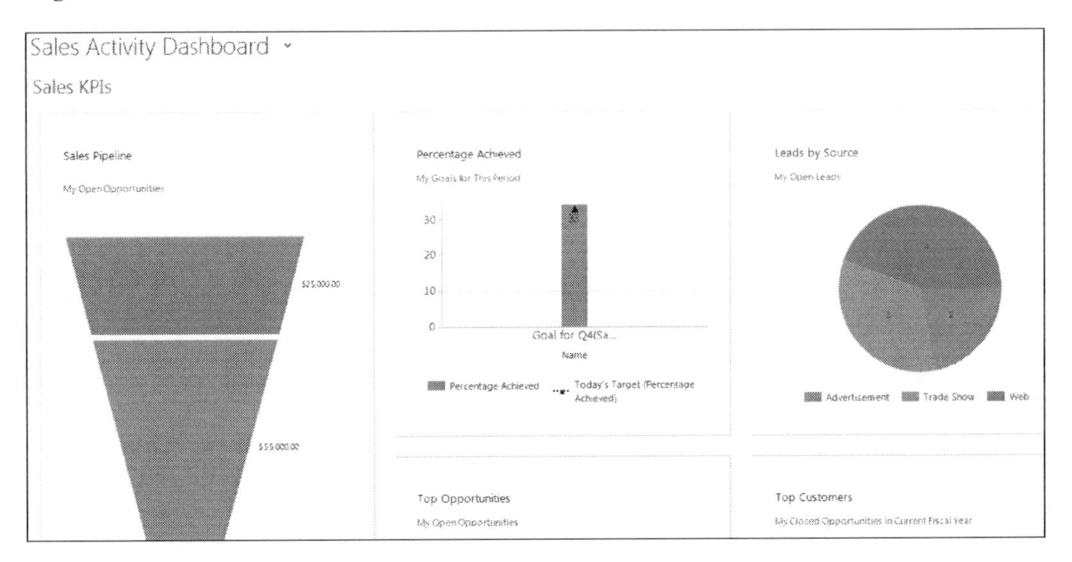

Entity Relationships

Entity relationships are the representation of relations between various Dynamics CRM entities. The customization tools included with Dynamics CRM make it easy for system customizers to create new entities, modify existing entities, and create the relationships between them.

The entity relationships define associations from one entity to other entities or to itself. A new relationship is represented as a new table relationship in the database.

The simplest example of an entity relationship is the creation of a lookup to an entity. This creates a one-to-many relationship between the two entities. This allows you to associate multiple child records to a parent record.

Within Dynamics CRM, there are three types of relationships. They are as follows:

- One-to-Many
- Many-to-One
- Many-to-Many

One-to-Many (1:N) and Many-to-One (N:1) Relationships

This kind of relationship defines an entity record that can be associated to many records of a different entity. The difference between 1:N and N:1 is the direction of the relationship.

When viewing a primary entity record, you can see a listing of the related entity records defined by the relationship.

Defining a custom 1:N relationship involves defining the following four parts: **Relationship Definition**, **Lookup Field**, **Navigation Pane Item for Primary Entity**, and **Relationship Behavior**.

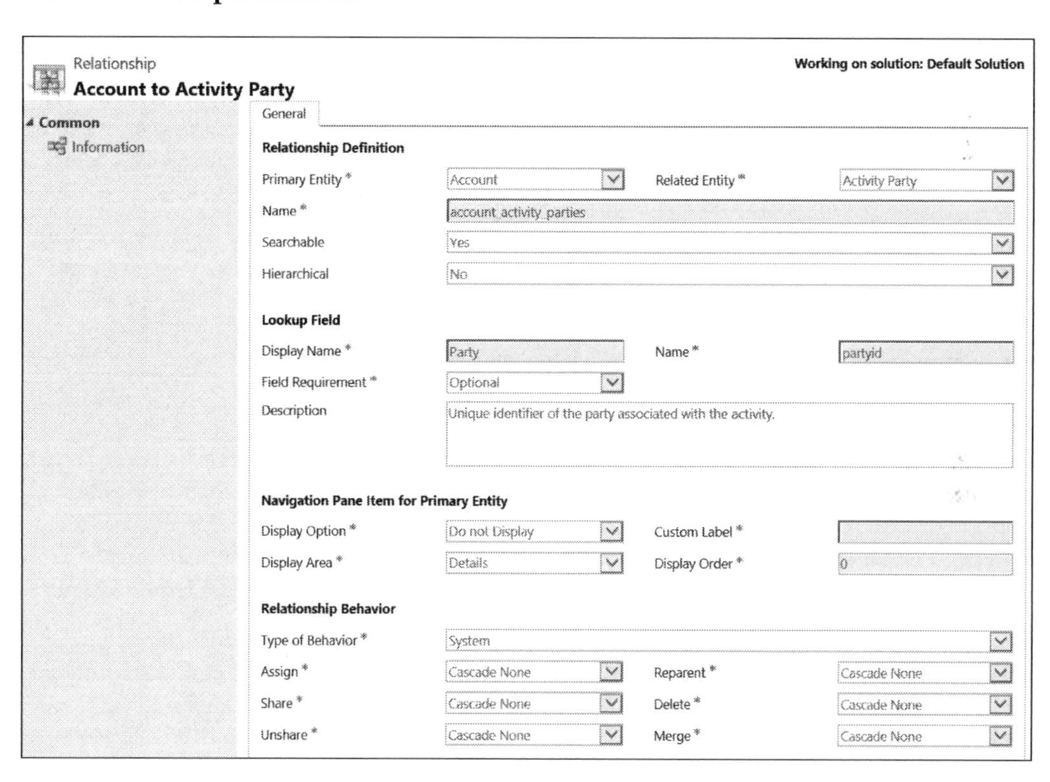

Many-to-Many (N:N) Relationships

The N:N relationships is a special type of relationship, that depends on an intersect entity to create a relationship. This allows us to relate many primary entities to many child entities.

When viewing record of the parent or the child entity, in a N:N relationship, you can see a listing of any record of the related entity.

Creating a new Many-to-Many relationship involves defining the parent and the child entity, and naming the relationship.

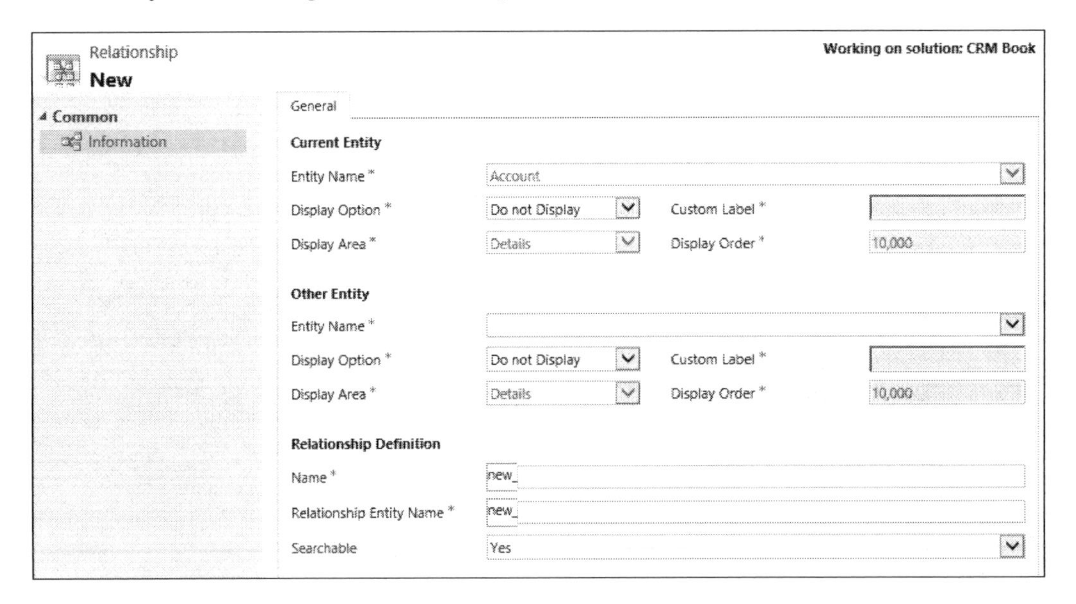

N:N relationships do not generate a hierarchy between related entities. In such a relationship, you do not define lookups or behaviors. The relationship is reciprocal.

The intersect entity is generated automatically by the system, and it is not customizable. As such, you cannot add custom fields to it.

When creating entity relationships, close attention should be paid to the Relationship Behavior settings. This influences how the relationship behaves and how changes are cascaded to the related records. For example, a Parental relationship cascades all changes to the related records.

For more details on relationships, see the documentation provided in MSDN:

`https://technet.microsoft.com/library/dn531171.aspx`

Once you have a relationship created, review the field mapping to make sure you are bringing in the correct fields and values from the related entity.

> Make sure to publish all changes to the solution. Publishing is the process that makes all changes available to all users. Changes made to a solution but not published are not visible to users of the organization until they are published.

When customizing relationships, pay attention also to **Navigation Pane Item** for the **Primary Entity** section. The **Display** option allows you to customize the label on each relationship to avoid confusion with multiple relationships using the same name, as well as to hide this particular relationship. **Display Area** and **Order** also help customize how and where this relationship is made visible to the system users.

Messages

Messages are customizable snippets of text that appear throughout the entity form. By default, there is a set of predefined messages, and they can be edited and replaced as needed.

Do not confuse **Messages** with the plugin execution messages. That is a development topic, completely different from what we cover in this book.

A standard **Messages** configuration window looks like this:

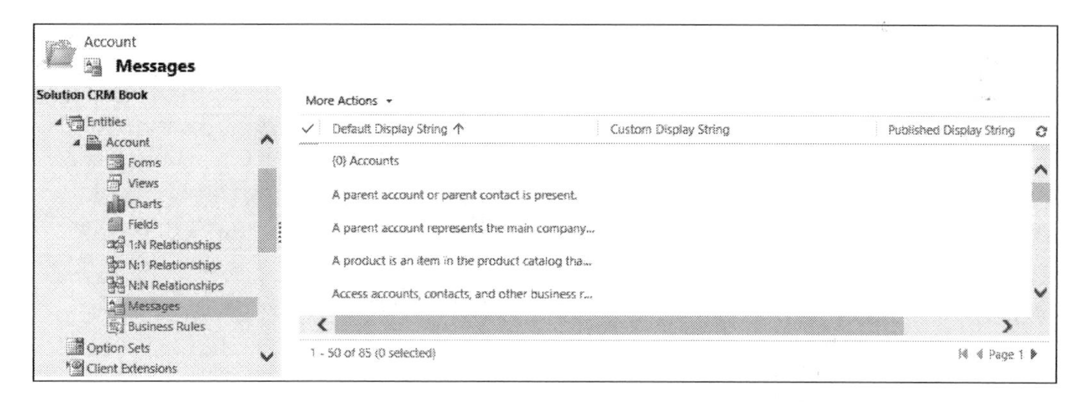

All messages that are being changed from the default must be published before they become visible to all users.

The view presents **Default Display String**, **Custom Display String**, which is the string we have modified, and **Published Display String**. The **Published Display String** can be different from the **Custom Display String** if we have modified a message several times, and the latest change is not yet published.

When working with multiple languages, only the base language messages can be modified through this interface. For additional languages, you can export the base language messages, translate them, and then reimport the translation for the additional languages.

Composite fields

Composite fields are another feature introduced with version 2013. They group a set of fields together, resulting in optimized screen real estate usage. Some examples of composite fields include the **Name** field, comprised of first, middle, and last name, or the address field. Once the user selects one of these composite fields, a *fly-out* ID is presented with each field editable separately as permissions allow.

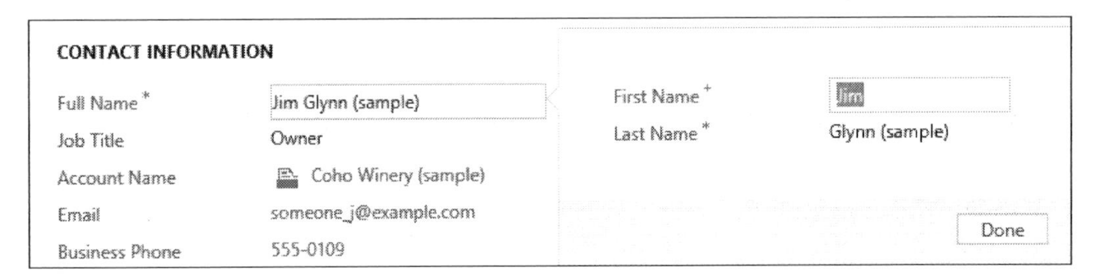

Composite fields are only provided with the platform. We do not have the ability to create our own composite fields. Also, we do not have the ability to customize existing composite fields by adding, removing, or relabeling fields. One thing to note is that, since the fields in a composite field are not actually on the form, standard events such as **OnChange** will not trigger on a particular field. They will however trigger on the composite field as a whole.

A workaround to that is to add the individual fields on the form in a hidden section. That way, when a field is updated, the hidden field takes the update and triggers the change.

Specific Business Rules can be configured against composite fields, but the conditions must be against the composite field to be associated correctly. You can have, for example, a condition where if the composite address field contains City, and the City value is a certain value, then perform an action. We will have an in depth look at Business Rules in the following chapter.

Calculated Fields

Calculated fields were introduced with Dynamics CRM 2015. The purpose of these fields is to provide automatically calculated field values based on other existing firm field values. Before version 2015, we used a lot of customization to generate this behavior. In addition, all change request involved reaching out to the development team again, process a change request, and all the associated hoops.

Calculated fields bring the ease and usability found in Excel to Dynamics CRM. The process also does not require a developer any more, and any power user with permission to edit the system can create these fields as well as Rollup Fields described next.

In order to create a Calculated field, you create a field in a Solution just like any other customization. On the field properties form, look for the **Field Type** definition. From the drop-down list, select **Calculated**. Once the field is configured as Calculated field, you can click on **Edit** to change the way the field behaves.

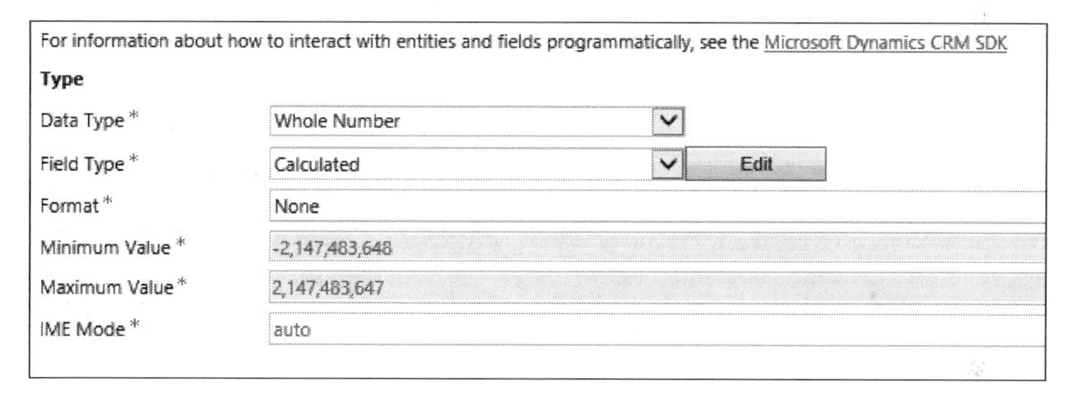

The interface to Configure calculated fields is very intuitive. You are presented with an **IF...THEN** condition. You set up your conditions, and upon validation of these conditions the configured Actions are executed.

This interface is common across multiple configurable elements. You will become very familiar with it when using not only Calculated fields, but also Rollup fields and Business Rules.

When working with Calculated fields, it is important to understand that, depending on the data type of the field selected, various functions are presented. For example, a field of data type of **Floating Point Number**, **Multiple Lines of Text**, or **Lookup** does not get an option for a Calculated field. For the ones that accept this option, functions around working with date and strings are available. Some of this include adding and/or removing days, months, years, concatenating strings, and so on. In order to do actual numeric calculations, you can generate formulas similar to the way you do it in Excel, with some limitations. You will have to write the formulas manually, automated generated functions such as sum, sin, and others are not predefined.

Once the field is added to a form and the changes are published, navigating to the respective form will show the newly added calculated field, as the following screenshot shows:

Rollup fields

In the same category as features with Calculated fields is the Rollup fields. Generating this type of field is quite similar to adding Calculated fields. The purpose of Rollup fields is to aggregate data from multiple child records. This addition is extremely helpful to reduce a lot of previous code complexity when performing such actions. An example is calculating the number of closed Opportunities in the last six months. In previous versions before Rollup fields were available, this scenario was handled by a develop function creating this functionality custom through code. Now, this can be replaced with a simple customization.

Adding a **Rollup** field is an option made available to only certain field data types. The ones that do not accept **Rollup** field are as follows:

- **Single Line of Text**
- **Option Set**
- **Two Options**
- **Image**
- **Floating Point Number**
- **Multiple Lines of Text**
- **Lookup**

Selecting a data type that supports **Rollup Field** allows us to select the **Field Type** as **Rollup**, as shown in the following screenshot:

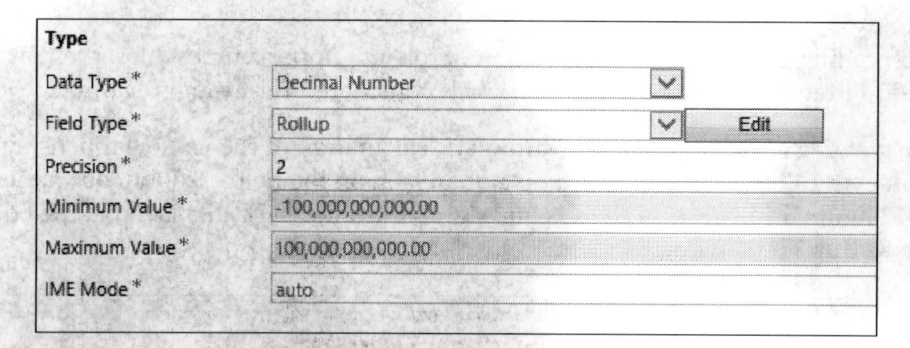

Select **Edit** to configure the behavior of the newly created **Rollup Field**. This presents the already familiar interface that we've seen before in Calculated fields.

In the configuration screen, the **SOURCE ENTITY** is usually preselected based on the entity we started the configuration of the field from. We get to select **RELATED ENTITY** and the **AGGREGATION** type, as shown in the following screenshot:

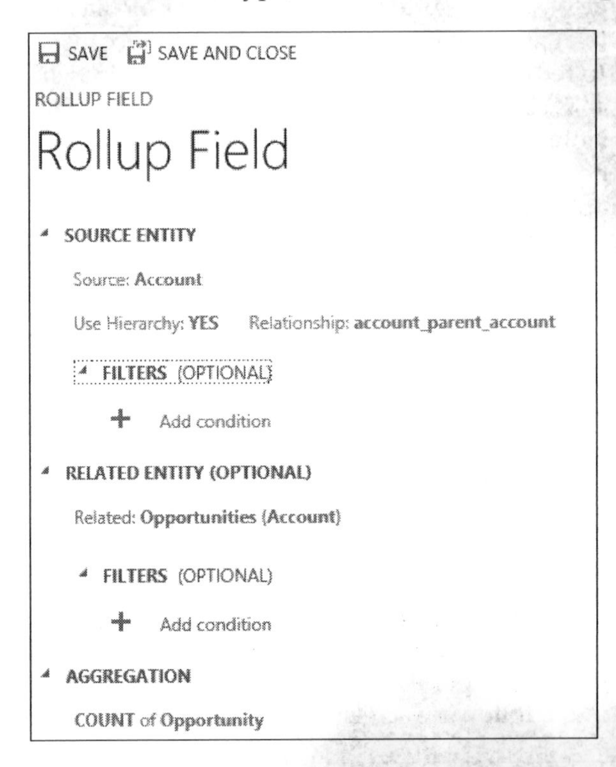

The preceding example shows a selection of related Opportunities. Observe that we can add **Filter** to limit the amount of records considered for the aggregation.

When creating a **Rollup Field**, the automatic calculation of the value happens by default every 12 hours. The first run is not, in fact, on the field creation, but rather after 12 hours from creation. This is highlighted in a message displayed at the bottom of the **Rollup Field** editor window.

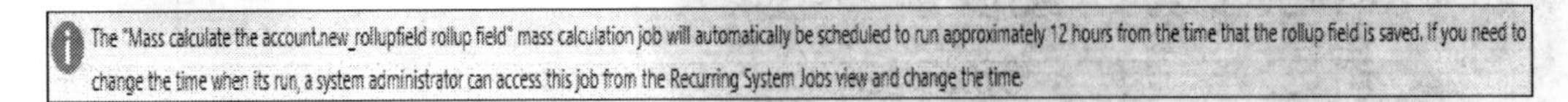

The final **Rollup Field**, once added on a form and published will look like the following screenshot:

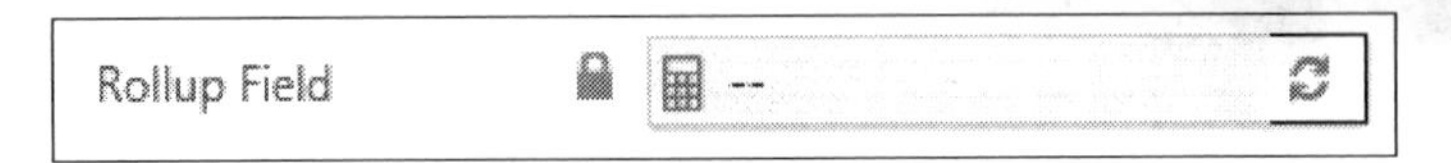

Observe the option to manually refresh the value. This will trigger an immediate refresh, which allows a user to manually refresh a rollup field value when they know a change of values has occurred.

An invalid formula will be flagged by the system. On the actual form, such fields with an invalid formula are presented as in the following screenshot:

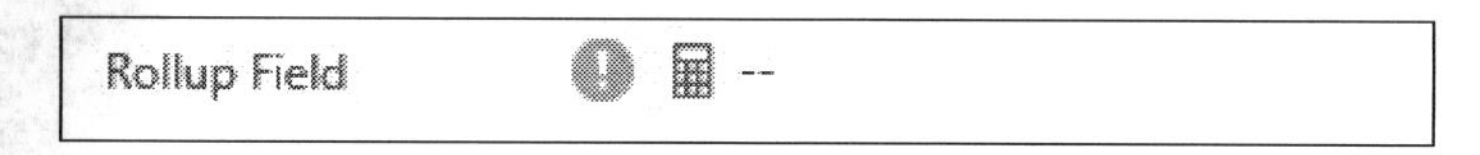

Observe the exclamation mark presented. Fix the formula and republish the correct values.

SLAs and the Timer Control

SLA stands for Service Level Agreement. This functionality in Dynamics CRM allows us to define the level of support and commit to respect this agreement. SLAs also allow us to track performance for client services in accordance with set expectations. We have the ability to define measurable metrics to push to the service team's timely warnings with regards to various support scenarios.

In Dynamics CRM, SLAs work in conjunction with entitlements if need be. Alternatively, SLAs can be defined across an organization. When used with entitlements, we define various levels of entitlements for groups of customers. These entitlements define the related SLAs, and all service and interactions with these customers are regulated through these new SLAs.

One simple example is to define company XYZ Inc. as a Gold level customer. Our Gold level customers receive special treatment. Their inquiries and requests must be fully addressed within a time frame of 24 hours. Thus, XYZ Inc. is entitled to this. A representative of this company opens a case with us with regards to a product they have purchased. The product turns out to be defective and needs to be replaced. Because of the current entitlement, we need to dispatch a technician to replace the defective product within 24 hours. Once the Case is opened, the SLA is associated with the case. The timer control is triggered, and starts counting down from 24 hours. We could also have notifications at, let's say, the 12-hour mark to remind the service team to review the case if no action was performed on this case.

We had the ability to achieve this with custom code before Dynamics CRM 2013. With the Dynamics CRM Online Spring 2014 update and the CRM 2013 Service Pack 1 on-premise version, Standard SLAs were introduced. It has evolved over the next few versions, and enhanced SLAs were added.

Standard versus Enhanced SLAs

Enhanced SLAs have followed after Standard SLAs, and have added a few additional features. These include items such as:

- Ability to pause an existing SLA: An SLA can be paused by the user if needed, to reflect waiting for input from a customer. While the SLA is paused, the time is not counted against the entitlement.
- Provide the ability to create success actions on an SLA: We can trigger specific actions when a case has been resolved resulting in a successful SLA. These actions could include both external and/or internal communication.
- Default SLA tracking on Cases: With enhanced SLAs, the default Case forms include the timer control, not requiring us to make this customization.

An SLA is configured at the Organization level. This is not a component of a solution.

In order to customize SLAs, navigate to **Settings** | **Service Management**. In the **Service Terms** section, you will find the configurations for both **Service Level Agreements** and **Entitlements**.

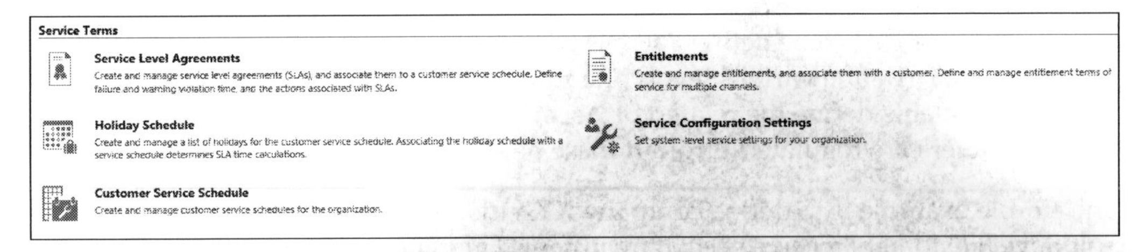

Let's navigate to **Service Level Agreement** and see how we can create our first SLA. We will pick a very simple SLA example.

On the **All Service Level Agreements** view, select **+New** from the ribbon. This brings us to the **New SLA** form.

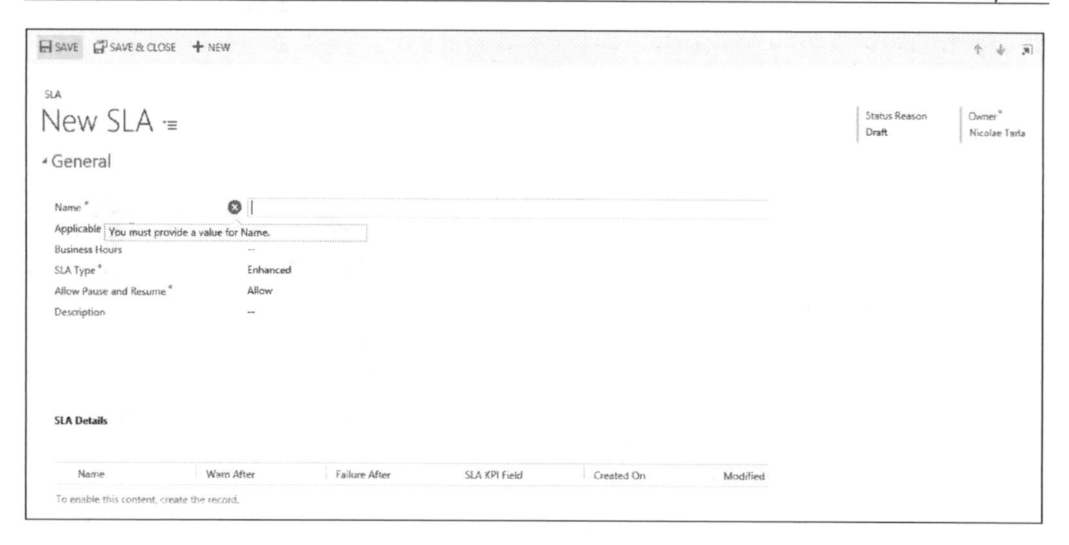

Here, we must define at least, the **Name**, **Applicable From**, **SLA Type**, and **Allow Pause and Resume** fields.

The **Applicable From** field defines the starting time when the timer commences the count. The default value is **Created On**, which represents the time the Case with this associated SLA is created. If this is not necessarily the time when you want the SLA to commence, other values available include the following:

- **Modified On**
- **Follow Up By**
- **Record Created On**
- **Resolved By**
- **First Response By**
- **Escalated On**
- **Last On Hold Time**

The SLA type is nothing more than a selection of the type of SLA you intend to create.

Observe that with the introduction of enhanced SLAs, this is the default value in this field.

Allow Pause and Resume tells the system exactly that. The default is set to **Allow**, but it can be changed on SLA creation.

Setting up Business Hours allows the SLA to be aware of working schedules, and only count against these schedules. For an organization that does not run 24/7, this is an important configuration.

Once the SLA is created, the following fields are not changeable any more:

- **Applicable From**
- **SLA Type**
- **Allow Pause and Resume**

If the configurations you have made are in fact not correct, to correct any of these fields, you must recreate the SLA from scratch.

Note that an SLA is not available and applicable until it is **Activated**.

Once activated, an SLA can be applied to specific records, or it can be set as **Default** through the available ribbon buttons.

SLA Details represents the specific **Key Performance Indicators (KPIs)** or metrics for the respective SLA. You can also define the success and failure actions related to this SLA.

The default new **SLA Details** form called **New SLA Item** looks like the following screenshot:

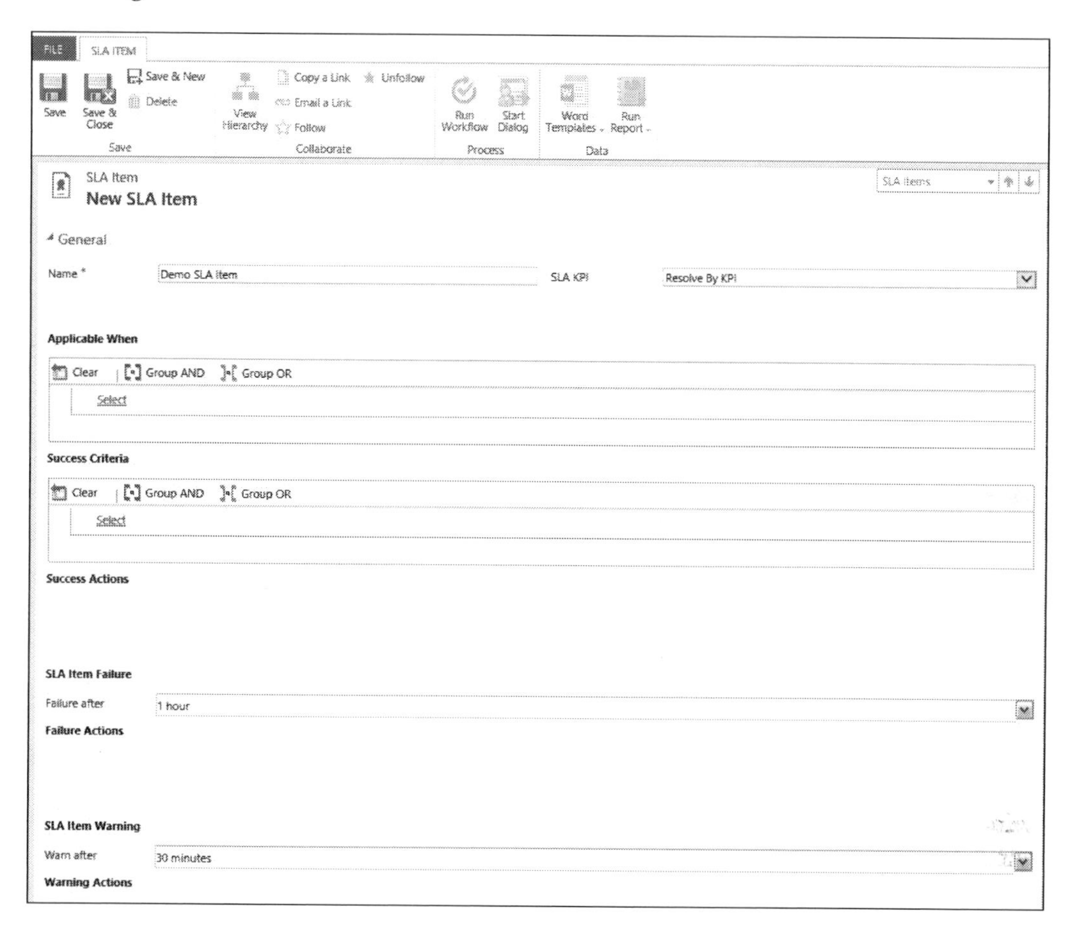

The SLA KPIs are trackable performance indicators. These are available to be selected from the drop-down at the top of the form. The values include the following:

- **First Response By KPI**
- **Resolve By KPI**

By default, there are two predefined values only. If you need to track other KPIs, you must create new case fields of type lookup that refer to that particular KPI instance entity.

You can add as many SLA items as necessary, and you can order them as needed. The condition in **Applicable When** defines when an SLA items is triggered.

Only the first SLA item that matches the condition in **Applicable When** is applied.

SLAs have behind the scenes corresponding Workflows that get triggered. When activating an SLA for the first time, the corresponding workflow is also created based on the definition of the SLA. From a permission stand-point, when you have permissions to trigger actions in an SLA, you must have the same permissions to perform the actions in the workflow.

Not all actions available in workflows are also available when defining the failure and warning actions. Only the following actions are available:

- **Send Email**
- **Create Record**
- **Update Record**
- **Assign Record**
- **Change Status**

When defining **Applicable When** and **Success Criteria** clauses, if no `AND` or `OR` grouping is defined, the system defaults to the `AND` grouping.

In order to be able to define **Failure Actions** and **Warning Actions**, you must first save **New SLA Item**. You must define at least **Success Criteria** for the SLA to make any sense. This validation is automatically performed by the system. Clicking on **Save** before having **Success Criteria** defined results in the following warning:

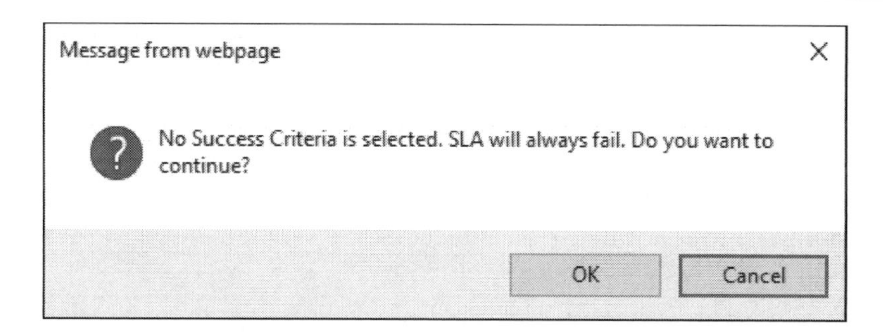

Defining **Success Actions**, as well as **Failure** and **Warning Actions** is done in a very visual way—by selecting from the **Add Step** drop-down menu provided by one of the previously mentioned options:

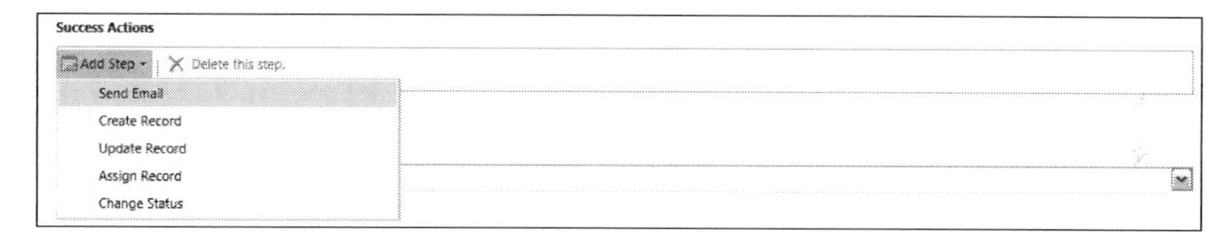

You have the ability here to define multiple steps as needed. If a step is not required any more, it can easily be removed by selecting it and clicking on **Delete this step**.

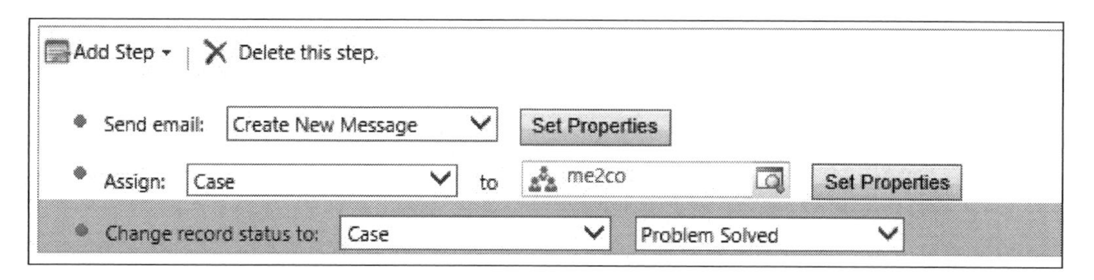

Working with SLAs during maintenance periods is a task to be considered carefully. When performing bulk data updates that trigger SLAs, and you don't want the SLAs to be triggered, you must disable the SLAs for the organization and re-enable them once the maintenance work completes.

How SLAs are applied

SLAs are applied on Case creation if enabled, either by default or triggered by an entitlement. The SLA is reapplied if any of the **Applicable When** fields are updated. This could potentially result in failure or warning actions being retriggered. You can prevent this behavior by adding a custom tracking flag field and adding it to the **Applicable When** condition. This will check to see whether the flag was raised already, and not trigger the actions a second time.

SLAs can also be applied on demand, or through the use of workflows. In order to apply an SLA manually to a Case, you must add the SLA field to the Case form, as shown in the following screenshot:

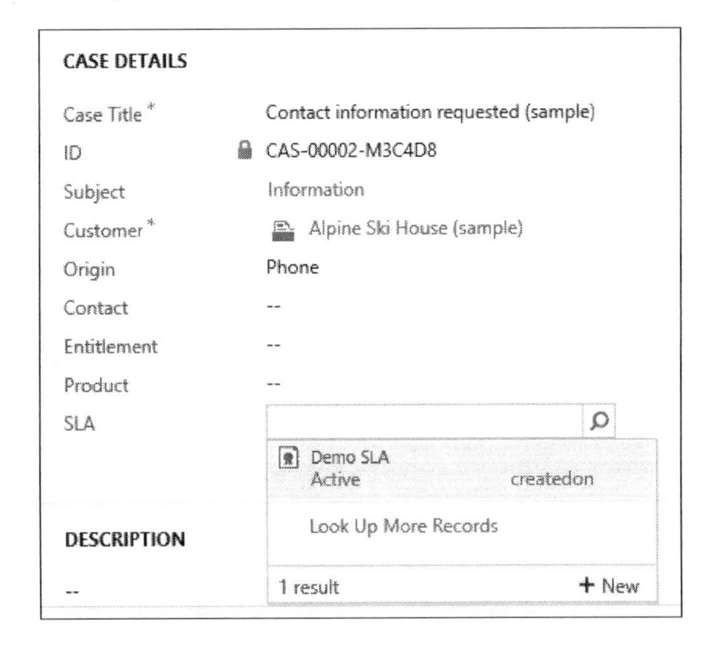

This allows the user to manually select an SLA to be applied to each case. Adding this Enhanced SLA to an existing case makes the **Enhanced SLA Details** section on the Case form light up with SLA specific information. The following screenshot shows an expired SLA, which triggered various actions as customized:

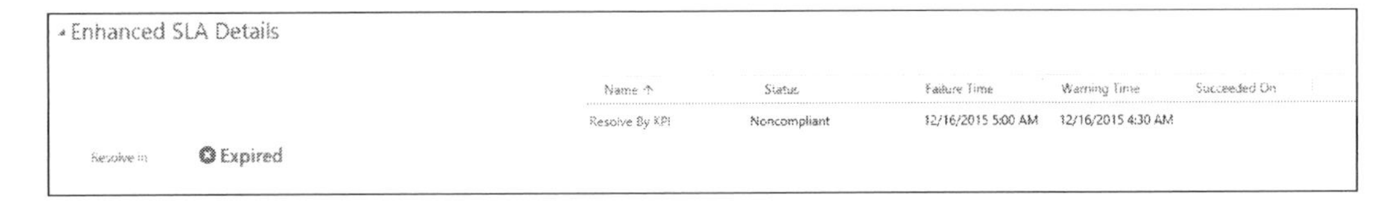

Working with Documents

Document management has been a feature available with the Dynamics CRM platform for a very long time—one of the first iterations dealt with storing documents directly into the Dynamics CRM database. This is still available, as we can add various document types to a Notes field. While this is available out of the box, and relatively easy to use, there are various drawbacks to making this the default document management strategy. As a matter of fact, this approach should probably be discouraged as much as possible.

Notes, once enabled on an entity, is behind the scenes as a reference to an entity called **Annotation**. This entity stores the file attachment along with note details and a reference back to the entity that the attached document is referenced to. For some of the out of the box entities **Notes** is enabled by default, but for all new custom entities this must be enabled as needed.

In order to enable **Notes** on an entity, navigate to the entity configuration, and find the **Communications & Collaboration** section. Make sure the **Notes (include attachments)** checkbox is selected. Note that once enabled, **Notes** cannot be disabled.

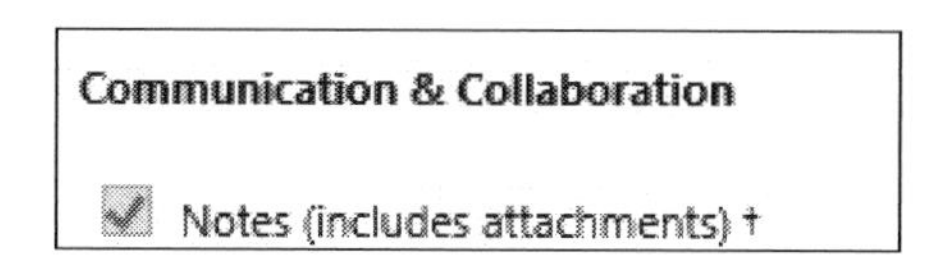

While this configuration is very simple, and it might be tempting to use, there are some very important factors why this is not necessarily the best approach. They are as follows:

- Inability to track various versions of documents
- Inability to search for a document
- Inability to create document metadata, or search through document content
- Rather difficult process to manage documents or export/import from one environment to another using only the out of the box tools

As the platform evolved, integration with other offerings brought us support for SharePoint document libraries. This brings a new level of performance, and the ability to manage document metadata, various enhanced search capabilities, document versioning, as well as the ability to handle and manage documents and document backup processes.

Microsoft SharePoint Server is a Content Management and collaboration platform (CMS). When integrating with SharePoint, all documents are stored outside of the Dynamics CRM database, and into SharePoint, in the context of a Microsoft Dynamics CRM record.

With the current Microsoft Dynamics CRM 2016 version, two types of SharePoint integration models are available. They are as follows:

- Client to server integration
- Server to server integration

Client to Server Integration with SharePoint

Using the client to server integration, we can integrate Microsoft Dynamics CRM with SharePoint both on-premise and online. This approach requires the installation of the Microsoft Dynamics CRM list component on the SharePoint server. This is a SharePoint specific component that needs to be deployed prior to configuring the integration.

Server to Server Integration with SharePoint

This approach is used when integrating Microsoft Dynamics CRM Online with an Office 365 subscription. The SharePoint services from the Office 365 subscription are used to perform the integration with the Dynamics CRM Online organization in the same Office 365 instance. This approach does not require the use of the Microsoft Dynamics CRM List Component.

> Once server to server integration is enabled, there is no way to revert to client to server integration in the same environment.

This integration is supported only from Dynamics CRM Online, against SharePoint online or on-premise. This support was added to Dynamics CRM with version 2015 Update 1 in the fall of 2015.

As far as version support, SharePoint is supported starting with version 2010.

> Server based integration with SharePoint must be enabled manually in Dynamics CRM Online.

Once you have the integration enabled with SharePoint, the following tasks must be performed in order to take advantage of document management features with SharePoint:

- Configure the target SharePoint server
- Enable entity document management

Configuring the target SharePoint Server

Before you can actually store any document into SharePoint, you must configure the target server. This allows you to point to a specific SharePoint Site Collection, and configure how the documents are to be structured on the target server. You do this by specifying the URL to the SharePoint server that will host your organization's documents.

These configurations are available from the **Settings | Document Management** section in your Microsoft Dynamics CRM Organization.

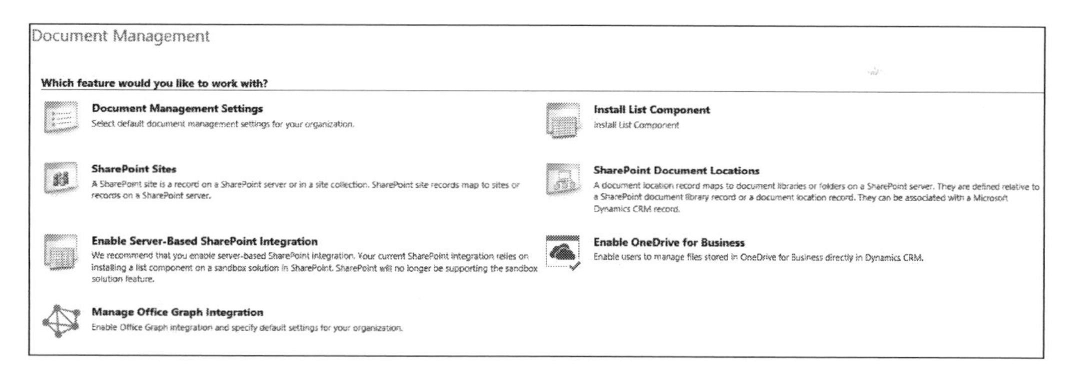

In order to configure in Microsoft Dynamics CRM Online, the server to server integration, start from the **Enable Server-Based SharePoint Integration**. This wizard will guide you through configuring this integration. The first screen of the wizard describes clearly the features and actions available once this is enabled.

Enable Server-Based SharePoint Integration

After you enable server-based SharePoint integration, you'll notice the following changes if you used the previous SharePoint integration:

- You can perform SharePoint actions in the CRM command bar.
- SharePoint documents display in Microsoft Dynamics CRM lists.
- There's no list component installation required for the SharePoint site.

If you're already connected to SharePoint sites, all the sites must be valid for server-based SharePoint integration.

Following the wizard, you can choose whether the target SharePoint server will be an online or on-premise deployment. When integration into the same Office 365 tenant, choose **Online**, otherwise choose **On-Premise**.

Next, specify the URL to the SharePoint site collection that will be used to store your organization documents, and then, validate the site.

Once a connection is established and the URL is validated, your configuration is saved. If you encounter any issues, make sure that the URL is valid and accessible.

After you enable server-to-server integration, you cannot go back and use client-to-server integration.

Once you complete this configuration, you must run the **Document Management Settings** wizard, as prompted by the final wizard screen. You can start it directly from this wizard, or you can go back to **Settings** | **Document Management** and start **Document Management Settings** from there.

Enable Server-Based SharePoint Integration

Congratulations!

Server-based SharePoint integration is now complete!

You've added a new SharePoint site URL, but you'll need to go to the Document Management Settings Wizard and enable the automatic folder generation for the site before you can view your documents in CRM.

☐ Open Document Management Settings Wizard

Finish

Enable entity Document Management

Navigate back to **Settings | Document Management** once this is configured and you will see that the option is not available anymore. This is normal, as once server-based SharePoint integration is configured, we cannot revert.

The **Document Management Settings** wizard is where we configure the entities that will take advantage of SharePoint document management features. Since we can create various SharePoint URLs to be used for document storage, in this wizard, we are prompted to also provide the SharePoint site URL.

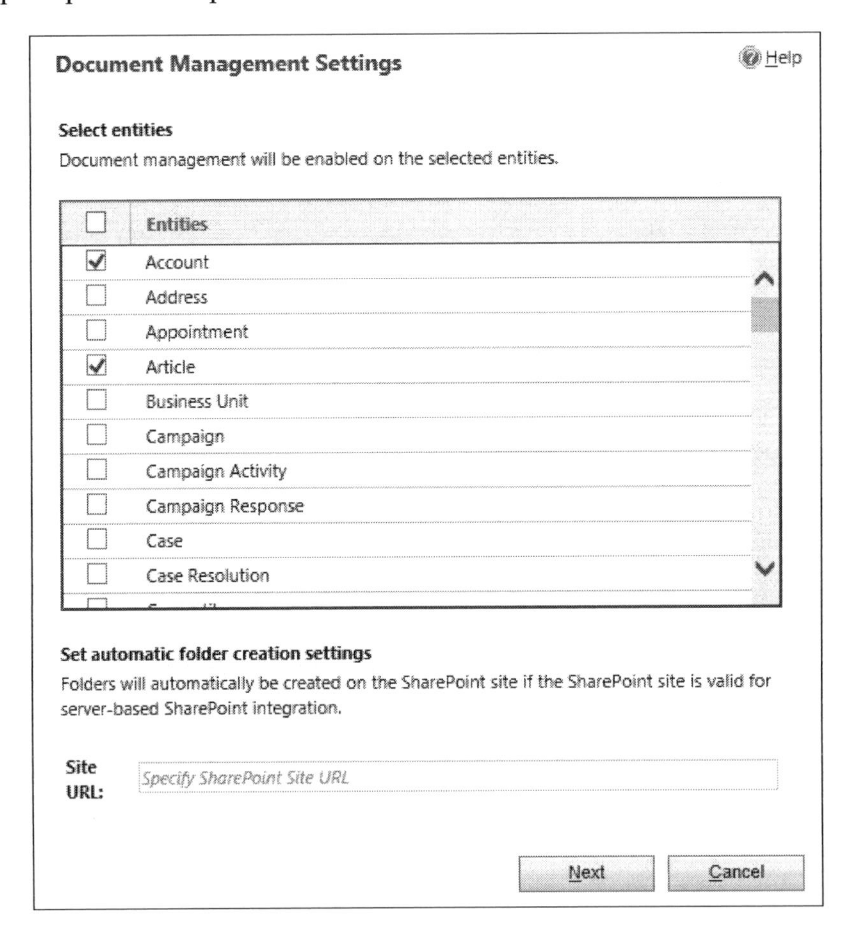

The URL is validated, and we are provided with an option to structure the documents based on a specific entity. This allows us to configure basic taxonomy in SharePoint in such a way that allows users easier access to the documents when browsing the SharePoint site directly.

If permissions allow, you can browse to the Dynamics CRM documents stored in SharePoint directly in SharePoint. You can also surf this document library on a SharePoint intranet site.

You can choose not to define a folder structure by an entity. This will create and store all documents in folders based on the entities enabled for document management.

The process to create the proper folder structure in SharePoint will take a few minutes, and when completed, a status of **Succeeded** is presented for each entity.

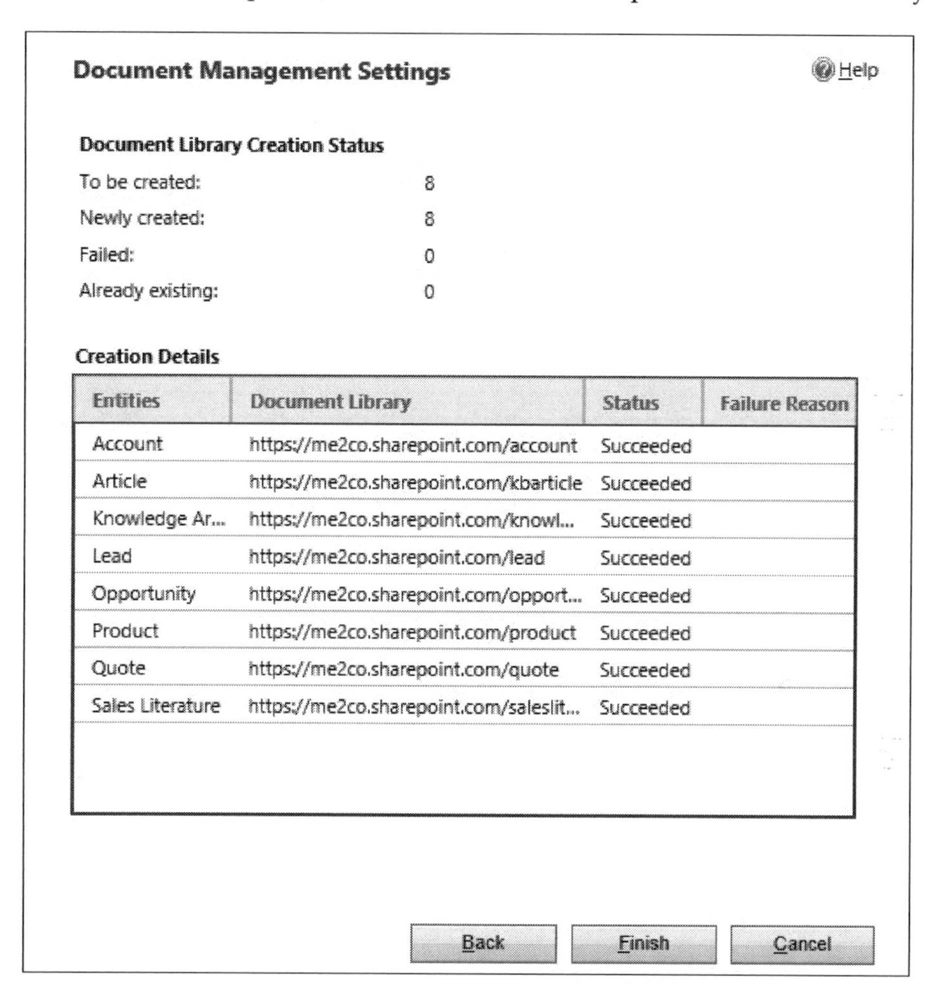

Once you complete this setup, you can navigate to a record of one of the entities enabled for document management. This is the first time getting to such record, since the folder structure is not yet created in SharePoint, so the user is prompted to create it.

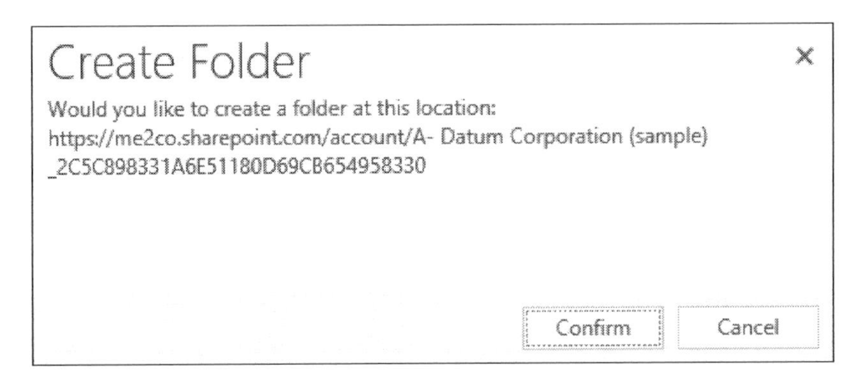

Once you have created the folder, getting to the documents on this record you are presented with a view into the list of documents stored on SharePoint and associated with this record. The ribbon presents options that work with these documents, including options to create new documents and upload new documents.

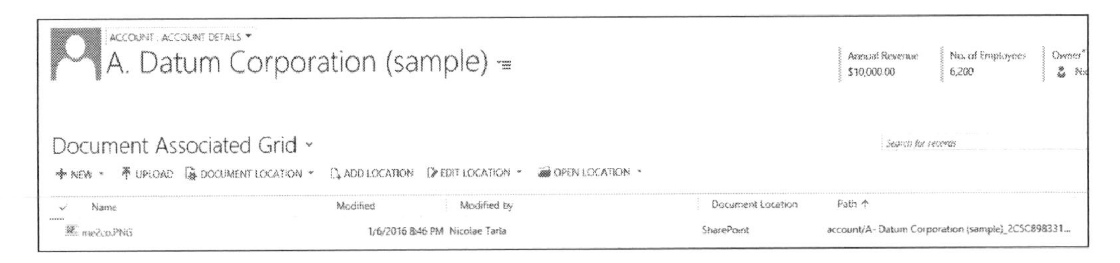

Now we have a fully functional integration with SharePoint, and we can start taking advantage of all the additional features offered by SharePoint.

OneDrive Integration

Starting with Microsoft Dynamics CRM 2016, we now have the ability to also store documents in our OneDrive for Business folders. We also have this functionality to complement how we use the existing document management features. From within the documents view, we have visibility into a merged list of documents stored in both SharePoint and OneDrive. However, when do we use one over the other, you ask?

OneDrive is meant for private documents, drafts not ready to be released, and so on. As such, the documents stored in OneDrive are not shared with other users that have access to a particular record. Other users will only see the documents shared through SharePoint.

Configure OneDrive for Business by navigating to **Settings | Document Management**. An option is presented to **Enable OneDrive for Business**. It is as simple as checking the **Enable OneDrive for Business** checkbox.

If you encounter an error, as in the following screenshot, make sure your OneDrive for Business account is initialized. All you need to do is navigate to your Office 365 tenant, to OneDrive for Business. The first time you access it, it will provision the document library on SharePoint.

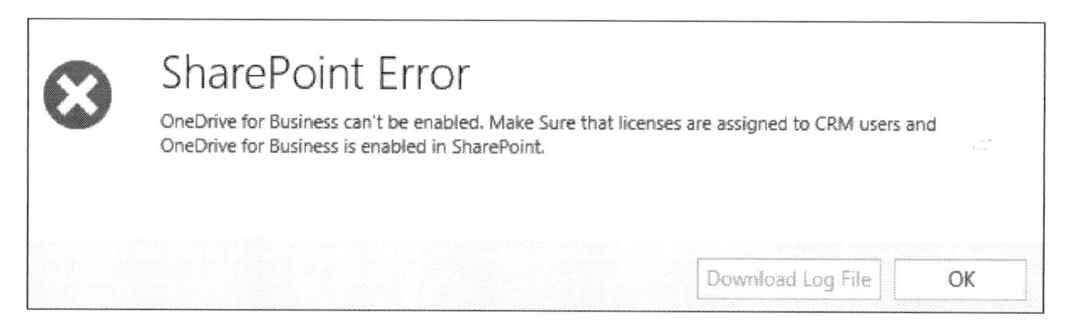

Once enabled, you can go ahead and configure the folder settings if necessary. You can decide to have all Dynamics CRM-related documents in a folder inside your OneDrive called by the default **CRM**.

With OneDrive for Business configured, navigate back to a record and add a new document in your OneDrive for Business this time. Going to **Upload Documents**, select the **OneDrive** option from the CRM folder drop-down menu.

Now have another look at **Documents Associated Grid**. Observe the two documents loaded as well as target **Document Location**. One is in **SharePoint** and the other, in **OneDrive**.

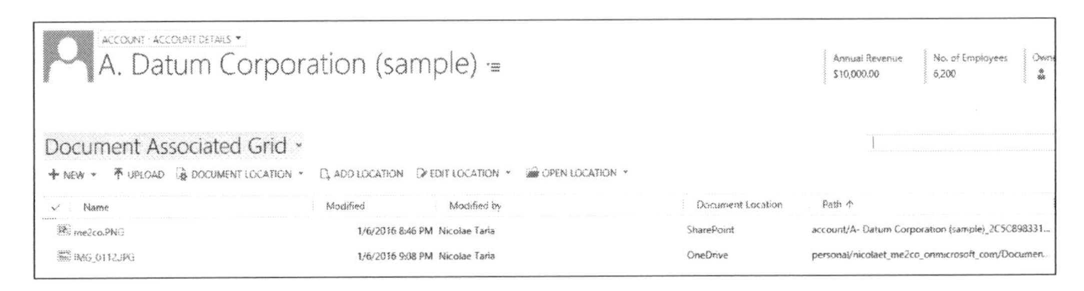

Office Graph Integration

Office Graph Integration is another new feature introduced with Microsoft Dynamics CRM 2016. It is based on the trends analysis provided by Office Delve.

For additional details on Office Delve, see the following site:

`https://support.office.com/en-us/article/What-is-Office-Delve-1315665a-c6af-4409-a28d-49f8916878ca`

In order for this aggregation to be significant and relevant, the use of various Office 365 features is very important. Email, OneDrive for Business and Office Sites are some of the sources used for aggregation.

Relationships to content, topics, and users are analyzed and a board-like rolodex of cards is presented as a result based on the analysis. This information can be presented on custom dashboards, as shown in the example later.

Office Graph Integration is configured from **Settings | Document Management**. Select the **Manage Office Graph Integration** option. The configuration is again a simple **enable** option. Once enabled, you can navigate to **Solution**, go to **Dashboards**, and add a new dashboard. Select a simple Dashboard, we will look at the Interactive Experience Dashboard in a following chapter when we talk about the Service module in detail.

In the Section configuration, you will observe a new icon to add a **Trending Documents** item.

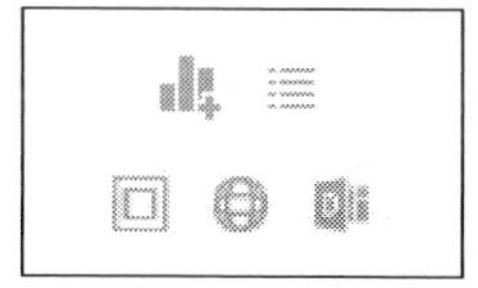

Once the dashboard is saved and published, we can navigate to it, and we will observe a section as shown in the following screenshot:

The more you work with documents and Office 365, the more relevant your Delve stream will become.

Geolocation

The geolocation features have been available for a few versions now. While not greatly popular, out of the box, we have the ability to map elements on a Bing map. There are, however, a few small configurations required to enable it.

In order to use this feature, in Microsoft Dynamics CRM 2016 and Online, you must enable it from **System Settings**. Some previous versions had this enabled by default, which caused additional customization requirements to hide it when not in use.

Navigate to **Settings** | **Administration** | **System Settings**. Scroll down on the **General** tab until you find the **Enable Bing Maps** section. Select **Enable Bing Maps** on forms to **Yes**.

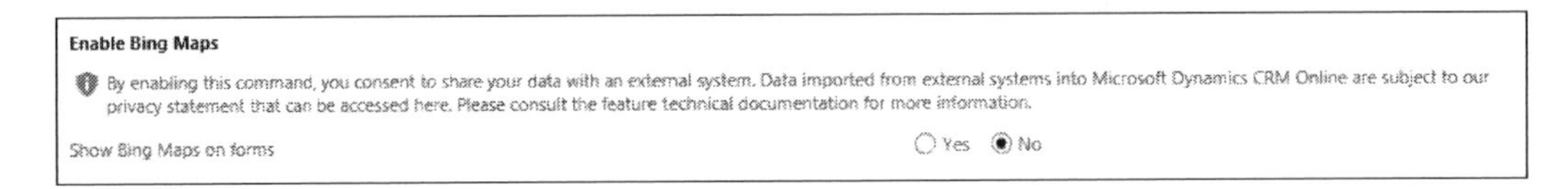

Once enabled, check which address fields it is using. For the out of the box Account for example, Address 1 is used as the source.

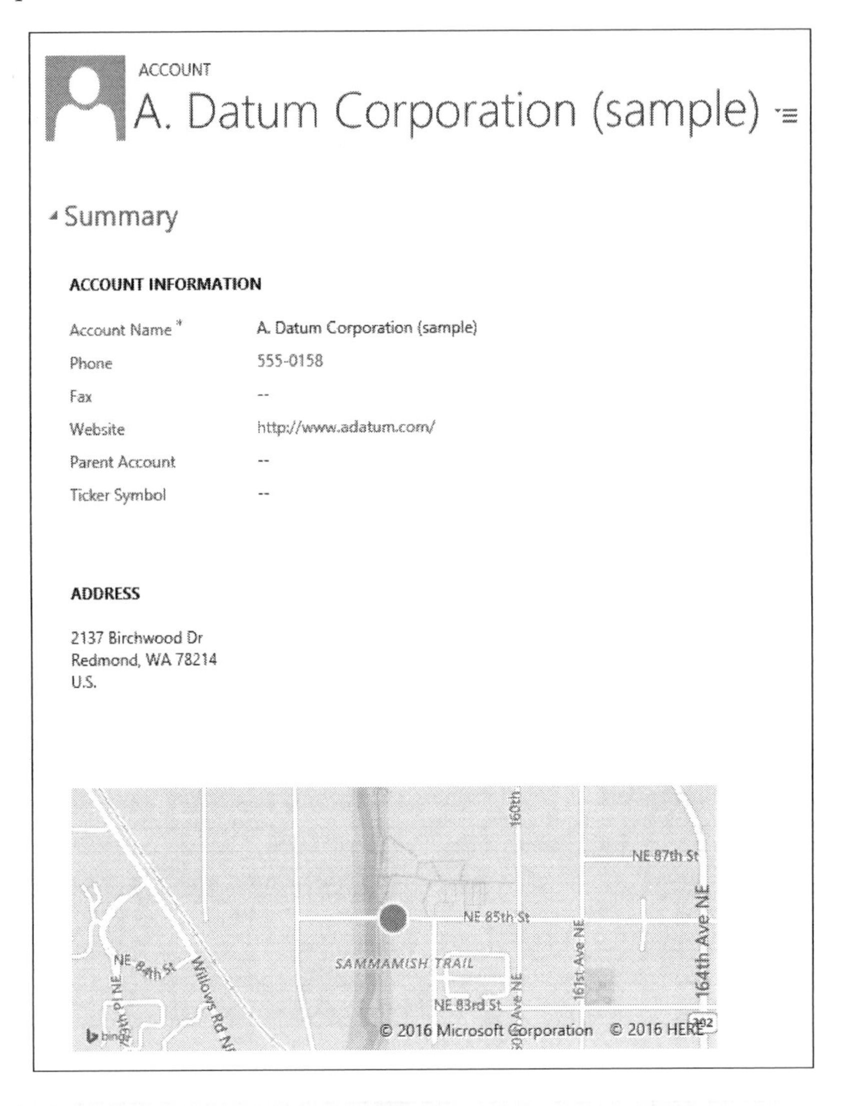

Make sure that when using this feature, the proper required licensing is in order. Bing Maps has its own licensing model in place.

Additional geolocation features can be built on other platforms, such as Google Maps, but most of them have a licensing cost associated.

One other option, if customizing this functionality, is to look into Open Street Map, available at `http://www.openstreetmap.org/#map=5/51.500/-0.100`.

This is a freely available set of mapping data licensed under Open Data Commons Open Database License by the **OpenStreetMap Foundation** (**OSMF**). Unfortunately, there is no customizable module to be simply added to your Organization. You will require a partner to help you build this integration.

Summary

Throughout this chapter, we looked at the main component of the three system modules, the entity. We have defined what an entity is, and we have looked at what an entity is comprised of. Then, we looked at each of the components in detail, and we discussed ways in which we can customize the entities, and we can extend the system. We have investigated ways to visually represent the data related to entities, and how to relate entities for data integrity. We have also looked at various new field types, such as rollup and calculated fields, which now reduce the amount and effort of customization to simple Excel-like configurations. We've seen the SLA functionality, and we've looked at various available document management options, and trending analysis. We closed this chapter with a quick look at enabling the out of the box geolocation features.

The next chapter will take you into the business aspect of the Dynamics CRM platform, with an in-depth look at all the available business processes. We will look at Business Rules and we will see other ways to enforce business specific rules and processes using wizard-driven customizations available with the platform.

4
Building Better Business Functionality

In the previous chapter, we looked at the basics of working with entities in Dynamics CRM and the essentials of customizing these entities. Now it's time to look at how the Dynamics CRM platform impacts our business, and how can we tailor it to fit most of, if not all, our business needs.

In this chapter, we will be looking at the following topics:

- What are Processes?
- Types of Processes
- Dialogs
- Workflows
- Real Time Workflows
- Business Rules
- The Business Process Flow
- Excel Enhanced Integration
- Automated Document Generation Templates
- The Mobile and Task Based Experience
- Dynamics CRM for Outlook
- The Dynamics CRM App for Outlook
- An Enhanced Search Functionality

We'll be looking at how to work with each of the elements comprising the Sales, Service, and Marketing modules. We will go through the customization options, and how we can extend the system to fit new business requirements. We'll also have a peek at the mobile experience, as well as the Outlook integration options.

What are Processes?

In the context of Dynamics CRM, Processes are a generic category that cover a few functional features all grouped together. A process is any type of automation introduced as part of customizing the system, and it involves multiple actions grouped together. As such, some examples of processes supported by the platform include Dialogs, Workflows, Actions, and Business Process Flows.

In the context of customizing Dynamics CRM, processes are created and grouped as part of one or more solutions. Within the solution, processes are listed as a separate category, and are accessible on their own configuration tab.

Working within a solution, we can add new or existing processes, remove processes, or completely delete them. Other options include the Activation and Deactivation of a process. Any process, in order to be available to users, must be activated. While a process is active, it cannot be removed and/or deleted.

When working with a large number of processes customized in a solution, you can order the processes view by any of the columns available, either ascending or descending. You can also apply filters to sort and reduce the number of processes displayed in this view. This will help a lot when retrieving a specific process from a large number of customized items.

Processes can have defined specified dependencies. As such, a process could be related to another process, in a parent/child relationship. A process can have one or more child processes, depending on the complexity of the business requirements. Splitting a large process into parent and child processes is a good practice to help manage functionality in smaller and more manageable chunks.

There are three ways to create processes in Dynamics CRM:

- The most common method used by power users and administrators is interactively through the user interface. The process builder in Dynamics CRM is a pretty robust and simple-to-use tool that allows building of custom processes with no code. This will be quite appealing to power users who can customize aspects of the system without having to call for support from a development team, and wait for the features to be implemented.
- Another method is by creating custom processes using code. This method is targeted to developers, and is using workflow-related classes from the **software development kit** (**SDK**). This is a very developer-focused approach, and it involves planning, designing, developing, testing, and deploying custom code solutions. Usually this approach involves a strict deployment process, and tends to involve various teams in producing proper packaged solutions.
- Finally, the last method to create processes is by importing already-developed processes from other environments or solutions. These processes come packaged in a solution. They can be either internally created, or can come from an external source such as a system customizer or **independent software vendor** (**ISV**).

Dialogs

One of the common processes customizable in Dynamics CRM is the **Dialog**. A dialog is a type of process used to create an interactive data entry form that guides the user step-by-step through a scenario. This process relies on continuous user interaction, and requires user input to run through to completion.

A dialog presents the user with an interface similar to a wizard. The user can make appropriate selection at each step of the dialog, and progress through all the steps to completion. A dialog can be used for data capture, as well as for guiding the user through a predefined scenario. It can include branching logic based on user input, thus allowing us to handle more complex business scenarios. This can be very helpful in call center scenarios, where, based on specific customer responses, a path can be automatically selected to guide the service representative to the best solution.

A dialog is usually launched by the user, or it can be customized to be triggered by an action on the form. Launching a dialog by the user is done by navigating to a record, and selecting **Start Dialog** from the ribbon:

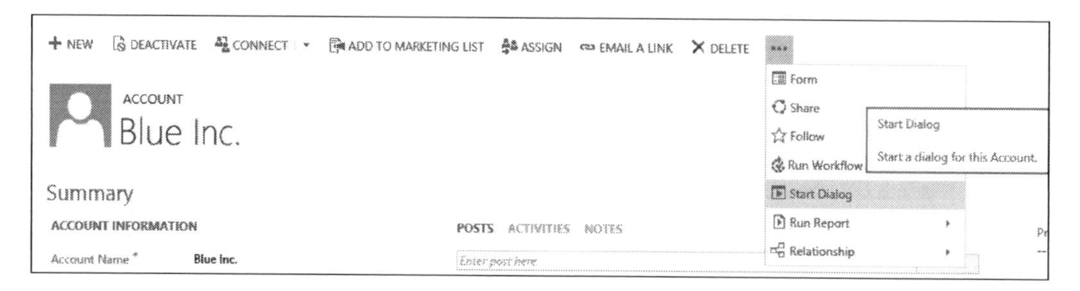

Once you select the **Start Dialog** option, you are presented with a Dialog selection window. Here, you can select any of the **On Demand Dialogs** options available for the specific type of record:

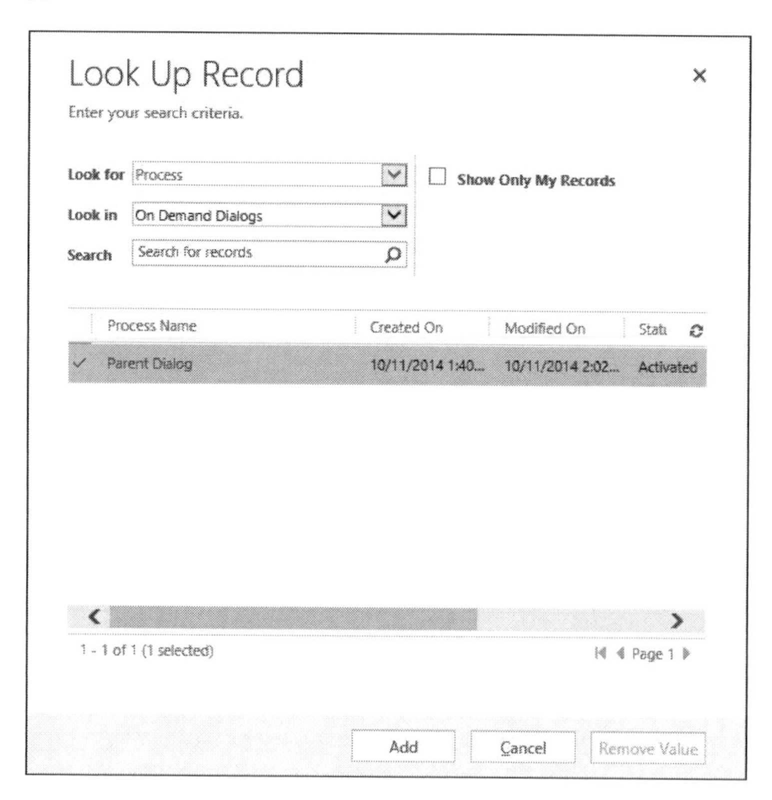

Dialogs can be configured to be **On Demand Processes** or **Child Processes**. An **On Demand Process** option is available to be run directly by the user or automatically started through customization. **Child Process** can only be triggered by **Parent Dialog**.

Dialog information is stored, in the context of the running process, in an entity called **ProcessSession**.

As opposed to workflows, dialogs cannot be created outside of Microsoft Dynamics CRM. They must be created within the platform, and exported as part of a solution.

Creating a Dialog

Dialogs should be created as part of an existing or new solution. We can start creating a new Dialog by navigating to a solution, and finding the **Processes** section in the solution **Components** listing:

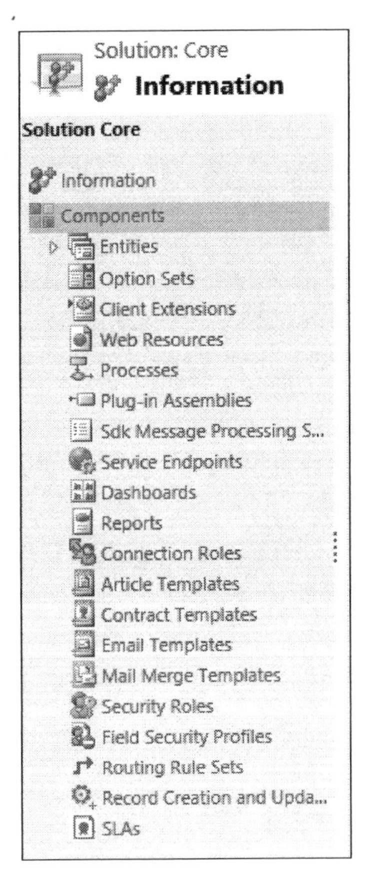

The **New Process** window gathers the minimum necessary dialog properties we need to define. These are as follows:

- **Name**: This is the name of the Dialog process. It does not require to be unique, but it should be at least distinct enough from other dialogs, and representative of the functionality expected. Prefixes or naming conventions could be used to reflect the use of these dialogs, and allow easy filtering and grouping.
- **Entity**: The entity defines the default entity the Dialog is applicable to. Once a Dialog is created, the entity cannot be changed. If the Entity needs to change, a new Dialog must be created.
- **Category**: This defines the type of process. For Dialogs, it will be obviously Dialog.

Dialogs are available to the entire Organization. Related records, such as the entities the dialog modified and the dialog session record, must be editable by the user running the dialog, otherwise errors will occur.

Once these properties are defined, click on **OK** to create the dialog.

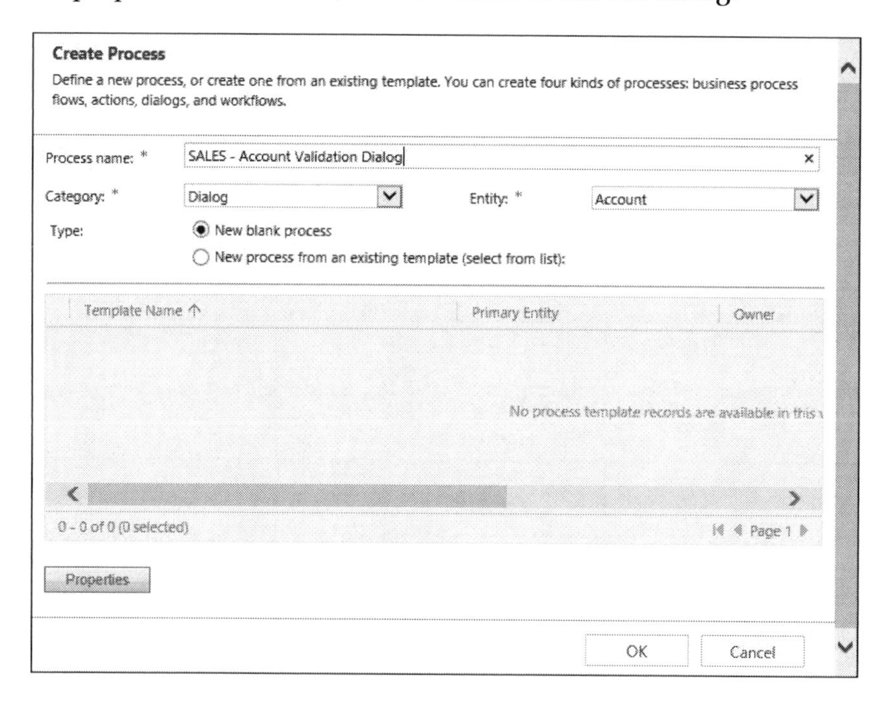

This results in the creation of the dialog template, and launches the Dialog configuration window. Here, we can start adding the necessary steps to be executed.

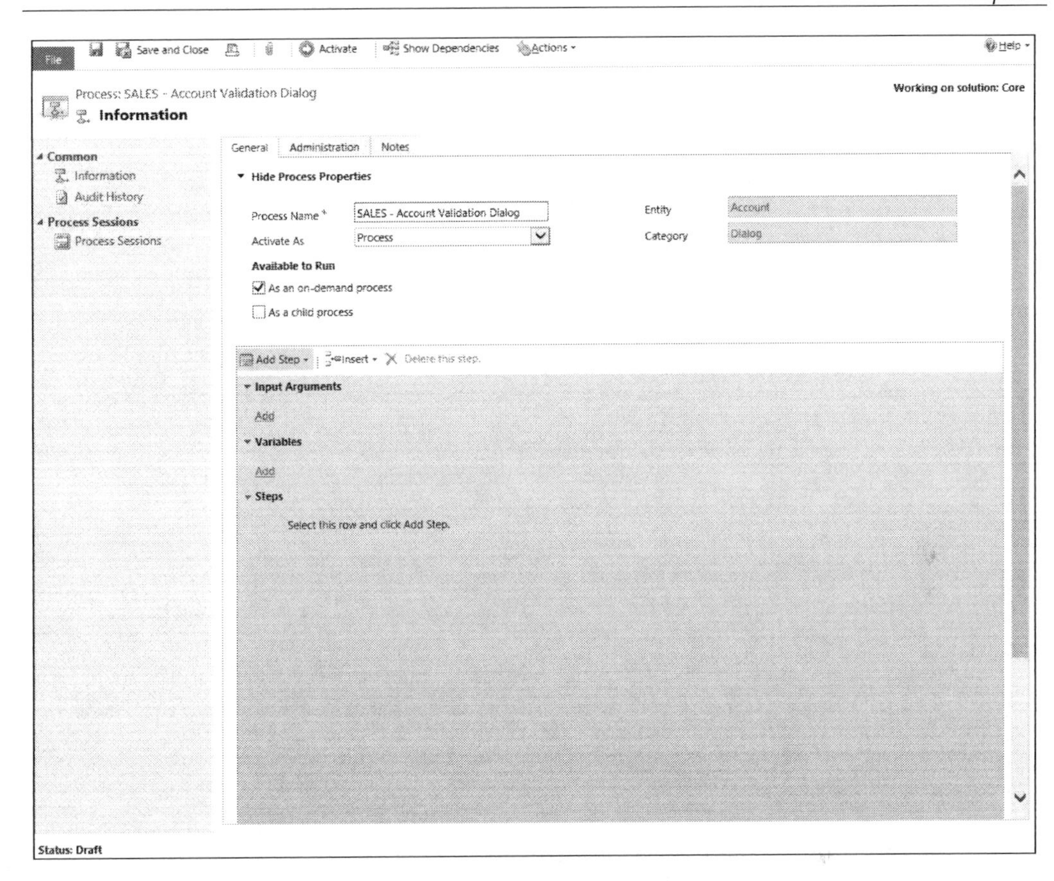

First off, observe that at the bottom left of the window the **Status** of the Dialog is a **Draft**. A Dialog is editable while in Draft, but is not usable by the system users in this state. Once we are done editing this Dialog, we can click on the **Activate** button on the ribbon to make it available to all system users.

The **Available to Run** section provides us with the ability to configure when and how this Dialog can be triggered. We can configure it to be triggered only by users manually, only as a child of another Dialog, or both.

The next section allows us to configure the content and steps of the Dialog. We can configure the following three items:

- **Input Arguments**: These are used to transfer data between parent-child dialogs
- **Variables**: These are used for temporary data storage throughout the dialog execution
- **Steps**: These are the actual windows and prompts presented to the system user interacting with the Dialog

Dialog Steps

You can add new steps to a dialog by selecting the step type from the **Add Step** drop-down menu in the editor window.

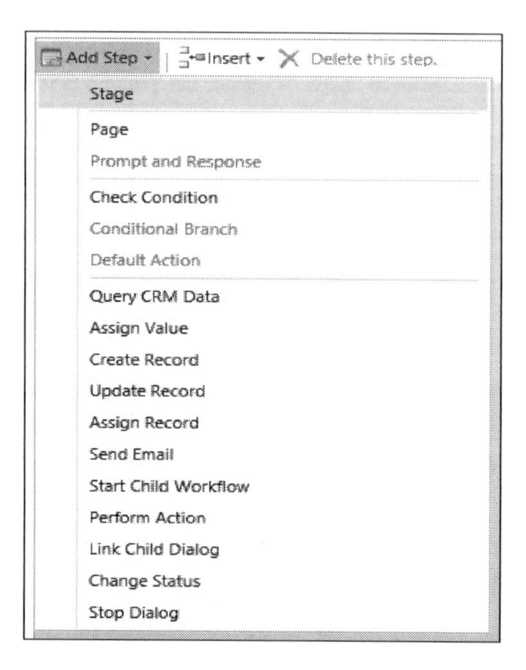

For the purpose of this example, we'll create a simple prompt to capture a Yes/No answer to a question. For more complex scenarios and details on all the available steps, see the documentation on Technet:

`https://technet.microsoft.com/en-us/library/dn531180.aspx#BKMK_DialogComponents`

The following are the steps to add dialog from the **Add Step** editor window:

1. Select **Page** from the **Add Step** drop-down menu. Once a Page record is added, give it a description, and select the row as instructed here:

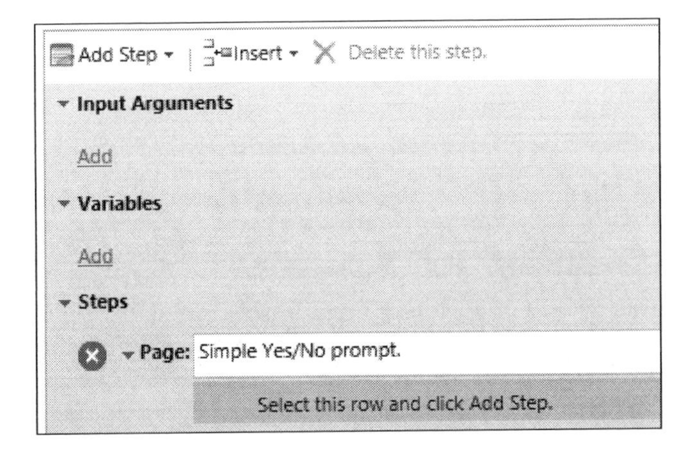

2. Click on **Add Step** again and this time observe that **Prompt Details** and **Response Details** are available for selection. Select both. Give the new record a description, and then click on **Set Properties** to define the actual question and answer:

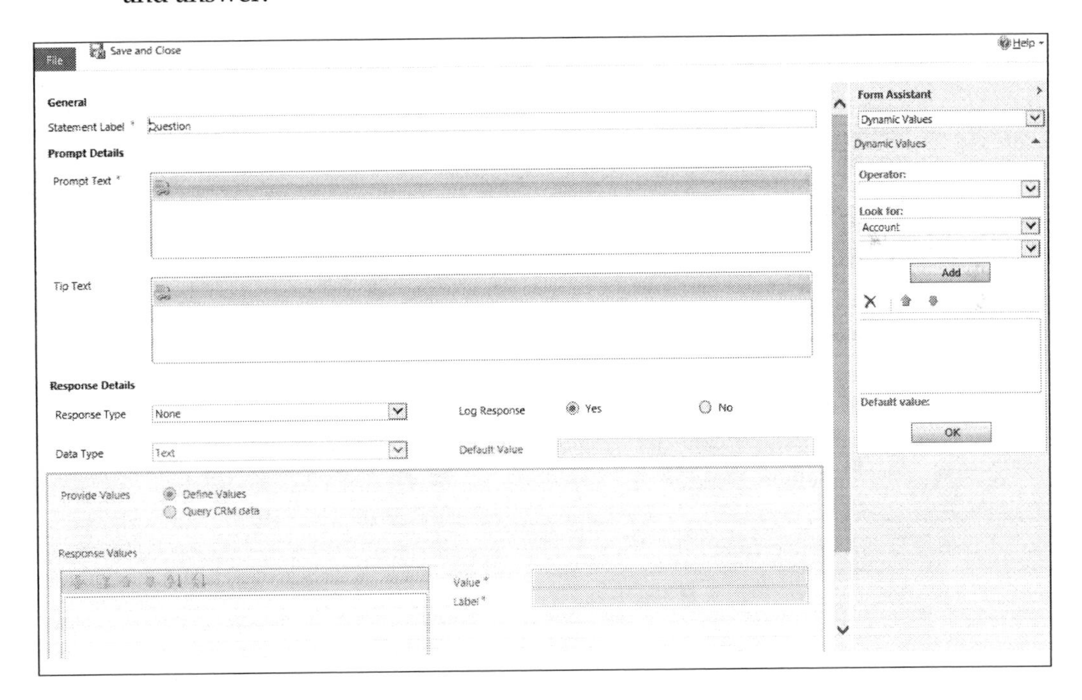

3. **Statement Label** is taken from the previous input. Fill in the **Prompt Text** field, which is the actual question to be asked. You can add **Tip Text** with additional information.
4. In the **Response Details** section, select **Response Type** as **Option Set (radio buttons)**. Leave **Data Type** as **Text**, and further down in **Provide Values** make sure **Define Values** is selected. Here, you can also configure a system query to retrieve data dynamically from the system by selecting **Query CRM data**. Queries are built using FetchXML, and they are beyond the scope of this book. For additional details on FetchXML queries for Microsoft Dynamics CRM, see the MSDN documentation available at `https://msdn.microsoft.com/en-us/library/gg328117.aspx`
5. To complete this step, add the **Yes** and **No** values in the **Response Values** by selecting the **+** symbol on the ribbon. Define the **Value** and **Label** properties for each, as shown in the following screenshot:

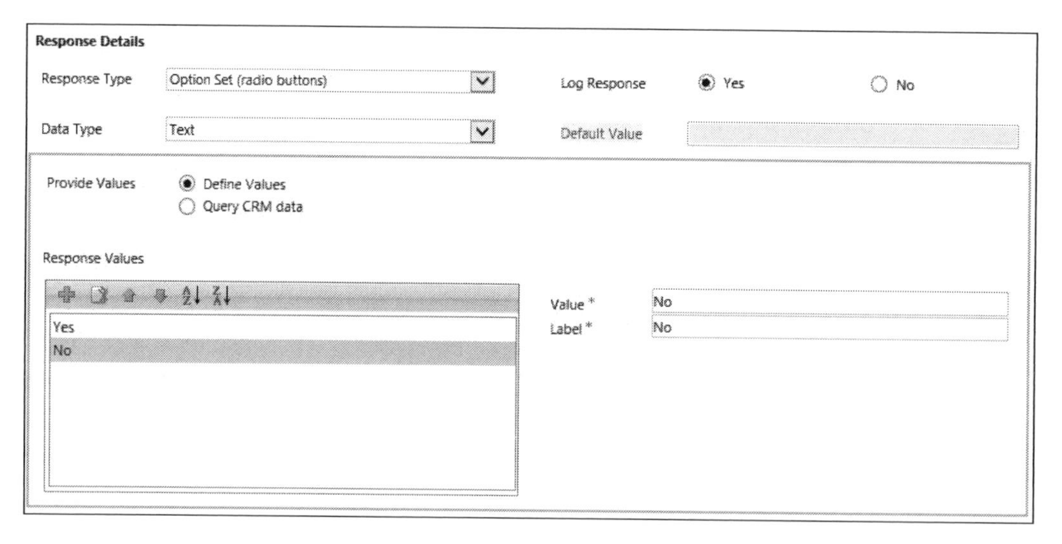

6. Once done, click on **Save** and close the window from the top ribbon. You are returned to the process configuration window, and the step is displayed as configured:

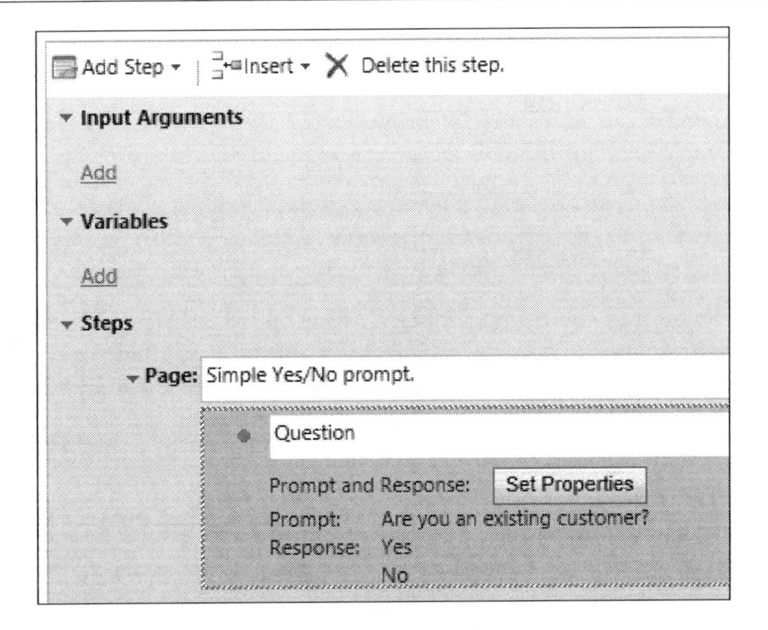

7. You should now continue to build the Dialog with additional steps. Once complete, **Save** and **Activate** the Dialog. You are prompted to confirm Activation. Once activated, you cannot edit or modify the Dialog. In order to make changes, you must Deactivate it first, make your changes, then reactivate it.

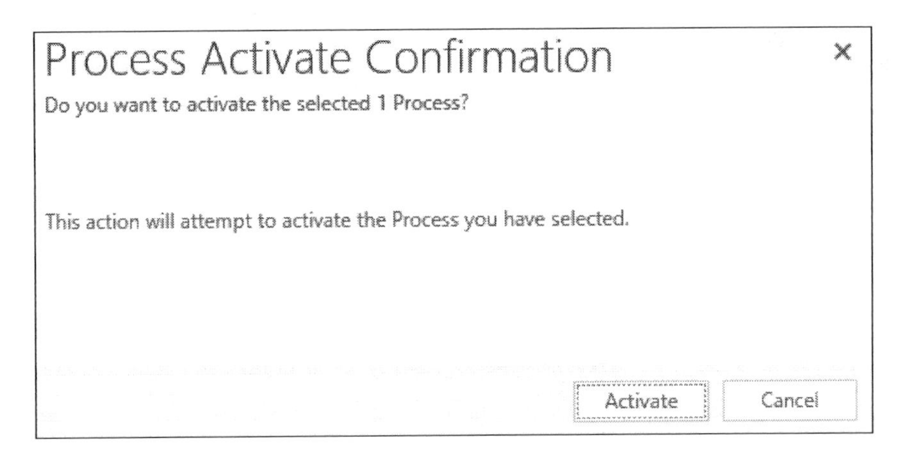

8. With the dialog activated, navigate to an Account, since this Dialog is related to the account entity. From the **Account** ribbon, select **Start Dialog**, as seen in the following screenshot:

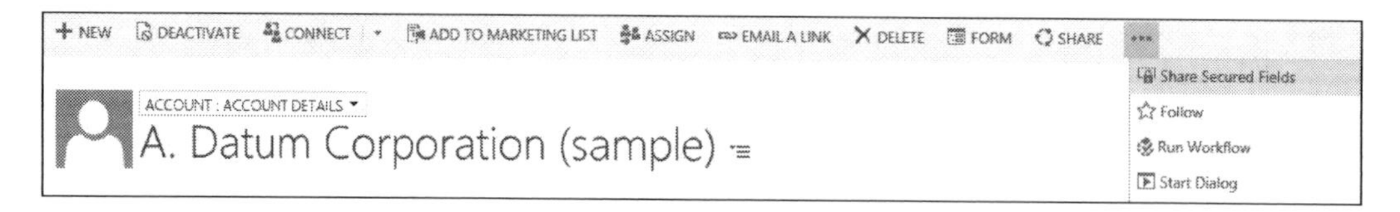

9. This brings a lookup window listing the available Dialogs in the Organization. We see here the Dialog we just created in the following screenshot:

10. Select the Dialog and click on **Add**. This launches the Dialog and displays the first prompt we added, as seen in the following screenshot:

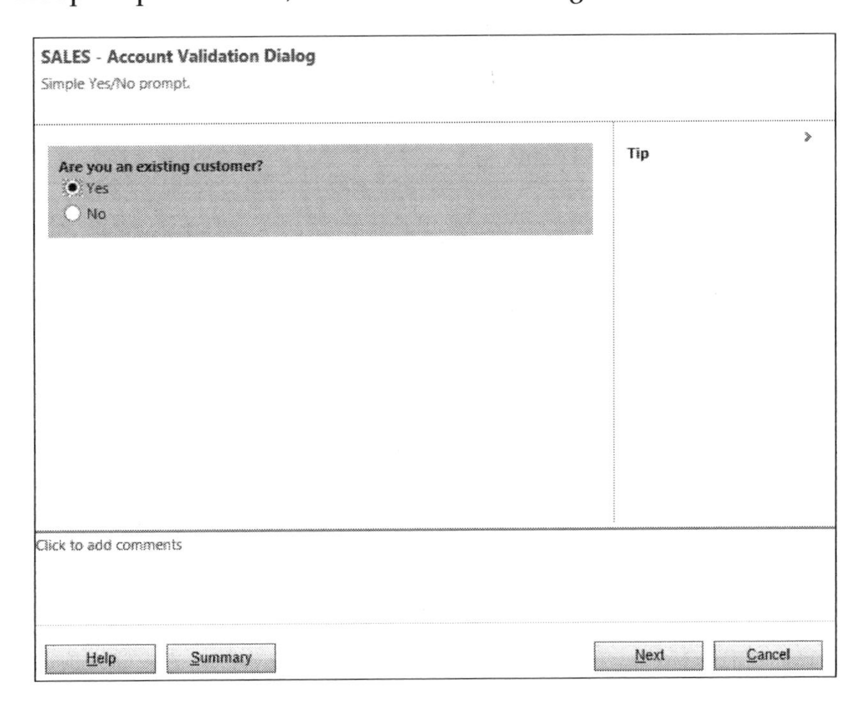

11. Click on **Next** to proceed through all the steps of the dialog, and then click on **Finish** to complete it. Depending on the level of complexity created, you could be adding and modifying record data, creating new records, triggering child workflows, and performing other actions.

Managing Dialogs

The process of managing dialogs revolves around the principle of solutions and activation. Dialogs should be created as part of the solution in Microsoft Dynamics CRM. This allows them to be moved from one environment to another, as well as exported for solution backup purposes.

On creation, a Dialog is in Draft mode. In order to make it available to users, it must be activated. Activating a Dialog makes it non-editable, and available to system users to execute.

To make a Dialog unavailable, deactivate it. Once deactivated, a Dialog can be further edited and customized, then reactivated when needed.

Workflows

A workflow is another type of process that can be defined within the Dynamics CRM platform. This process is used to model and automate business processes.

There are two types of workflows customizable with Dynamics CRM 2016:

- Background workflows (async)
- Real-time workflows

Workflows run in the background. They are triggered either automatically based on certain triggers on the entity forms, based on specific conditions, or they can be started manually by a user. Starting a workflow manually is done by navigating to a record and selecting the **Run Workflow** option on the ribbon.

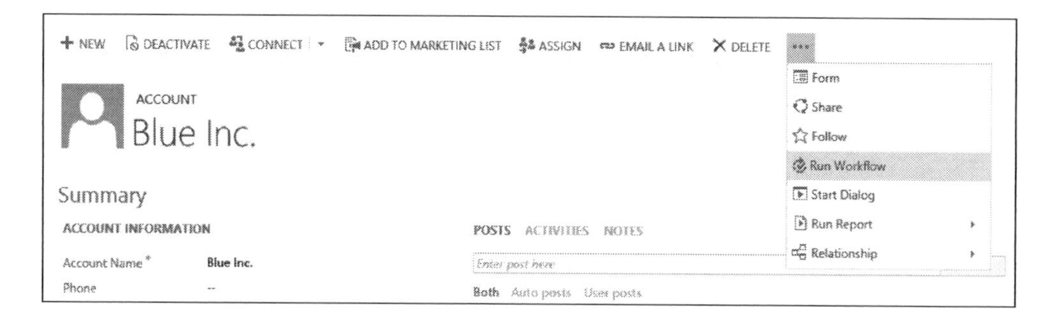

Once the **Run Workflow** option is selected, the user is presented with a dialog to select **On Demand Workflow** to be run.

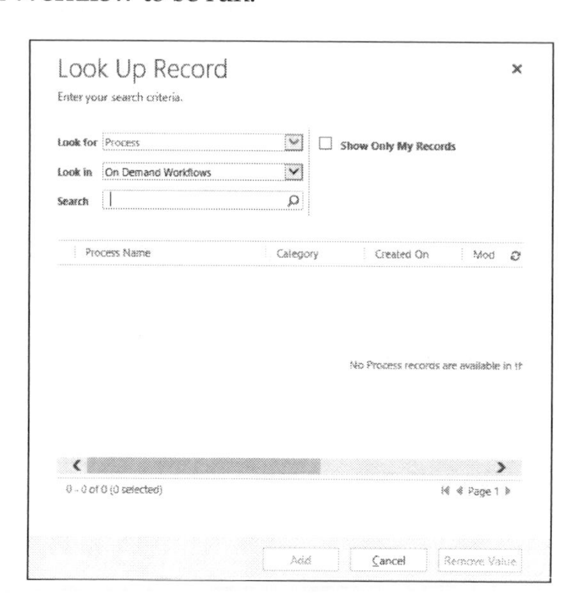

If no workflows are customized for this specific entity, or no workflows are enabled, the **Look Up Record** view will not display any records. For records to be available in this view, a few conditions must be met:

- The workflow has to be enabled
- The workflow has to be targeted to the entity we are trying to run the workflow against
- The workflow must be an on demand workflow

No child workflows can be selected to be run this way.

Workflows can be created in the same fashion as dialogs, using the Dynamics CRM process builder wizard, by creating them in custom code, or by importing them from other solutions. In addition, workflows can be created declaratively. This process does not involve writing any code, and you do not have to compile them. Using this approach you declare the workflow definitions using a language called XAML. This is a declarative markup language used mostly to simplify creating user interfaces for .NET applications.

XAML workflows are not supported in Dynamics CRM Online.

While workflows can perform almost the same operations as custom coded plugins, there are certain situations where a workflow is recommended over a plugin. These include situations where the business logic needs to be updated regularly by non-developer users, or when we need the ability to start a process manually.

Workflows can be distributed from one environment to another as part of a custom solution. There are, however, some considerations to be aware of. If your workflows reference specific entity instances, the unique IDs of the entity will differ in a new environment. Dynamics CRM only resolves system user and currency records based on the full name property, while all other entities do not get resolved. For this reason, if you deploy workflows as part of a solution to another environment, you must verify after deployment to make sure all workflows are enabled. Workflows where the above condition is encountered will remain in a Draft state, and will require the user doing the deployment to correct the references and reactivate the workflows.

Just as Dialogs, Workflows are in a Draft state while they are being worked on. Once you are ready to make them available to users, you must activate them. On activation, the workflow subscribes to specific events, and listens for them to be triggered. Once triggered, the workflow creates a new asynchronous operation and adds it to the asynchronous service queue. As such, workflows are running asynchronously.

Asynchronous operations can be suspended and restarted by users.

Running a workflow asynchronously allows Dynamics CRM to queue execution and process operations at a later time. This allows the platform to manage resources efficiently, and allows long running processes to be paused and resumed as needed.

Using the asynchronous service, long running processes can be safely paused and resumed while the state is being saved. This allows the system to restart without losing the process state. This save is taking advantage of the persistence service by saving the state on the disk. This also allows a process that crashed to restart from the last persisted point.

Creating a Workflow

The process to create a workflow in Microsoft Dynamics CRM is somewhat similar to the one described previously when creating a Dialog:

1. Within the solution package, navigate to **Processes**.
2. Here, select **New**. Give it a relevant Name, choose the **Entity** that will trigger the Workflow, and in **Category** select the **Workflow** option, as shown in the following screenshot:

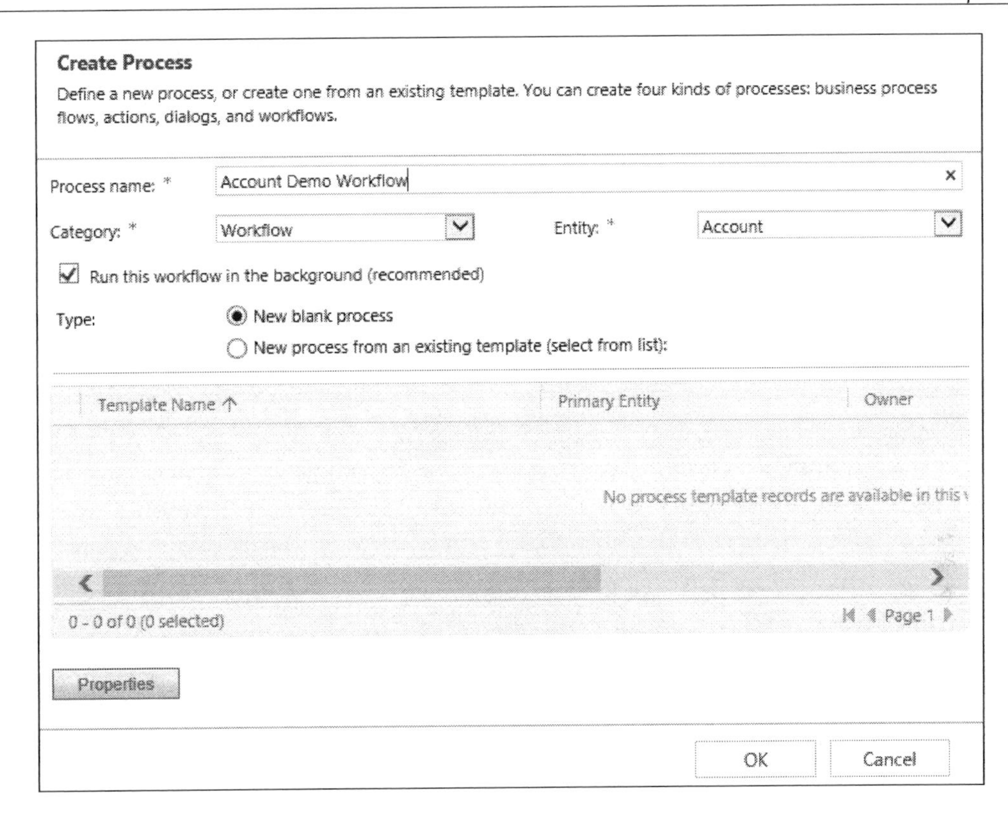

3. When clicking on **OK**, you are presented with the Information screen. Here, we can now define the scope of the workflow.

> Note that a workflow, as opposed to a dialog, allows us to define a scope. The available choices are **User**, **Business Unit**, **Parent: Child Business Unit**, and **Organization**.

The purpose of defining a Scope for Workflows is to further restrict access to the records affected. It works in conjunction with the user's permissions on the system. For example, selecting a scope of User makes only the records owned by the current user available to the process, no matter the organizational-level access the user has configured through permissions.

The **Start when** option allows us to define when the workflow is automatically triggered. We can trigger a workflow manually, just like we described earlier with a Dialog, or we can configure it to be triggered automatically when an action takes place on a record. The choices available are as follows:

- **Record is created**: When a new record is created and saved initially, a workflow can be triggered.
- **Record status changes**: When we change the status of a record, for example, from **Active** to **Closed**, we can trigger a workflow to perform closing actions.
- **Record is assigned**: This triggers a workflow when the owner of a record changes.
- **Record fields change**: This gives us the option to trigger a workflow when we modify the value of a filed on the record form. We have the choice to select which fields are available to trigger the workflow execution.
- **Record is deleted**: When a record is removed, we can trigger a workflow. For example, we can create an audit record when a Contact record is deleted from the system.

The **Available to Run** section allows us to define when the workflow can be triggered. For example, selecting **As an on-demand process** makes the workflow available to be triggered manually by a user. **As a child process** makes it available to be triggered from another workflow. Finally, unchecking **Run this workflow in the background (recommended)** is what allows us to define a Real-time workflow. This option was introduced in Microsoft Dynamics CRM 2013, and replaces many situations where we needed to write simple custom code plugins.

The default selection has this checkbox selected. Unchecking this option makes it a Real-time workflow. You cannot change the option directly; you have to select the **Convert to a real-time workflow** option on the ribbon.

Workflow Job Retention allows us to configure whether to keep a record of the successfully completed workflows. For situations where this stores too much data, you can select to have this information removed on successful execution of each workflow.

The process of adding steps is similar to the one we described previously in the Dialogs section. We do get a few additional options specific to workflows, such as **Start Child Workflow** or **Stop Workflow**, which are self-explanatory.

Real-time Workflows

Real-time workflows are by nature very similar to regular workflows in Dynamics CRM. The creation process is identical to regular workflows. This type of workflow was introduced with Dynamics CRM 2013, and involves a change in the backend of how the information is processed. These processes are not queued, but they execute immediately or in response to a message.

Real-time workflows execute in the same stage as synchronous plugins. They can execute before, after, or during the main operation. They can also be ranked within a stage, same as plugins.

These workflows can run either in the context of the current user, or the workflow owner. When running a workflow manually, it only runs in the context of the current user.

A limitation of Real-time workflows is that they cannot contain any delay or wait activities.

A Real-time workflow can be converted to asynchronous and back to real time. The workflow must be in draft mode to be able to modify it.

Actions

Actions are a special type of workflow in Dynamics CRM. They have been introduced with version 2013, and are used to define custom messages. Actions are used to add new functionality to the organization's web service or to combine multiple organization's web service message requests into a single one.

The basic actions in most systems are defined by verbs such as Create, Update, and Delete. CRM systems add Assign to this list. Through Actions, we can define additional functionality such as Escalate, Approve, Schedule, Route, and so on. By combining processes based on the core actions, system customizers can create new actions for specific business needs.

The Actions are defined by implementing workflows. The action workflows are registered in the core operation of the execution pipeline.

Actions are supported in both on-premise and online Dynamics CRM organizations, but just like workflows, when defined using declarative XAML, they are only supported in Dynamics CRM on-premise and **internet facing deployment** (**IFD**) scenarios.

One main difference between actions and regular workflows is that actions can be declared global, where they are not associated to a particular entity. Also, actions can be triggered from a JScript.

> Actions always run in the context of the calling user.

One aspect to be aware of when defining actions is that they are not supported with offline clients. If the expectation is that offline access is required for certain actions, a more creative approach must be taken and possibly plugins may be used.

Actions can be created in two ways: through the process builder just like any workflows and dialogs, or through custom code. The first approach is targeted mostly at power users, as a no code approach, while the latter requires a developer to be involved in the creation of the action definition.

Just like Workflows and Dialogs, Actions can be added to a packaged solution and transferred to another environment.

The steps to create an action through the process builder are explained as follows:

1. In the context of a solution, navigate to **Processes**.
2. On the processes listing view, select **New** to create a new process.
3. In the **Create Process** window that pops-up, define the required fields and select **Action** from the **Category** drop-down. For the entity definition, you can create an action against a specific entity, or a global action.

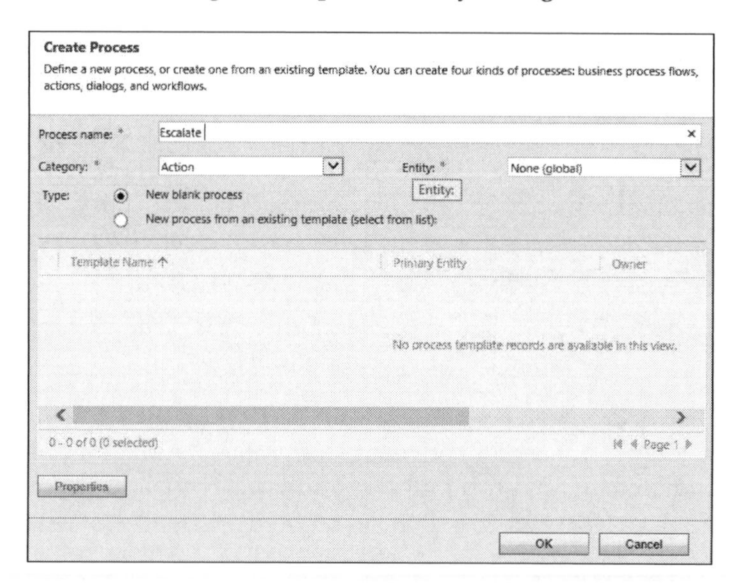

With the selections in place, you are ready to create the new Action. Select **OK**.

The creation of the action from this point forward is quite similar to creating a workflow. The main difference is the ability to define a multitude or arguments of various data types, as well as the direction of arguments.

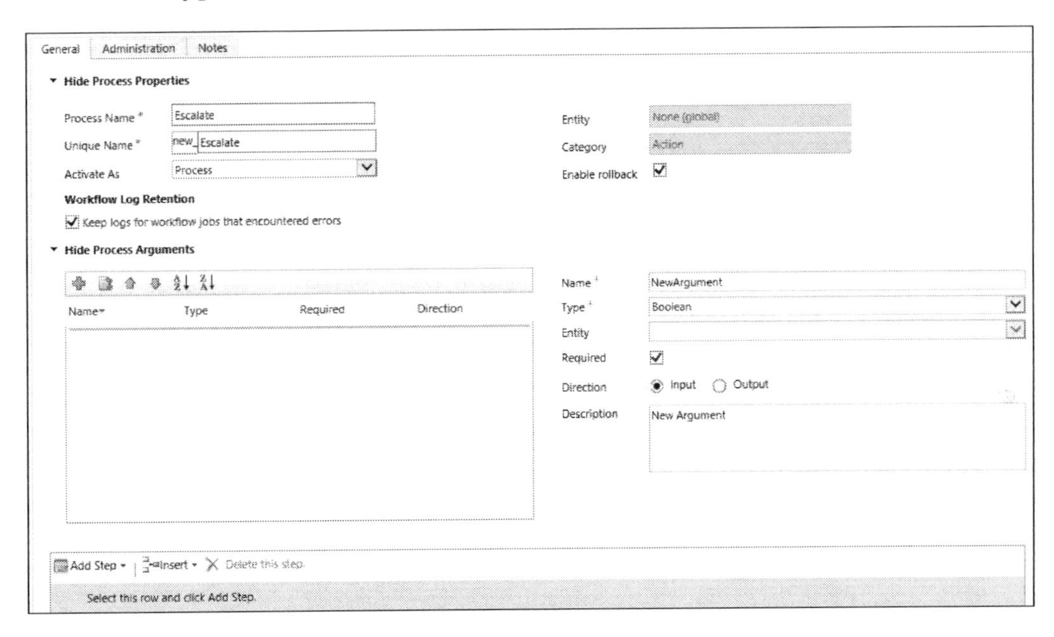

The **Enable Rollback** configuration on the Action creation screen allows us to define when we disable the Rollback feature. There are situations when the code goes beyond the scope of CRM. These actions cannot be rolled back, and so we can disable the option in the Action configuration form.

Using Actions allows us to run custom business logic using server-side events.

Quick View and Quick Create Forms

Entities in Dynamics CRM can be accessed from various parts of the system, and their information can be presented in various formats. This feature contributes to the 360 degree view of customer data.

In order to achieve this functionality, the entities in Dynamics CRM present a variety of standard views available for customization. These include standard entity forms, quick create forms, and quick view forms. In addition, for mobile devices, we can customize mobile forms.

Entity Forms

As we have seen in the previous chapter, each entity can be customized with a multitude of views. We can have role-based views, which change based on the user's security role, and we can also have more than one form available to users to select from. We can customize which view is presented to the user based on specific form rules, or based on other business requirements.

It is good practice to define a fallback form for each entity, and give all the user view permissions to that form. Once more than one main forms has been created for an entity, you can define the order in which the forms are presented based on permissions. If the user does not have access to any of the higher precedence forms, they will be able to access the fallback form.

Working with contingency forms is quite similar, in that, a form is defined to be available to users that cannot access any other forms in an entity. The approach to configuring this is a little different though. You create a form with minimal information displayed on it. Only assign a System Administrator role to this form, and select **Enable for fallback**. With this, you specify a form that will not be visible to anybody other than a system administrator. In addition, configuring the form like this, it also becomes available to users whose security roles do not have a form specified. With such a configuration, if a user is added to a restrictive group that does not allow him/her to see most forms, they will have this one form available.

Quick View Forms

The quick view forms are a feature that was added with Dynamics CRM 2013, and allows system customizers to create a minimalistic view to be presented in a related record form. This form presents a summary of a record in a condensed format that allows you to insert it on a related record's form.

The process to using a quick view form comprises two steps:

- Create the quick view form for an entity
- Add the quick view form to the related record

Creating a quick view form is a process similar to creating any other form. The only requirement here is to keep the amount of information minimal in order to avoid taking up too much real estate on the related record form.

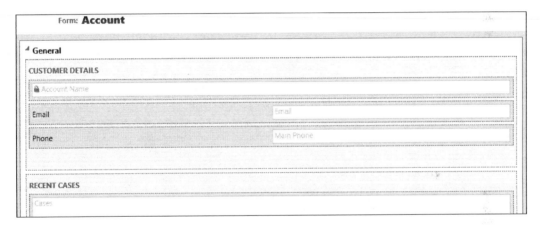

A very good example is the quick view form for the **Account** entity. This view is created by default in the system. It only includes the account name, e-mail, and phone number, as well as a grid of recent cases and recent activities.

We can use this view in a custom Project entity by performing the following steps:

1. On the project's main form, add a lookup field to **Account** to define the account related to the project.

2. On the project form customization add a **Quick View Form** from the ribbon.

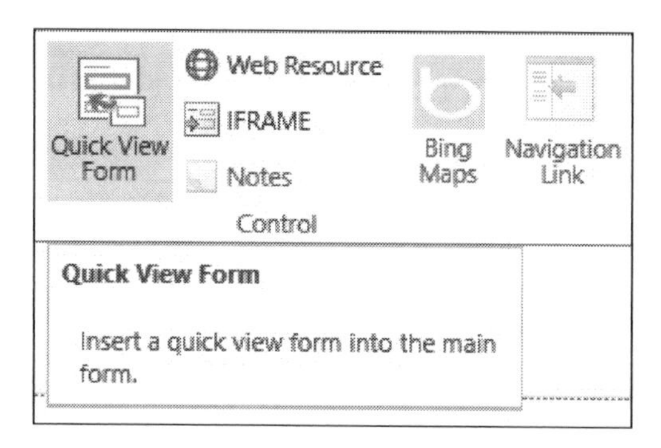

3. Once you select **Quick View Form**, you are presented with a **Quick View Control Properties** window. Here, you define the name and label for the control, and whether you want the label to be displayed on the form.
4. In addition, on this form, you get to define the rules on what is to be displayed on the form. In the **Data Source** section, select the lookup field and related entity to show **Account**, and in the **Quick View Form** drop-down menu, select the **account card** form. This is the name of the account quick view form defined in the system.

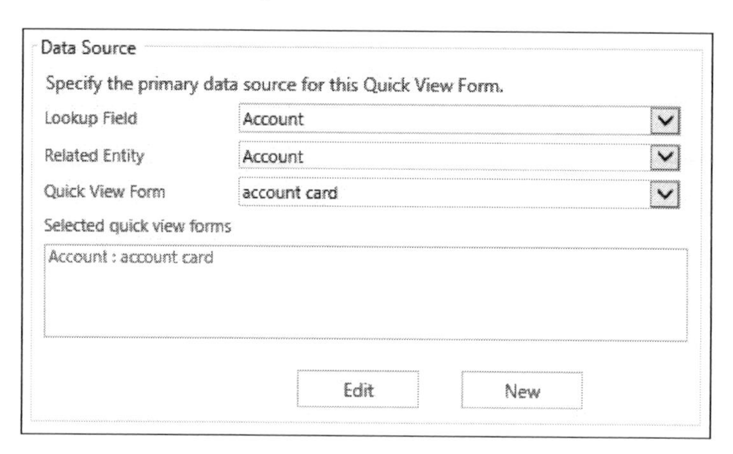

5. Once complete, save and publish the form.

Navigating to a Project record now, we can select the related Account and the quick view will be automatically displayed on the Project form.

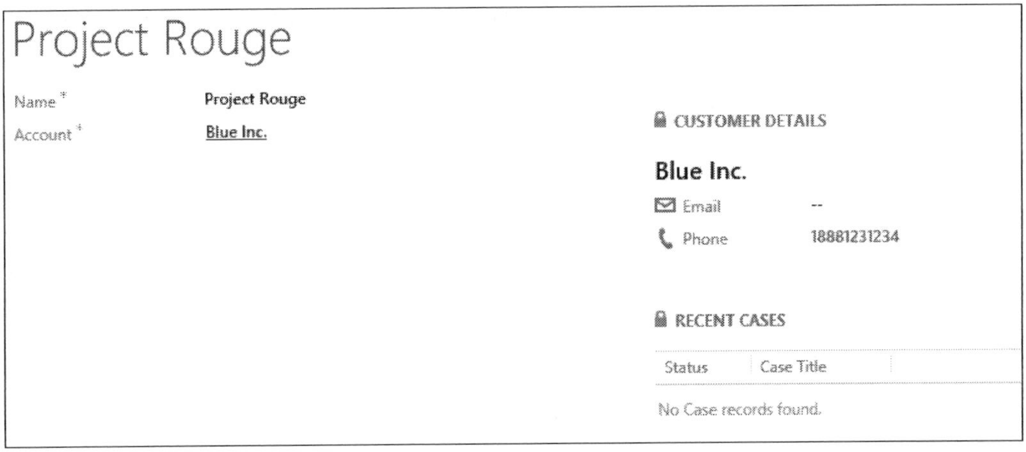

Project Rouge

Name * Project Rouge

Account * Blue Inc.

CUSTOMER DETAILS

Blue Inc.

Email --

Phone 18881231234

RECENT CASES

Status | Case Title

No Case records found.

The default quick view form created for the **Account** entity is now displayed on the Project form, with all the specified Account related details. This way, any updates to the Account are immediately reflected on the Project form.

Taking this approach, it is now much easier to display all the necessary information on the same screen, so that the user does not have to navigate away and click through a maze to get to all the data needed.

Quick Create Forms

Quick create forms, while serving a different purpose than quick view forms, are confined to the same minimalistic approach. Of course, a system customizer is not necessarily limited to a certain amount of data to be added to these forms, but rather should be mindful of where these forms are being used, and how much real estate is dedicated to them.

On a quick create form, the minimal amount of data to be added are the required fields. In order to be able to save a new record, all business required fields must be filled in, and they should be added to the quick create form.

Quick create forms are created the same way as any other type of form:

1. In the solution package, navigate to entities, select the entity where you want to customize an existing quick create form or add a new one, expand to the views section, and you will see all the existing view for the specific entity.
2. Here, you can select the view you want to modify, or click on **New** to create a new one.

3. Once the view is open for editing, the process of customizing the view is exactly the same for all views. You can add and remove fields, customize labels, rearrange field on the form, and so on.

In order to remind the customizer that this is a quick create view, a minimalistic three-column grid is provided by default for this type of view.

Pay close attention to the fact that you are limited by the type of control you can add to a Quick Create Form. Items such as iFrames and sub-grids are not available.

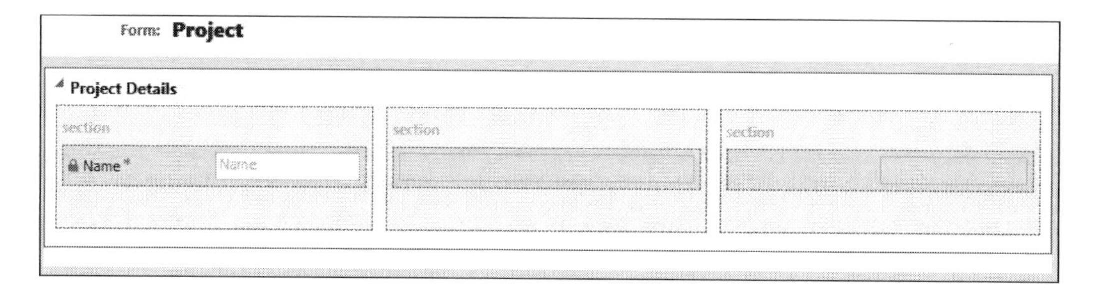

That is not to say that the layout cannot be changed. You can be as creative as needed when customizing the quick create view.

Once you have the form created, save and publish it. Since we have earlier created a relationship between Account and Project, we can add a grid view on the Account displaying all related child Projects.

Navigating to an Account now, we can quickly add a new child **Project** by going to the Projects grid view and clicking on the plus symbol to add a Project. This will launch the Quick Create View of the Project we just customized.

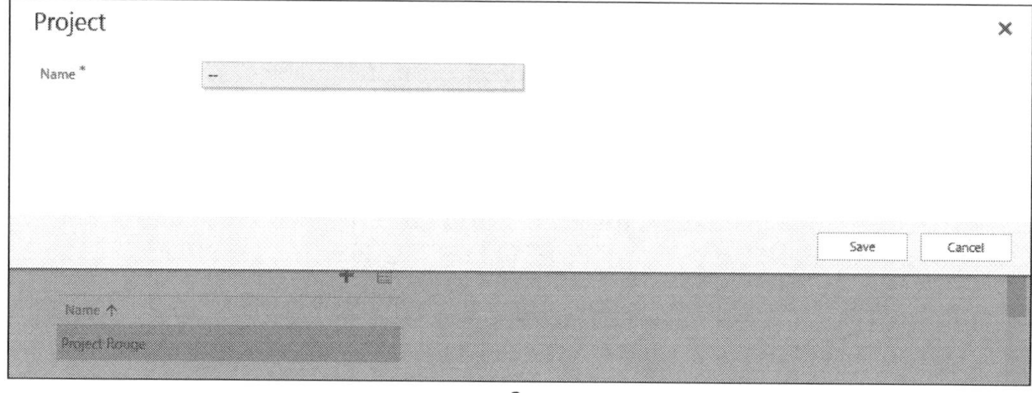

3

As you can see in the preceding screenshot, the quick create view is displayed as an overlay over the main form. For this reason, the amount of data should be kept to a minimum. This type of form is not meant to replace a full-fledged form, but rather to allow a user to create a new record type with minimal input and with no navigation to another record.

Another way to access the quick create view for an entity is by clicking on the **Create** button situated at the top right of most Dynamics CRM pages, right before the field that displays your user name. This presents the user with the option to create one of the most common record types available in the system.

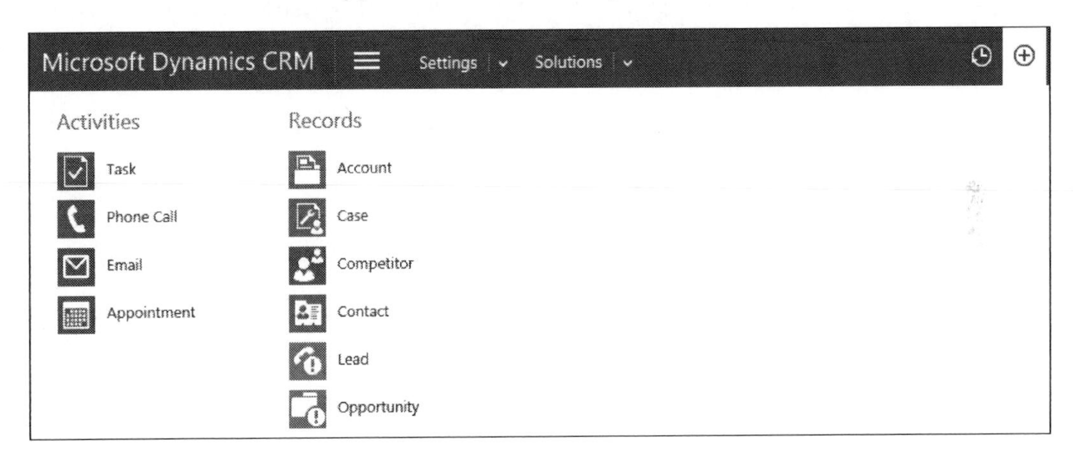

Selecting any one of the **Records** options presents the Quick Create View. Selecting to create Activities this way will not present a quick create form, but rather will take you to the full activity form.

Once a quick create form record is created in the system, the quick create form closes and a notification is displayed to the user, with an option to navigate to the newly created record.

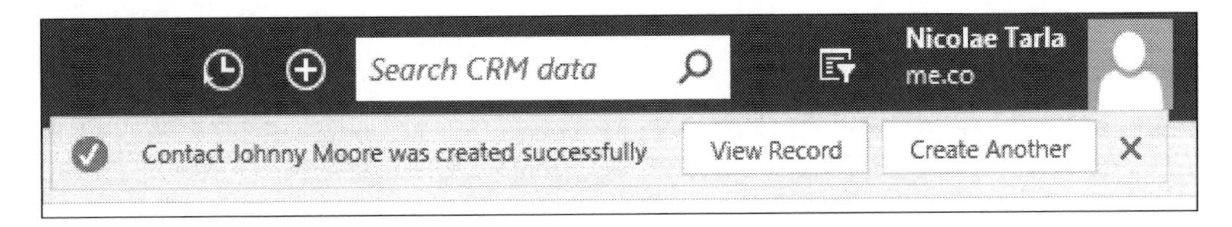

Business Rules

Business rules is a new feature added to Dynamics CRM with version 2013. It allows power users and nondevelopers to create automated processes without the use of custom code. It is a very powerful feature that's been added to the system customizer's toolbox.

With the use of business rules, now we can apply form logic to replace some of the JavaScript code we previously used for customization. For situations where we want to validate fields, show or hide fields based on values of another fields, or simple form manipulations, we can now implement Business Rules. These rules can be applied in a pseudo-code format. No code is required, as the whole creation of business rules wizard based.

While this is a step in the right direction, business rules will not replace JScript completely. For complex validations and implementation of complicated rules, you will find that certain limitations will still require a JScript developer to be involved.

The main difference between workflows and business rules is the location where the process runs. Business rules are primarily meant as a client side logic, and the result is expected to directly and immediately influence the user's interaction with the system.

The most common application for Business Rules involves the following processes:

- Set or clear a field's value
- Set the required/not required level on a field
- Enable or disable fields
- Show or hide fields
- Validate field data
- Show error messages to users

Business Rules are included in a solution at the entity level. This way they can be deployed from one environment to another.

Business Rules can be applied not only to the main entity form, but also to quick create forms.

In order to customize Business Rules, you must at least have a System Customizer role. Furthermore, to activate a Business Rules you must have the **Activate Business Rule** privilege.

When creating Business Rules, you can set the scope to either a specific form, or to all forms. Selecting **All Forms** applied the business rule to all main and quick create forms for the entity. You have no ability to only select specific forms.

Creating a new business rule involves the following steps:

1. From the solution package that will hold the customizations, navigate to an entity and expand the options. Click on **Business Rules**.
2. In the business rules grid, select **New** to create a new business rule. You are presented with a new window that allows you to customize the business rule definition.

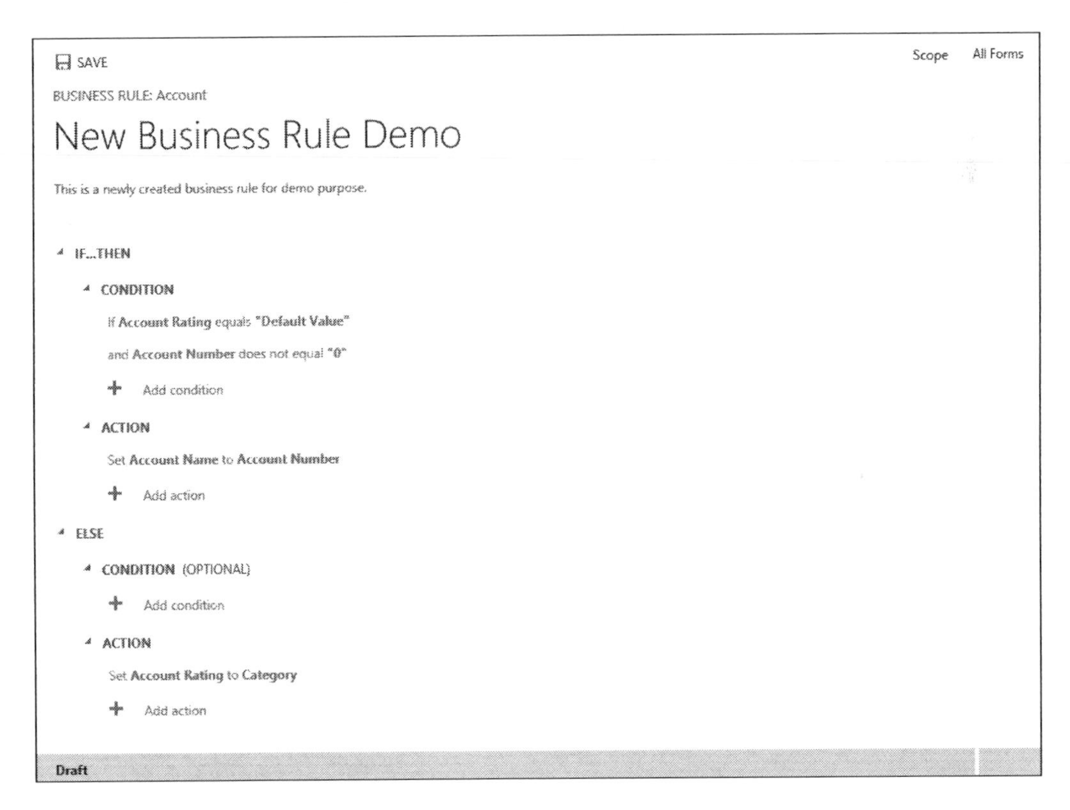

3. Provide a name for your new business rule. Make sure the name is descriptive enough to allow other users customizing the system in the future to quickly understand the purpose of this business rule.

4. Next, configure the conditions for execution. Here, you can set various conditions, by selecting the **Add a condition** option represented by the **+** sign. Selecting this opens up a grid where you can select the field against the condition it is running, the operator, type, and field.

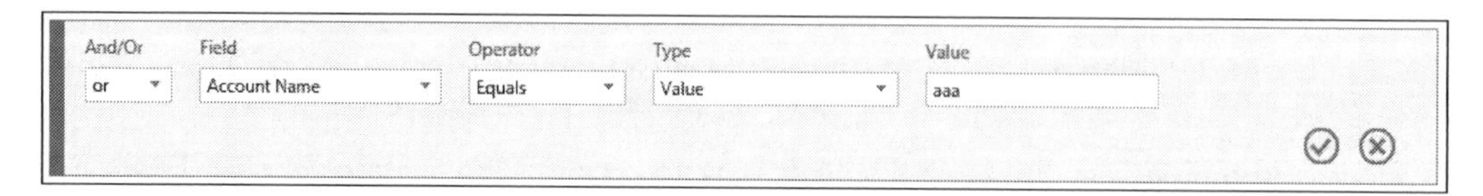

When adding multiple conditions, you can define AND or OR operators. You cannot, however, define a combination of both AND and OR operators in the same condition. You can define an ELSE operator with a new set of conditions as part of the same logic, as described in the preceding screenshot.

Operators used within the condition include most of the common conditions, such as **equals**, **does not equal**, **contains** and **does not contain**, **begins with** and **does not begin with**, **ends with** and **does not end with**, and **contains data** and **does not contain data**.

The type allows us to define a condition against a field or the value of a field.

A simplistic example of a condition can be described in pseudo-code as *Account Number does not equal 0*:

1. Once you have the conditions defined, we can move on to defining the Actions. We can configure one or more actions, as required. All actions associated with a set of conditions will be executed together.
2. Adding an action is similar to adding a condition, by clicking on **Add Action** represented by the **+** symbol. Performing this action presents us with a drop-down menu of available actions to be configured.

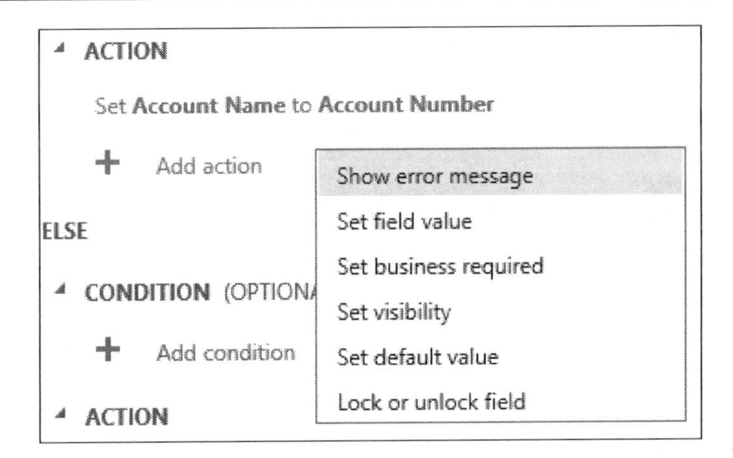

3. Through these preconfigured actions we can generate and display a defined error message, we can set a field's value either as a fixed value or the value or another field, we can set a field as business required or not, set a field's visibility or lock or unlock a field.
4. As we can observe, some of the limitations include the lack of ability to set a field as **Business Recommended**, or set the value of a field to a **Calculated** value. For these situations, we still need to revert the JScript or take advantage of other features such as calculated fields.
5. Finally, provide a description of the business rule in the description field. This will help future system customizers to determine the reasons for creating this business rule, as well as the business logic. Here, you can also track the updated performed while customizing the system.
6. Once your business rule is fully customized, save it. In order to make it available to users, you must activate it. Later on, if you need to modify it, you must deactivate it before any modifications can be made.

> You can create a business rule based on another existing business rule by performing **Save As** and modifying the new rule as required.

When using business rules to customize a system, you must be aware of the order of execution. First off, all system scripts are executed, followed by custom scripts on the form, and then the business rules logic. When multiple business rules execute against the same fields, the business rules are applied in the order in which they were activated. The oldest activated business rule is applied first.

Limitations of Business Rules

While business rules are a very handy customization option for power users, we must take the following limitations into consideration:

- Business rules do not run on record save. They are triggered by the **OnChange** message of the field, or by the form **OnLoad**.
- If a field associated to a business rule is removed from the form, the business rule will not run. No error message is presented to the user or logged in the system.
- Interaction of business rules is limited to form fields only. No other form elements can be manipulated through business rules.
- When performing a field value change using business rules, the **OnChange** event is not triggered. If you have scripts set to run on the **OnChange** event of that field, they will not run when the value is updated by a business rule.
- Certain whole number fields cannot be used in business rules. They include **Time Zone**, **Duration**, and **Language**, and they are not presented in the rule editor.
- Nevertheless, business rules are an important advancement that has been added to the system. They enhance the ability of nondeveloper system customizers to create rules through a visual editor and implement logic with no code.

Business Process Flows

Starting with Dynamics CRM 2013, Microsoft introduced Business Process Flows. They are a feature similar in design to other processes, but provide very different capabilities to the system. Business Process Flows provide users with a visual way to guide a system user through a predefined business process to get work done. The user experience is greatly enhanced and streamlined. They provide visual guidance through a predefined business process, highlighting the user interaction with the system, and defining the steps and the requirements at each step in order for a user to complete a process. These processes can easily be customized through a wizard-based, no-code approach. They also allow a user the ability to select the process type to be used when performing an activity.

Business Process Flows are used to define a process and the required steps for users to take to achieve a desired outcome. Each step is visually indicated through graphical representation on the record, and include a listing of required fields at that step. A user has the ability to navigate through the defined steps, determine what needs to happen at each step, and make decisions regarding the best approach to take to complete a process. Users also have the ability to advance the process to a new step if certain business requirements are met.

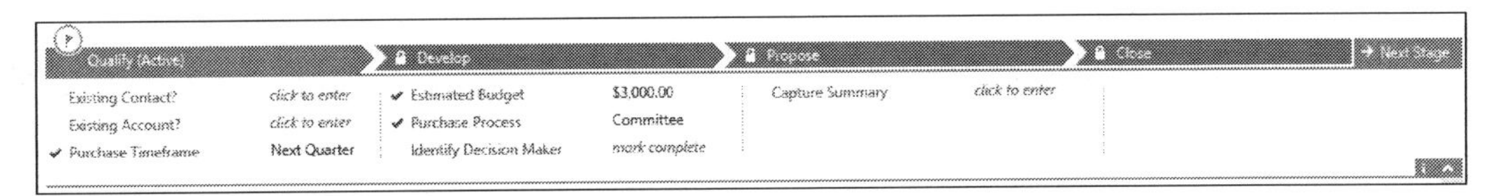

An example of a predefined Business Process Flows is the Lead to Opportunity Sales Process. This is one of the standard defined processes in Dynamics CRM, and provides a good representation of the potential of Business Process Flows on the platform. All existing Business Process Flows can be customized to match existing business requirements, and new processes can be created from scratch.

The main purpose of Business Process Flows is to reduce the amount of user training, by enhancing the ability to guide the user through predefined steps:

- Business Process Flows can be configured to support sales methodologies specific to each business and group, as well as service response processes. You can also customize Business Process Flows for any other business requirements involving standard or custom entities defined in Microsoft Dynamics CRM.
- Following a specific predefined Business Process Flow greatly reduces the amount of mistakes a user can make when performing his/her duties, and allows users to quickly and efficiently correct mistakes. This results in increased customer satisfaction.
- With the help of Business Process Flows, a system user can easily determine where he/she is in the process, what needs to be done next, and what was already completed.
- Each Business Process Flow defines a collection of stages and steps. They are visually displayed at the top of the records that have Business Process Flows enabled.

- Stages are the main groupings, and contain a set of steps. They are represented visually by the chevron headers. The current step is highlighted and marked with a flag in a circle icon. The completed stages are represented with a check mark before the stage name. All stages other than the current stage are represented with a grey background. A user can navigate to past or future stages by clicking on the chevron for each stage. Doing so, they will see the steps associated with each stage.

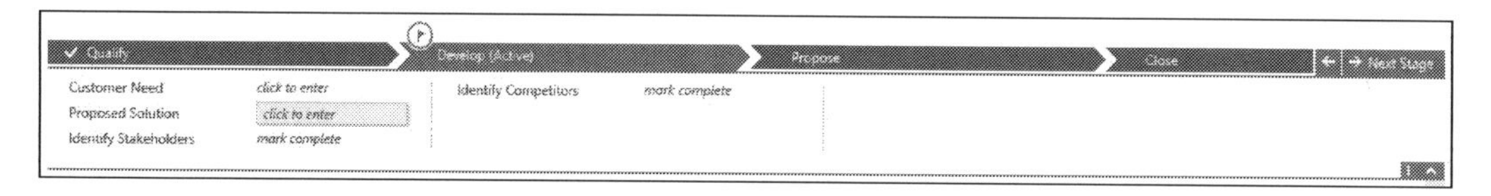

You advance to a next stage by performing a required action that automatically advances the process to a new stage, or by clicking on the **Next Stage** button at the top right of the Business Process Flow representation.

Within each stage, the completed steps are represented with a check mark in front of each field, while the remaining steps are color coded and marked with the **click to enter** message.

Business Process Flows provide a streamlined experience for capturing user input at each defined stage. A complete solution can mix Business Process Flows with other system processes to enhance and validate the user interactions with the system, thus creating quite complex scenarios with absolutely no involvement from developers. Thus, power users can create and add complex business requirements and scenarios to the system, and maintain them without having to rely on a development group or partner.

The data captured in the Business Process Flows is also replicated on the form fields, where other custom processes or customizations can be triggered to execute validation or any other type of customized processes. This gives us the ability to not only visually guide users but also validate that the work performed is correct and in line with the current company business processes, requirements, restrictions, and service level agreements.

Business Process Flows can set field values for fields that are not present on the form. Thus, the form can be kept simpler, while still collecting all the necessary information on the record.

The order of execution is very important when designing Business Process Flows. Other processes that are initiated by changes to Business Process Flow fields are only triggered when the data in the form is saved.

With the December 2012 update to Dynamics CRM online and on-premise, Microsoft has added three system Business Process Flows. They are as follows:

- Lead to Opportunity Sales Process
- Opportunity Sales Process
- Phone to Case Process

These three processes are hard-coded, and some of the capabilities are not available when creating new Business Process Flows.

With Microsoft Dynamics CRM 2016, there are three additional Business Process Flows added. They all revolve around managing Knowledge Articles, and are part of the newly added Interactive Service Hub experience. We'll take a look at this new functionality later on.

When creating and working with Business Process Flows, they can span across one or multiple entities. Processes can be created to being in an entity, and continue through other entities to completion. For example, you can start a Business Process Flow at the Opportunity record level, and progress through to Quote, Order and Invoice. You can also return in the last step to update the Opportunity record with the final conclusion of the process.

One limitation of Business Process Flows is that they cannot span for more than five related entities.

From a user perspective, we have the ability to define which Business Process Flow is required when working with a specific record. As a customizer, multiple Business Process Flows can be created for the same entity. When creating a new entity record, the user then has the ability to select which Business Process Flow applies to the particular scenario used.

Up to 10 Business Process Flows can be activated per entity.

In Dynamics CRM, Business Process Flows can be associated with specific security roles. This way, specific users can be restricted from using specific Business Process Flows. The functionality is quite similar to restricting forms by security role. The default Business Process Flow assigned to an entity is the oldest activated on the entity that the user has permissions to use.

When multiple Business Process Flows are activated on an entity, the user has the ability to choose which one to use. He/she can choose Switch Process from the command bar, and follow the onscreen steps to change to a different Business Process Flow. On changing the process, the newly assigned process starts at the first step.

If a user opens a record with a Business Process Flow assigned that he/she does not have permissions for, the Business Process Flows will be displayed, but it is disabled. Thus, the user cannot modify anything on the process itself.

Another limitation of Business Process Flows is in the number of stages available. For performance and usability reasons, a Business Process Flow cannot contain more than 30 stages.

Also, Business Process Flows are only available for entities that use an **Update** form. This limits the use of Business Process Flows to custom entities and the following standard system entities: Account, Appointment, Campaign, Campaign Activity, Campaign Response, Competitor, Contact, Email, Fax, Case, Invoice, Lead, Letter, Marketing List, Opportunity, Phone Call, Product, Price List Item, Quote, Recurring Appointment, Sales Literature, Order, User, Task, and Team.

For custom created entities, the Business Process Flows must be enabled on the entity definition. Once this option is enabled, it cannot be disabled.

Creating Business Process Flows

The process to start creating Business Process Flows is quite similar to creating any other process in Dynamics CRM, but the process definition is quite different:

1. We start by navigating to the solution that will store our customizations.
2. We go to the **Processes** section. This section will display all existing processes customized in this solution. This includes not only Business Process Flows, but also workflows, dialogs, and actions. We can easily see the status of each customized process in the processes view. We can also sort and filter by any of the columns in the view.

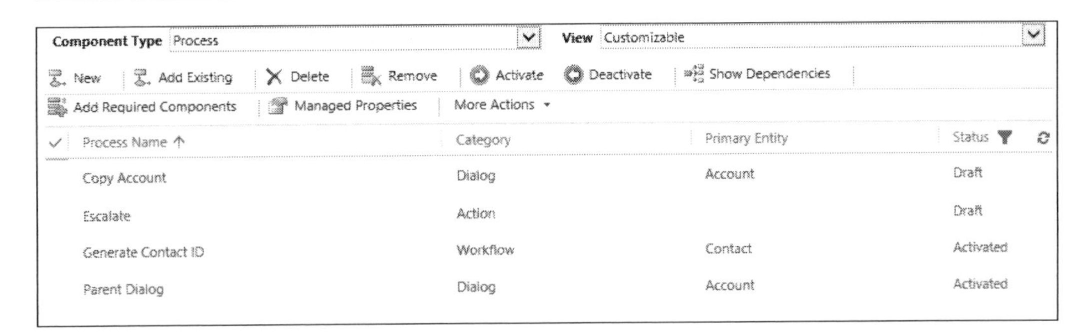

3. In here, we click on **New** to create a new Business Process Flow. We are presented with a new **Create Process** window.

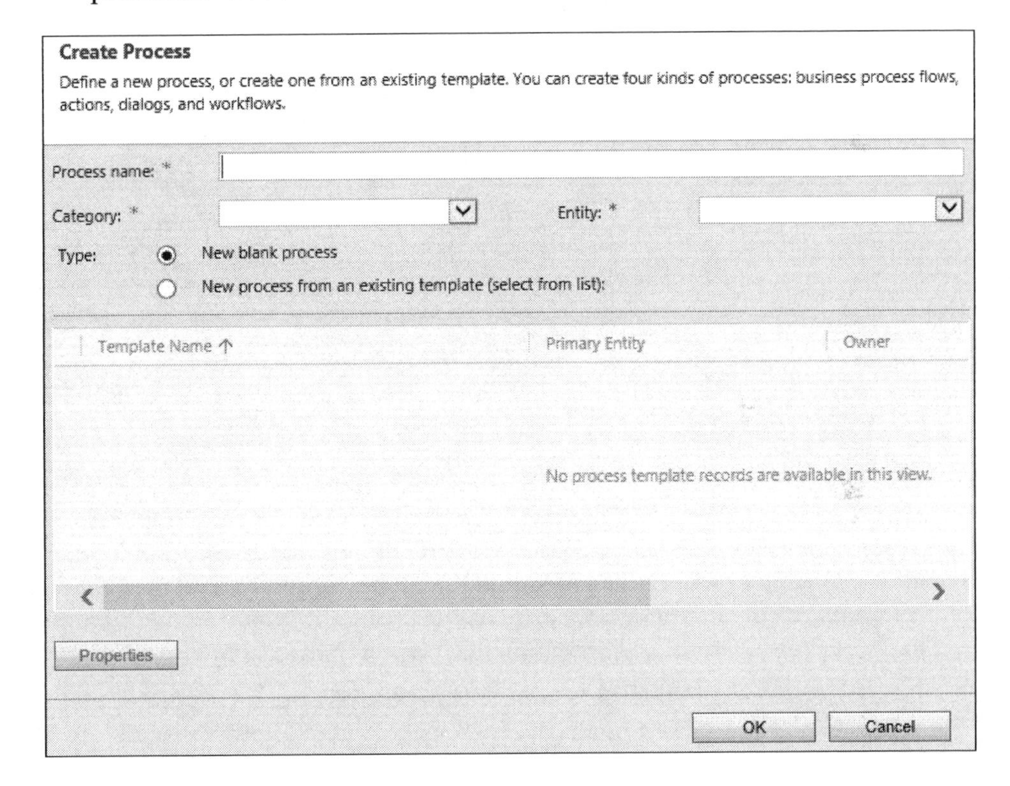

4. Populate all required fields, defining a name for the process, the entity it's being applied to, and from the **Category** drop-down menu, select **Business Process Flow**. If a template is created in the system, you can use the template as a starting point for your new process.

5. Next window presents us with the options to define the Business Process Flow stages and steps, as well as generic properties:

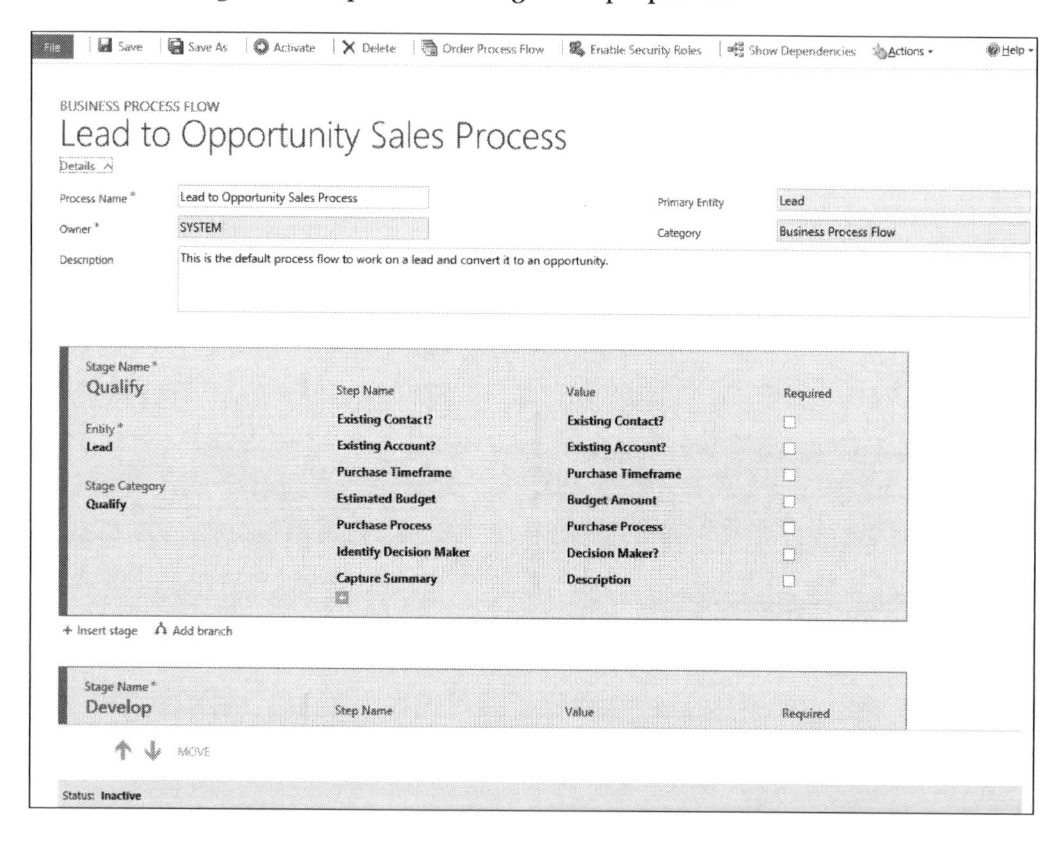

6. In this window, at the top, we have the controls to manage saving, activating, deleting, and other features. While we can still modify the process name in this view, we can no longer change the entity. A description field is also provided. While not mandatory, it is a good practice to put in details about the expected business requirements this process handles.

7. The next section on this form presents us with the options to create and manage stages. As mentioned earlier, stages are represented visually as chevrons, and they contain one or more steps.

8. Name each stage with a concise and clear name that describes where in the process the user is. Next, select a stage category from the available options.

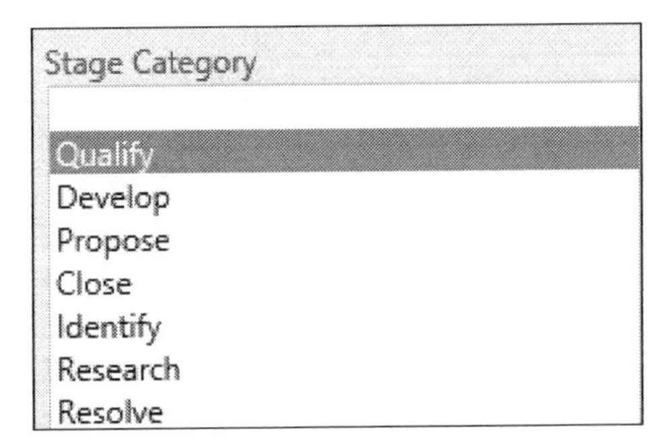

9. These stage categories are in fact customizable, and they are available as a global option set. You can add it to your custom solution by adding an existing option set.

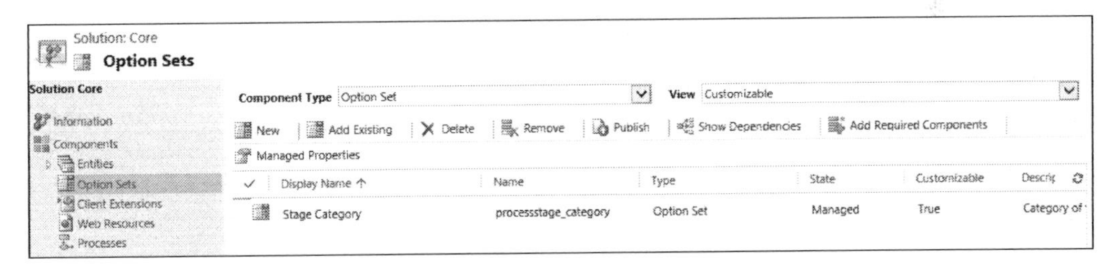

10. Next, define your steps by providing a step name, a field, and whether the field is required or not. Define as many steps as needed per stage.
11. Once you have your first stage defined, define the rest of the stages. This will conclude the definition of your Business Process Flow.
12. In order to make the process available to users, don't forget to activate it. Once activated, it will become available to users that have permissions to execute it.

13. To define a Business Process Flow for a specific security role, click on the **Enable Security Roles** button on the ribbon. This opens up a new window that allows you to enable the process to everyone or to select one or more specific security roles to have access to this process.

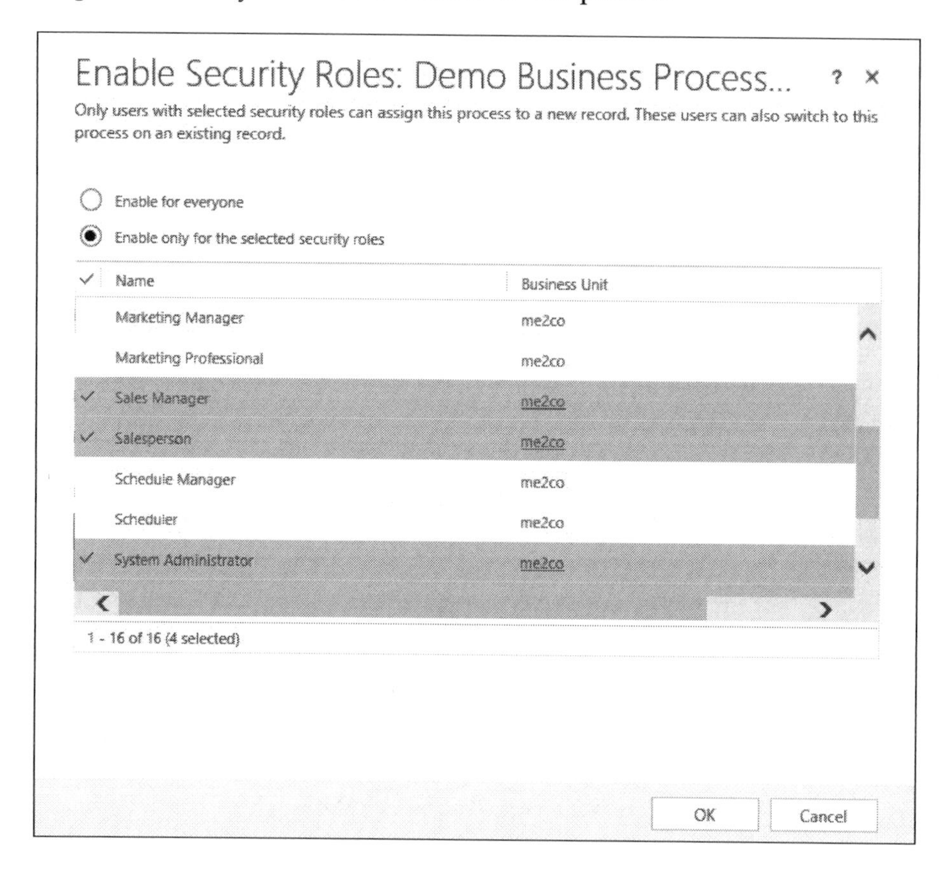

One other important customization option presented to power users is the ability to create a new Business Process Flow from an existing one. You can open an existing process, and click on **Save As** on the ribbon. This creates a copy of the existing Business Process Flow, and allows you to change **Process Name** and then modify any of the stages or steps to suit your new business requirements.

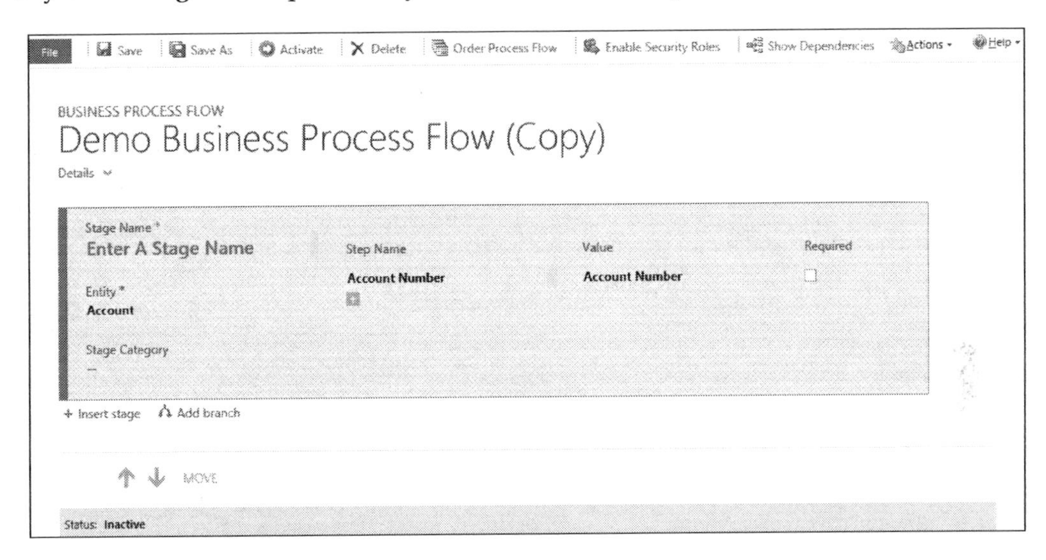

Note that the newly created Business Process Flow retains the same properties as the original, but the name has the **(Copy)** suffix appended.

Triggering Workflows on Business Process Flow Stage change

The beauty of Business Process Flows is that they allow a system customizer to declare workflows that are being triggered by a change of stage in a Business Process Flow. The whole configuration lies with the custom workflow, and a workflows can be added and/or removed at a later time without affecting the original Business Process Flow.

1. In order to achieve this functionality, create a new workflow. In the workflow definition, select the **Start when** to be on **Record fields change**.

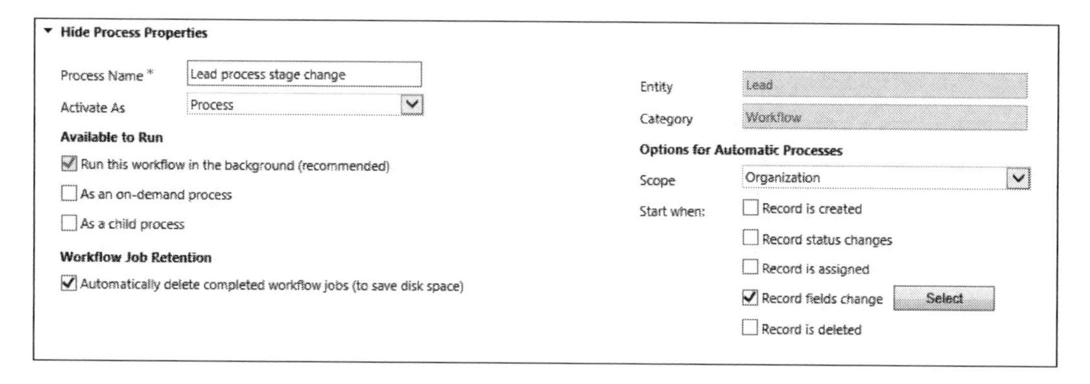

2. Click on the **Select** button, and in the new window that opens up, scroll until you find the **Process Stage** option. Select the checkbox in front of it, and click on **OK**.

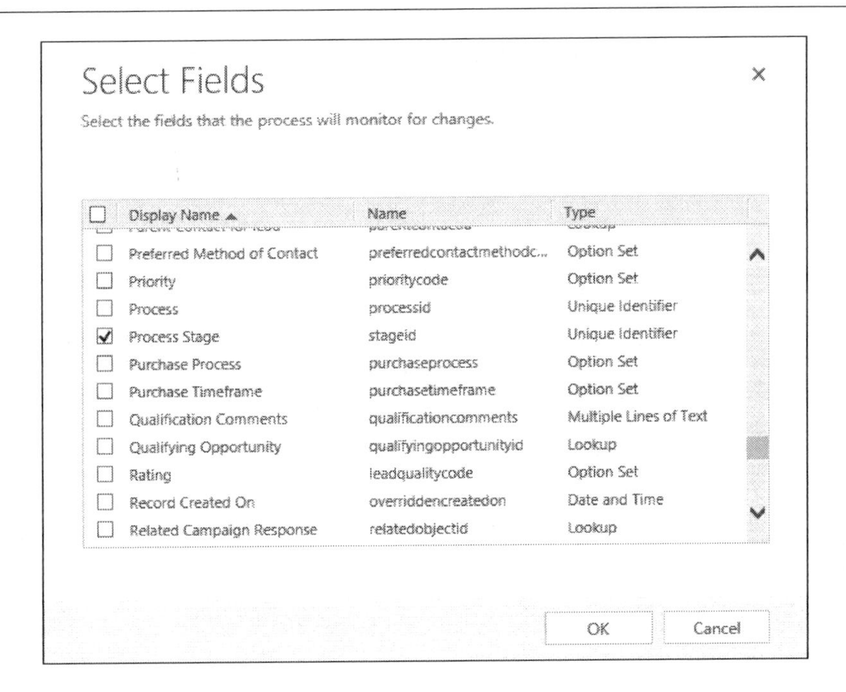

3. Now, build the rest of the workflow as described in the **Workflows** section earlier in this chapter. This can be either a real-time (synchronous) or asynchronous workflow.
4. With both the Business Process Flow and the workflow now published, you can test and see that each process step change in the Business Process Flow now triggers the workflow to execute.

Excel Enhanced Integration

The tight integration with the Office suite of applications has always been one of the strengths of this platform. Each new version built on top of existing features, adding new ways to interact, bringing the tools closer to the platform, and making the platform into a core service for the client applications.

With Microsoft Dynamics CRM 2016, the Excel integration has been greatly enhanced furthermore. While we had the ability to export data to Excel for further analysis, and to have the data ready for reimport in a blink of an eye, with the tight integration with Office 365, now client applications can be substituted by the online versions. For details on the online apps, see the main Office landing page at `https://www.office.com/`.

With these capabilities, now we can render Excel data directly in a record in Microsoft Dynamics CRM. When working with Excel, instead of spending time and clicks switching between applications, a system user can stay on the same record page and analyze data in Excel in the same view. All changes made to the data this way are being captured and saved back to the platform.

To further enhance these features, we can use Excel templates to format data, present it graphically in the context of the Dynamics CRM record, and analyze changes and the impact in real time.

The ribbon presents the new **EXCEL TEMPLATES** options next to the former **EXPORT TO EXCEL** options, as seen in the following screenshot:

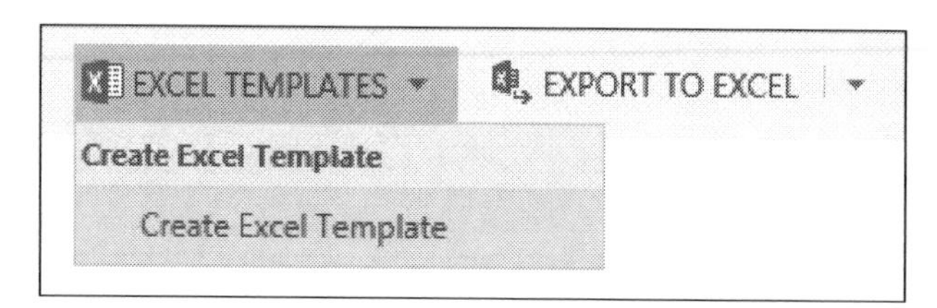

Document Templates

Document templates are a new feature added with Microsoft Dynamics CRM 2016. As seen previously, we can use templates for both Excel files as well as Word documents. These templates can be created outside of the system and uploaded, or generated while working in Dynamics CRM.

From any ribbon option where we are presented with the **Create Template** menu, we can trigger the template creation process. This starts with a selection of the template type we will be working on, as well as defining the data source, as seen in the following screenshot:

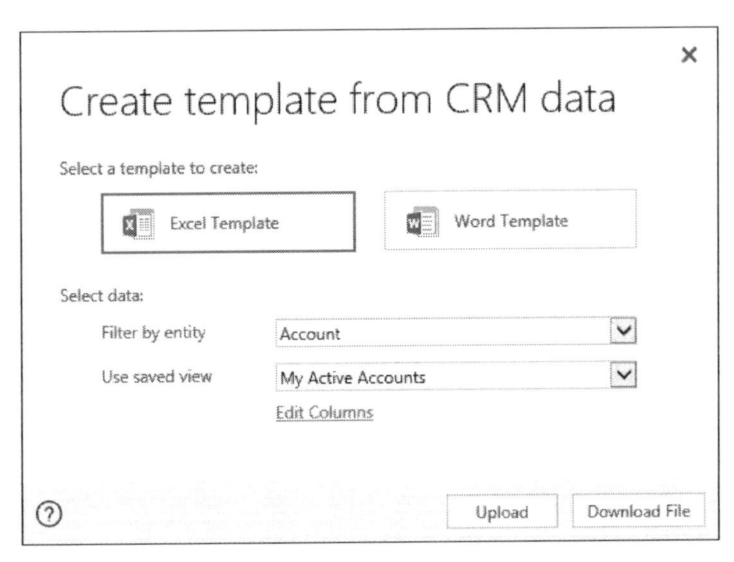

Choosing a document template type and selecting **Upload** allows us to load a predefined template created outside of the current Dynamics CRM organization. The **Download File** button allows us to take the template out of our Dynamics CRM organization, modify it, and either reimport it in the same organization, or port it to a new organization. With the template exported, we can now take advantage of the various graphs and rendering options in Excel to create more interactive templates that can be used for extensive analysis.

Automated Document Generation Templates

Document Generation Templates have also been added with Microsoft Dynamics CRM 2016. Where with older versions we had to create either custom reports or various programmable processes to be able to generate a branded and well formatted document such as a Quote or an Invoice, now we can do all that with a single click. Once the templates are generated and loaded in your organization, they are made available to the users.

From a record where you want to generate a document based on a template, navigate to the extended ribbon options, and find the **Word Templates** option. Here, you can either create a new word template if permissions allow you to, or you can use an existing one if available.

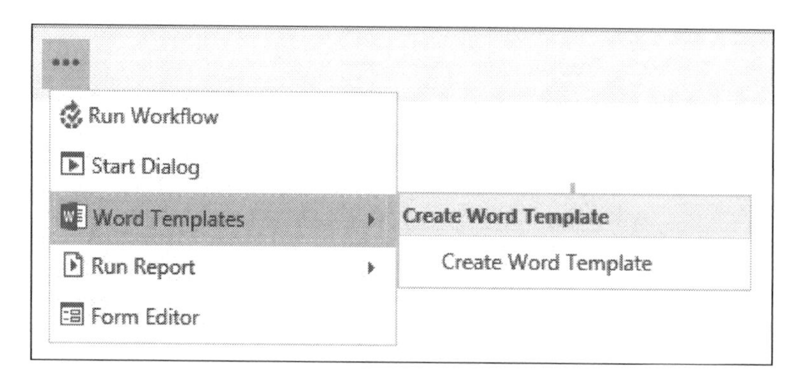

Once a document is generated, it can be downloaded and saved, printed, shared, or e-mailed to other users or clients.

This bypasses the rather complex process of using the default Office Mail Merge functionality.

Mobile and Task-based Experience

The mobile experience has seen great improvements with each new version of Microsoft Dynamics CRM. Starting with a very simplistic and trimmed-down mobile page, the mobility functions have evolved to a full-blown and very usable alternative to using the platform. We now have support for all mobile platforms, both tablets and smart phone. Furthermore, the user experience is similar on all mobile devices, no matter the platform. The application is configured once, and when deployed, presents the same functionality everywhere.

Starting with Microsoft Dynamics CRM 2016, users of the mobile apps now also have full offline capabilities. This feature is available to Microsoft Dynamics CRM Online users on an Enterprise license or Professional license where more than 30 users are part of the Organization. For all other license models, offline cache mode and drafts will be available. This is the functionality that was made available with the previous version, and enables users to access the records that they accessed previously while online and have the data cached, as well as create new records.

With full offline mode in Dynamics CRM 2016 Online, users can now create, change, and delete records while offline, as long as permissions allow them. All related actions are queued and played back once they go online. This helps synchronize the local changes with the online organization.

When starting the mobile application for the first time, or after changes were configured on the server, the mobile application will go through a refresh of configurations and data. While this is happening, the user is prompted with the following screen:

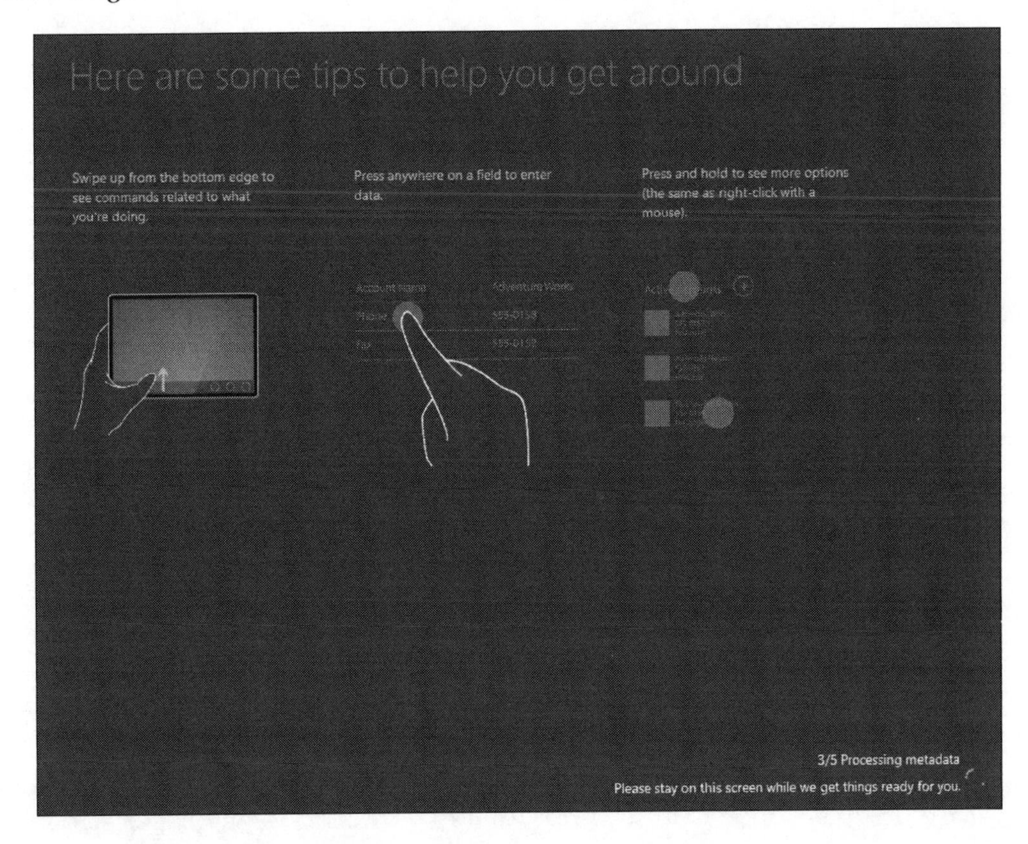

Once all configuration is downloaded and the application is ready, the following screen is presented to the user:

This interface will become quite familiar, as it is common across all mobile devices. It does scale a little more compact on smartphones, but the concepts are very similar. This is a very touch-friendly interface, with enhanced functionality and support for gestures. Contextual menus are presented when swiping up from the bottom. On a Task record, for example, the contextual menu will look like the following screenshot, and will be different from the contextual menu for other record types:

The main menu and home button are always visible in the top left of the screen.

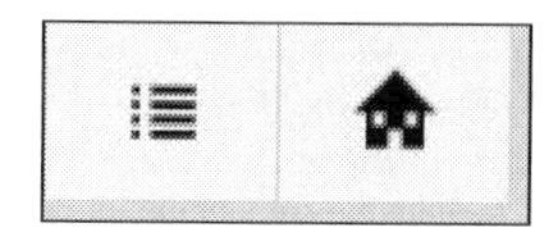

Clicking on the home icon will always bring you to the default dashboard view, while the menu button will present the following options:

The **Search** functionality is accessible from the top right of the screen, and presents the results structured in the same multiple format column, with results grouped by various records. The following screen shows the results when searching by a person's name:

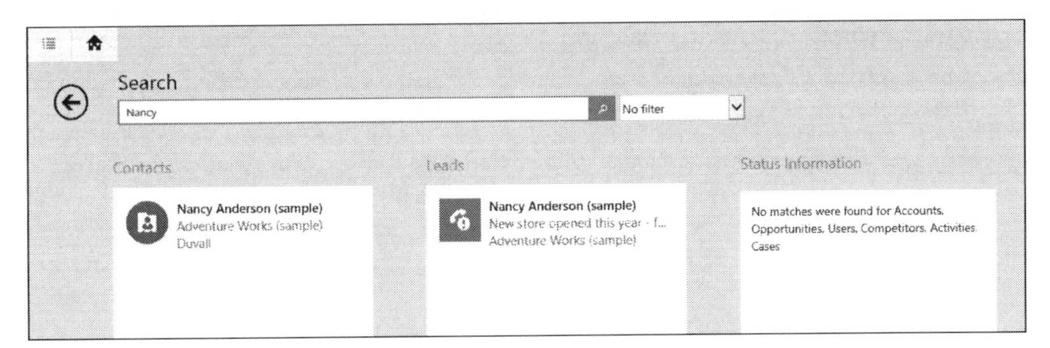

When in **Offline** mode, the application presents the **Offline** side flag clearly, as shown in the next screenshot:

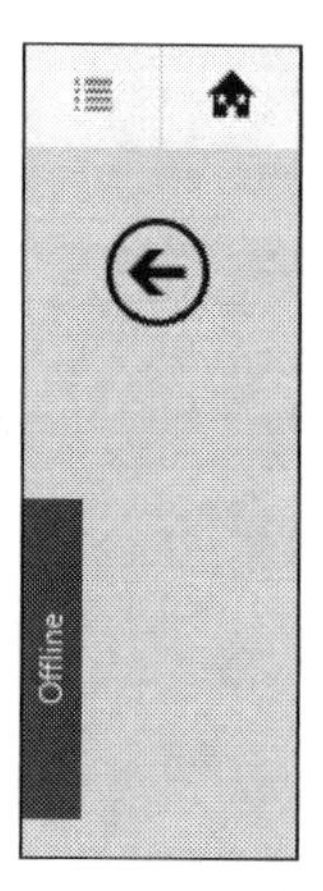

Once connectivity is restored, clicking on the **Offline** tab brings up a menu with the **Reconnect** option. Tap on **Reconnect** to go back online and start synchronizing all changes made while offline.

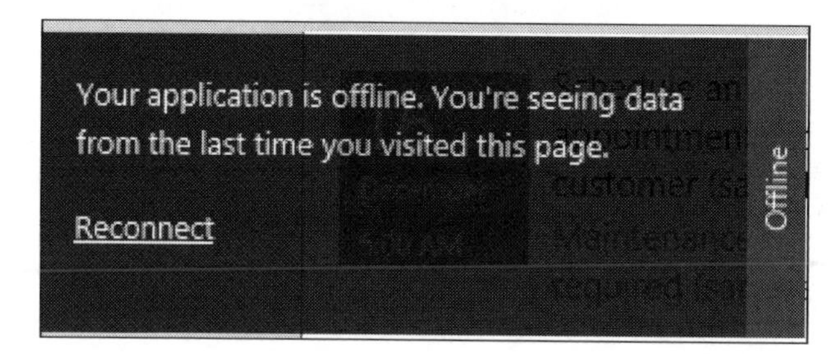

With the new version of the client application for Dynamics CRM 2016, we now can view documents in the context of a record, and open them in the respective application on mobile clients. With the availability of Office 365 on all mobile platforms, this integration is now seamless. The following screenshot presents the **DOCUMENTS** view in the mobile application.

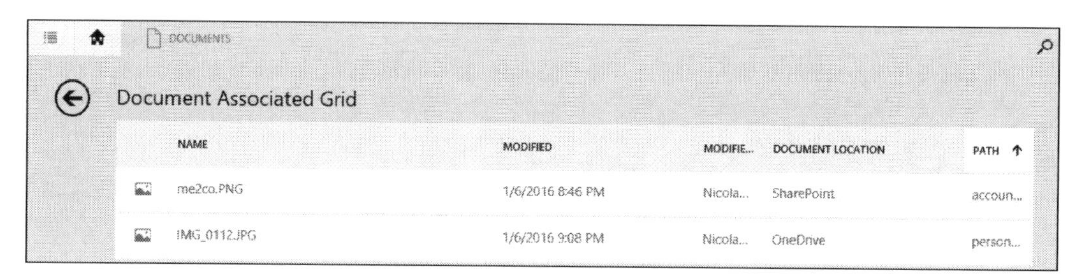

New to Dynamics CRM 2016 Online, we have the **Task Based Experience** functionality. In this initial release, it is still offered as a preview feature, and must be specifically enabled.

A preview feature is not supported by Microsoft, and is made available as an opt-in feature.

In order to enable this feature, navigate to **Settings | System Settings**. Find the **Previews** tab to the far right, and select to enable **Task Flows for Mobile Preview**. This provides a new icon on the bottom-left side of the mobile application screen. Clicking on it presents the user with direct access to the various Business Process Flows available to drive functional processes. The following screenshot shows the **Task Flows** menu opened in a default instance:

The Task Based Experience is a way of allowing users to focus on the business relevant processes they need to execute rather than the structure of the information. Data from the various entities that the process spans across is brought forward for a cohesive user experience. This not only simplifies usage, but also guides the user through the required actions they need to perform. Behind the scenes, the same logic is available as what we have seen when customizing the Business Process Flows that drive this.

Dynamics CRM for Outlook

Microsoft Dynamics CRM has been available to be used through the familiar Outlook interface for several versions now. This provides users the ability to work from a familiar application, and have direct access to the platform while taking advantage of functionality such as direct tracking of e-mails, synchronization of tasks and events, and so on.

This functionality is made available across all recent versions. Various clients are provided with each release, containing various enhancements and performance optimization.

When upgrading the Organization to a new version, make sure you plan to upgrade Dynamics CRM for Outlook clients. You will thus take advantage of all enhancements brought forward by the new versions.

In order to connect Outlook to Microsoft Dynamics CRM, you must install an add-on for Outlook. This installer is available for download from the Microsoft's site:

`https://www.microsoft.com/en-US/download/details.aspx?id=50370`

Select the appropriate client that matches the version of Outlook you have installed. For example, if you have Office 32-bit installed, select the 32-bit version of the client.

The process to install and configure CRM for Outlook has been covered in detail in *Chapter 1, Getting Started*. Please refer to that section for additional details.

Dynamics CRM App for Outlook

In its stride to reach out to salespeople across various platforms and devices, Microsoft has recognized that the desktop Outlook application is not the only medium in which they retrieve their e-mails anymore. Key capabilities have been added starting with Microsoft Dynamics CRM 2016 Online to allow users to interact in a similar manner from both Outlook on the desktop as well as mobile browsers. Contextual information has now surfaced using the CRM App for Outlook directly into the user's inbox.

The CRM App for Outlook makes it easy to manage contacts and track e-mails directly from within the message interface.

Currently, this feature supports the Internet Explorer and Chrome browsers, with support for Firefox, Safari for Mac, and Outlook for Mac coming soon.

The most important features of the CRM App for Outlook include:

- Access CRM data from within your inbox
- Track e-mails from within a browser
- Link e-mails to an existing CRM record
- Convert e-mails into a new CRM record

CRM app for Outlook is currently available only for Dynamics CRM Online. It is based on an exchange online and server-side synchronization, as well as specific privileges in the system.

To push the CRM App for Outlook, follow these steps:

1. Navigate to **Settings** | **CRM App for Outlook**.

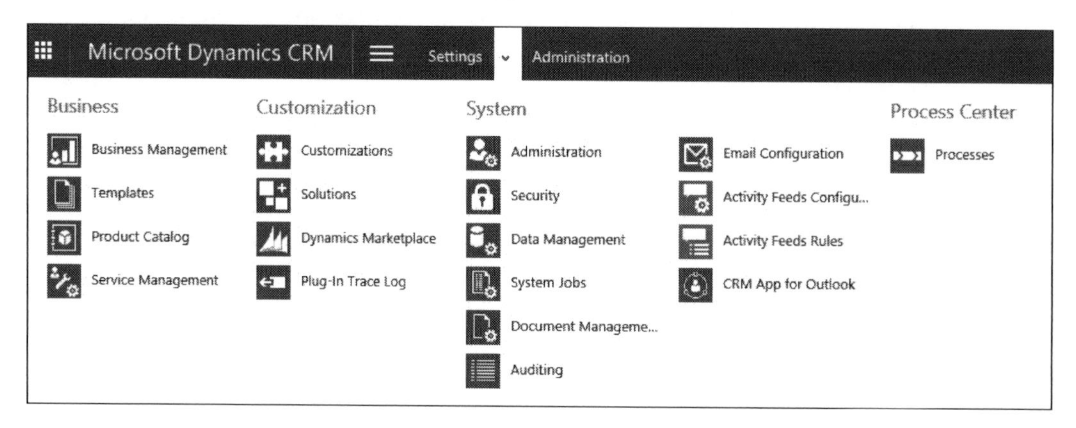

2. This triggers the configuration wizard. Here, you are reminded of the configuration needed on the user profiles in order to be able to use this feature. Check the **Automatically add the app to Outlook** checkbox, then click on **Save**.

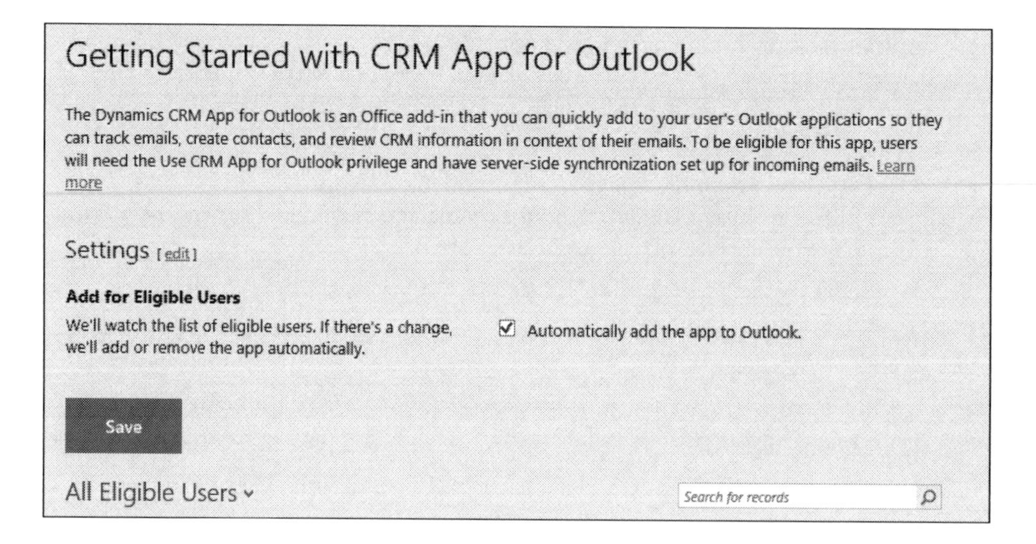

3. Once done, you have the ability to identify the users where you want this feature deployed. As mentioned previously, make sure the requirements are met so you can add this feature.
4. In order to give a user permission to use CRM App for Outlook, in the respective security role, or in a new role, navigate to the **Business Management** tab and in the **Privacy Related Privileges** section find the **Use CRM App for Outlook** setting. Enable it from here, as in the following screenshot:

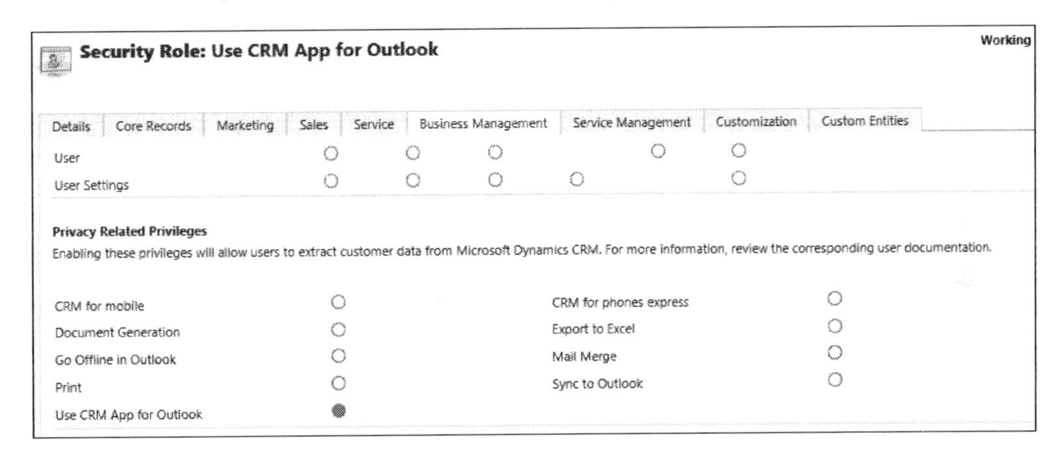

5. For details on configuring user permissions, roles, and groups see the security roles section in *Chapter 6, Dynamics CRM Administration*.
6. Once your users are configured properly, selecting **Add App for all eligible users** triggers the configuration for users, and a status is presented in the following list.

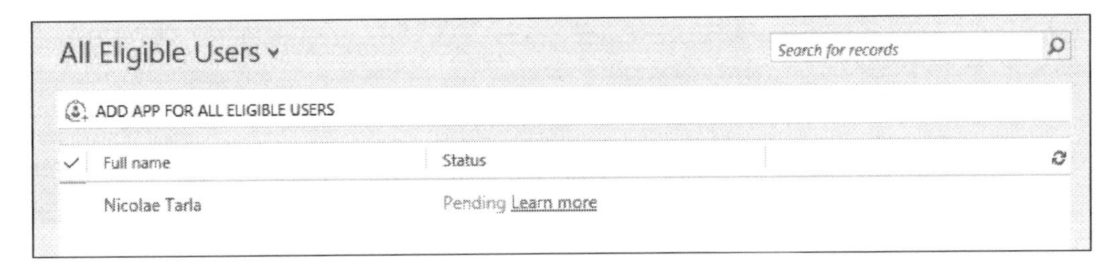

7. Once enabled, a user navigating to his inbox is presented with a view similar to the one in the following screenshot:

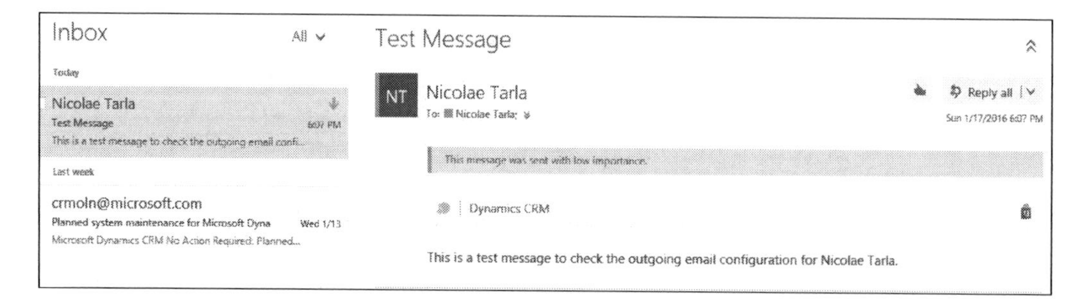

8. Click on the Dynamics CRM link to expand the CRM app for Outlook window, as shown in the following screenshot:

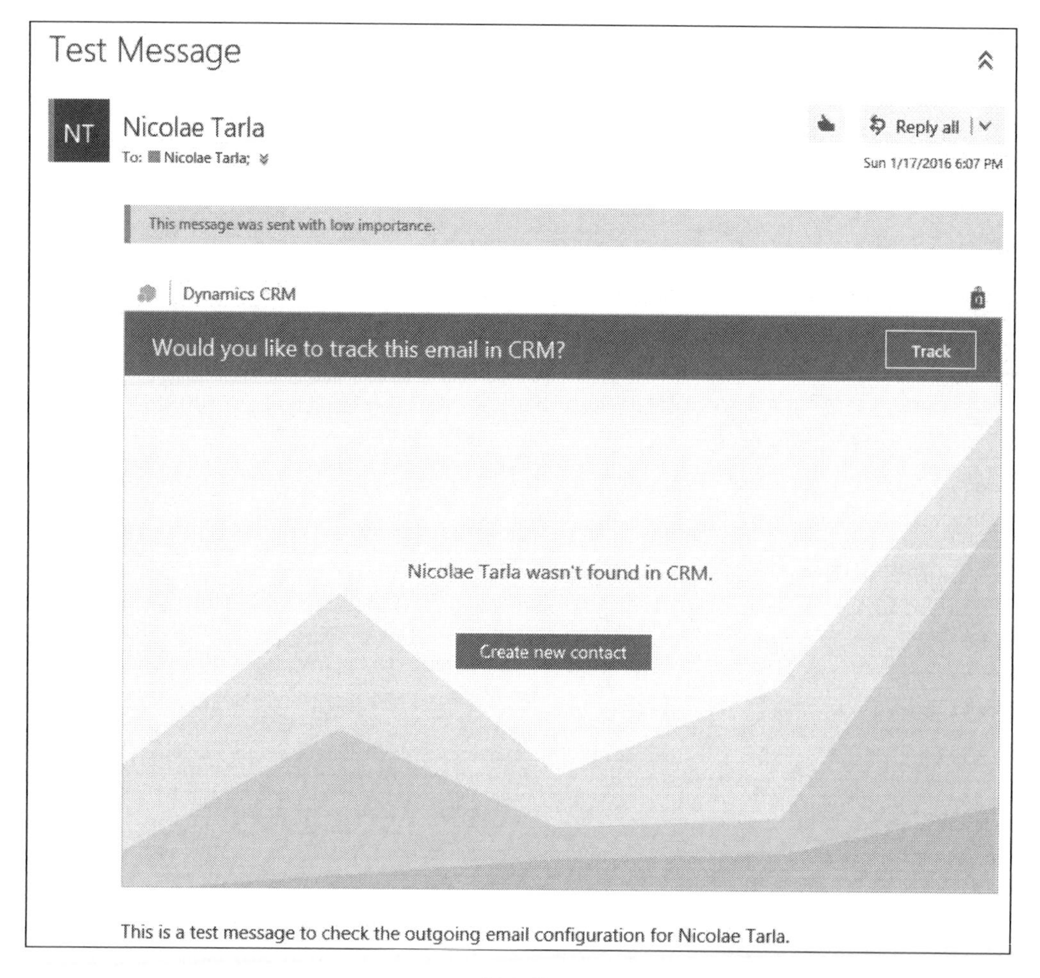

9. Now, we can start working with this message, by tracking it, or creating a new contact. Clicking on **Create new contact** brings up a new wizard that allows you to edit the contact details.

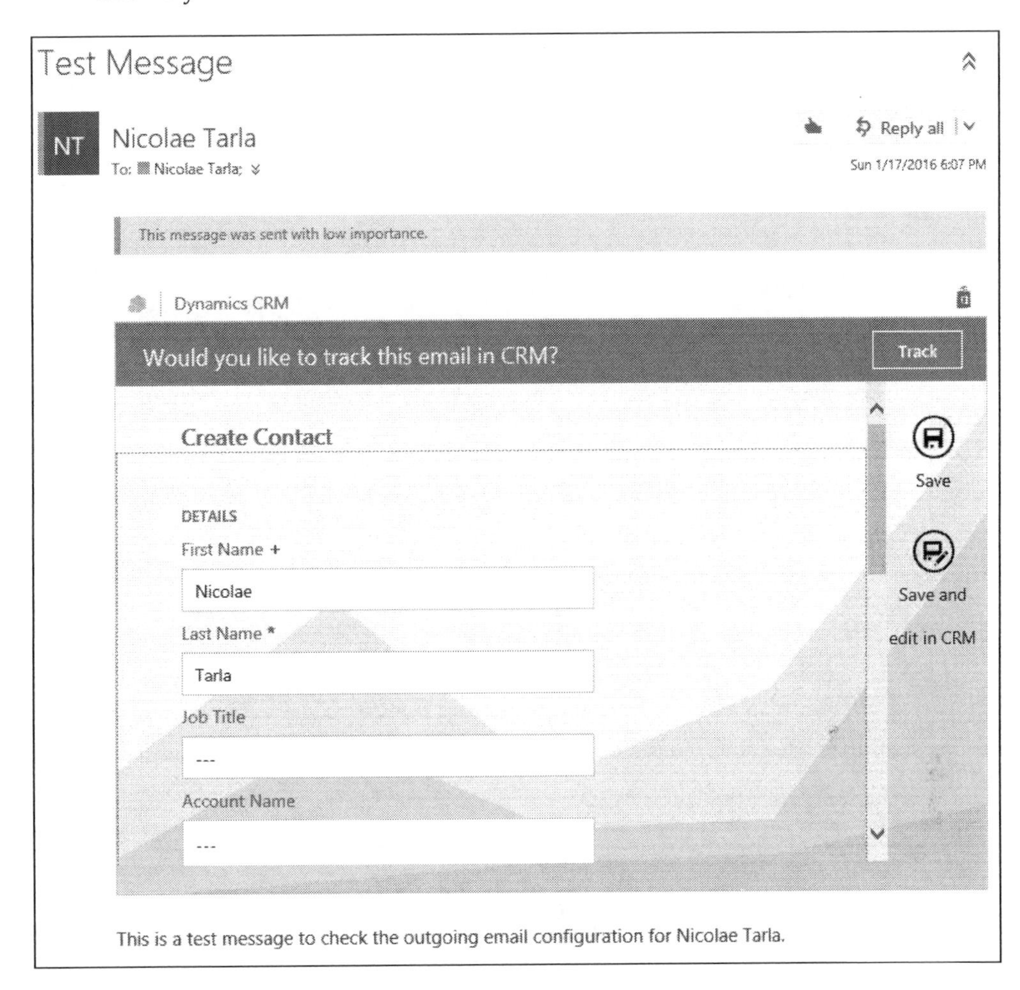

Selecting to Track the message allows us to associate it with a specific record type.

Once we have a contact created, and the message tracked, we can see additional details on the contact and the activities existing in my organization. The next screenshot shows the message tracked, with options to change tracking or untrack, as well as additional details retrieved from my Dynamics CRM organization about the particular contact we are tracking against.

In this case, we can see that we have a case already opened with this contact. We can navigate directly to the case by clicking on the case. This brings up a new window with all the case details.

An Enhanced Search Functionality

Search has been at the core of this platform from the early days. It has evolved with the platform, and today it provides extensive features that greatly enhance the user experience and usability.

There are various ways to search in Microsoft Dynamics CRM 2016. They are as follows:

- Searching in a view
- Searching across the entire Organization
- Advanced Find
- Search using voice on mobile

Each one presents a different set of data, and each one has its best scenario to be used. Let's look at each one individually and see what their strengths are.

For all searches, the results are returned based on the fields we have already defined as searchable. For any data in fields not marked as searchable, no match will be identified.

Searching in a View

One of the simplest ways to search in Microsoft Dynamics CRM is to search in a view. This is available from any entity view, and is presented in the top-right side of the view, as shown in the following screenshot:

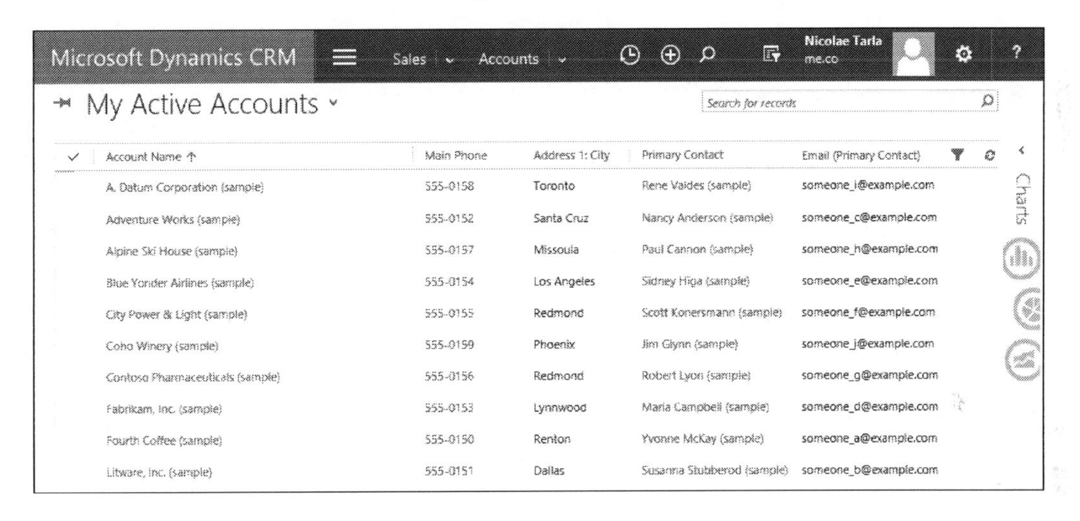

The search box, when not selected, is marked with the **Search for records** text.

This type of search is performed against the entity to which view are we seeing. The results are always security trimmed, meaning we only see the records we have permissions to see.

Searching Across the entire Organization

To perform a search across the entire organization, on the top ribbon, we are provided with a different search box, as seen in the following screenshot:

This is available pretty much anywhere in the system, and it performs a search across multiple entities, and returns the results grouped by entity:

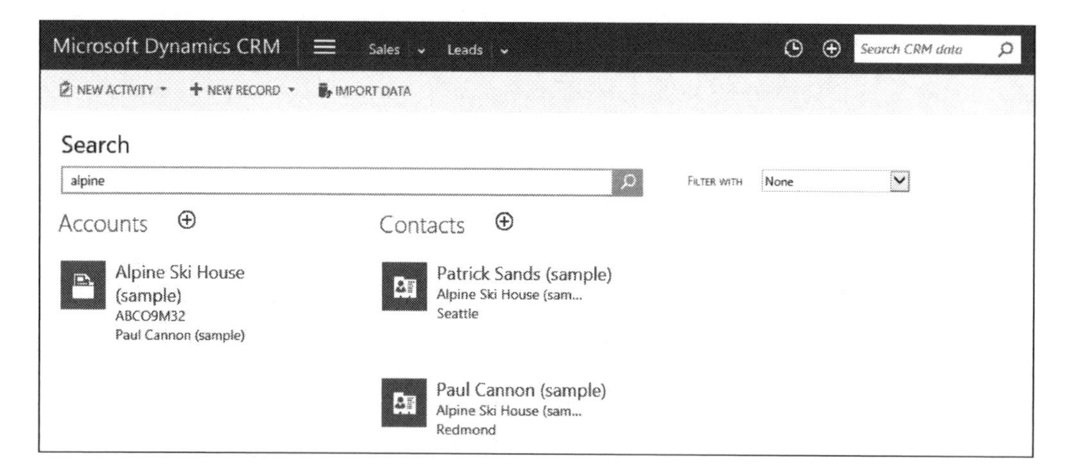

Advanced Find

Advanced find is a feature that allows us to not only retrieve data, but also can be used as the starting point for creating a new view.

We can also access Advanced Find from the top ribbon, to the right of the Search Box. The icon for Advanced Find looks like a page with a funnel overlapped, and is shown in the following screenshot:

This brings up a new window where you can configure the target and parameters of your search. You define the entity you search against in the **Look for** drop-down menu, as well as an existing view if you want to search using an existing view. If not, your search will be performed across all the records for the selected entity. The following screenshot shows the default **ADVANCED FIND** window:

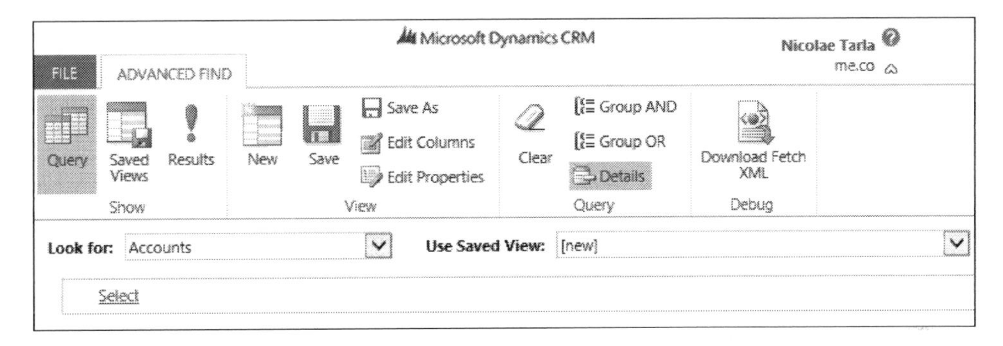

In the following section, you start defining the conditions and filtering parameters. Click on **Select**, and choose a field. Then, define a condition. For example, if I want to retrieve all accounts with **Account Name** containing the text **Blue**, my search filters will look like the following screenshot:

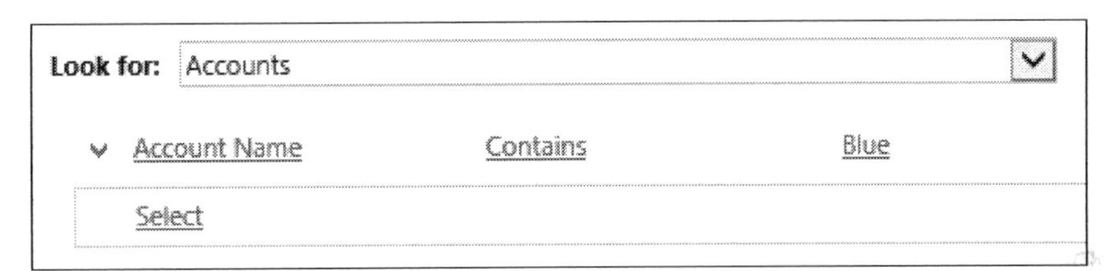

As you can see on the ribbon, in the **Query** area, we have options to group our defined condition either as **AND** conditions or **OR** conditions. We can configure the **AND** condition along with the **OR** condition, as seen in the next screenshot:

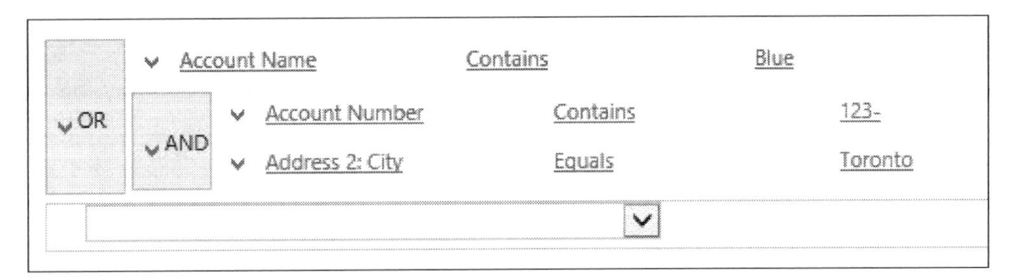

Click on the **Results** ribbon button to see how your search parameters behave. Once you are satisfied, you can save this search as a new view. Clicking on **Save** brings up the following screen, prompting for **Name** and **Description**:

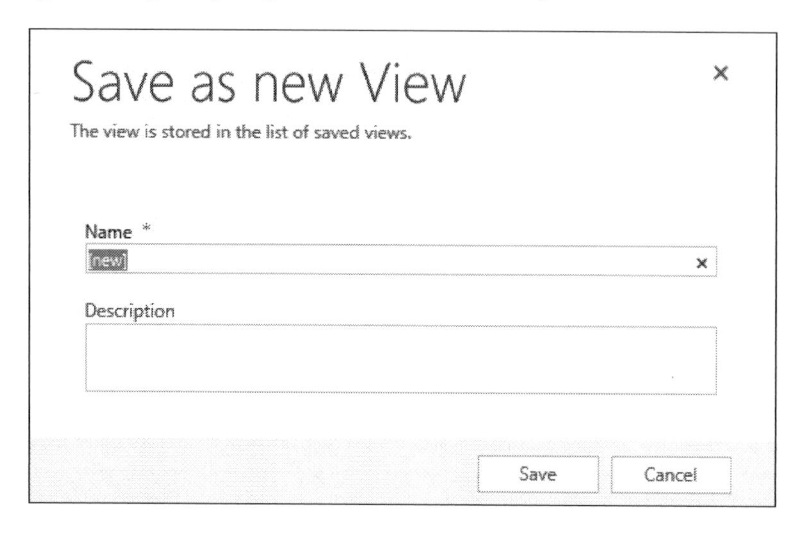

The **Edit Columns** button allows us to select which columns are displayed, and to define the order in which they are shown.

Search using voice on Mobile

With the extended support for mobile, on the Windows platform, we now have the ability to use Cortana, the mobile digital assistant, to interact with the Dynamics CRM platform. A series of commands have been customized for support and integration with CRM. Some of these include actions such as:

- Opening a record
- Showing a view
- Searching for an item
- Creating a new record

To find a record in CRM, the Cortana command is as follows:

```
CRM find <item> called <name>
```

For example, to retrieve a contact called James, we would ask Cortana the following:

```
CRM find Contact called James
```

For more details on the available commands for Cortana integration with Dynamics CRM, see the following URL in the CRM help and training:

`https://www.microsoft.com/en-us/dynamics/crm-customer-center/use-cortana-voice-commands-in-crm-for-phones.aspx`

Summary

Throughout this chapter, we have looked at the processes available for customization in Dynamics CRM. We determined which type of process applies to which scenario, and when one type is better suited than another. We also looked at business rules and the Business Process Flow, and how to use them to enforce and visually enhance user experience. We also saw examples of creating these processes, and building complex relationships where one process can be triggered from another.

We also looked at working with documents and document templates. Finally, we looked at various ways to interact with Microsoft Dynamics CRM, using Outlook, the App for Outlook and mobile. We also quickly saw the search capabilities provided with the platform.

The next chapter will look at some of the external features that integrate with the platform, and some of the new tools introduced with the newer versions of Microsoft Dynamics CRM.

5

Dynamics CRM – Additional Features

In the previous chapter we looked at business processes, and how business affects the behavior of the platform. We looked at how to map and enforce business rules on the platform, and how to customize the system by creating guided paths for users, thus making sure the platform works with the user. Some of the new features and integration points were also highlighted.

In this chapter we will look at the following topics:

- Social Pane
- Office 365 Features and Integration
- OneNote Integration
- Interactive Service Hub
- Enhanced Knowledge Management
- Office Delve Recommendations
- Field Service Capabilities
- Voice of the Customer
- Insight by InsideView
- Yammer
- Web API
- Microsoft Social Listening Integration
- Microsoft Dynamics Marketing Integration
- Power BI and Dynamics CRM

We'll be looking at both the internal and external inner workings of the platform. We dive first into the internal social aspects of the platform, then at external sources integrated into Dynamics CRM. We are also looking at the analytics options available with the platform.

Social Pane

Social Pane in Microsoft Dynamics CRM is the place where you can see all business interactions related to a particular record. It also shows the activity feed with record related activities, posts, Yammer if integrated, and notes with document attachments. New tabs have been added along the various versions. Yammer was a later addition supported with the Yammer integration, while the Notes tab has been enhanced around the 2013 version. Now with the newer version, the OneNote integration finds its place as part of Social Pane.

What it is, where it is, and how it works

The Social Pane was introduced on the Microsoft Dynamics CRM platform in version 2011. It made its debut with the December 2012 update (Polaris) to Dynamics CRM Online, and was introduced at the time on Leads, Opportunities, and Case. The purpose is to enhance business interactions and allow a user to review and create *social* posts directly at the record level. Posts can be either user-created, or automatically generated by the system. Some of the automatically generated posts include the record creation, or assignment information.

The Social Pane presents all interactions related to a specific record, across entities such as Account, Contact, Lead, Opportunity, Case, and so on, and ensures they are all being presented in a unified manner.

Along with this information, the Social Pane is also the place to find Notes, and to track activities on a record in a much simpler interface. This makes it so much easier for the system user to see all the interactions with a specific record without the need to navigate to other tabs or views.

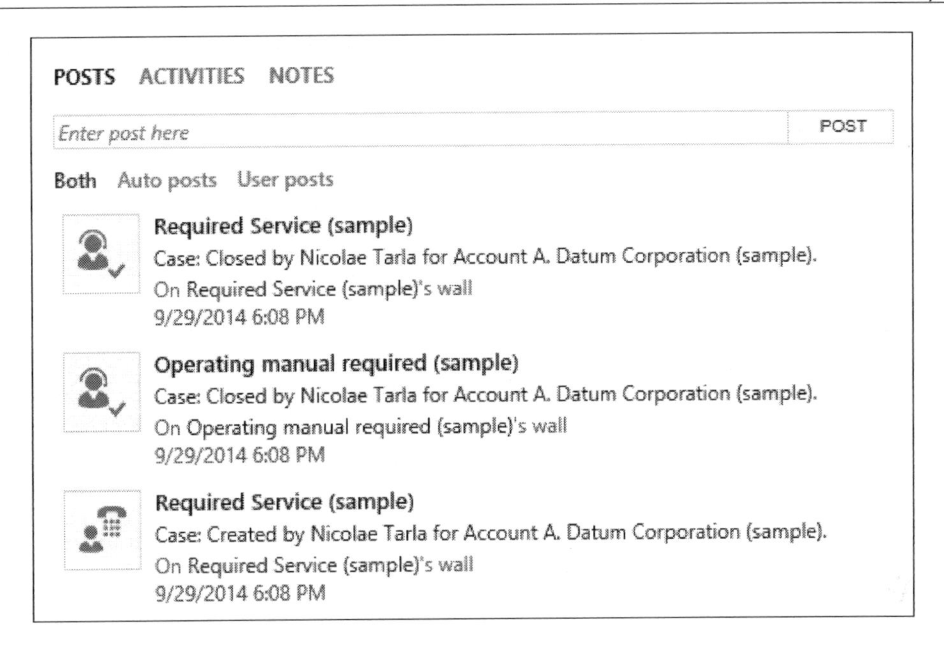

Since the initial introduction of Social Pane, we can now find it on all the main system entities, and by default it is placed on the entity's main form. This way, the users can now interact with all record types by adding either new Activities or Notes.

The Social Pane is a structure with three main category tabs. These will vary based on the entity setting; they are as follows:

- Posts
- Activities
- Notes

Any one of these can be hidden based either on the entity configuration, or through customizations. For example, if Notes are not enabled on the entity, the **NOTES** tab will not be displayed on that particular entity's records.

When integrated with Yammer, the Social Pane is also the place to find the Yammer activity feed. It presents a new tab for all Yammer social interactions, as shown in the following image:

Social Pane – standard configuration options

The standard configuration options of the Social Pane are quite limited. The configuration wizard presents us with the standard field customization options, along with an option to select the **Default tab** for this pane to present:

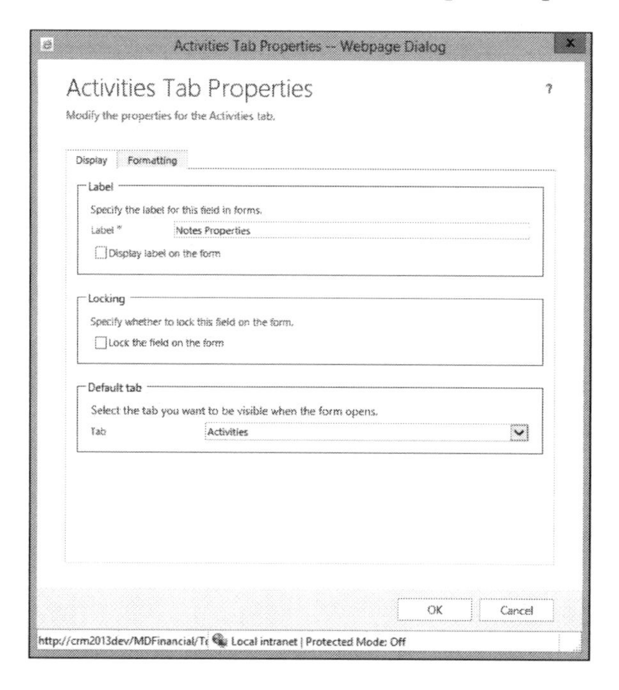

The default value is **Activities**, and this can be changed to **Posts** or **Notes**, when Yammer is not configured.

Adding Social Pane to custom entities

While the Social Pane comes with most of the standard entities in Dynamics CRM, for new custom entities it must be added to the entity form.

Customizing the Entity

On the entity customization screen, enable both **Notes** and **Activities**:

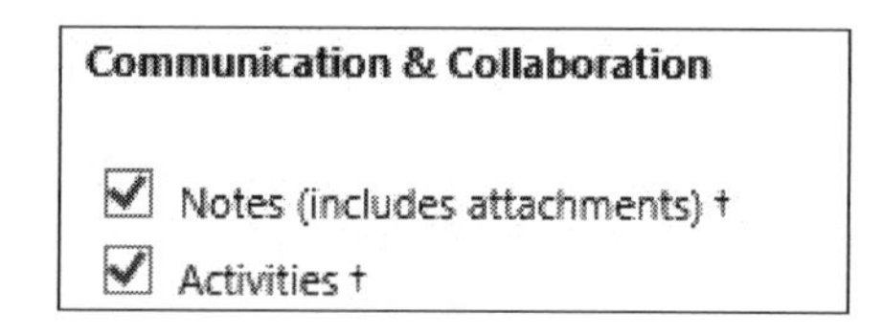

Configuring Post Configurations

In order to record posts, we need to configure the following steps:

1. Navigate to **Settings** | **Post Configurations**.
2. Make sure the new entity has the **Wall Enabled** option selected:

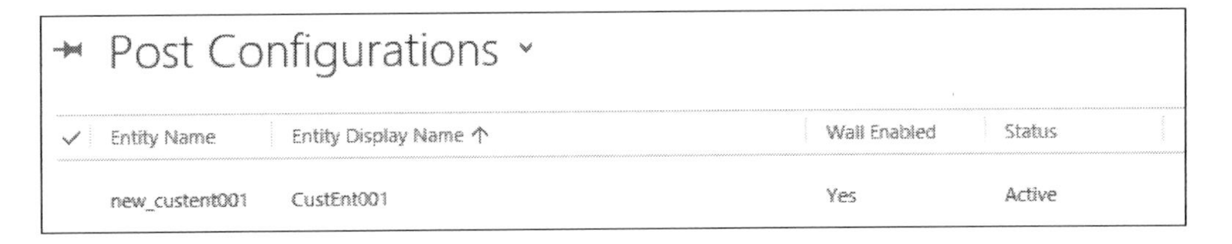

Customizing the form

For forms upgraded from CRM 2011, the Social Pane cannot be added. You must create a new form after upgrading to CRM 2013.

Once a CRM 2011 form is upgraded, only the **NOTES** tab will be displayed.

On a new CRM 2013, or newer form, **POSTS**, **ACTIVITIES**, and **NOTES** will be displayed.

Creating a custom new Activity Feed Post

For situations where a new set of Posts must be added to the Activity Feed, they can be created using a custom process (workflow). These are the steps to add a new set of posts to the Activity Feed:

1. Select your trigger condition – for each entity where you want to add new custom Posts, create a new workflow and set the starting condition. This could be either a field change, a record save, or any other custom condition, as required.

2. Add a step to create a record, and select **Post** as the record type. Insert your **Text**, **Source**, **Regarding**, and select the **Type** of post:

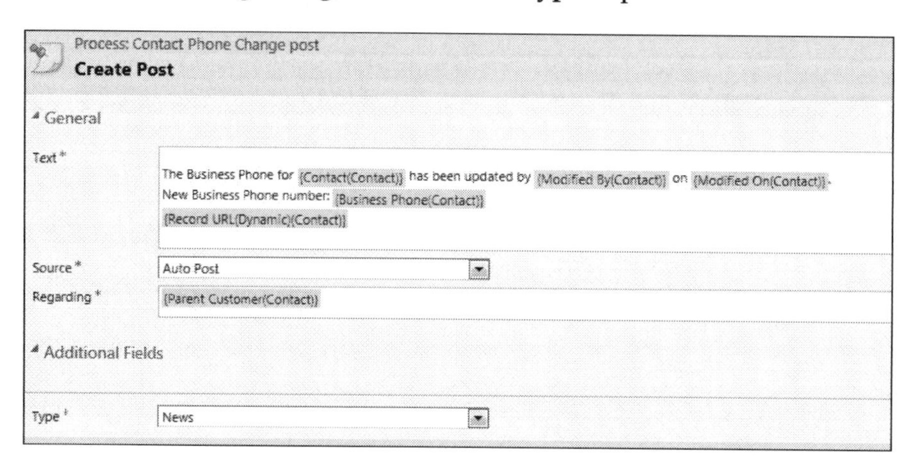

3. Activate the workflow and test it on a record.

Office 365 Features and Integration

With the growing popularity of cloud services and Dynamics CRM Online, Office 365 has become a component that is necessary for a lot of functionality. Starting with the enhanced analytics functionality provided through Power BI, along with the real-time, anywhere collaboration features available with Office Online, the teams using the Dynamics CRM platform become more effective and efficient every day.

The familiarity of the Office suite of tools is what drives this adoption. A large majority of enterprise customers are already familiar with these tools, which makes for an easier adoption of the platform. Access to the sales, service, and marketing tools is now available through these products, anywhere, from a large variety of devices.

Some of these service integrations have been covered in previous chapters. In *Chapter 3, Dynamics CRM Customization* we have looked at the section *Working with documents*. This section covered the integration with SharePoint services for document storage and management. We have looked at configuring this integration and the folder structure to be created in the SharePoint site collection. Next, we looked at one of the new features added in Microsoft Dynamics CRM 2016 to enhance working with documents. This is the support for OneDrive for Business. OneDrive for Business is part of Office 365, and is made available with enterprise packages. There is a difference between the regular OneDrive and OneDrive for Business, which is also based on SharePoint. For this integration, only OneDrive for Business and part of the Office 365 subscriptions are available for integration.

OneNote Integration

OneNote integration has been added with Dynamics CRM 2015 Update 1 to support a more in-depth way to collect and organize notes on records enabled for this functionality. This integration is based on and requires SharePoint integration to be already configured in your Organization. The `OneNote` file will be created and stored in a SharePoint document location assigned to the respective record:

1. To enable **OneNote**, once you have SharePoint configured as described in *Chapter 3, Dynamics CRM Customization*, in the section *Working with Documents*, navigate to **Settings** | **Document Management**. Since we already have SharePoint configured, your screen will look like the following screenshot:

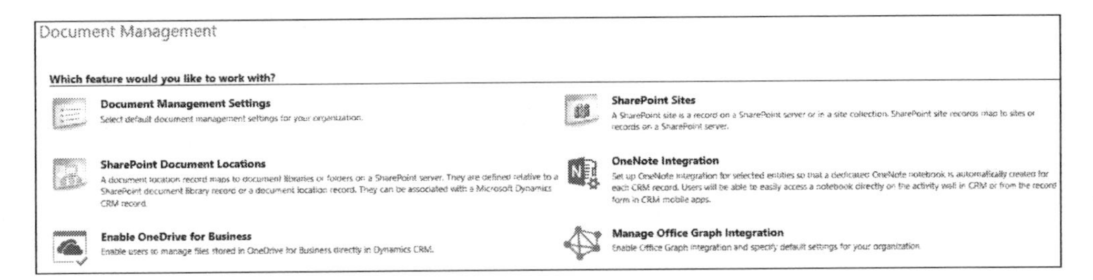

2. Here, select **OneNote Integration**. You are prompted to select the entities where the OneNote functionality is enabled, as shown in the following screenshot:

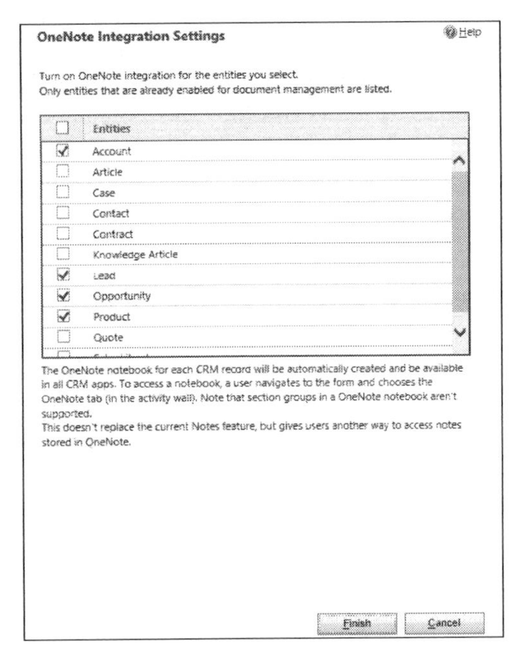

Be aware that only entities that are configured for SharePoint document management can support OneNote integration. If one of the entities you need OneNote enabled is not in the displayed list, make sure it is configured for SharePoint first.

3. Once you are satisfied with the selection of entities, click on **Finish**. The configuration process completes, and now you can start adding and editing OneNote files for individual records.
4. Once you navigate to a record, looking at the Social Pane described earlier in this chapter, we can now observe a new tab called **ONENOTE**. Click on it and you will find a newly created document called **Untitled**, as shown in the following screenshot:

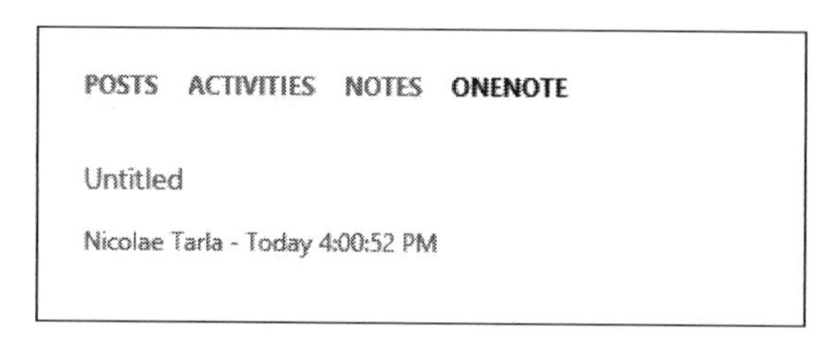

5. Click on the **Untitled** link, and the document will open in OneNote. Now you can start editing and taking notes. They will all be associated with your record automatically:

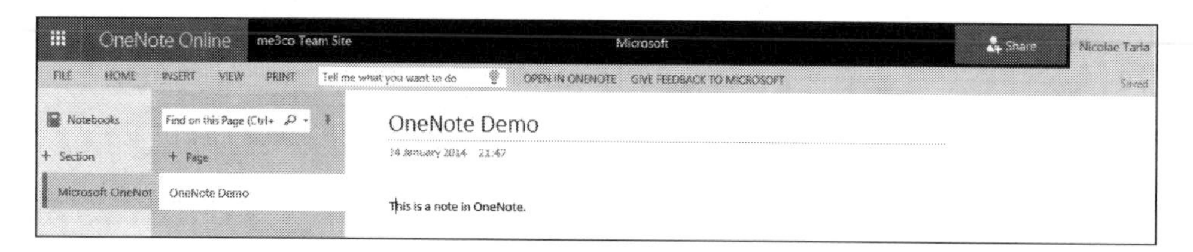

Make sure to rename the section and then refresh the record view to force the refresh of the name of the link to the `OneNote` file. The name **Untitled** will be replaced with the name you gave to your section tab.

Interactive Service Hub

New with Microsoft Dynamics CRM 2016 is the **Interactive Service Hub**. It was designed with a simplified interface based on the tablet and mobile application. This service hub is specifically built around the functionality used mostly by customer service representatives.

The design revolves around functional requirements and ease of access to information. The functionality around the **Service** tab is brought forward, with access to Accounts, Contacts, Cases, and a few other entities, along with specifically designed interactive dashboard for Tiers 1 and 2 of customer service:

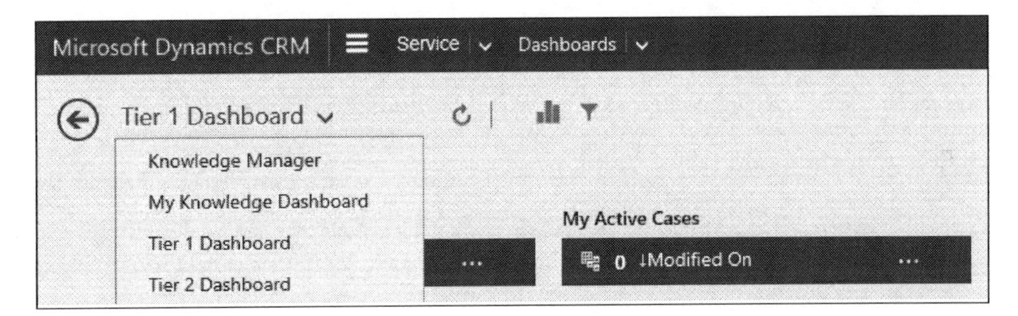

Tier 1 Dashboard brings an interactive experience, which allows a customer service representative to interact with the various elements directly on the dashboard. Various **Streams** present grouped information in vertical columns on the dashboard. Data in Streams is aggregated from views or queues.

The Streams comprise multiple **Tiles** which present various record specific data. Tiles can be expanded to show all the information, or can be selected to reveal a ribbon of available actions, as seen in the following screenshot:

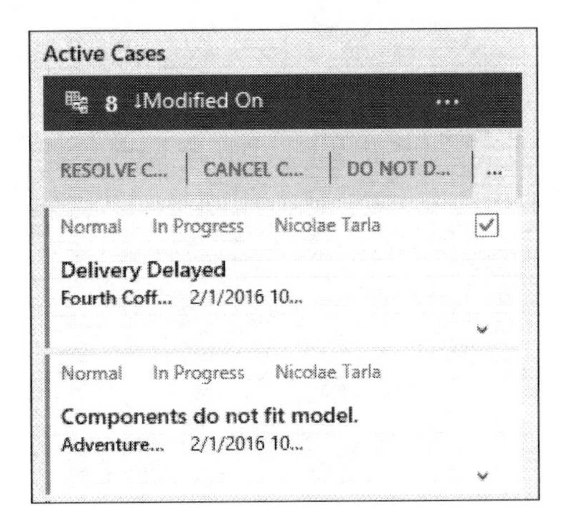

Within this dashboard we have the ability to restrict the presented data to a specific period of time, as shown in the following screenshot:

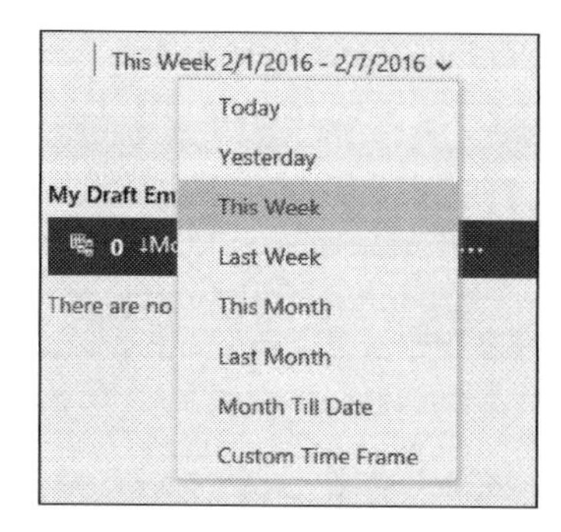

In addition, we can create global and visual filters to restrict the amount of data shown on the dashboard. We do this from the icons to the right of the refresh button, as shown in the following screenshot:

The **Tier 2 Dashboard** brings more visual elements to the table. By default, this dashboard includes a single **Stream**, as seen in the **Tier 1 Dashboard**, along with various visualization Tiles, as seen in the next screenshot:

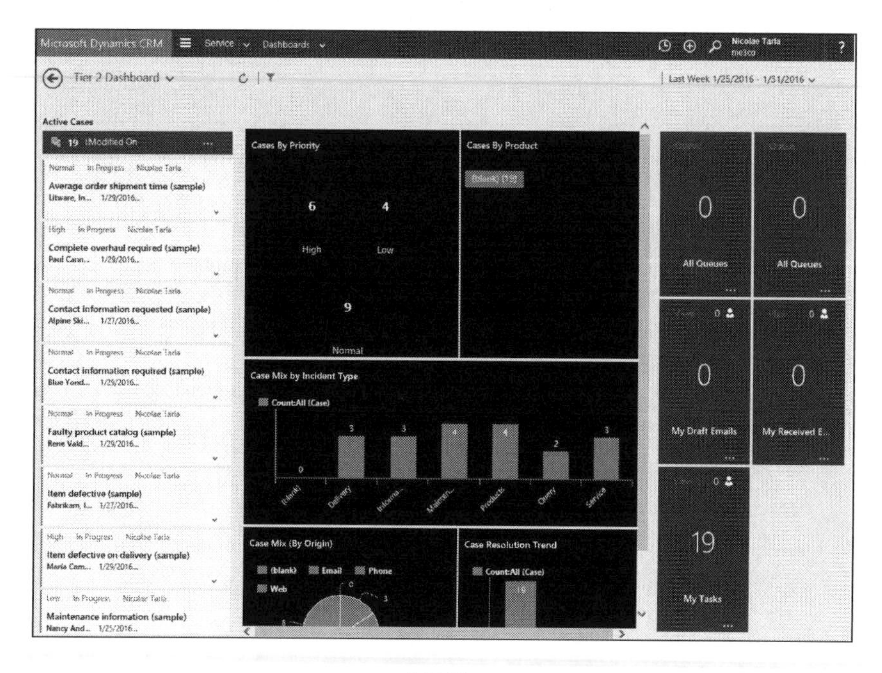

The additional tiles allow a user to drill down into the data, and the entire dashboard refreshes to reflect the additional subset of data selected. As such, drilling down into Product-related cases by case type, the refreshed dashboard will look like the following screenshot:

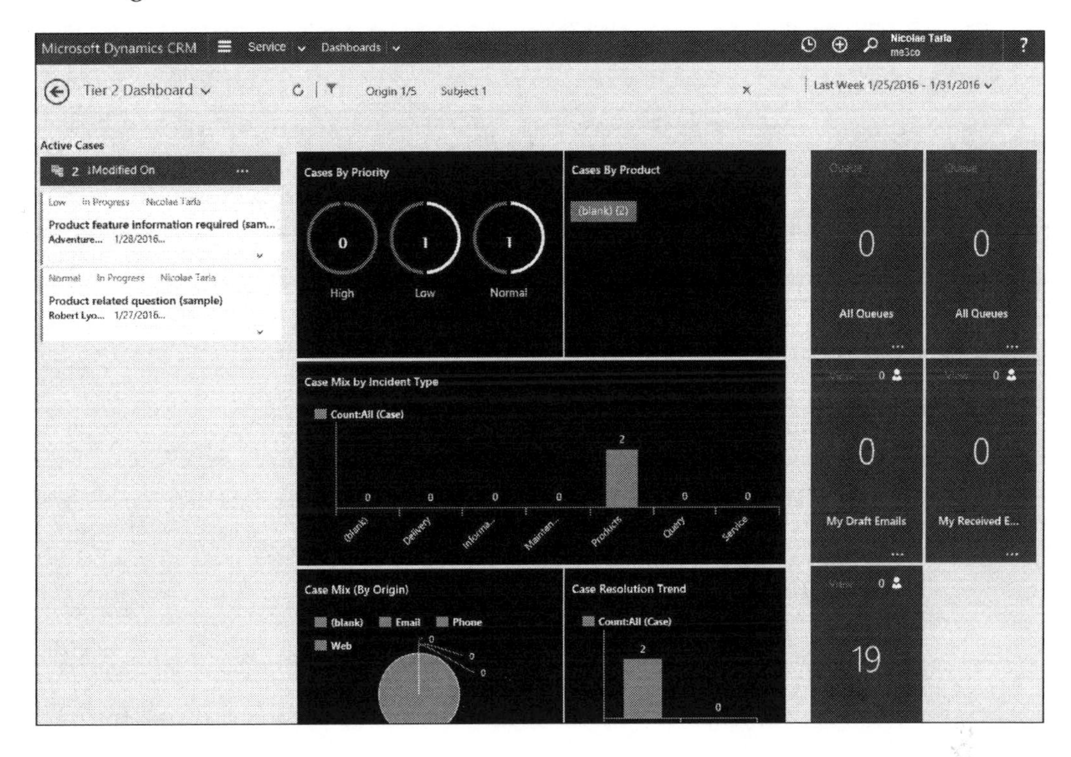

In addition to drilling down on the graphical tiles, using the Interactive Service Hub, we can drill down on a **Stream Tile** to get to a specific record. For example, selecting a specific Case in the Active Cases stream takes us to a streamlined view of the Case, as described in the following screenshot:

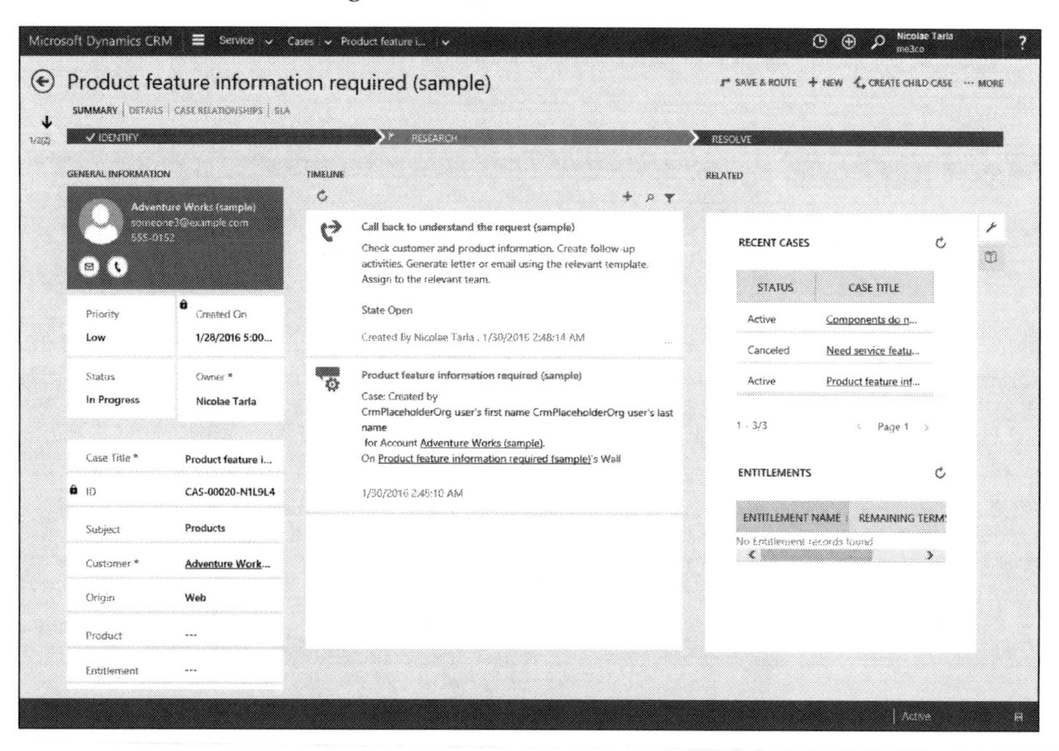

The new streamlined Case view is now comprised of various tiles presenting Case-related entities data. The Business Process Flow shows minimized at the top, presenting only the stage names. Clicking on any of the stages expands the list of fields related to the respective stage as described in the following screenshot:

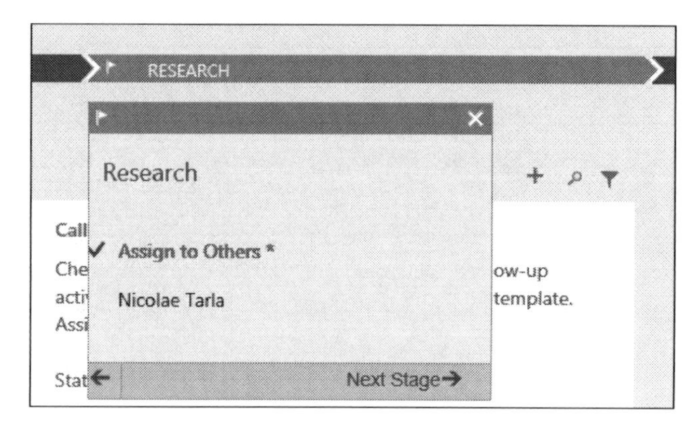

On the current stage you also get the options to navigate to the next stage, or to a previously completed one.

Record navigation is related to the Stream we started from, with the ability to navigate to the previous or next Case in this example by clicking the up/down arrows, as well as showing the location in the stream, as seen in the following screenshot:

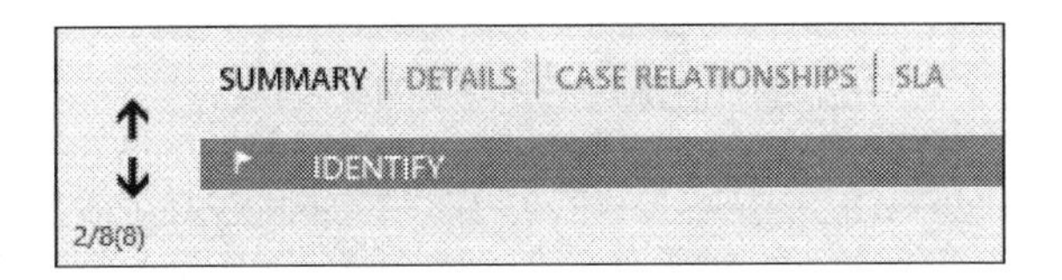

An open record can be easily processed and interacted with by taking advantage of the functionality presented to the top right of the record screen, as seen here:

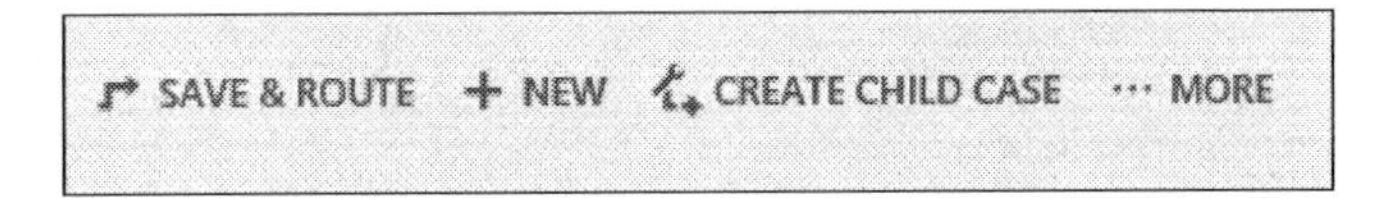

Here we have options to route a record to another team or user for processing, create new records, create child records, or interact directly with the record through the available actions. We can also change the process assigned to a record from this location.

Various sections on this record layout can be accessed as tabs under the record name. All forms include one or more tabs, depending on the record type. The default options when looking at a Case include **SUMMARY, DETAILS, CASE RELATIONSHIPS**, and **SLA**, as seen in the following screenshot:

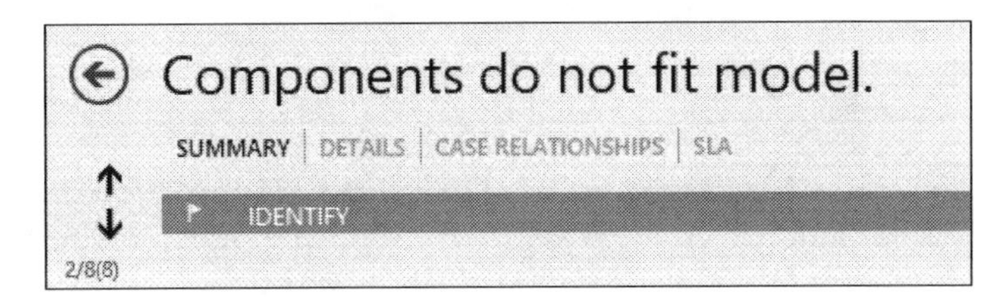

The actual record form is divided into several distinct sections. On the left side is the **GENERAL INFORMATION** section including the main customer card, presenting generic information about the customer and options to contact him/her, as seen in the following screenshot:

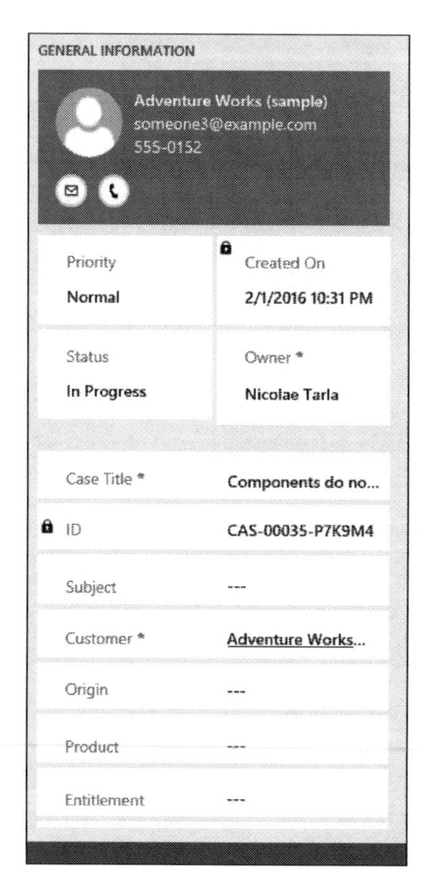

It is followed by several tiles and the generic record details.

Next, in the center of the form, we find the **TIMELINE**. This section captures all activities and interactions related to the current record. This functionality is quite similar to the Social Pane described at the beginning of this chapter. The layout and design is enhanced to match the new form layout, as seen in the following screenshot:

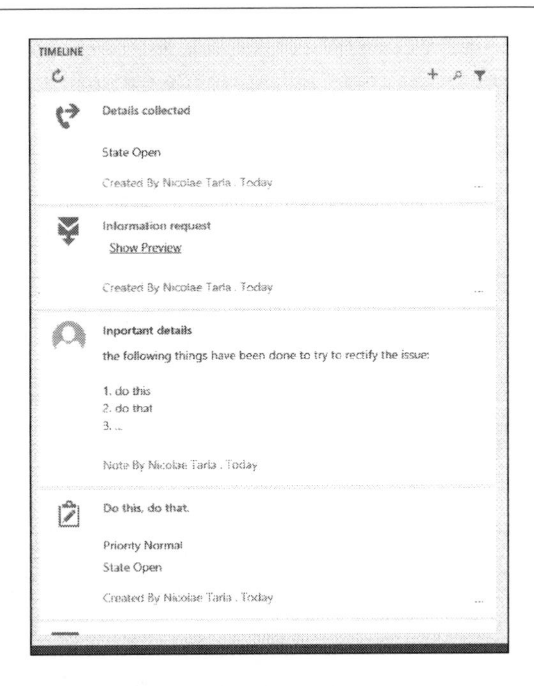

Further to the right on the Case form we have the **RELATED** section. In here we can find information about related **records, cases,** and **entitlements,** as seen in the following image:

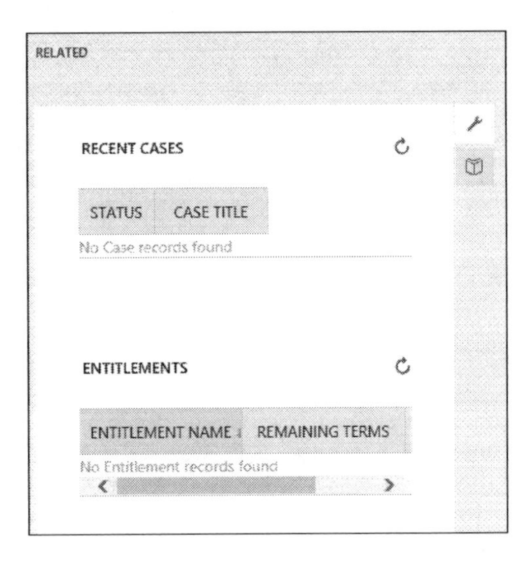

Observe the little tab on the top right-hand side of the section. This allows you to navigate into the **Knowledge Management** section. We will be looking at this functionality in the next section.

These tabs are sensitive to the type of record they surface on, and various tabs are presented depending on the record type we are currently working with. For example, on a Contact form, the tabs will include the **Recent Opportunities**, **Recent Cases**, and **Entitlements**, as depicted in the following image:

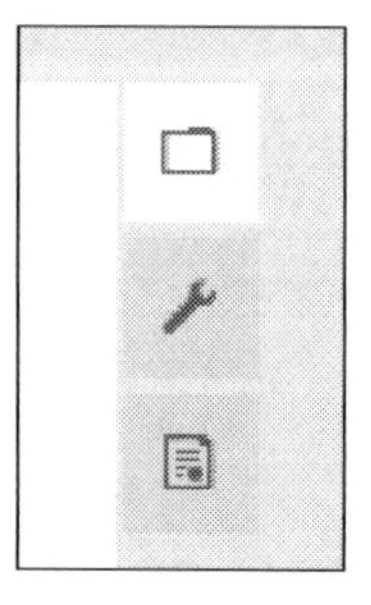

As mentioned earlier, the Interactive Service Hub revolves around the service functionality. As such, the navigation is restricted to functionality available as part of the business requirements and actions in scope. The default navigation looks like the following screenshot:

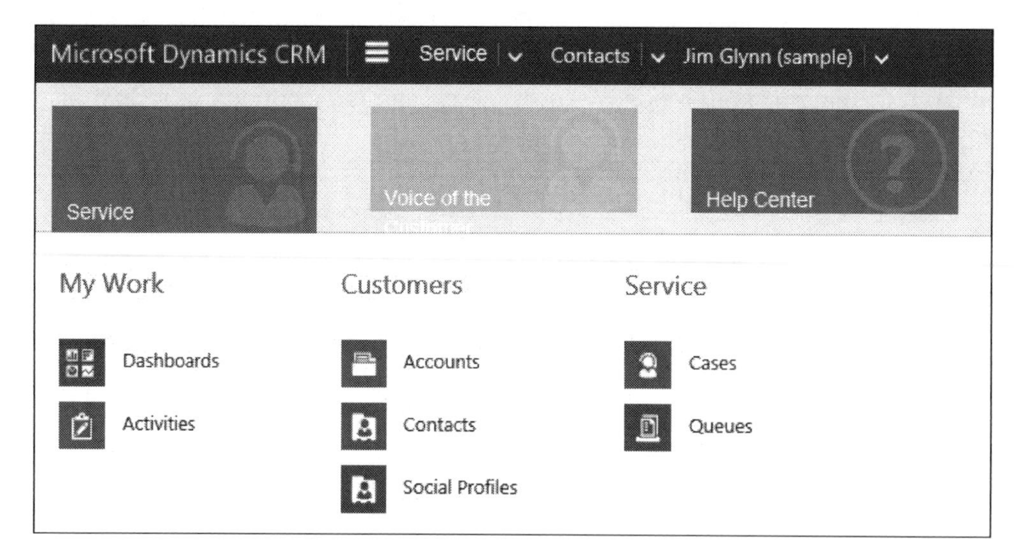

Navigating to an entity, such as Activities for example, presents the familiar views already configured and made available in the new interface. It is easy to change the default view to any of the views available in the Organization, as seen in the following screenshot, showing **My Activities**:

Views present the familiar filtering options, with the ability to sort by any of the visible columns, as well as, in this case, due dates. The standard search in a view is available, as well as filtering by letter at the bottom of the view.

On an Activities view we have the option to generate new records at the top right of the screen. We can create from here new records for the various activity types available.

Overall, the Interactive Service Hub has been built to give service personnel the ability to interact directly with data in a streamlined and simplified manner, built around business processes rather than structured organization entities. The interface is built based on the previous mobile user experience, with large form elements that work really well for touch interaction. As other parts of the platform adopt this interface, we will possibly be seeing a lot more functionality made available to users.

Enhanced Knowledge Management

Added with the Interactive Service Hub presented above, the **Knowledge Management** section has been completely revamped. This version gets us closer to an actual CMS functionality, where we can now create complex articles with various formatting possibilities and images. Furthermore, an enhanced knowledge management process has been added to handle the publishing and approval process.

As one of the most important aspects of customer service, knowledge management gets a boost with Microsoft Dynamics CRM 2016. Rich content authoring enhancements now allow copy and paste from other formatting applications such as Microsoft Office Word, as well as support for source code and HTML editing. This greatly enhances the capabilities of formatting articles. Along with formatting, we now finally have the ability to embed images and videos in our knowledge-based articles. Along with formatting, we can now create visually appealing articles that look just like a well-designed brochure or web page.

With all the formatting and visually enhanced capabilities, we now need a way to track our changes. For this reason, versioning now becomes part of the new Knowledge Management. We can create major and minor versions of documentation. We can thus publish one version while working on the new version.

But what good are all these features if we can't target our multilingual client base? Now, starting with this new incarnation of Knowledge Management, we can do just that. We have support for article translations in 164 languages at the time of writing. All translations are linked, to relate them together as needed. A knowledge manager can select all the required translations and assign them to various third parties tasked with producing the translations.

And to wrap all this information together and make it easier for content managers to keep track of the entire knowledge base, the Knowledge Management Dashboard surfaces contextual information and provides a quick glimpse of the authoring process. The following screenshots shows the **Knowledge Manager** dashboard:

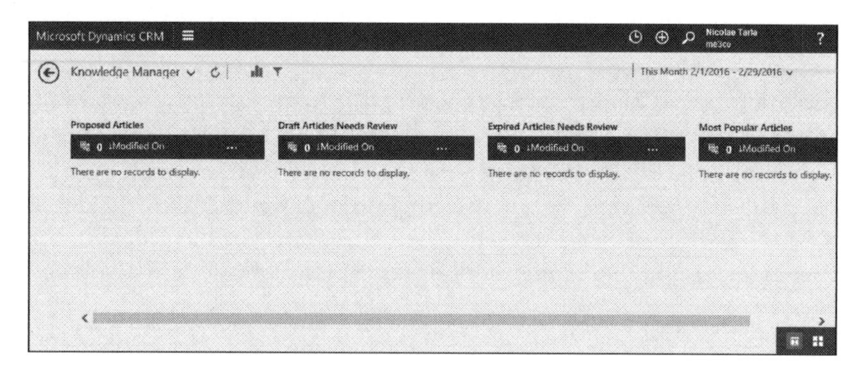

We can also re-format this dashboard by switching from Stream View to Tile View, using the selection at the bottom right of the screen. Tile View is shown in the following screenshot:

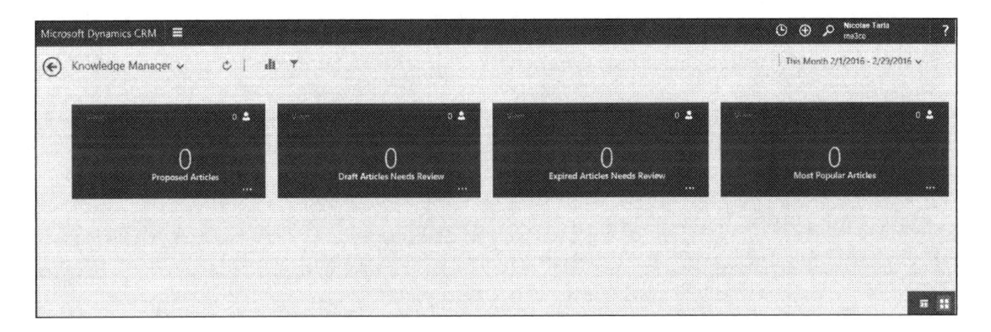

For the Knowledge Base editors, a separate dashboard presents the aggregated information required in a tiled format. Here we get quick access to relevant information for this specific role, including an active articles stream and several tiles with articles categorized by various metrics. The following screenshot shows this dashboard:

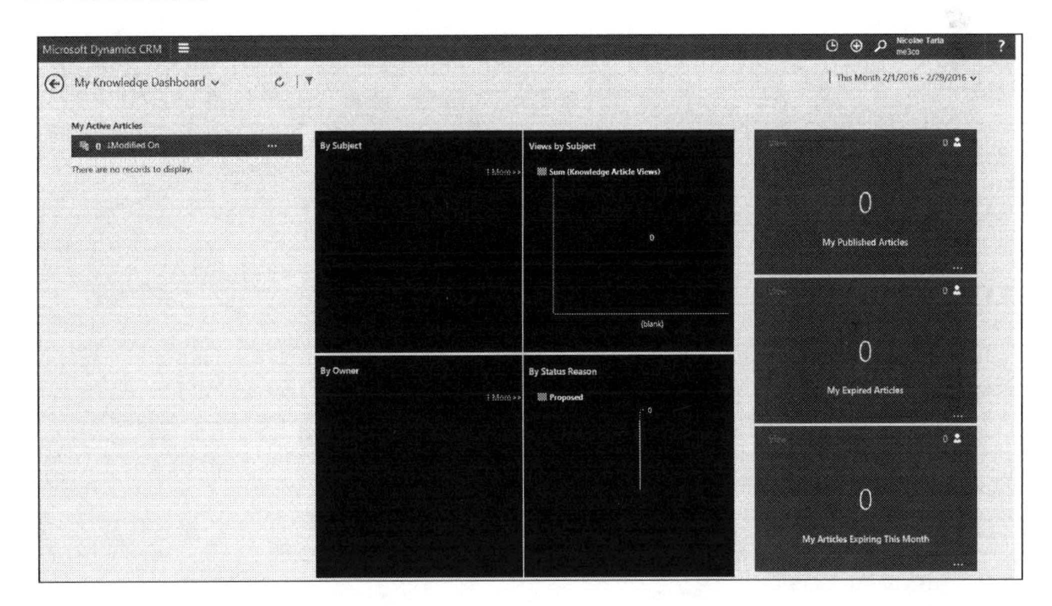

Article Life Cycle

The process of creating and managing articles has now received a face lift with Microsoft Dynamics CRM 2016. A pre-defined process flow has been provided with the platform to guide developers and system customizers in the right direction. The beauty of it is that it's a very functional process that in many cases is sufficient for the task at hand.

We can start this cycle from the **My Active Articles** view. We get to it by navigating to **Service | Knowledge Articles**, as shown in the next image:

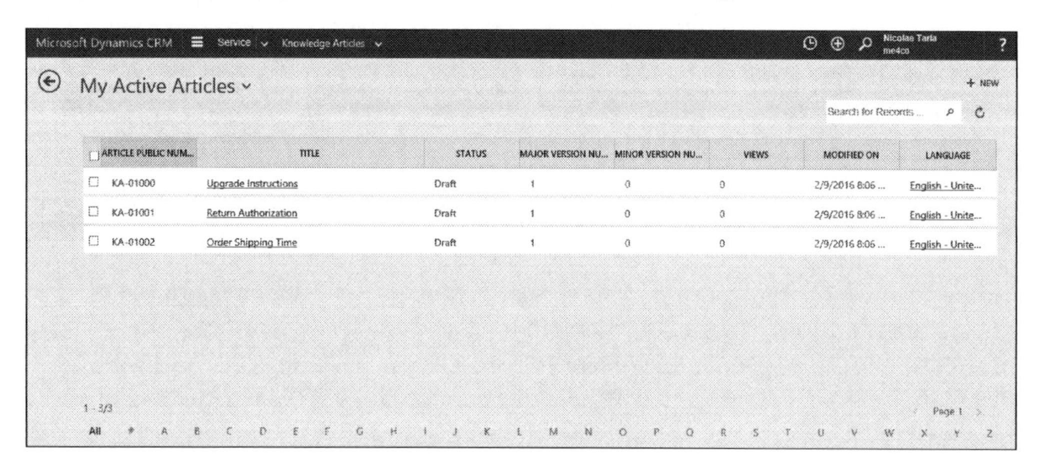

Observe the ability to filter by letter at the bottom of the view, to search for a record at the top right, and most importantly to select one or more records at the same time. Having the ability to select multiple records presents us with an extended menu of options at the top right of the screen, including the following options:

- **Delete**
- **Assign**
- **Create Major Version**
- **Create Minor Version**
- **Approve**
- **Publish**
- **Revert to Draft**
- **Archive**
- **Send to Trash**
- **Add to Queue**

This menu is presenting options depending on the selection type and the number of items selected.

Creating a new article is as simple as clearing all selected articles. The menu changes to present us with a single option for a New article. Click **New**.

The **New Knowledge Article** screen is presented, as seen in the following image:

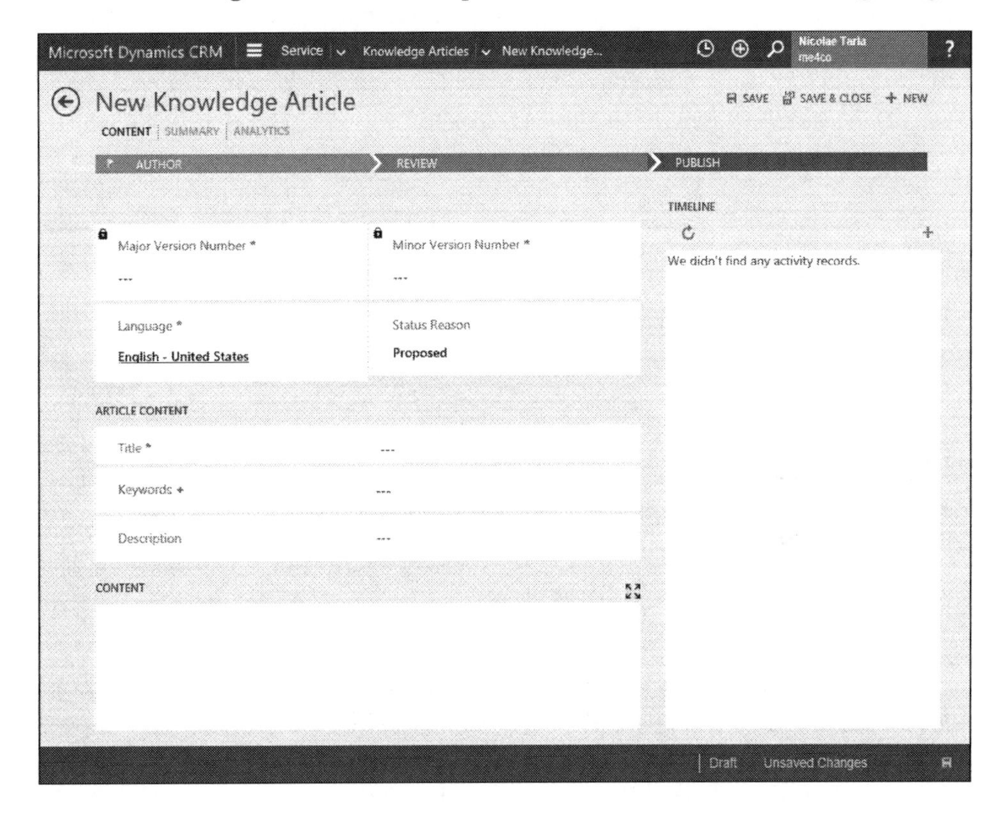

Let's pause for a moment and look at the various elements of this form.

First off, we have the tab navigation right under the article title. On a default new article, the out of the box options include the following:

- **CONTENT**
- **SUMMARY**
- **ANALYTICS**

We can navigate through the tabs to get access to additional data fields, as well as related records.

Next, to the top right of the form we have options for working with the current record. We can perform actions such as saving the record, saving and creating a new one, or simply creating a new article. Clicking on **New** without saving the current record prompts for confirmation to determine if the current record can be discarded or needs to be saved, as seen in the following screenshot:

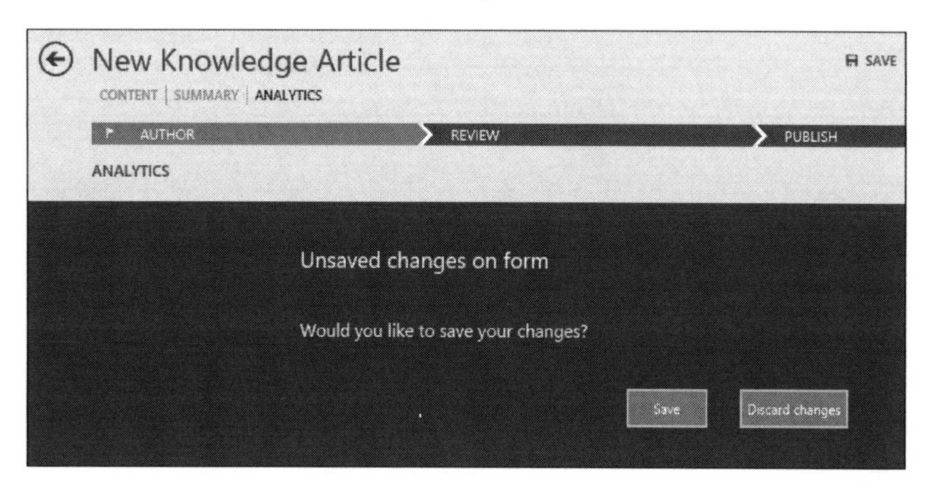

Further down, at the bottom of the form, we see the article status, in this case Draft, as well as the save status and command. Once we save the article, the major and minor version numbers are generated automatically, starting with a major version 1 and minor version 0. To adjust these values as we work with the article, we have options to Create Major and Minor Versions as needed.

The **CONTENT** of the article is where some of the most exiting features are for most content publishers. The **CONTENT** area is presented in the following screenshot:

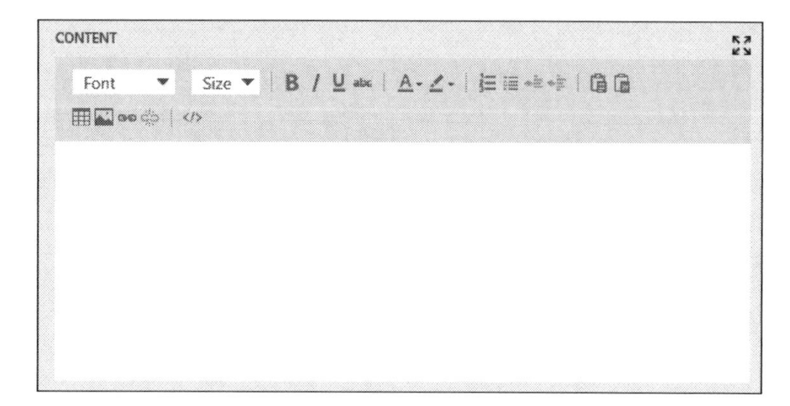

Here we now have a ribbon to allow us to format text, as well as options to drop down into code for additional formatting behaviors.

Keep in mind that in this window we can now also copy and paste already-formatted text and images from Microsoft Office Word documents.

Editing an article now becomes a job as simple as creating a nice word document. This functionality is in line with most modern **Content Management Systems** (**CMS**). A formatted article with included artifacts is presented in the following screenshot:

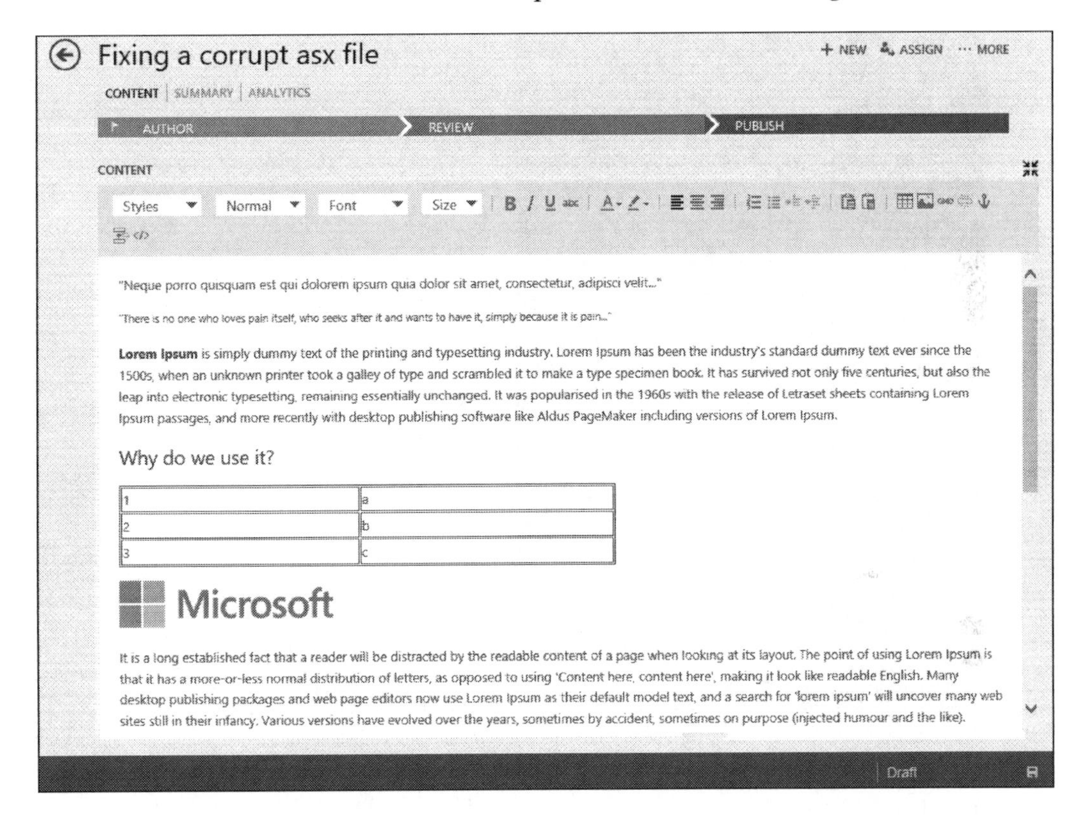

Observe how the Content area is maximized to take the entire form, thus making it easy for the author to focus on the content creation. This can be achieved using the four arrows icon at the top right of the area. When completed, we can minimize it back using the same button.

Once we are satisfied with the content created, we can proceed into the review stage. Go to the process flow at the top of the form, expand the **Author** stage by clicking on it, and at the bottom of the pop-up window, click on **Next Stage**. Make sure the article is marked for review before proceeding to the **Review** stage, otherwise you will be prompted to do so.

For reviewing the article, it should usually be assigned to a content reviewer. You can do that from the ribbon by selecting the **Assign** option.

The reviewer now has the ability to inspect the article and decide if it needs additional work or if it's ready for publishing. Clicking on the **Review** stage expands the window with the options to mark the article as either **Approved** or **Rejected**. If you select **Rejected**, you are prompted to communicate a reason for rejection, as depicted in the following screenshot:

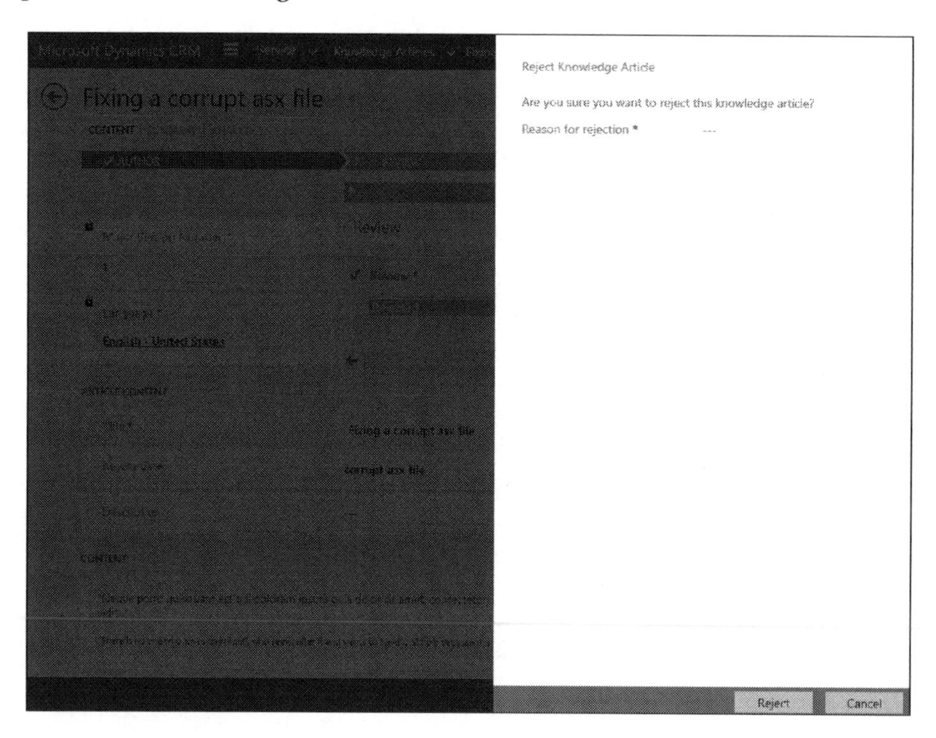

Once an article is rejected, you will observe the Rejection comments showing up on the timeline, and the process flow changes to add an **Update Content** stage.

Upon update, mark the content as updated and proceed to the next stage. Here we can go into setting the publishing information, scheduling the articles and setting an expiration date.

Schedule, Publish, Expire

Scheduling articles to publish is as simple as selecting articles from the **Active Articles** view and selecting the **Publish** option in the menu. Once we do this, we can start scheduling the publishing process. The following screenshot depicts the options we are presented with on publishing:

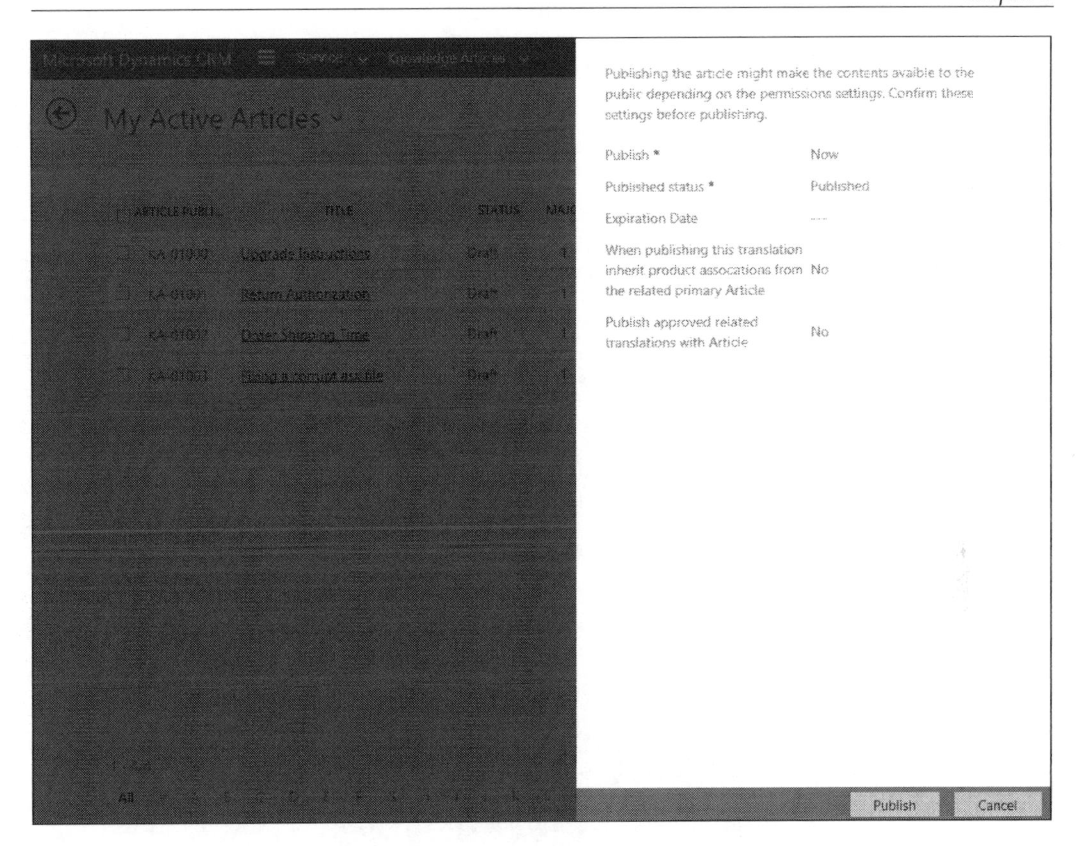

If you want to publish in the future, select the option from the **Publish** drop-down menu, and select the date and time when the article will become available.

Setting up an expiration date allows us to define the last day and time when the article will be available for users to consume. This is usually a good idea for time-sensitive materials that require a refresh at timed intervals.

Article Context Search

Besides the default search on a view of articles, we have the ability to drill down into specific articles from either the **My Knowledge Dashboard** or the **Knowledge Manager Dashboard**. We can do this by adding a dashboard global filter, in the streams by re-ordering the items, or in the graphical tiles by clicking on a specific section. For example, on a tile showing two different status reasons for articles, clicking on one filters the entire dashboard elements to the new selection. The next screenshot shows the tile for selection:

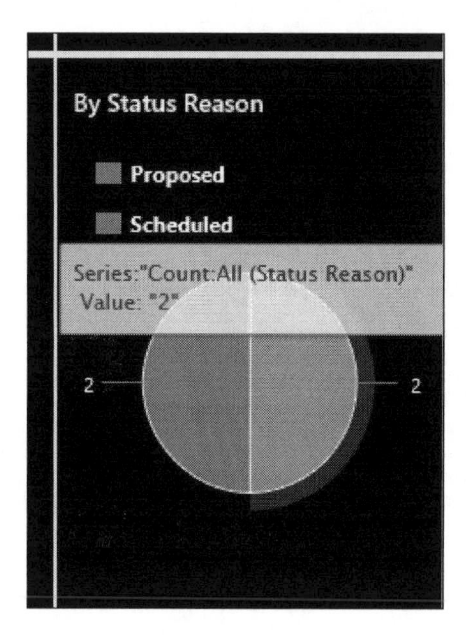

For additional details on the Knowledge Management process and working with the new Knowledge Management features, see the documentation provided by Microsoft:

`https://www.microsoft.com/en-US/dynamics/crm-customer-center/user-s-guide-for-the-new-interactive-service-hub.aspx#bkmk_KMProcessinCRM`

Office Delve recommendations

Office Delve is part of Office 365, and it allows us to surface personalized content from Office 365 based on the items you are working on, the people you are collaborating with, and filter all based on the permissions you have in the organization.

This tool is one of the more productive applications when used by the entire organization. Based on Office Graph, it allows a user to find the most relevant content in the smallest amount of time.

In order to take advantage of these features, the new Interactive Service Hub allows us to create dashboards in Microsoft Dynamics CRM to surface this same content. This way, a user working on this platform does not have to leave the screen to go to another application; he/she can find the information needed directly from within CRM.

The following items are required to enable Delve integration with Dynamics CRM:

- Microsoft Dynamics CRM Online
- Office 365 Subscription
- SharePoint Online with at least one SharePoint site
- Server-Based SharePoint Integration configured

The following are the steps required to enable Delve integration with Dynamics CRM:

1. In order to enable Delve, go to **Settings** | **Document Management** | **Manage Office Graph Integration**, as seen in the following screenshot:

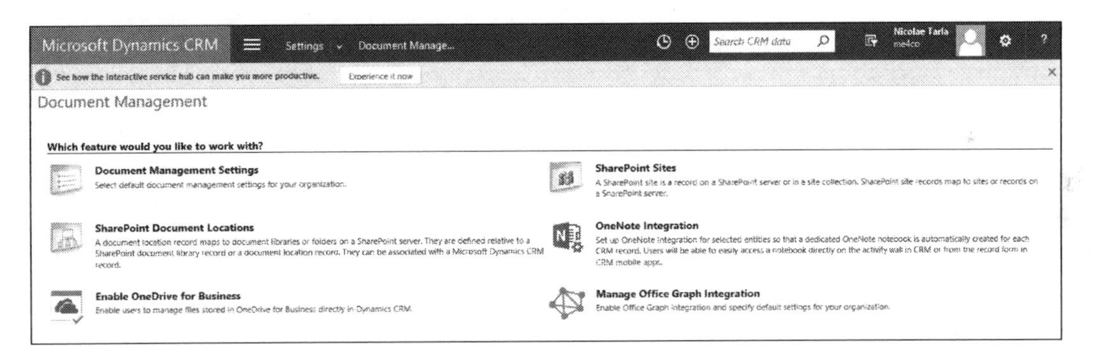

2. In the pop-up window, check the **Enable Office Graph integration** check box, and click **Next**. Click **Finish** on the next screen. With this setting enabled, you are now ready to create a Delve dashboard.

As mentioned at the beginning of this book, all configurations and customizations should be structured in a solution package. As such, create a new solution package or open an existing one:

1. In order to create a Dashboard that can host the Delve stream, go to Dashboards.
2. From the **New** button, select the **Dashboard** option. Observe the new option added with Microsoft Dynamics CRM 2016 and the Interactive Service Hub. This allows you to create dashboards with streams. The following screenshot shows this option in the context of a solution:

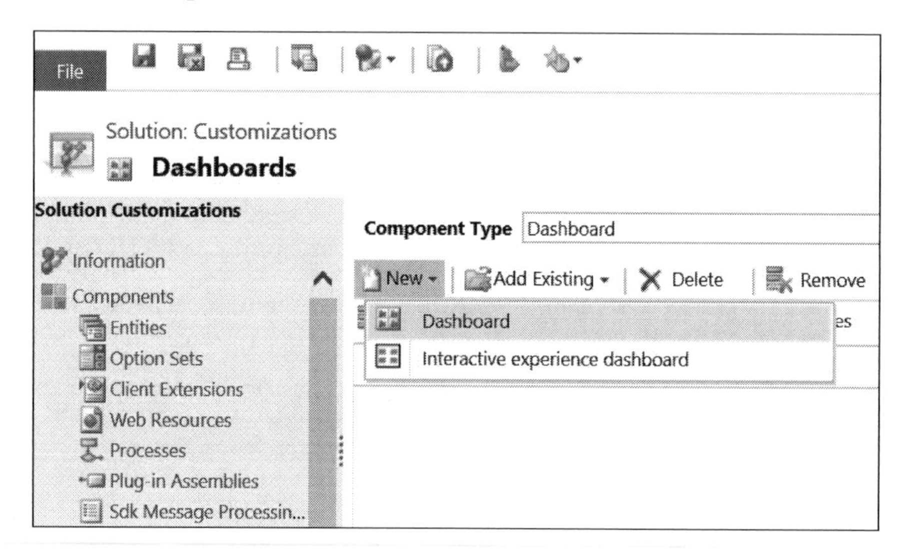

When you choose to create an Interactive experience dashboard, observe the additional dashboard options presented. We are no longer limited to a maximum of six elements on a Dashboard. In addition, we have choices for **Multi-Stream** and **Single-Stream** dashboards. In a **Single-Stream** dashboard we now have formats for five, three, and two columns, as seen in the following screenshot:

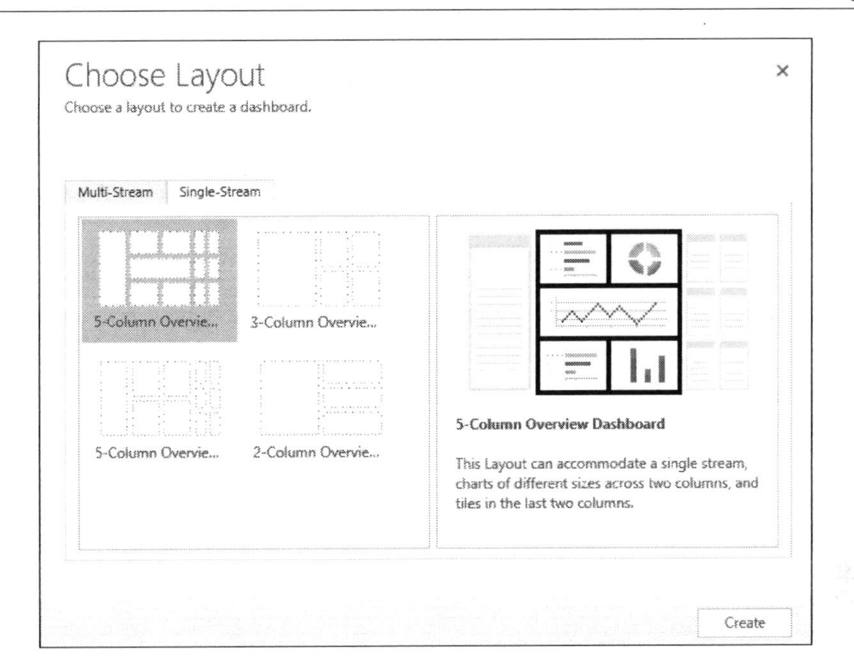

In order to create a Dashboard that contains a Delve stream, you need to complete the following steps:

1. Select **New | Dashboard** and choose one of the available classic layouts.
2. In the new screen that pops up, observe, both on the ribbon and within each dashboard section, the new option for **Delve**, as seen in the following screenshot:

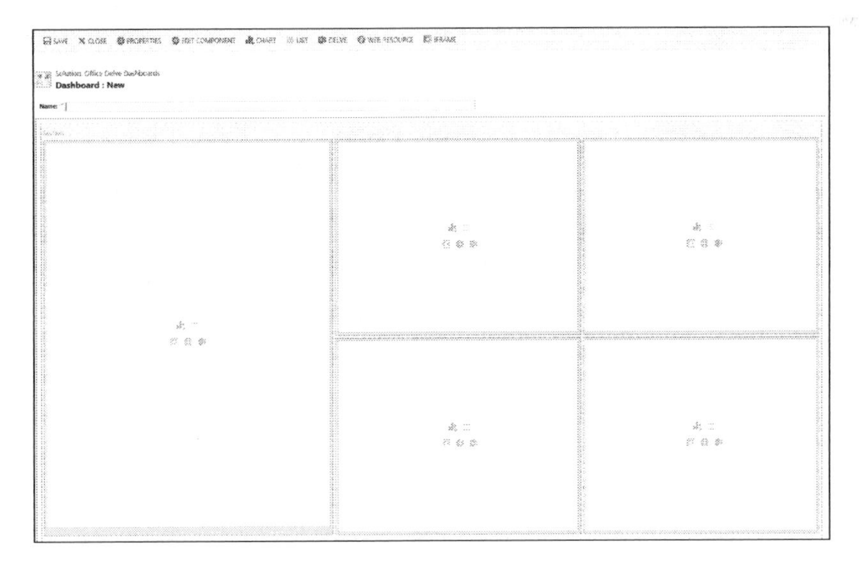

3. Clicking this option turns the dashboard section into a **Trending Documents** section. This will render a new stream on the dashboard, as shown in the following screenshot:

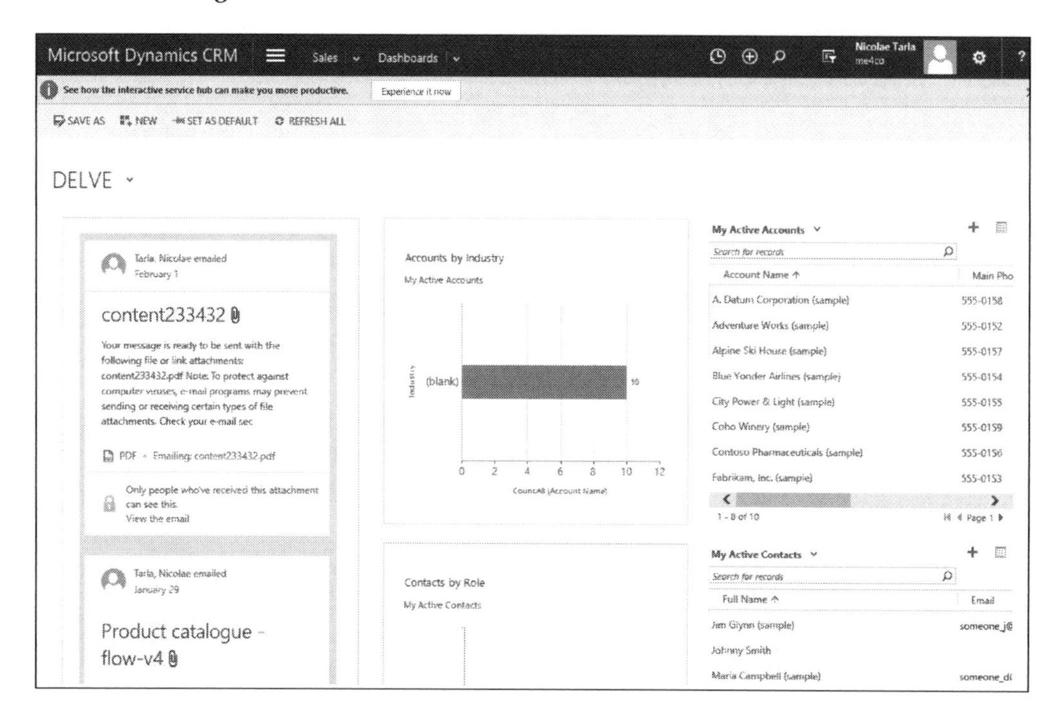

For more details on Delve integration, see the CRM help and training portal:

`https://www.microsoft.com/en-us/dynamics/crm-customer-center/view-relevant-and-trending-information-with-office-delve.aspx`

Field Service Capabilities

After the acquisition of FieldOne by Microsoft, the solution became available to be installed on a new instance of Dynamics CRM Online 2015, Update 1 or newer.

FieldOne Sky is an intelligent field service management solution. Its functionality revolves around enhanced management and scheduling for work orders. The scheduling engine is the highlight of this solution, where we are presented with three types of actions:

- Manual scheduling
- Schedule assistant
- Automated routing scheduling

The friendliness of the UI and the ability to provide drag and drop on a scheduling board makes using this product very easy and intuitive. Coupled with a powerful backend engine to validate and recalculate schedules, this is an ideal solution for field service. Add to that extensive support for mobile, and you have a complete end to end package for managing resources in the field.

The amount of business insight that can be gained using this solution is of great value. Starting with a real-time view into the performance of your business and field service, analyzing of large amounts of data to determine patterns and issues with standard scheduling as well as extensive reporting capabilities for operations analysis and strategy, this solution is a great add-on to the Dynamics CRM family.

The process of adding the FieldOne solution is the same as adding the previously available Insights and Office 365 Groups solution:

1. From the Office 365 portal navigate to CRM. In the Manage all CRM Online instances select the trial or production instance where you want the solution added. Click on **Solutions**:

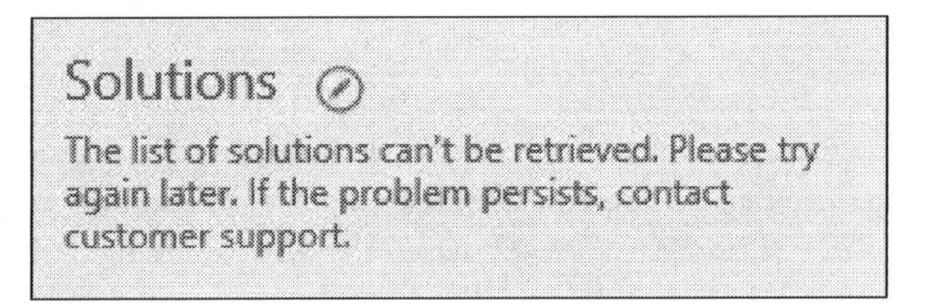

2. On the next screen, select the **FieldOne Sky** solution and click **Install**. Note that the installation will take a short while:

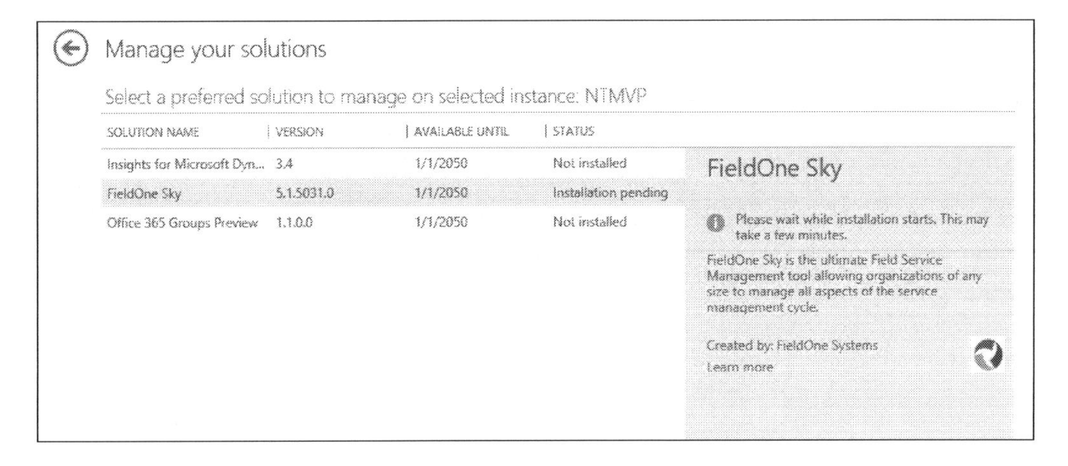

3. Once the solution is installed, navigate to your CRM instance and validate that FieldOne Sky is installed. If your standard navigation is not customized, you can do that by looking for a new tab, added to the top navigation and named FieldOne Sky.

For additional details on the functionality and customization of FieldOne Sky, see the following documentation:

`http://www.fieldone.com/products`

Adxstudio Portals

Adxstudio solution has been one of the best portal solutions on the market for a long time. Before the release of Microsoft Dynamics CRM 2016, Microsoft acquired the Adxstudio solution. This is a much anticipated feature, but at the time of writing, an updated version built under the Microsoft umbrella is not yet available.

Adxstudio provides an advanced portal platform and **Application Lifecycle Management** (**ALM**) solution built entirely on Microsoft Dynamics CRM. As such, it makes total sense to see this solution coming in the near future.

For features and details, see the documentation provided for the current version:

`https://www.adxstudio.com/adxstudio-portals/`

Voice of the Customer

Another new feature added to Dynamics CRM 2016 is Voice of the Customer. This provides us the ability to collect customer feedback directly in Dynamics CRM. We can now design surveys, collect results, invite people to participate in our surveys, and also trigger various actions on the Dynamics CRM platform based on the collected results. We can analyze these results, report on them, and present our results in dashboards for monitoring.

Voice of the Customer is another one of the add-on solutions that must be installed in your organization by an administrator. We do this by navigating from the Office 365 Admin Center to **Admin** | **CRM**. A new window opens and we see our organization(s) listed here. Select the organization where you want this solution to be added, and click on **Solutions**:

CRM Online Administration Center

INSTANCES | UPDATES

Manage all CRM Online instances

NAME	STATE	TYPE
me3co	ready	Production instance

me3co
PRODUCTION INSTANCE
Microsoft Dynamics CRM Online 2016
EDIT NOTIFICATIONS
Purpose
Add purpose by editing instance
Solutions

Among the listed solutions, find the one called **Voice of the Customer**. At the time of writing, this solution is at version 8.0.301.2.

Select **Install** to get this solution configured in your Organization:

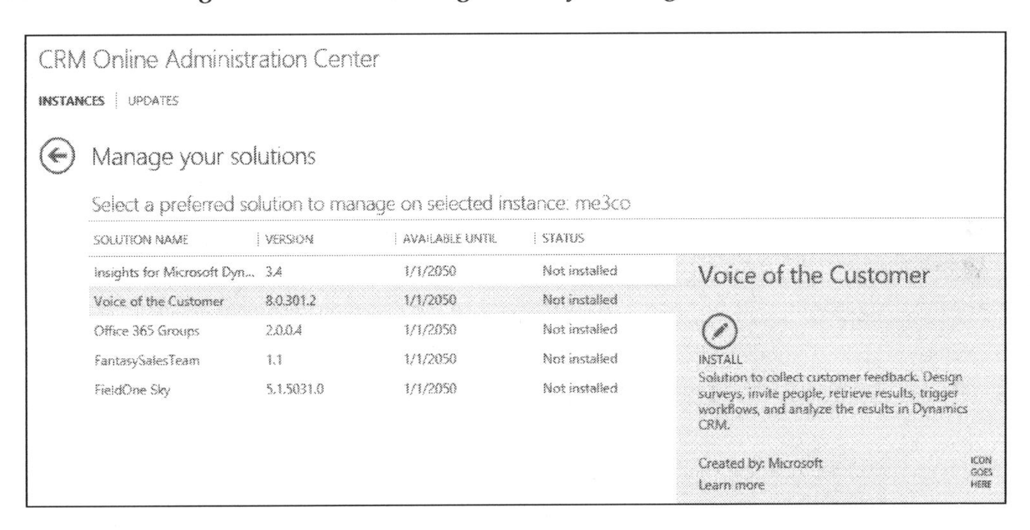

Accept the **Terms of Service** and click **Install**. This will configure the solution in your organization, and will take a moment. The status of **Installation Pending** is displayed in the **Manage your solutions** view until completed.

To verify the solution is installed, you can navigate within your Dynamics CRM organization to **Settings | Solutions** and make sure that the **Voice of the Customer** solution is installed. You will also observe that the entire organization navigation has been re-organized.

> The survey functionality is tightly integrated and requires an Azure account. When a survey is published, the definition is stored in Azure Storage. The responses are passed through Azure Service Bus before they are retrieved and stored in Microsoft Dynamics CRM. All these configurations are available by navigating to **Settings | VoC Configurations**. This being a preview feature, configuration might not be as straightforward as other features. For a trial setup of this functionality, reach out to a technical partner for assistance.

When creating a survey using Voice of the Customer, the following steps are involved:

- Loading and defining images
- Designing themes
- Planning and designing the survey
- Distributing the survey

Working with images in surveys requires all the images to be loaded in Dynamics CRM first:

1. You do this from the navigation menu, by going to **Voice of the Customer | Images**. Select **New**, and on the new form, add information for **Name** and **Image Title**:

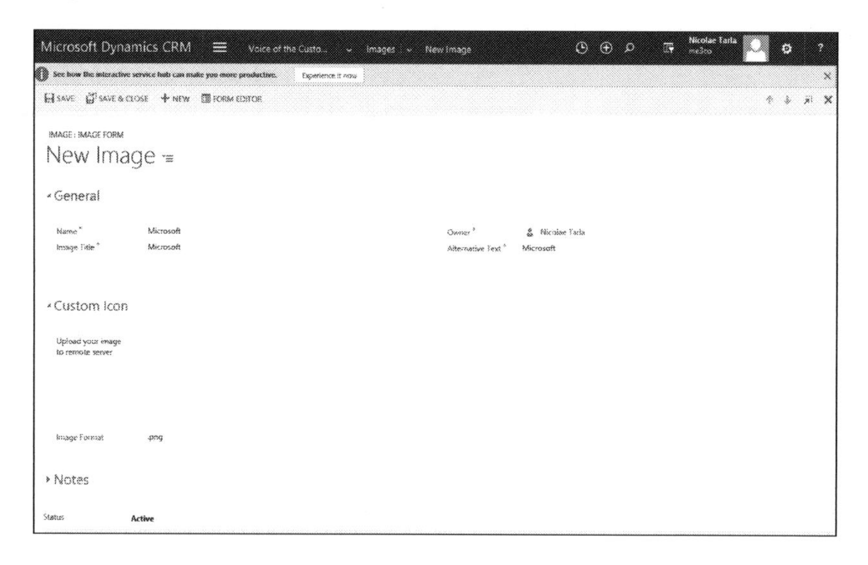

2. Once you click **Save**, you can browse to the image you want to upload, as seen in the following screenshot. Once done, click **Save**. Repeat the process for all the images you want to use in surveys.

Designing a survey theme is a process that requires a little bit of knowledge of web safe color definitions in hex values. Luckily, W3schools provides a chart at the following URL:

`http://www.w3schools.com/html/html_colorvalues.asp`

If you work with a web designer, or you have knowledge of CSS, you can further customize the look and feel of the survey. Don't worry, this is an optional step; you can create simple surveys without any web design skills:

1. To customize a survey theme, start by navigating to **Voice of the Customer | Themes**. Click on **New** to create a new one, or select an existing theme. You can also edit the default theme by selecting **Default** in the list of themes, as seen in the following screenshot:

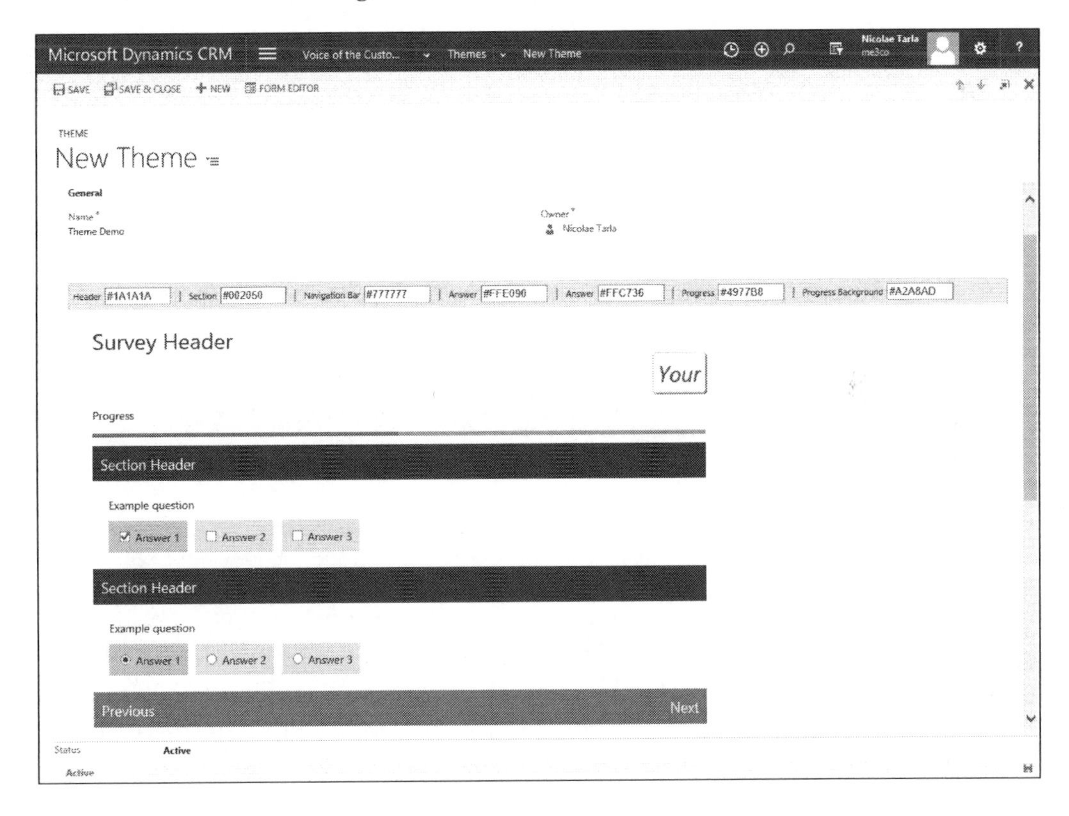

2. Give the theme a **Name**, adjust the colors as needed, edit the CSS if desired, and click on **Save**. Now you have a new customized theme.
3. With **Images** and **Themes** configured, we are now ready to create our first survey.

4. We do this by navigating to **Voice of the Customer | Surveys**. Select **New** to create a new survey. On the survey form, complete the necessary fields, as shown in the following screenshot:

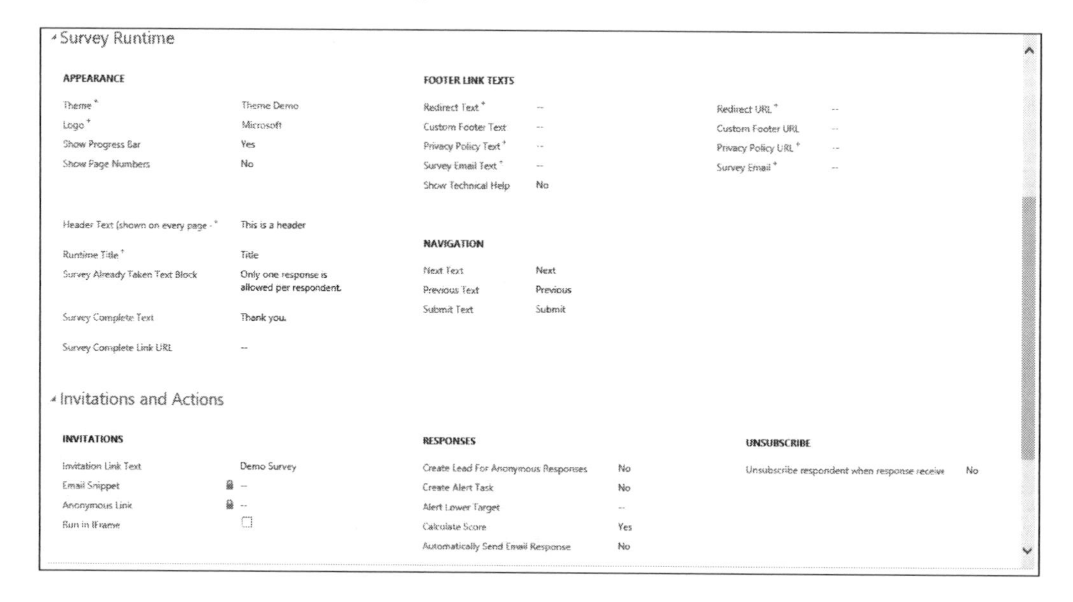

5. When done configuring the survey, you can preview it from the **Preview** ribbon button. Before you can make it available to users, you must **Publish** it. The options are on the ribbon, as shown in the following screenshot:

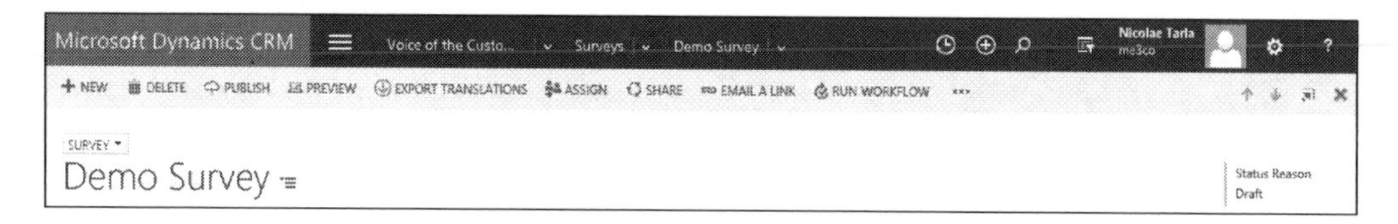

6. Once a survey is published, responses can be collected and reviewed on the **Survey Responses** views available, accessible by navigating to **Voice of the Customer | Survey Responses**.
7. Survey Outcomes are also accessible by navigating to **Voice of the Customer | Response Outcomes**. In addition, we have access to a pre-configured survey dashboard, as well as the ability to run reports on surveys by selecting a survey, and from the **MORE COMMANDS...** option, selecting **Run Report**.

Insight by InsideView

Microsoft Dynamics Insight is an add-on provided by Microsoft and powered by InsideView. It is included with Microsoft Dynamics CRM Online with a Professional license, and available as an add-on for Dynamics CRM On-Premise.

Insight is the equivalent of the InsideView for Sales Professionals edition. The functionality is made available in Dynamics CRM through integration with the InsideView platform. This package is available for Dynamics CRM version 4.0 or newer, and is available for both On-Premise and Online.

Insight is a data enriching tool that allows users of Dynamics CRM to validate and enhance their data, as well as generate new leads and close more opportunities.

Once configured, the Insight solution presents data within Dynamics CRM on the Account, Lead, Contact, and Opportunity entities in an iFrame on the actual record form. This makes it easy for users to get access to all the additional data provided by the solution.

Installation and Configuration

Depending on the type of Dynamics CRM deployment you have, the installation process is slightly different. An on-premise deployment involves additional configuration with regard to preparing the environment and configuring the necessary infrastructure.

For an Online deployment, a lot of this is already handled for you, so the process is simplified. The following section will look at both an online deployment versus an on-premise deployment.

Dynamics CRM Online

For Microsoft Dynamics CRM Online, you can take the following steps to install and configure the InsideView solution:

1. First off, download the managed solution provided by InsideView on their site.
2. Next, proceed to **Settings** | **Solutions**, and install the solution you just downloaded.

3. Once installed, open the solution and navigate to the **Configuration** tab:

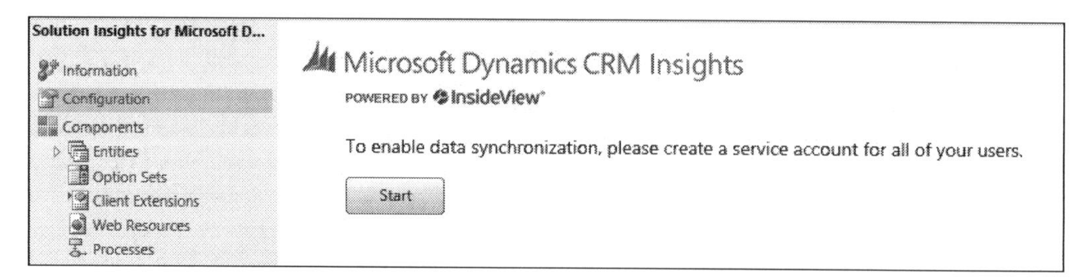

4. Click on the **Start** button to enable data synchronization, and follow through the wizard to complete the initial configuration.
5. Once you complete the wizard, you are returned to the Configuration screen in Dynamics CRM, where the data synchronization configuration progress continues:

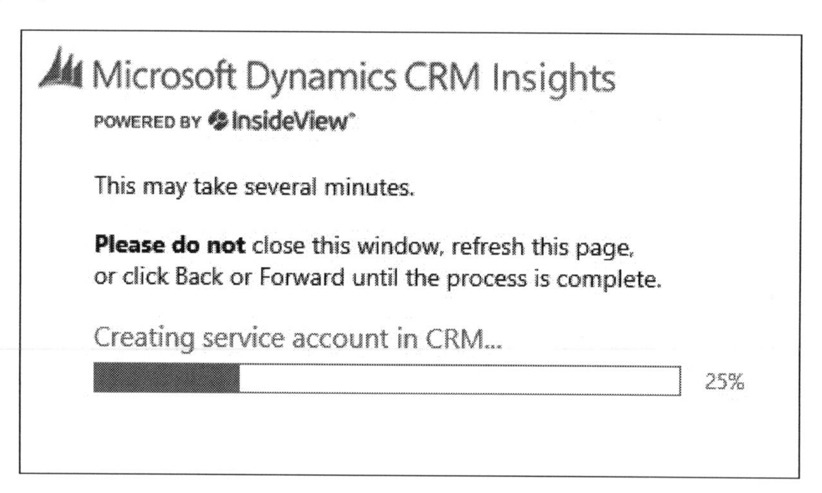

6. Once completed, you will be presented with a confirmation message:

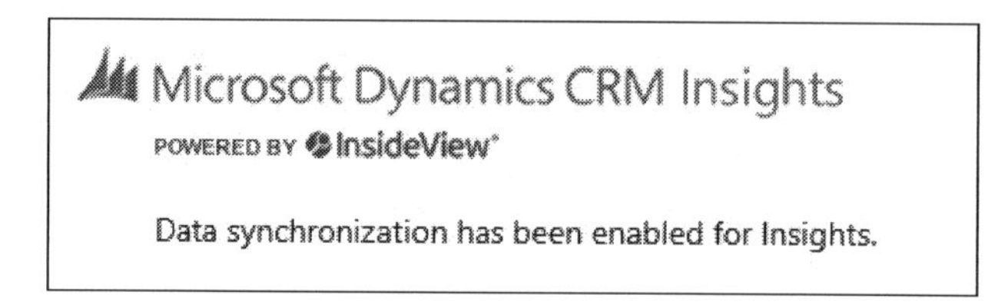

7. Once the data synchronization has been completed, you are ready to start using the Insight functionality. To validate, you can navigate to an account and make sure you have a new tab called **Insight**.

Dynamics CRM On-Premise

For On-Premise deployments, the process is similar, but the data synchronization is not handled through the solution configuration page. Instead, you need to set up a proxy CRM user in order to provide your application users with the ability to synchronize and export data. For the updated instructions for setting up a proxy CRM user, please follow the instructions provided by InsideView on their website.

Once your synchronization is complete, just as with Dynamics CRM Online, you can validate that the installation is successful by navigating to an account record and looking for the **Insight** tab on the form.

Insight Feature Set

Once the configuration is complete, navigating to an Account, Contact, Lead, or Opportunity will display a new tab called **Insight** with additional data about the specific record.

The data is structured in various tabs. The **Overview** tab presents generic information about the selected record. In the case of an Account record, we can see the address and phone number, the ownership and industry, revenue, number of employees, and a description.

In addition, we get a set of company insight information. We can see news articles, structured by the various categories, including **Leadership Changes**, **New Offerings**, **Acquisitions**, **Partnerships**, **Expanding Operations**, and so on:

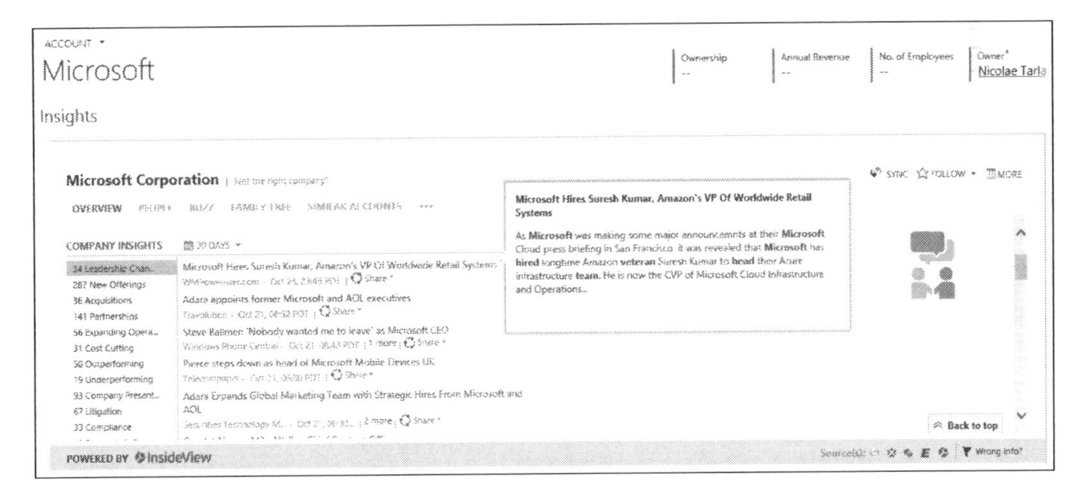

The **People** tab presents details of various resources associated with the selected record. These resources are populated based on various social network profiles and augmented data by InsideView. You can sort and filter the list of these resources as needed, based on job level or job function, as well as by your relationship to the respective contacts.

You can also search for a specific contact by name or role/title.

Hovering over a contact in the list brings up the extended user profile:

Navigating to the **Buzz** tab, you do a one-time authorization of the app for Twitter and Facebook. Once that's done, you can see all related social network posts on this tab:

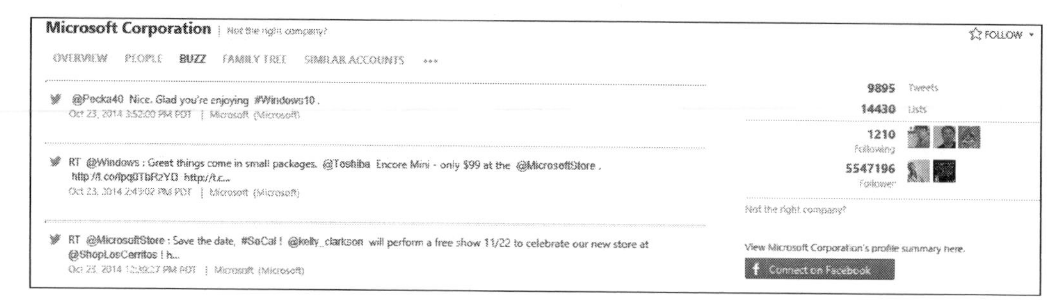

The Twitter connection brings in not only tweets related to the record selected, but also tweet statistics and followers:

From the tweet window you can directly interact with the tweets, by Retweeting and Replying to any of the existing tweets captured.

The **Family Tree** tab presents a list of related companies as well as acquisitions. You can hover over any of the companies presented to get additional details.

The **Similar Accounts** tab lists companies related to the selected account record, as well as header details on each company.

Expanding the navigation shows other options to see company news, jobs, financial details and the industry profile:

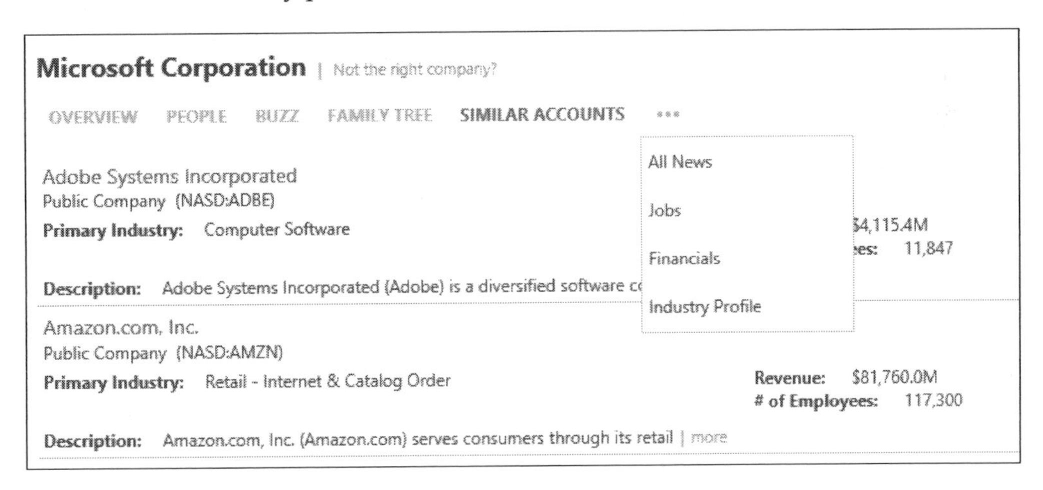

There is a very rich set of additional information presented through these tabs. All these details collected in one easy to find place can greatly enhance the ability of a salesperson to generate new leads and close new opportunities.

You can choose to follow any record or related records. This allows the system to surface data as needed.

One great feature of Insight is the ability to synchronize data and refresh your Dynamics CRM records. From the **Overview** tab, in the top right of the window, you can find the **SYNC** button:

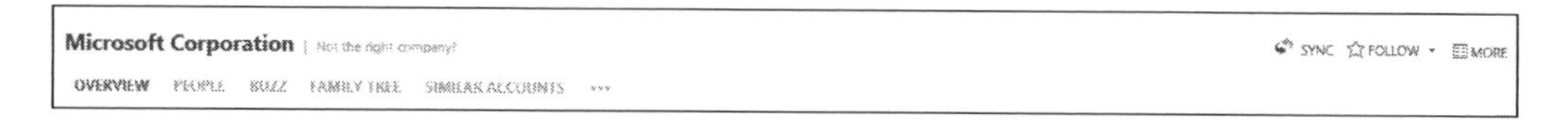

Clicking on **SYNC** allows a Dynamics CRM user to select which information can be refreshed in Dynamics CRM:

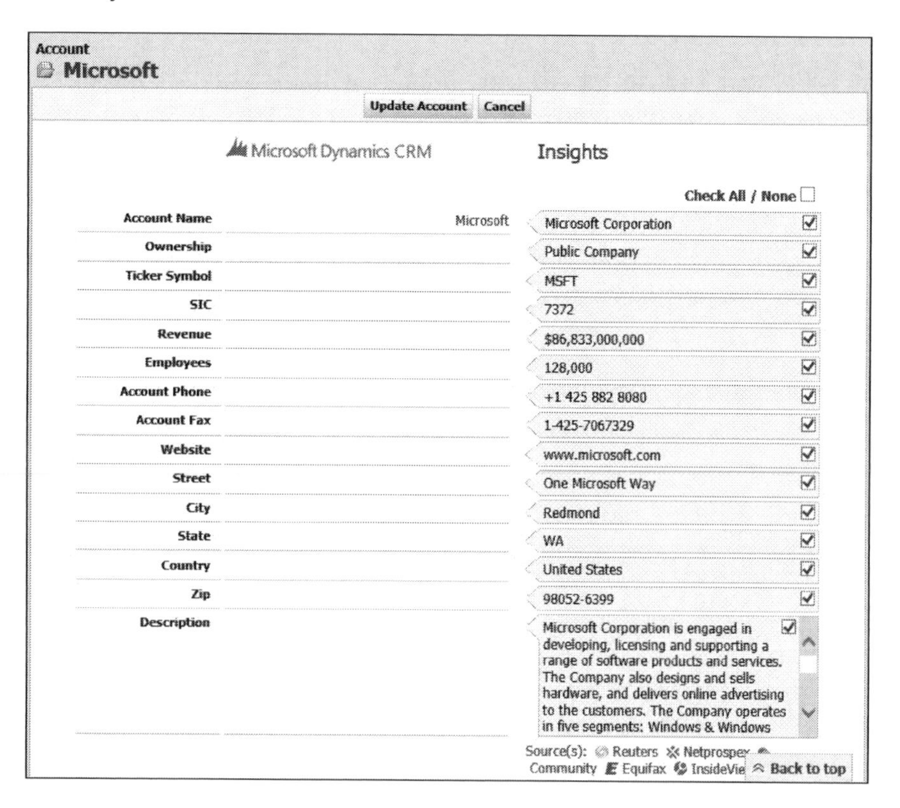

Select the specific records to be updated in Dynamics CRM and click on **Update Account**. The data from Insight will be transferred automatically into your CRM record.

You are prompted by a screen notifying you if the operation was successful, and after five seconds you are returned to the Dynamics CRM record. All data is refreshed with the new information from the selected data source.

You can perform the same operation on Contact records from within the Account record.

Yammer

Yammer comes integrated into your Dynamics CRM instance. You just need to configure the connection to get it running.

Yammer is the enterprise social network. The company was created in 2008 and bought by Microsoft in 2012. The social network is a corporate-friendly social media network. Any user can join the network with a business email account, as long as the company's domain is registered. Once joined, you can create internal and external networks for employees, customers, suppliers, and so on.

The application structure is quite similar to Facebook when accessed online, outside of Dynamics CRM. You have a newsfeed on the main page, and the ability to follow users and send and receive private messages.

Yammer and Hashtags

Yammer's architecture is built around a very robust search function. Using hashtags greatly increases the findability of posts. Hashtags are posted using the # symbol followed by a word or combination of words. An example is **#CustomizationEssentials**.

Mentions are also supported on Yammer. You use the @ symbol. An example is **@JohnDoe**.

Other Yammer Features

Yammer sports a people directory, which enhances the search ability and easily surfaces details about your colleagues. Furthermore, user profiles can be searched, thus making it easy to retrieve, for example, a Dynamics CRM specialist in your company.

In order to enhance the business appeal of the network, you can use Yammer for file sharing. Files can be attached to posts, or they can be uploaded to a file repository and made accessible to other users. In addition, for teams, Yammer introduces the concept of Pages. They are used for collaboration on documents, and can be locked to read-only if needed.

Yammer and Dynamics CRM

Since Yammer was included under the Office 365 umbrella, there has been a big push to integrate it into most, if not all, business applications. Yammer integration has been built into Dynamics CRM both On-Premise and Online editions.

Configuring the integration can be achieved easily, thus giving the Dynamics CRM users the ability to collaborate more productively within the teams.

In order to configure the integration with Dynamics CRM, the following prerequisites must be met:

- For Dynamics CRM to integrate with Yammer, you need the Enterprise version of Yammer
- The user account configuring the integration must be a System Administrator in both Dynamics CRM and your organization on Yammer
- Dynamics CRM must be updated to the latest available version if possible

Configure the Integration

In order to configure the integration, complete the following steps:

1. Navigate to **Settings | Administration**.
2. In the **Administration** section, you will find the **Yammer Configuration** section. Click on the link to take you to the configuration section for Yammer integration:

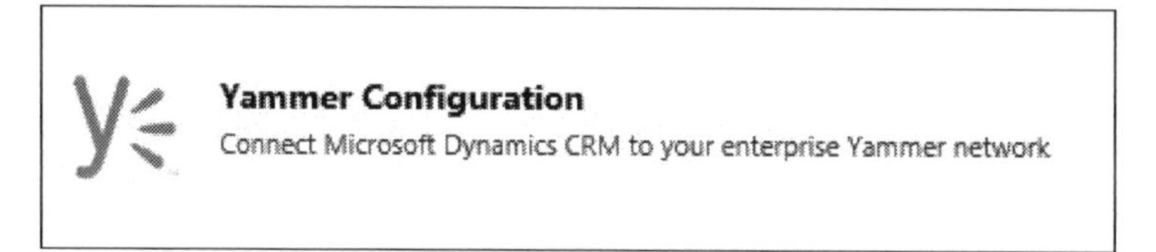

3. First you are prompted with a disclaimer page. Click on **Continue**:

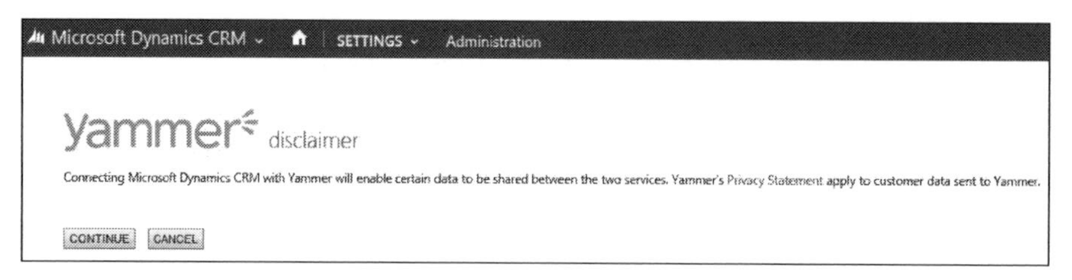

4. Next, you are taken to a configuration page. On this page, only the first option to **Authorize Microsoft Dynamics CRM OnPremise to connect to Yammer** is enabled at this point. For Online instances, the message will be **Authorize Microsoft Dynamics CRM Online to connect to Yammer**:

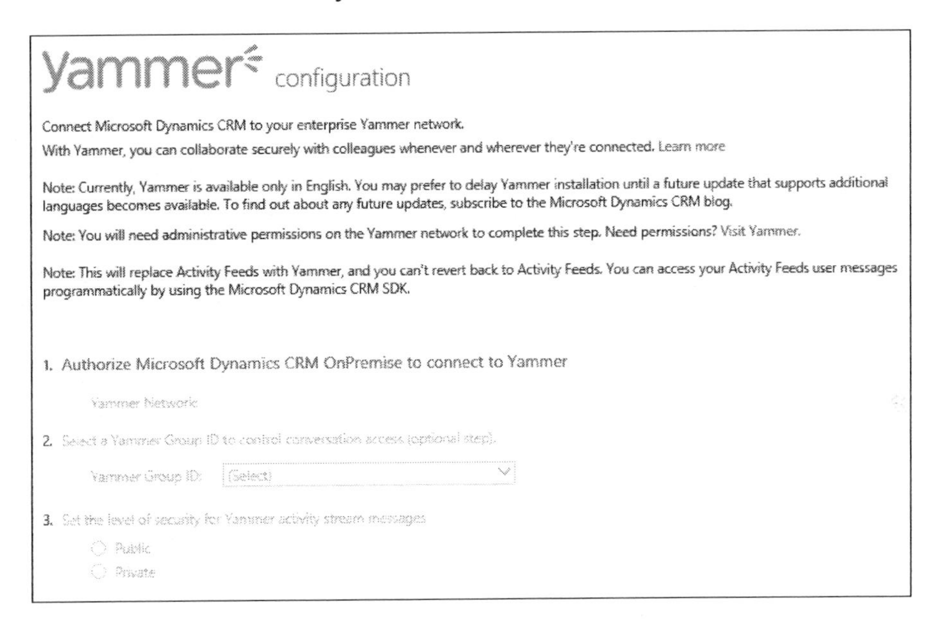

5. Click on the link, and you are prompted to log in to Yammer. Here is where you must use an account which has **System Administrator** rights in your Yammer organization:

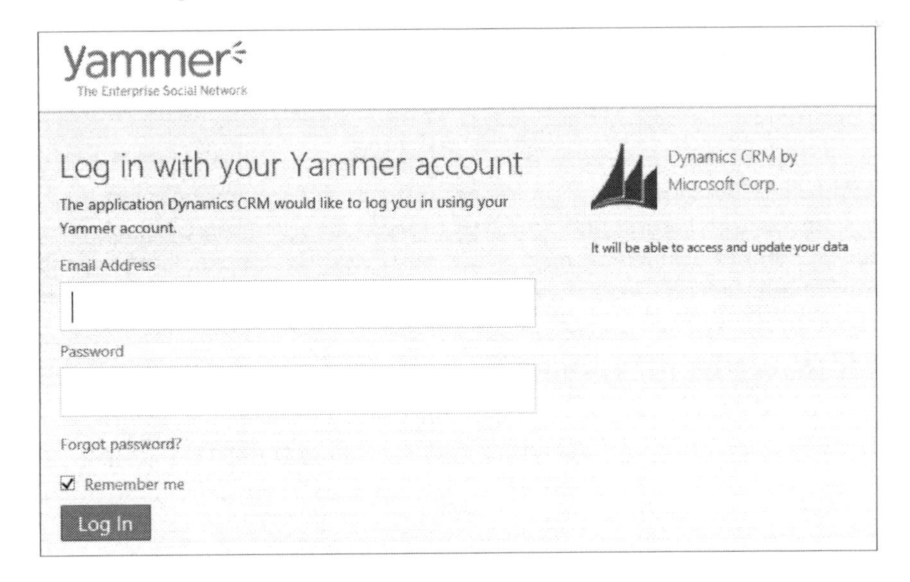

Failing to provide such an account results in an error message stating that the required permissions are not valid:

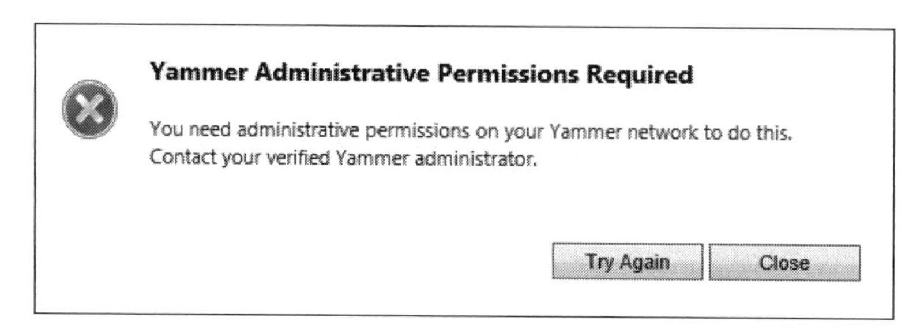

Once you provide the correct credentials, the next steps of the wizard walk you through the authentication portion, and when completed, returns you to step two on the configuration page:

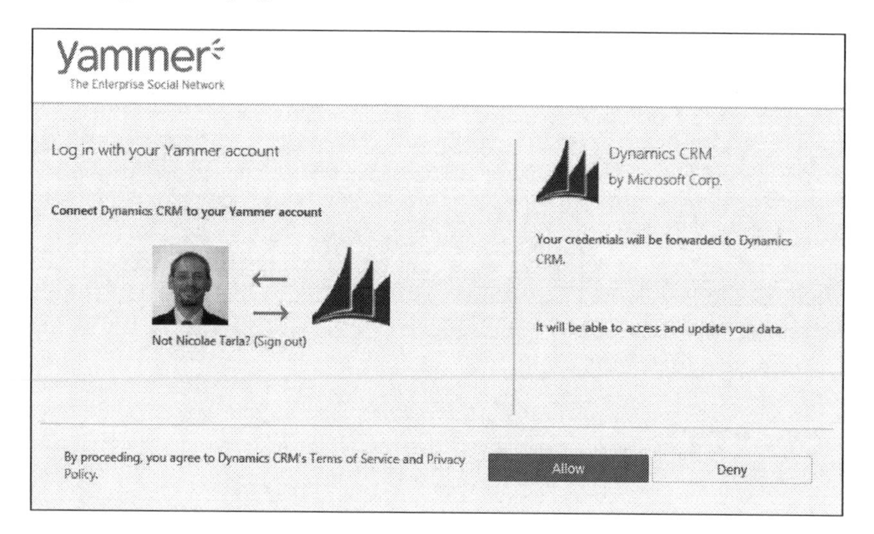

At this point, steps two and three on the configuration page are enabled. Note that these steps are optional, and allow you additional configuration of the integration. At this point, the integration is complete, though, and Dynamics CRM now has access to the Yammer network. In order to verify this, you can navigate to a record that has Social Pane visible and the entity enabled for Yammer, and confirm that a new Yammer tab is displayed at the top.

Step two on the configuration page, while optional, allows us to configure a specific Yammer group to be used for the Dynamics CRM integration. This allows us to restrict conversations and not pollute the entire All Company Group area with Dynamics CRM messages. It is a good practice to separate the Dynamics CRM messages from the other Yammer group communications.

The third step, also optional, allows us to configure the security for Yammer messages. In this step we can configure if the Dynamics CRM messages are made available to the public (everyone) or are set to private. Setting this option to private restricts visibility of the messages to users that follows the specific Dynamics CRM records.

Entity Configuration

Now that the integration with Yammer is complete and functional, there is one additional step required to surface Yammer into our Dynamics CRM environment. We need to tell Dynamics CRM which entities are enabled for Yammer. Without this configuration, no entities will support the Yammer integration:

1. We do this by navigating to **Settings** | **Post Configurations**:

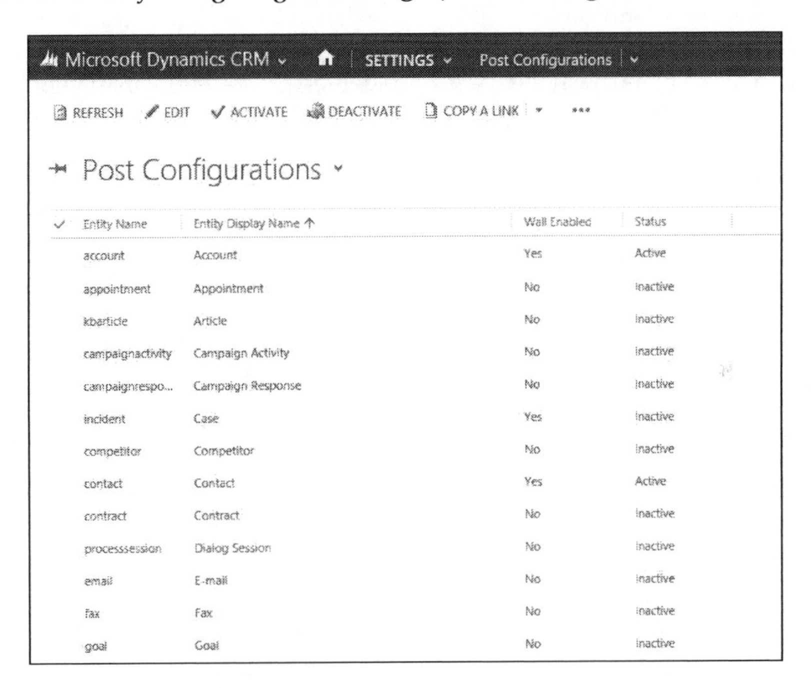

2. Here we can select the entities where Yammer will be available, and then click on **Activate** on the navigation bar. Once activated, make sure you publish all customizations.

If an entity is deactivated, the Yammer integration will be removed from the entity records. The messages, however, will remain in Yammer. All messages posted to Yammer remain stored in Yammer, and if the entity is re-enabled, the messages can be re-surfaced.

Additional Configuration

In some situations, you might encounter unexpected behavior when using entities integrated with Yammer. If that is the case, make sure that the Yammer URL is added to the browser's Trusted Sites, along with the Dynamics CRM URL.

Web API

While presented as a developer-oriented enhancement added to Microsoft Dynamics CRM 2016, the Web API is one of the features that even non-developers should be aware of when evaluating the platform's ability to integrate and communicate with other tools.

The Web API provides the ability to communicate with various other programming languages, platforms, and devices. The protocol implemented is **Open Data Protocol (OData)**, version 4.0. This is a standard used for building RESTful APIs, and allows resources to be published to various web-enabled clients using simple HTTP messages.

For technical details on the standards, see the protocol documentation provided by OASIS:

`http://docs.oasis-open.org/odata/odata/v4.0/os/part1-protocol/odata-v4.0-os-part1-protocol.html`

Due to the no-code nature of this book, we will not cover in detail the various aspects of this protocol, but it is important to remember that this is what enables various applications, on a multitude of platforms, to communicate with Microsoft Dynamics CRM 2016. Various components and libraries are already built to support this protocol using a multitude of platforms, including the Microsoft .NET platform, Java, JavaScript, C++, Objective C for the iOS, and other libraries on the Linux platform.

Microsoft Social Listening Integration

Microsoft Social Listening is one of the more recent additions to the Dynamics CRM suite of tools, and is available to monitor and interact with various social media channels. This is a service that can bring your organization to the forefront by allowing a system user to track campaigns, track brand and product impact, and interact in real time with customers, thus putting your business in front of customers as a leader across the social web.

Social Listening can integrate with all three default application modules, as well into custom-created components.

For marketing professionals, this service can analyze and present customer perception of campaigns in real time. It also allows marketers to interact directly with potential or existing customers on media channels such as Twitter and Facebook. It also allows the marketing team to report in real time on brand and product sentiment. This allows for campaign adjustments to be made to the correct specific aspect in order to raise the success of a campaign.

In addition, and very important to marketing personnel, this service allows them to identify the top influencers, the most active people discussing your brand or products.

From a sales perspective, this service allows users to monitor specific customer accounts, and to gain a competitive advantage over competitors by analyzing their performance against yours.

In addition, this service can track social buying signals. This means more social-generated leads, and more targeted opportunities identified.

From a service perspective, this service allows users to identify in real time potential customer issues, and prevent a bad public relations campaign generated by negative reviews. The customer service team can be notified and can directly interact with customers to immediately identify and flag potential issues, engage with customers in resolving these issues across the various social platforms, and minimize the potential of a negative image created as a result of customer non-satisfaction.

Furthermore, social charts can present the social sentiment as an integral part of standard dashboards. This allows key management a direct view into the success of the company's overall image or a specific product line with the public.

Microsoft Social Listening lives as a completely separate application, but is integrated directly with Dynamics CRM.

Integrating Social Listening with Dynamics CRM

The process of integrating Social Listening into Dynamics CRM varies by the type of CRM implemented.

Dynamics CRM online

The simplest configuration is for CRM Online. Since all configuration is under Office 365, the system knows where the Social Listening instance resides, and presents it as an option on a drop-down menu:

1. Navigate to **Settings** | **Administration**:

2. In there you will find the link to **Microsoft Social Listening Configuration**. Click on it, and you are presented with a simple configuration page:

3. In here, simply select the instance from the drop-down list and click **Select**.

Dynamics CRM On-Premise

For Dynamics CRM On-Premise, the configuration involves settings on both applications. On the Social Listening side, you need to specify the allowed domain where your Dynamics CRM resides. Then you can go back to CRM, find the same link under **Settings** | **Administration**, and provide the wizard in the **Connect this CRM instance** section with the URL to the Social Listening environment. Make sure you check the **Allow social insights** check box, and click on **Save Settings** after testing the URL.

Application Layout

The application itself is designed based on the same layout as Dynamics CRM. This will make it very convenient for users to get familiar with navigating between the two platforms:

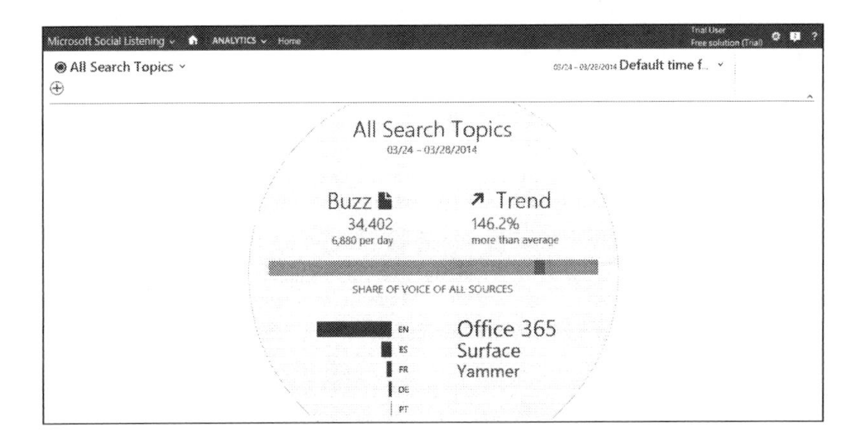

The main solution navigation presents the user with is the option to customize the tracking settings, as well as direct links to a comprehensive analytics package, social channels, and customizable alerts:

Targeting Sources

Microsoft Social Listening can target various social media channels. It can follow sentiment on Facebook, Twitter, YouTube, and various blogs.

Dynamics CRM environments, with the updates of spring 2014, can integrate the Social Listening charts and visuals directly into the environment into Dashboards. In addition, charts can be added to specific record types, such as Accounts, Contacts, and Competitors.

Configuring Analysis

Using Social Listening is mostly a wizard-driven configuration process. We can look at defining the time frame to be analyzed by selecting it from the top drop-down menu:

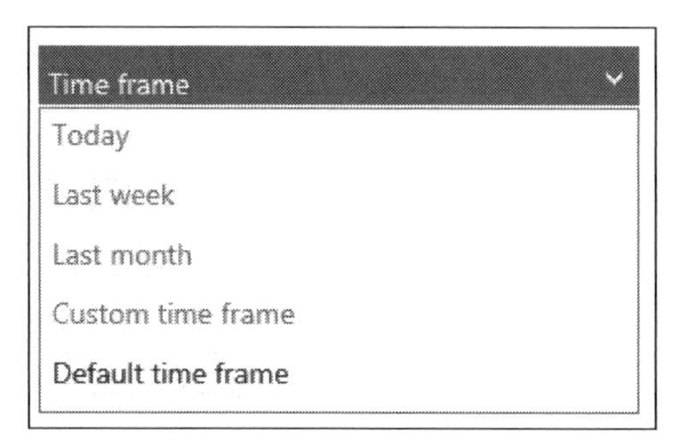

The main Analytics dashboard presents an overall view of all monitored sources. From here we can drill-down into the underlying data:

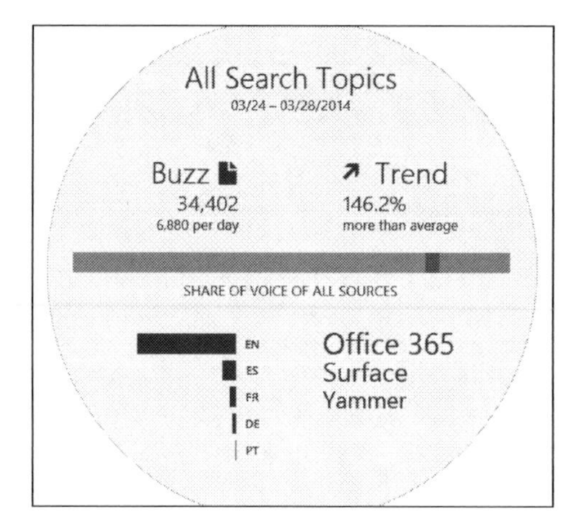

Hovering over a specific category allows us to look at specific details of the category:

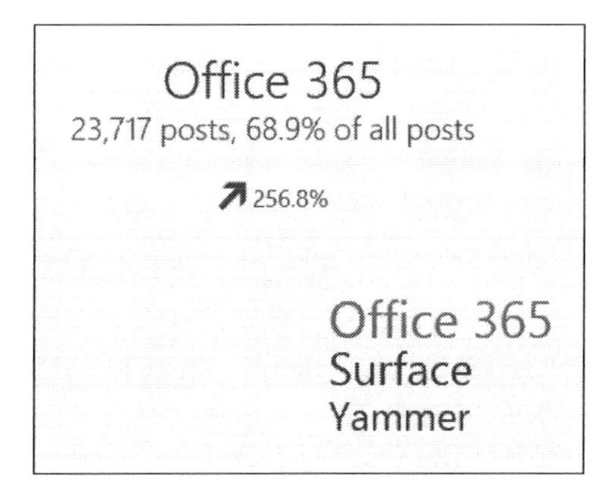

Clicking on a category allows us to get to the underlying data, the same way we work with dashboard in Dynamics CRM:

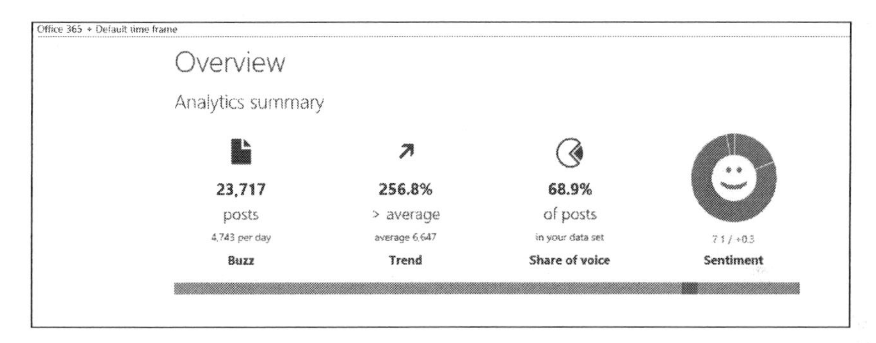

Within this **Overview** of the selected category, we can see an Analytics summary, along with details for **Volume history**, **Sources summary** and **Sources share of voice by language**.

Analytics Summary

The summary of analytics presents the data analyzed in the following four categories:

- **Buzz**
- **Trend**
- **Share of Voice**
- **Sentiment**

The **Buzz** is a generic presentation of the number of posts analyzed and captured during the specified period of time. This allows us again to drill down further to see the actual sources, item by item, and to interact with them.

The **Trend** is a calculated section showing us a comparison against the average. This allows users to determine if we encounter an upward or downward trend in the posts analyzed.

The **Share of voice** is again a calculated section, analyzing the posts in the current captured data set.

The **Sentiments** is the graphical representation of positive vs. neutral vs. negative comments, captured and analyzed in the selected data set. This allows further drill-down into the underlying data and the ability to interact with each post captured.

Interacting with the social channels

Once we drill down into the listing of analyzed posts, we can interact with each one. We can adjust and modify the sentiment associated by the system with each post:

In addition, we can respond to posts directly from this view, for the channels that support interaction, such as Twitter.

Other options include the ability to navigate to the original post, to forward it by e-mail, or to remove it from the overall analytics data set if it's not relevant:

For each tracked record, the source channel is clearly represented by the standard source logos.

Volume History

The **Volume history** is a representation of the total number of topic-related posts in the selected analyzed period. It displays graphically the volume, the trend, and a comparison against the average number of posts in total:

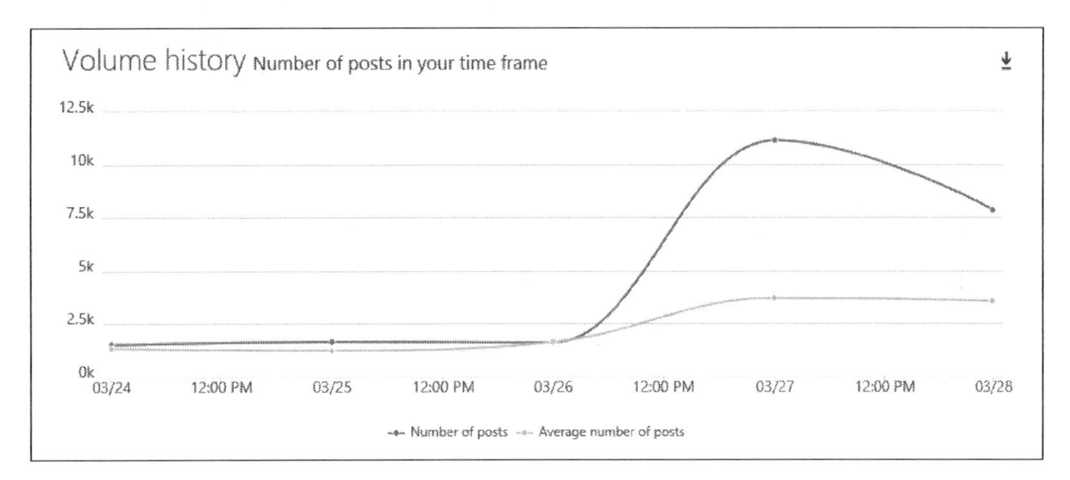

Source Summary

The **Source summary** splits the total number of posts by source channel, and renders this information in a graphical and easy-to-read format:

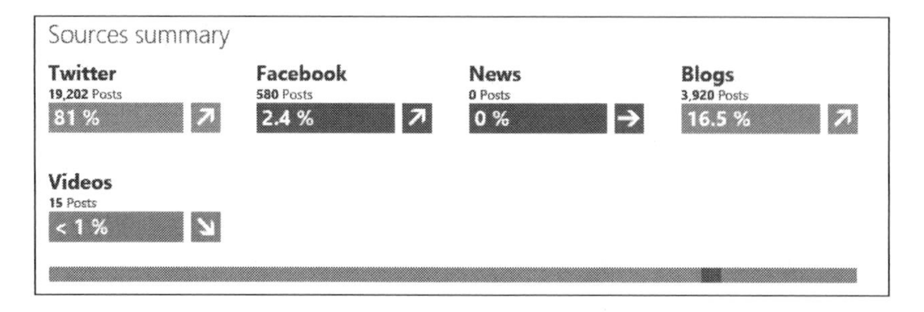

In addition, it provides specific numbers and calculates percentages by source channel.

Source Share of Voice by Language

Source share of voice by language allows users to analyze the social impact of a campaign or product not only by social channel, but also by language:

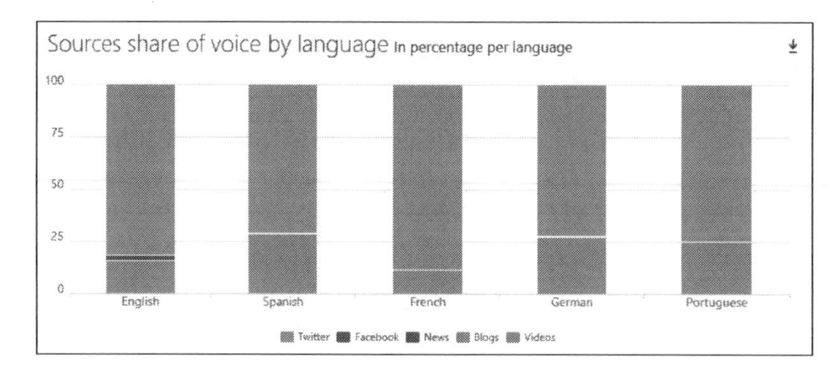

This information can prove crucial for companies managing campaigns and products globally, or across multiple markets.

Analysis Details

For additional analysis down to the individual level, Social Listening allows advanced drilling into the data, and can surface the most active users by social media channel. Navigating to **Analytics | Sources** presents the data not only by source, but scrolling down the page we can see the top overall contributors, as well as top contributors by media channel.

For the overall top contributors, we can display in the view the location, number of posts, percentage in the overall data set, as well as trend:

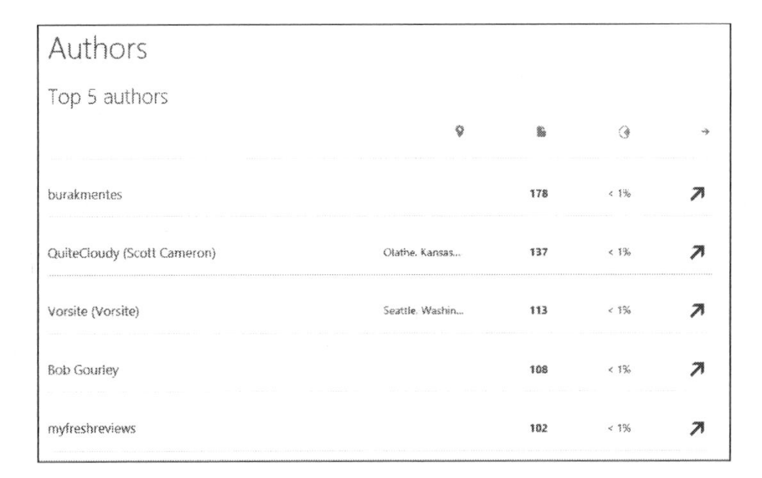

When analyzing by a specific social media channel, we can see in a similar formatted view the data specific to each media channel:

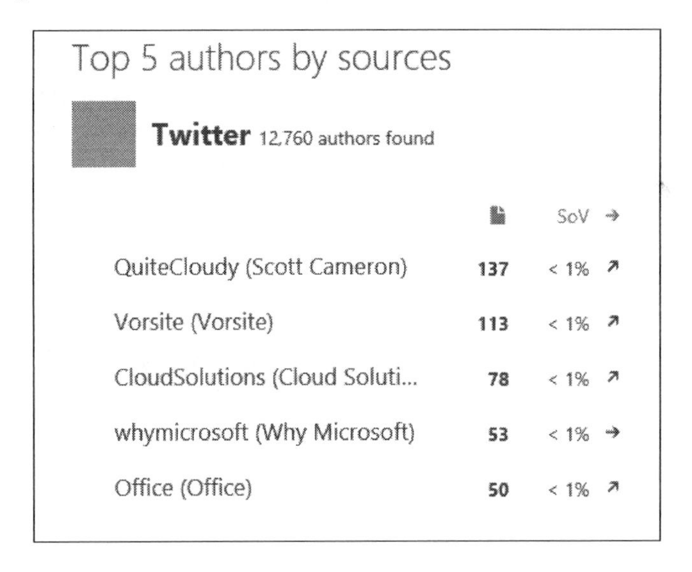

Configuring Alerts

In order to enhance the platform and make it more dynamic, Social Listening has the ability to not only monitor and analyze the data, but also to alert users of specific changes in trends. This can be achieved by configuring alert parameters and properties:

1. Navigate to the main menu and click on **Alerts**.
2. In here you will have a list of existing alerts configured, as well as the ability to create a new alert. Selecting **Add Alert** allows users to customize the alert specifics:

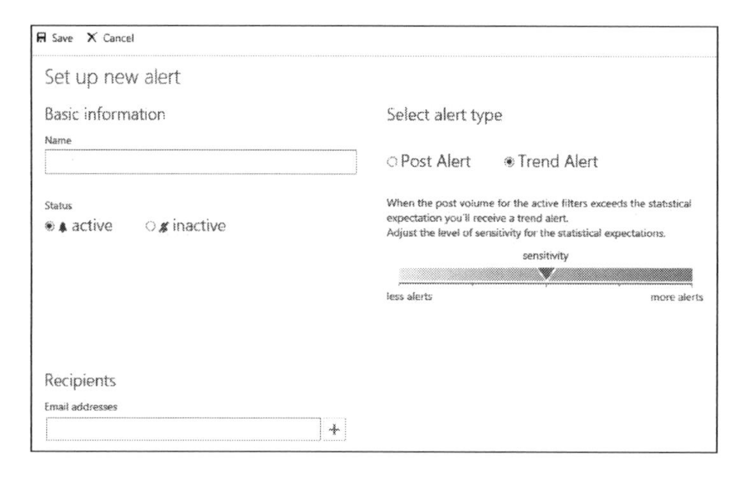

3. Once the alerts are configured, they can be reviewed and edited from the main **Alerts** screen.

Microsoft Dynamics Marketing Integration

Another product in the Dynamics family, Microsoft Dynamics Marketing is a dedicated marketing solution for planning and execution of marketing operations, as well as analytics of marketing performance.

This is a separate product on its own, but can be easily integrated to live side-by-side with Microsoft Dynamics CRM. This integration brings the ability to share resources, capture and surface marketing campaign results, as well as enhance the analytics data surfaced through the Microsoft Dynamics CRM platform.

With an enhanced graphical designer interface for workflows, this tool makes the process of designing and monitoring campaigns much easier. Sales pipeline analytics, along with lead management and scoring, are getting a major boost by integrating this solution with Microsoft Dynamics CRM rather than using the simplistic marketing functionality already built on the platform. For extended marketing needs, this product offers enhanced functionality, ease of use in campaigns design, and a complete set of extended functionality.

Enhanced reporting through dashboards, Excel, and Power BI makes it easy for marketing staff to get a clear picture of revenue and **return on investment** (**ROI**) for various campaigns.

Power BI and Dynamics CRM

Power BI, part of Office 365, is an analytics tool. It allows a user to monitor and discover trends through rich visualization dashboards. These dashboards can be rendered on various devices, making them available to all users across the organization.

We can use Power BI to connect to our Microsoft Dynamics CRM and extract data for analysis.

Starting the application, you are presented with the following screen:

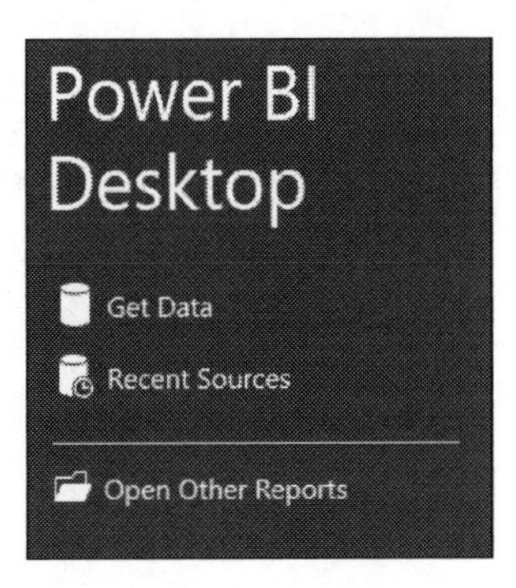

1. If you disabled the startup page, you can get to the same wizard by going to **Get Data** on the ribbon:

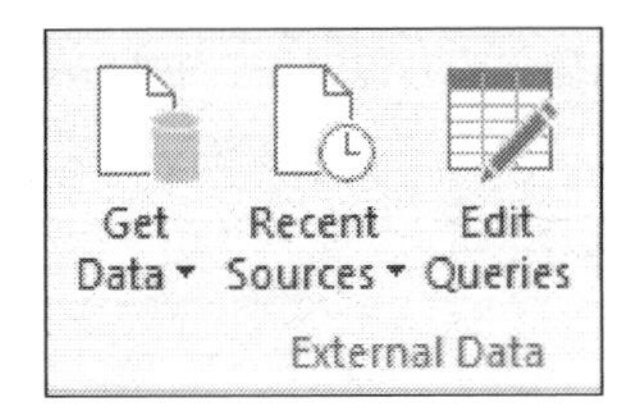

2. Select **More**, and in the window that pops up, find **Dynamics CRM Online**:

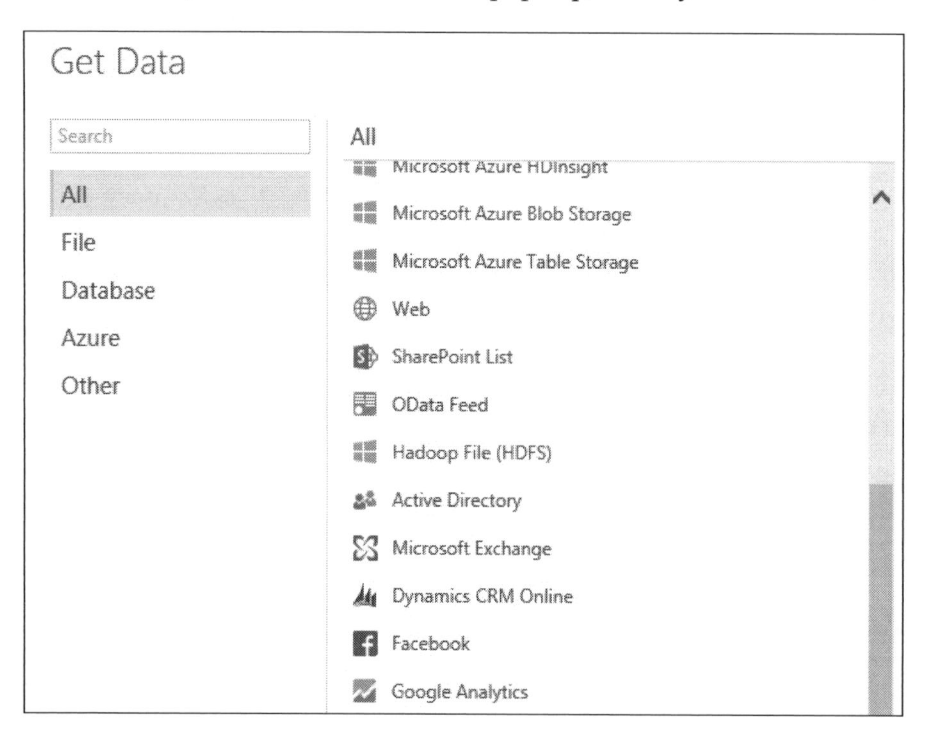

3. Once you click **Connect**, you are presented with the URL screen. Here's where it's easy to make a mistake, even though it's stated pretty clearly what URL you have to point to. Make sure it's the complete Organization Service URL, not just the Org URL:

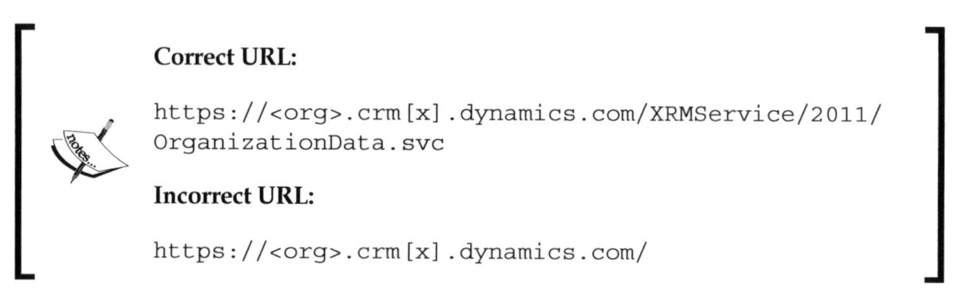

Correct URL:

```
https://<org>.crm[x].dynamics.com/XRMService/2011/
OrganizationData.svc
```

Incorrect URL:

```
https://<org>.crm[x].dynamics.com/
```

4. When using the incorrect URL, you are not prompted to provide the credentials later on, and thus cannot establish the connection.
5. Next, for authenticating to CRM Online, select **Organizational Account** on the next screen:

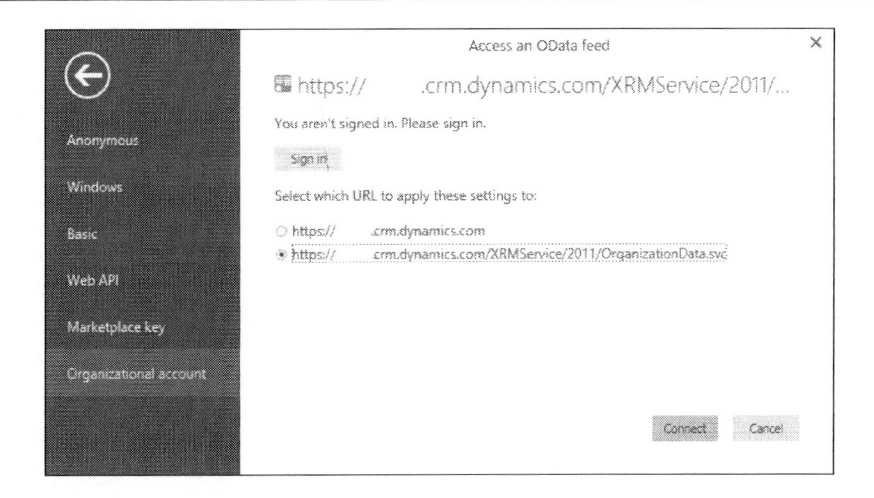

6. If you have provided multiple URLs before, including the incorrectly formatted one, select the correct one you want to use.
7. You will be prompted to sign in. Do so using a user with permission to access the organization.
8. Once everything is okay, click **Connect**, and you should be in. Now select your data set and start building the visuals.

For details on how to work with PowerBI, see the knowledge base:

`https://powerbi.microsoft.com/en-us/documentation/powerbi-service-get-started/`

Summary

Throughout this chapter, we looked at the various tools and services available for the Microsoft Dynamics CRM platform. From internal social integration, using Social Pane, to using the Microsoft Social Listening platform in an integrated manner, to the external integration achieved by bringing insight into Dynamics CRM, taking advantage of new features like voice of the customer, Power BI, platforms like Microsoft Dynamics Marketing, and finally, through using Yammer in a more dynamic way, we have a large variety of platform interactions available for Microsoft Dynamics CRM. All these enhanced features enrich the platform in ways that were not possible before.

In the next chapter, we will look at the administration aspects of the platform. You will be introduced to the basic administrative concepts of Microsoft Dynamics CRM, have a quick tour of the administration interface, and quickly pause to analyze the sections and processes an administrator is expected to use on a day to day basis.

6
Dynamics CRM Administration

In the previous chapter, we looked at the various solutions integrated into Dynamics CRM. From the Social Pane, to integration with Social Listening and Yammer, as well as the available Insight component by InsideView and the full blown solution provided by them. We have also done a quick overview of the new features added to the platform, including the OneNote integration, the all new Interactive Service Hub, as well as the newly added features brought by the acquisition of the field service solution from FieldOne.

This chapter will look at the following topics:

- Administration Concepts
- The Settings Area
- Business Management
- Service Management
- Case Settings
- Service Terms
- Entitlement Templates
- Service Scheduling
- Templates
- Product Catalog
- Administration
- Security
- Data Management

- Working with Data
- Data Loader Tool
- Data Reporting
- Monitoring System Jobs
- Document Management
- Auditing
- E-mail Configuration
- Configuring Activity Feeds
- Process Center
- Dynamics Marketplace
- Customization Principles
- Security
- User and Team Management
- Mobile Experience

This is by no means an exhaustive description of all the administrative options available in Dynamics CRM; a whole book could be dedicated to this topic. In this chapter, we will try to give a quick overview of the available functionality, as well as highlight the most commonly used configuration options an Administrator of the system will work with on a day to day basis.

Administration Concepts

Just like any other platform, Dynamics CRM requires constant care and attention. An Administrator of the system is tasked with monitoring the system, analyzing its performance, and intervening where necessary to make improvements.

In a standard, out of the box configuration, all the system management options are collected in the **Settings** area. You can reach this by going to the top navigation and selecting **Settings** from the presented options:

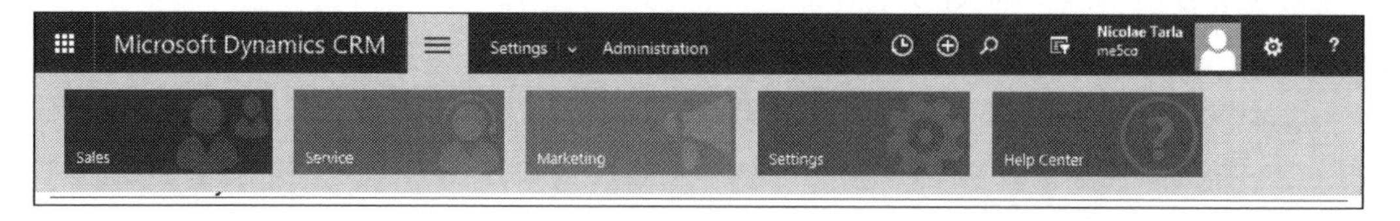

When working with a heavily customized system, the **Settings** area might be removed, renamed, or relocated at a different location on the navigation. In addition, some options could be entirely removed. The navigation and settings options are security trimmed, so that a user can only access the settings options they are allowed to.

The Settings Area

The settings area is structured in the following categories:

- Business
- Customization
- System
- Process Center

Each one of these areas contains links to the various configuration aspects of the application:

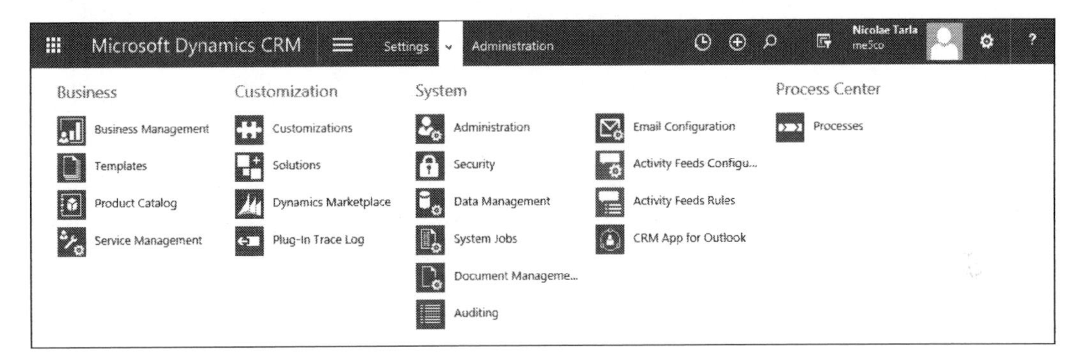

Business Management

The **Business Management** area is the place where we can handle most of the initial system configuration, as well as manage common aspects of the system. In here we can configure the **Fiscal Year Settings**. The Fiscal year is a setting usually configured at the system creation. Rarely in the life of a business The Fiscal year changes.

In this area we configure The Fiscal year start date and the period, as well as formatting options for display throughout the system.

Chances are that, once you've initially configured these settings, you might not have to touch it again for a very long time, if ever:

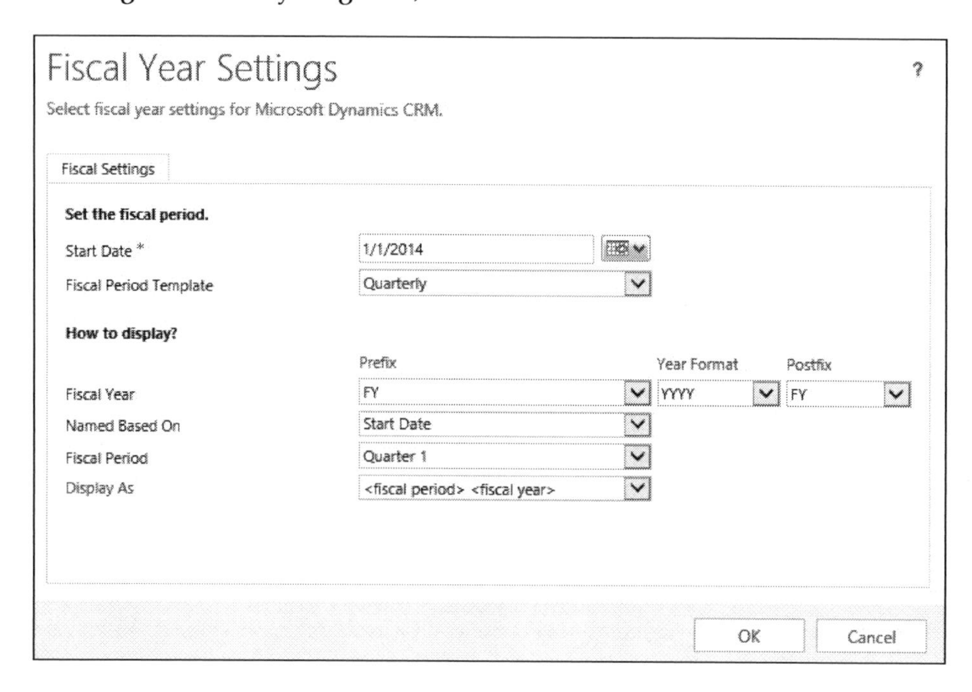

The **Business Closures** section allows us to define in the system the standard holidays for each year, as well as certain company specific closures. Usually these settings are configured at the beginning of a year. These settings work in conjunction with the Service module, and integrate into scheduling activities.

Once the business closures are configured, we have the ability to export them to Excel or print them.

Scheduling a new Business Closure involves the definition of a Name for the record, as well as start and end dates, and times if required:

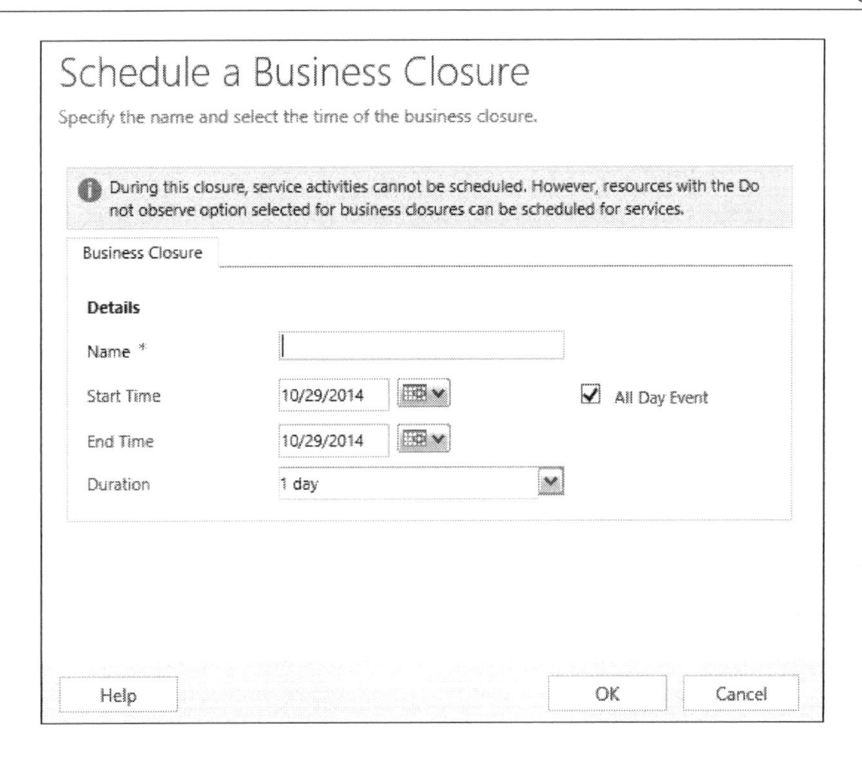

The **Queues** area allows us to manage system Queues. By default, queues are created for users and teams in the system, but they can be created for all customizable entities in Dynamics CRM.

Queues can be either public or private. Queue items residing in private queues are only accessible to members of that particular queue.

We can store multiple Queue Item types in a Queue. We can have items for entities like Cases, Tasks and E-mails in the same queue.

In addition to the standard information regarding the item placed in the queue, queues also store information about the user working on each queue item.

A very important aspect of automating queues is the ability to enable workflows and audit for queues. This helps with automating processes in order to validate specific business processes and rules around processing various queue items, improve productivity, and track progress. Auditing allows us to report on changes at various stages in processing queue items.

Starting with the introduction of Service Pack 1 for Dynamics CRM 2013, improvements to managing queues access now allow for private queues.

The **Services** area allows administrators to configure the capacity of a service activity. In order to modify these settings, you must have the Schedule Manager role.

Here we can select to assign resources based on various conditions based on work load and also to define capacity requirements.

The **Subjects** area allows us to define a comprehensive subject tree in order to hierarchically categorize various elements of the system. We can use this hierarchy to categorize products, cases, sales literature, or articles. We can also use this hierarchy for various custom entities.

The **Connection Roles** area allows viewing and defining new connections. The Connection Roles are used for defining relationships between entities based on specific defined roles assigned.

You can apply connection roles in three different ways:

- Apply the same connection role to both the source and the target records
- Apply a connection role from the source record to the target record only
- Apply reciprocal roles, which is a role from source to target and a related role from target to source entity.

The **Facilities/Equipment** section allows us to track physical equipment and facilities for scheduling services. These facilities and equipment can then be used in defining service activities.

The **Resource Groups** section is where we define groups and their membership. These groups can then be used in conjunction with the service module to schedule service activities.

The **Sales Territories** is where we define geographical areas or Sales, Service, or Marketing. To these territories we can assign managers and members. For example, we an create a Central territory and assigning a Sales Manager for this territory, as well as a team of sales people for all the sales activities.

The **Sites** section is where we can track various locations for conducting business. For example, in a manufacturing company, we could have various storage sites, various production sites, as well as various retail stores. Each one of these could be tracked as a different site.

The **Currencies** section is where we define the additional currencies used by the system. Each system will have a base currency defined on the creation of the Organization. On top of this base currency, we can define as many new currencies as needed. For example, if we have retail stored in two different countries, we can define, in addition to the base currency for one of the countries, an additional currency for the other covered country. This allows sales personnel from the other country to track sales in that country's currency. The conversion is done automatically by the system using the conversion rate defined.

The **Goal Metric** area allows us to define and track goals assigned to users. Using goals, we can assign teams- or user-specific goals, and track and measure their performance against these goals. In order to define a **Goal Metric**, a Goal must be created for a specific type of data to be measured. Once we have a goal created, we can define rollup fields to track a target's actual and in-progress values.

The **Relationship Roles** section allows the management of labels defining relationships roles. This type of relationship existed from previous versions of Dynamics CRM before the introduction of Connections, and is retained in the system for backwards compatibility. The Connections are much more versatile and should be used for all new customizations.

One of the major limitations of Relationship Roles is that they are only available to define relationships between Accounts,Contacts, and Opportunities.

The **Automatic Record Creation and Update Rules** section allows for customization of auto creation rules. Based on the settings provided, we can generate new records from incoming e-mails based on valid entitlements and from activities related to a resolved case. We can also configure automatic responses notifying customers that the provided information was successfully captured and queued for action.

The entire **Business Management** screen is presented here:

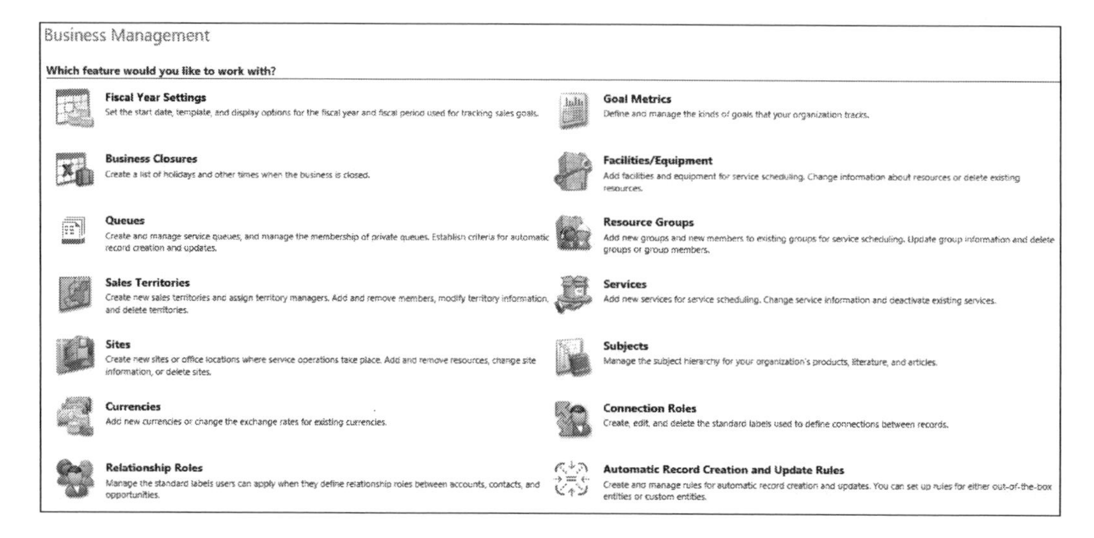

Service Management

The **Service Management** administration area has been introduced with Dynamics CRM 2013 Service Pack 1, and has received a slight reorganization with each subsequent version. In Microsoft Dynamics CRM 2016, the Knowledge Base Management was added here also. It groups together settings around the service module and defines the following functional groupings:

- **Case Settings with Record Creation and Update Rules**
- **Service Terms**
- **Knowledge Base Management**
- **Templates**
- **Service Scheduling**

Case Settings with Record Creation and Update Rules

The **Case Settings** area groups configuration elements around the case creation and routing processes available. This area is particularly useful in grouping and categorizing rules around Case processing.

The first option in this grouping, the **Queues**, allows us to view and manage the system queues. We can see a listing of the system queues by selecting the **All Queues** view, as well as manage the membership of private queues.

The **Routing Rule Sets** is where we manage specific case routing rules. Here we can define special rules on how a case is to be handled. For example, we can specify that, when a created case matches specific criteria, it should be forwarded to a particular team, user, or queue. In order to define these, we create a new **Routing Rule Set**, and within this set we create one or more **Rule Items**. Each **Rule Item** defines the **If Conditions**, meaning when this executes, as well as the **Then Condition**, meaning the action that will take place:

The **Subjects** area is leading to the same configuration of structured subject topics as the area from **Business Management**.

The **Parent and Child case settings** area allows us to define the information inheritance rules around related cases. Here is the place to define cascade operations on related cases. For example, we can define a rule to allow closing of all child cases when a parent case with the same **Case Title** and **Customer** is closed:

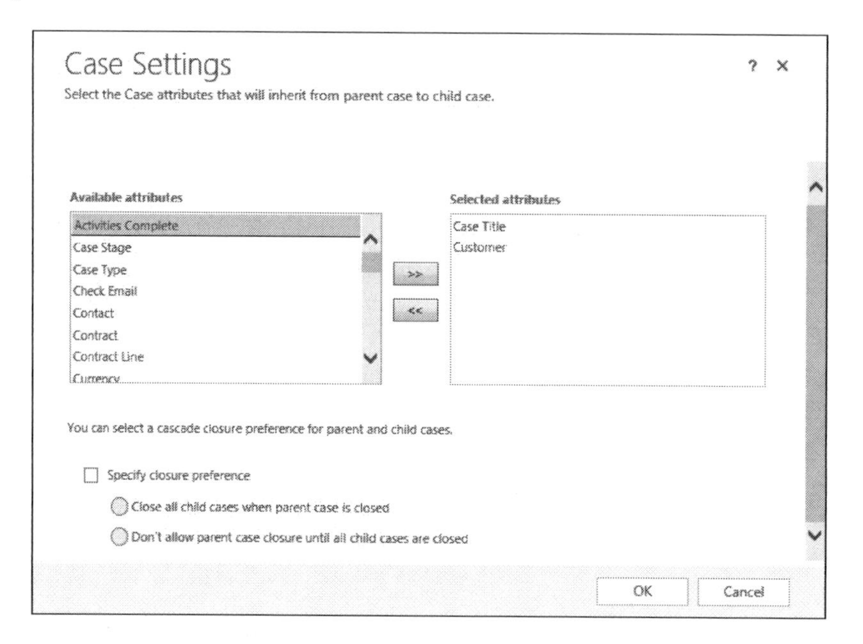

The **Automatic Case Creation Rules** area allows the definition of rules for automatic case creation from incoming e-mails and special social records. On each case creation rule defined we specify the conditions for case creation and the auto response setting. We can create new cases from incoming e-mails from senders not in the system, from customer entitlements, or from activities related to a resolved case.

For newly created cases through automatic rules, if there is no routing rule to handle it, the rule owner becomes the owner of the case.

The **Case Settings** area looks like the following image:

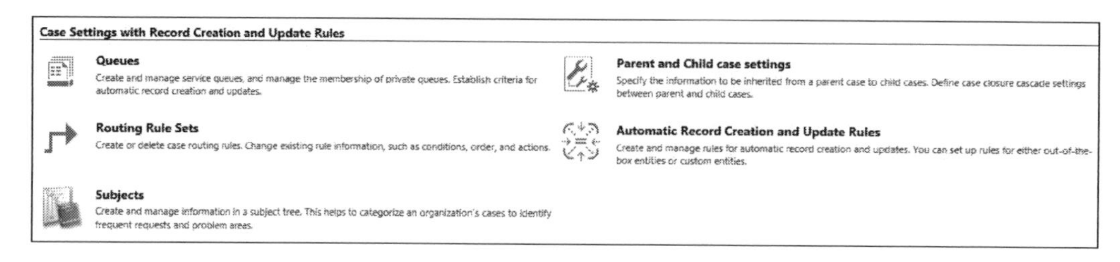

Service Terms

The **Service Terms** area houses specific settings for SLAs, customer entitlements, and scheduling. The **Service Level Agreements** section allows us to define specific SLAs and assign them to a service schedule. Part of SLAs involves the definition of specific failure and warning times, and the associated actions.

There are two types of SLAs available to be defined in Dynamics CRM. SLAs can be defined as Standard or Enhanced. The Standard option was introduced first to the platform, while the Enhanced option has added support for extra functionality. Some

of the features of Enhanced SLAs include the ability to pause an SLA when a Case is on hold, to add specific actions to an SLA, like the ability to notify when an SLA has succeeded, and the ability to track SLAs on a Case form by default.

The **Holiday Schedule** area allows us to define specific holidays that, once added to the system, are propagated into the service schedule and notify users if scheduled service events overlap with these predefined holidays.

The **Customer Service Schedule** area allows us to define and manage organization-wide service schedules. Here we define the business hours at the day level for the service activities. This can work in conjunction with SLA time tracking.

The **Entitlements** area allows us to associate to a specific customer a specific set of entitlements. Through entitlements, we define the customer support level based on either total number of hours or the number of cases. This entitlement can vary based on the product or service acquired by each customer:

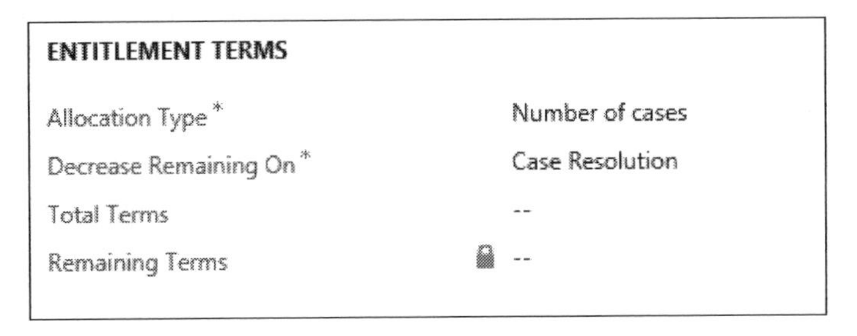

Finally, the **Service Configuration Settings** area allows us to define system-wide settings for the entire Organization. This basically links us back to **System Settings**, directly to the **Service** configuration tab. Here we can choose to enable or disable all SLAs, and if enabled, we can define on which case status an SLA is paused.

The entire **Service Terms** section looks like this:

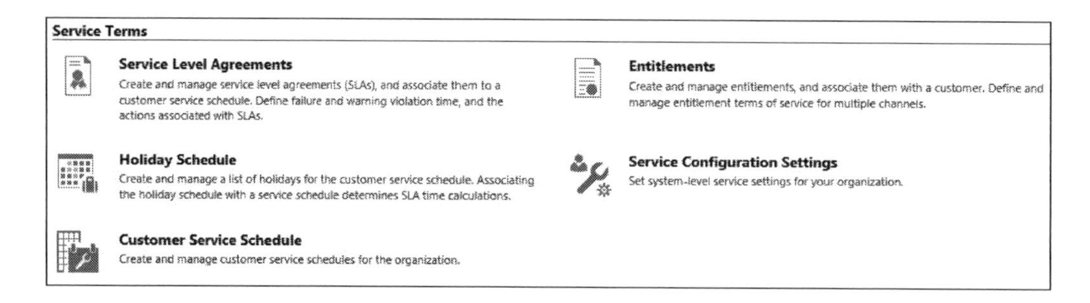

Knowledge Base Management

The **Knowledge Base Management** section was added with the newer version of Dynamics CRM and hosts the **Embedded Knowledge Search** configuration. This section is presented as the following screenshot demonstrates:

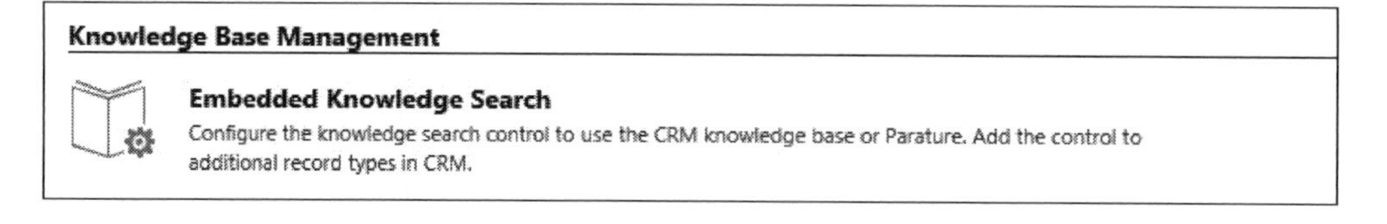

Once we click on the **Embedded Knowledge Search** link, we are presented with a new window where we can start configuring the record types to associate knowledge articles to. We have a choice here between knowledge articles hosted in Dynamics CRM or in Parature when integrating with the Parature Knowledgebase solution. In addition, externally hosted knowledge base articles can also be surfaced into Dynamics CRM by configuring the link to the source in the **Support Portal Connection** area:

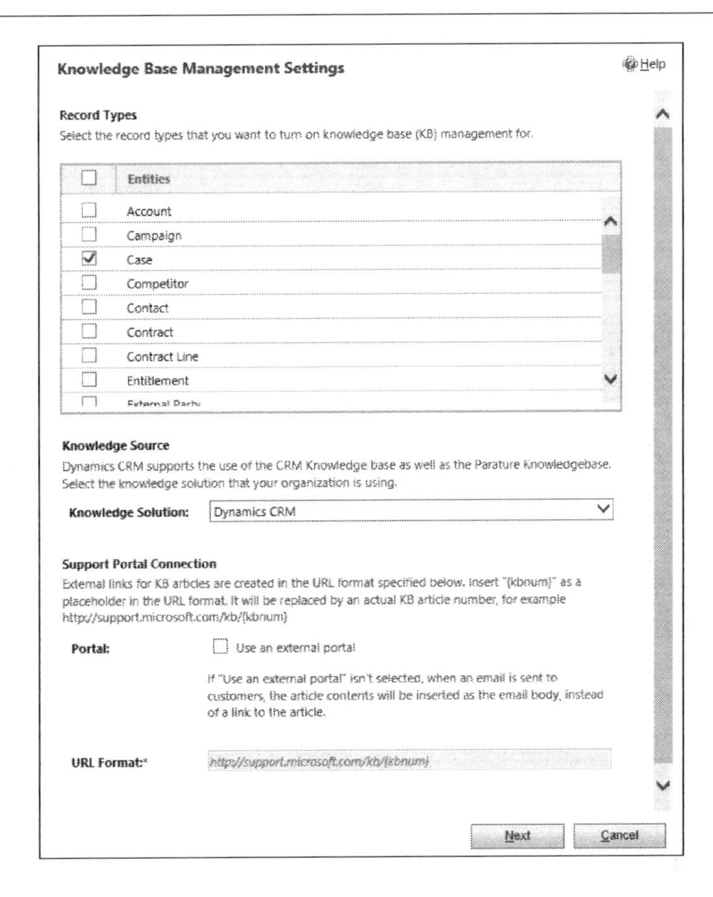

Templates

The **Templates** section of **Settings** allows us to define standard templates for knowledge base articles, templates for e-mail messages, contract templates, and mail merge templates.

The **Article Templates** section allows us, through a wizard-based interface, to create simplistic templates for knowledge base articles. We can create various sections within a template, and we have limited options to modify the text properties.

An article template must be activated before it can be used to generate new knowledge base articles.

The **Email Templates** area allows us to define specific dynamic templates to be used when e-mailing from the system. These templates can include dynamic data from the related records, as well as standard formatting supported by the most common e-mail clients.

Dynamics CRM already comes with a set of predefined e-mail templates. You can modify these, remove them, or create new ones as needed.

The **Contract Templates** area allows us to manage and create templates defining support contracts. Here we can define frequency for billing, service level, working hours/schedule, as well as the type of allotment. We can have contracts limited by number of cases, time, or coverage dates.

By default, a single Service contract template is created in the system. We can remove it, modify it, or create new ones as needed.

The **Mail Merge Templates** area allows us to upload mail merge templates created with Microsoft Word. Here we can define the template properties, including the associated entity, the language, and the base word document to be used.

The entire **Templates** section is presented as follows:

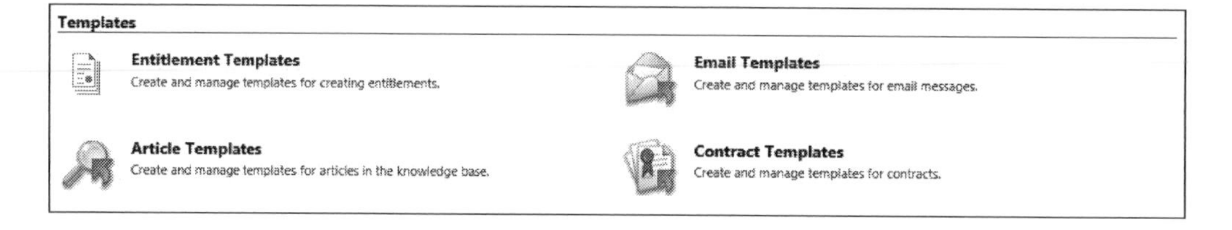

Entitlement Templates

The **Templates** section groups together some of the same settings that can be found directly under **Settings** in the **Templates** sub-menu with the newly defined **ENTITLEMENT TEMPLATES**. The **ENTITLEMENT TEMPLATES** allow us to define and manage standard templates for entitlements, and associate them to **Products**. This way, a customer can be assigned to an entitlement through the use of a template when a product is purchased:

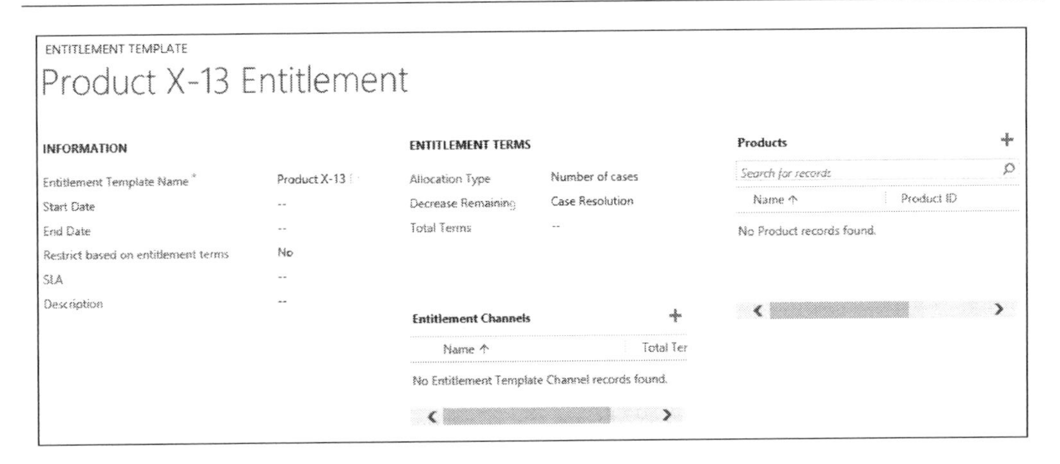

Service Scheduling

The last section of **Service Management** is the **Service Scheduling**. Here we have a collection of navigational menus collected from the **Business Management** section of **Settings** and grouped in here as they interact with the Service module in one way or another.

We can find in here options to define **Business Closures, Facilities/Equipment, Sites, Services** and **Resource Groups**:

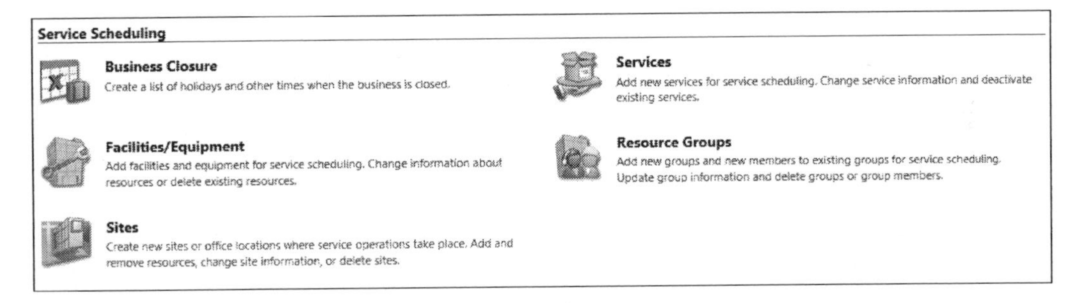

Product Catalog

The **Product Catalog** area is where we configure the products and services offered and tracked through the application. Here we configure products and/or services, prices, discounts, unit sizes, and price lists. Without these items set up, the functionality of quotes, orders, and invoices is crippled.

In order to configure the **Product Catalog** and to keep on track with all the dependencies, the items here must be configured in the following order:

1. If volume discounts are to be used, the **Discount Lists** must be created first.
2. Next, create **Unit Groups** and **Units**. Here we define the quantities that the products are being sold as. **Unit Groups** allows us to group by different categories of measurements. For example, if products are being sold by weight, length, unit or case of a specific number of units, these must be set up as available unit groups.
3. Create the **Price Lists**. Each **Price List** is a collection of items and the related price. **Products** can be added to the price lists later on, but you need to create the empty **Price Lists** at this point.
4. Create the **Products**. For each **Product** being sold, a **Product** record must be created. As part of the **Product** record creation, you link the **Product** to a **Unit Group** and a **Default Unit**. This allows you to define how the product is being sold. For example, if a product is sold by length, you associate it to the **Unit Group** defining lengths and to the default length it is measured in.
5. Associate the **Product** with the **Price List**. Each **Product** on a **Price List** is a **Price List Item**. In addition, here we can associate **Discount Lists**. There is a limitation of a single **Discount List** per **Price List**. The opposite, though, allows you to associate the same **Discount List** to multiple **Price Lists**.
6. Select the **Default Price List**. If an opportunity has an associated **Price List** that does not include a particular item, the **Default Price List** is queried and the item is retrieved from there. As such, the **Default Price List** should include all products and services available.

The **Product Catalog** area presents the options as per the following screenshot:

Families & Products
A product is an item in the product catalog that you want to sell to your customers. In this section, you manage products, set up product family hierarchies, create product bundles, and manage properties of product records. You can publish, revise, or retire product records, and also reclassify them to move them to other areas of the product catalog.

Price Lists
A price list specifies what prices can be charged for each unit in the unit group of a product. In this section, you create, manage, and delete price list line items and price lists in the product catalog. You associate and disassociate products with price lists. You also specify various pricing options in the price list line items, such as the quantity selling option, the pricing method, and the rounding options.

Discount Lists
A discount list contains the specific discounts that can be applied to a product, based on volume purchased. In this section, you create, manage, and delete discount lists in the product catalog.

Unit Groups
A unit group contains the base unit a product is available in, such as a liter, and then lists all the different increments that this base unit is packaged for sale. For example, if the base unit is a two-liter bottle, then that product could be sold individually as a two-liter bottle or in a case containing 6 two-liter bottles. In this section, you create, manage, and delete units and unit groups in the product catalog.

Starting with Dynamics CRM 2015, we now have the ability to create and group Products by Product Families. This lets us define relationships between products and product templates, and allows us to enhance the process of managing products and services. The new structure includes product families, product bundles, and individual products. We now also have a hierarchical visualization of products and services based on the predefined relationships. We can now see both a tree-like structure of products and a graphical display that can be reused on other forms:

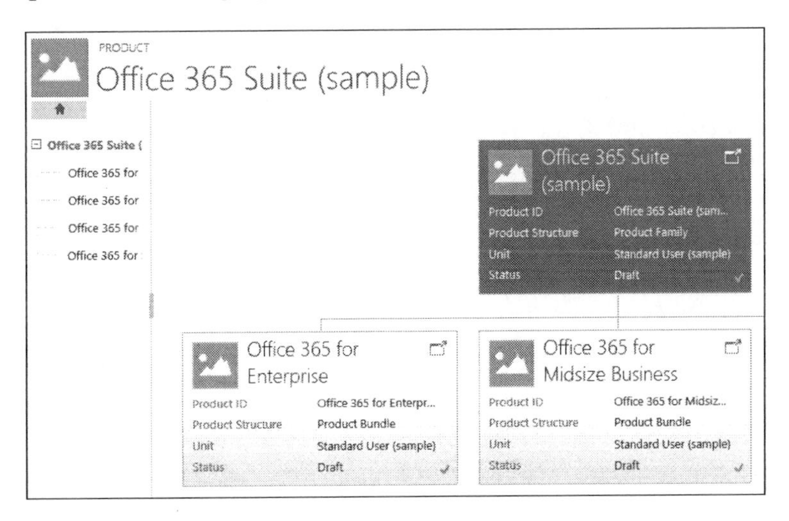

Administration

The **Administration** area is found under **Settings** and then **System**. Here we are presented with the general system settings for the Organization:

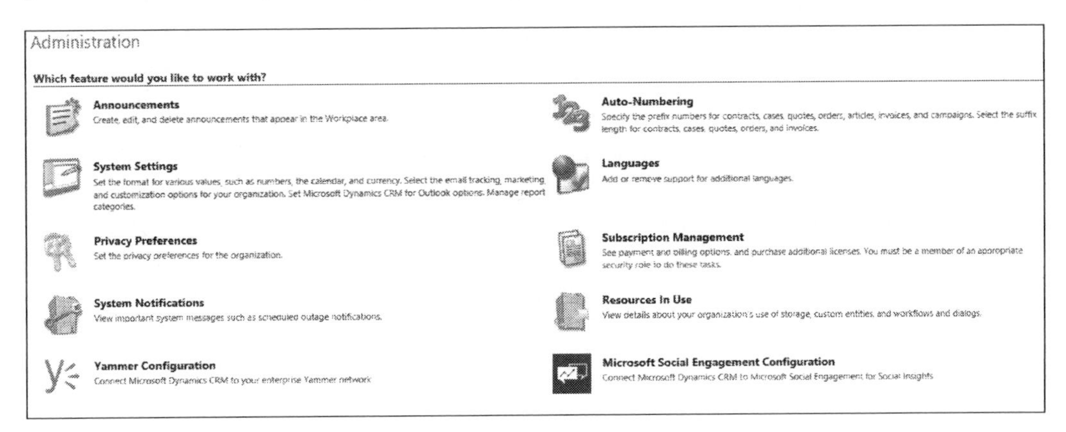

As you can see if you have worked with previous versions of the product, the options have been reorganized and streamlined. The **Administration** section now includes only organization administrative items, while all the configurations related to security and other items have been moved and relocated to their own respective areas.

Let's look at each option individually and see what they do.

The **Announcements** area allows us to define Organization-wide announcements. This can be used for notifications that all system users should receive. When defining an announcement, we must provide a title and a body containing the announcement details. We can additionally provide a URL that links to additional details or an external source, as well as an expiration date for when the announcement becomes irrelevant and should be removed.

This is a feature that was kept for backwards compatibility with Dynamics CRM 2011. For Organizations upgraded from Dynamics CRM 2011, the Workplace area can be kept, and that is where these Announcements are being displayed. With new Organizations created in Dynamics CRM 2013 or newer, the Workplace area has been removed. While you can still bring back the Announcements area, you need to customize the navigation in order to do so.

The **System Settings** area is where we can find all the necessary organization configurations. Here we have the settings organized in fourteen main categories or tabs. The newest one, added with Dynamics CRM 2016, is the **Previews** tab, which provides us with the ability to enable some of the newest preview features, like **Task Flows** and **Cortana integration**.

The **General** area of System Settings allows us to configure auto save on forms. Here we can enable or disable auto save globally. We can also enable presence through integration with Lync. This will show users the status of other system users when looking at their records. We can also define here the name formatting, currency precision, currency display options, and sharing of records on reassignment.

Also in the general area, we configure the file extensions that are blocked from the system. While Dynamics CRM supports attaching files to records through the **Notes** section, we should define limitations with regards to which files are allowed to be loaded in the system. By default, Dynamics CRM provides a list of file types blocked. That is a good starting point, but it can be edited and enhanced as needed.

Starting with Dynamics CRM 2015, we see enhancements with regards to search. The **General** area of **System Settings** allows us to configure the settings around **Quick Find**. We can enable a limit on the number of records displayed in search results, as well as the entities that we can perform a search across. The new search now returns results across up to ten different entities, and here is where we configure that:

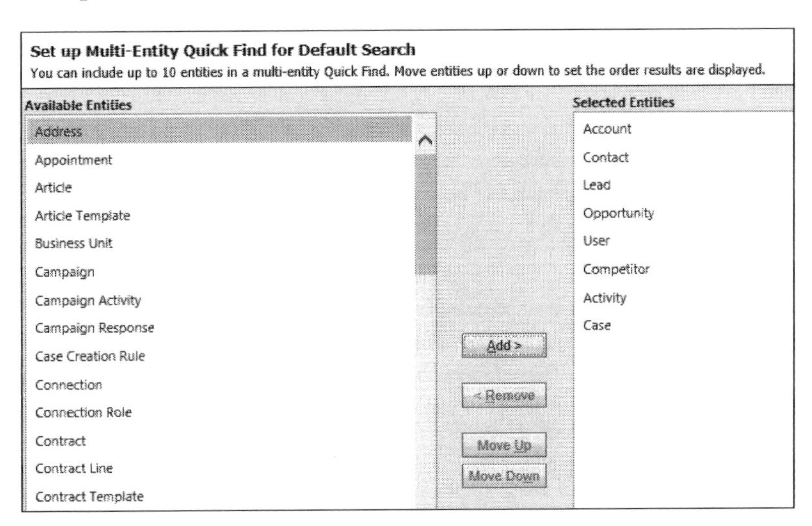

The **Bing Maps** area of the **General** tab allows us to enable Bing integration and input the Bing Maps key. If Bing Maps are not to be used, we can disable the functionality from here.

This section also provides settings around telephony. As before, both Skype and Lync are supported out of the box, and we can enable automatic prefixing based on country or region.

With Dynamics CRM 2015 and up, we now have the ability to include customized Help, and we can configure the custom help URL from here:

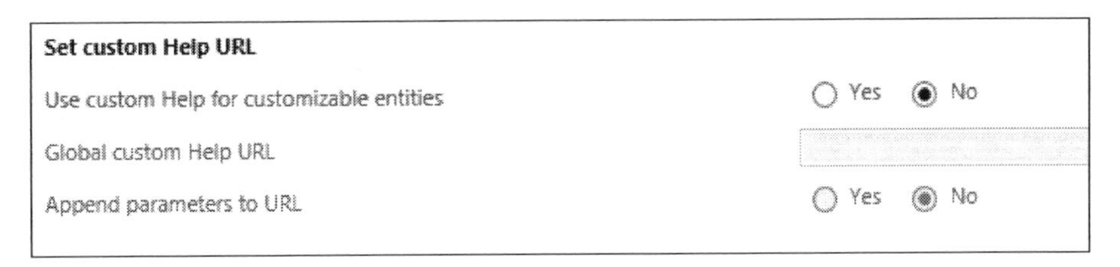

In addition, a new setting was added to the **General** tab to allow us to globally disable the navigation tour.

The **Calendar** area of **System Settings** presents us with a single option to configure the maximum duration of an appointment in days. This allows us to limit all users in the organization to a maximum duration.

The **Formats** tab presents global options for currency format and time and date, as well as numbering formats. We can select a predefined format, or customize our own as needed.

The **Auditing** tab allows us to globally enable or disable auditing, as well as configure auditing to be available to specific sections of the application.

Note that once **Auditing** is disabled globally, all the settings at the entity level are disabled. You can enable auditing globally, and then enable each entity as needed.

The **Email** tab presents options for globally configuring the e-mail processing method as Server-Side Synchronization or E-mail Router. We can select a predefined Server Profile, which will dictate the default settings for all newly-created users. In addition, we can configure here the e-mail tracking settings and the token to be used, as well as **Smart Matching** settings for capturing e-mails.

The **Marketing** tab allows us to configure mail merges and campaign responses, as well as unsubscribe settings.

The **Customization** tab allows us to configure Dynamics CRM to open in Application mode. This will allow users to see the Dynamics CRM system in a way that mimics a desktop application.

On the **Outlook** tab, we get options to configure Outlook synchronization. These are global settings, and they can be overwritten by the user settings. As such, these settings serve as a template for all new users.

The **Reporting** tab allows us to configure the main report categories. New reports can be added to these categories for easy management and display filtering.

The **Goals** tab presents options for roll-up expiration time and frequency. Here we can configure roll-ups to be recalculated at a set interval, and to expire after a set duration, in days.

The **Sales** tab deals with configuration around product state on creation, price list allocation, and discounts. In addition, we can find here settings for product bundle maximum values for products and product properties.

On the **Service** tab of **System Settings**, we configure if **Service Level Agreements** are enabled and when an SLA is on hold. This allows those of us now starting with Dynamics CRM 2015 to stop calculating an SLA while a case is either on hold or we wait for feedback from a customer.

Lastly, the **Synchronization** tab presents us with options to manage integration with Outlook and Exchange. We can get to the preconfigured filters for synchronization and offline from here. In addition, we can define if Appointments are to be synchronized, the type of address to be synchronized on Contacts, and if we need to synchronize Tasks.

Back on the **Settings | Administration** screen, the **Privacy Preferences** area is where we can configure the error reporting at the global level. We can now disable the error messages presented to users and choose to handle them automatically on behalf of the users:

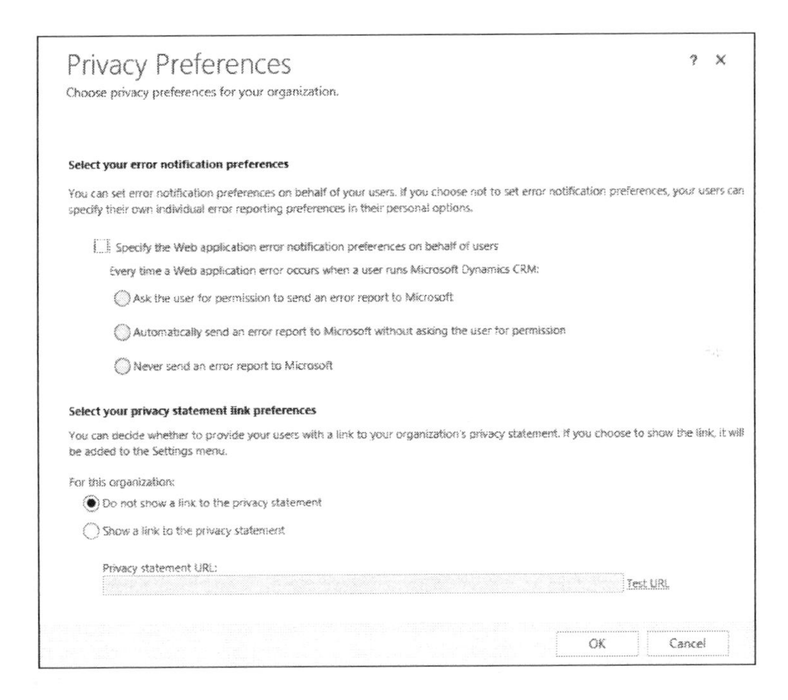

The **System Notification** area is specific to Dynamics CRM Online organizations and is where we are presented with details about possible scheduled outages or other important environment notices.

Yammer Configuration is where we configure the Yammer integration, as presented in *Chapter 5, Dynamics CRM – Additional Features*.

The **Auto Numbering** area allows us to configure the format for the auto numbering used in various places in the system. Entities supporting auto numbering out of the box include:

- **Contracts**
- **Cases**
- **Articles**
- **Quotes**
- **Orders**
- **Invoices**
- **Campaigns**
- **Knowledge Articles**

For each one of these entities, we can customize the formatting of the auto number generated:

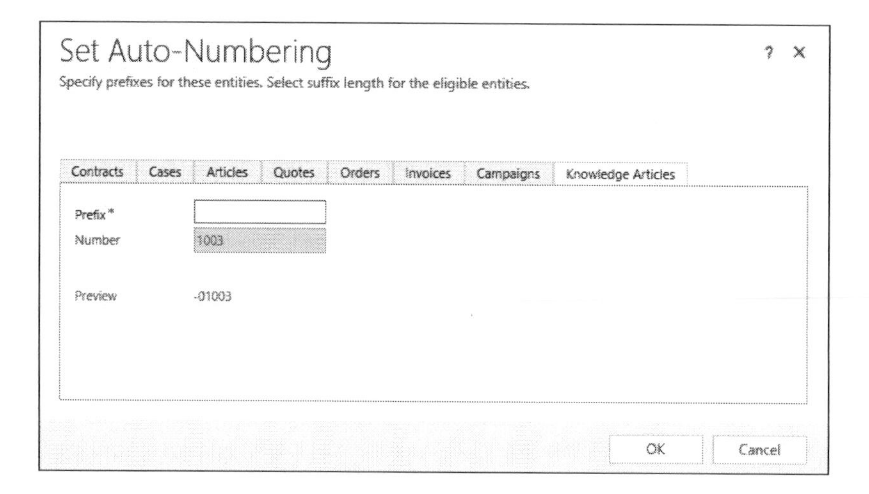

We can configure here the prefix to be used, as well as the length of the suffix.

Starting with Dynamics CRM 2016, we can now take advantage of the enhancements to Knowledge Articles functionality, and we can configure auto-numbering for these. We can only customize the prefix though, as opposed to all the other auto-numbering entities.

For more advanced rules around auto-numbering, it is recommended that a plugin is developed to generate these numbers. This way you can specify all the rules and the external sources you might need to use when generating this. For example, your unique numbers might come from an external system, or be mapped to specific records from other systems.

Languages is where we manage system languages. When creating our organization for the first time, we select the default language. In addition, we can add as many other languages as needed from the available supported languages. In order to be able to manage other languages, the specific language packs need to be installed on the Organization. When configuring this feature for Dynamics CRM Online, all available languages are already loaded and made available; you just have to check the additional languages to be used.

The **Subscription Management** area is only available for Dynamics CRM Online, and is just a link to the account and billing management for your current organization. Here is where you can manage licenses, add additional services, or remove licenses. You need specific permissions to access this section.

The **Resources in Use** area is again specific to Dynamics CRM Online, and presents a quick overview of Organization performance against standard limitations. Here you can see how much storage your organization is using against the maximum limit available, as well as how your organization is tracking against the limit of 300 custom entities created. You also have links to licensing management options:

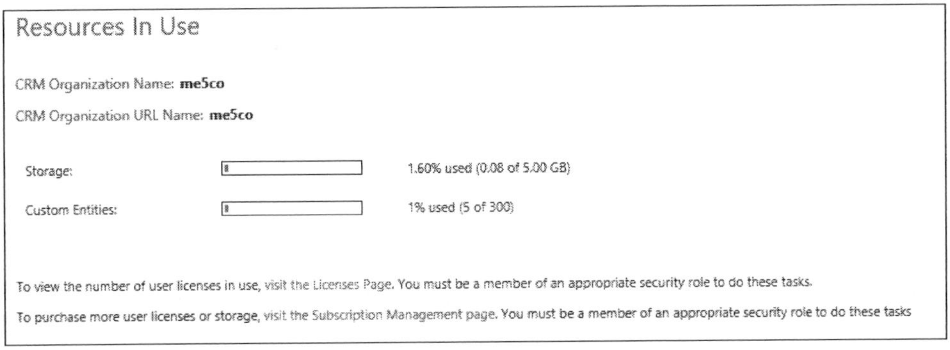

Resources In Use

CRM Organization Name: **me5co**

CRM Organization URL Name: **me5co**

Storage: 1.60% used (0.08 of 5.00 GB)

Custom Entities: 1% used (5 of 300)

To view the number of user licenses in use, visit the Licenses Page. You must be a member of an appropriate security role to do these tasks.

To purchase more user licenses or storage, visit the Subscription Management page. You must be a member of an appropriate security role to do these tasks

Microsoft Social Engagement Configuration allows us to configure the integration with Microsoft Social Listening. Social Listening has been presented in *Chapter 5, Dynamics CRM – Additional Features, Dynamics CRM Online* section.

Security

The next area of settings we are looking at is the **Security**. As a result of streamlining the administration of the platform, starting with Dynamics CRM 2015 we now have a new section called **Security**. We have now grouped in here all settings related to users, teams, and the related security roles:

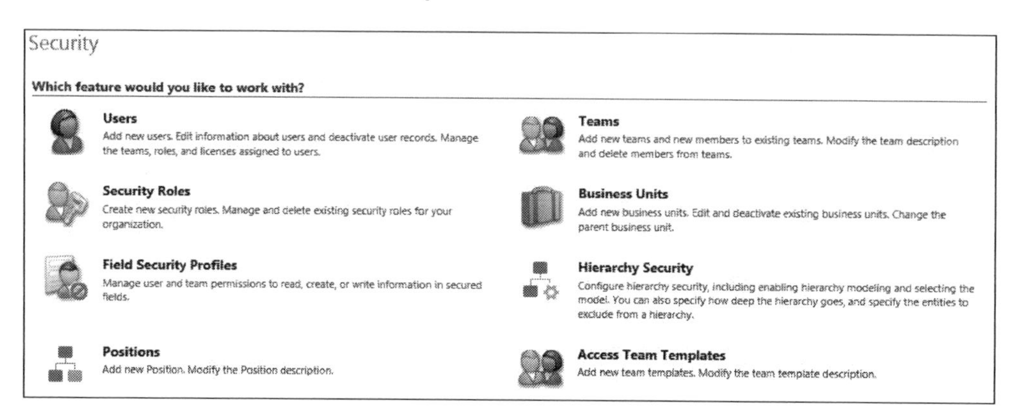

The **Users** area is where we can manage the system users. We have a large variety of views into the users listing, with various filter options already created. We can see users by their status, by ownership, by roles, by relationship, by team, or by social relationship. This area is also the entry point for adding new users to the system, disabling users, or updating their information.

The **Security Roles** area is where we can define specific roles and permissions. There is a tight relationship here with the **Business Units** configuration mentioned above.

We can create as many security roles as needed, and we can assign to a user one or more security roles. The final permissions are determined by merging all permissions allocated through all the security roles assigned to a user.

Security Roles can be assigned to either **Users** or **Teams**. Assigning a security role to a team will give all team members the same permissions as the team.

The **Field Security Profiles** area is where we configure the read, create, or write permissions for users and/or teams. In order to have the secured fields working properly, we need to define rules around who has what permissions on those fields. The process involves three steps once a secured field has been added to an entity form. First we need to create a field security profile. Then we associate users or teams to this profile. Lastly, we add the specific field permissions.

The **Positions** is a new feature added with Dynamics CRM 2015. This area now allows us to create not only the standard relationships between roles, but also a way to visualize these relationships. The default view is **Active Positions**, and it presents the listing of available roles in the organization. Observe that now we have a new column preceding each record, with a symbolic representation of a relationship:

This type of icon shows up in several places where we have visualization enhancements around relationships. Clicking on it allows us to see and navigate visually through the whole relationship tree.

The beauty of this new functionality is that we can also take these visual representations and reuse them on various records:

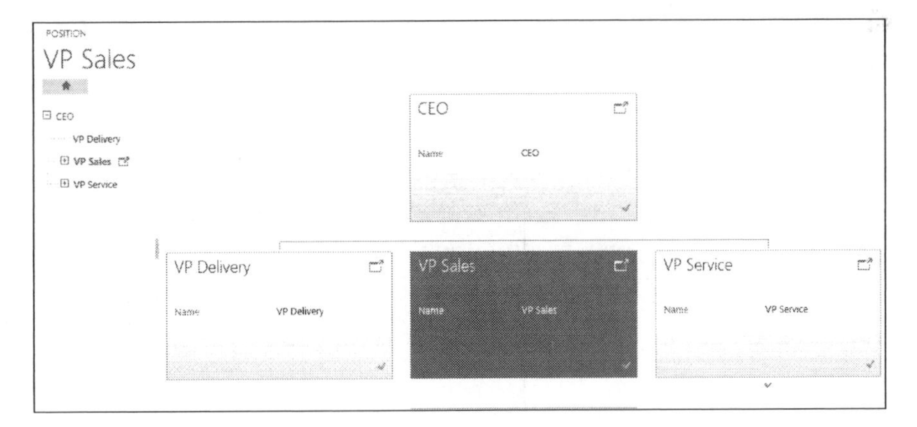

The **Team** section allows us to define and manage teams in the system. Defining a team involves naming the team, assigning it to a particular business unit, defining who the team administrator is - by default the user creating the team - as well as determining and assigning the team members. Once a team is created, going to **Manage Roles** allows us to associate one or more security roles to the team.

The **Business Units** area allows us to customize various Business Units and their relationships. Within every Dynamics CRM Organization there is one main Business Unit created on organization creation. Additional Business Units can be added as children of this main Business Unit, or children of its children.

With the Business Unit structure, we can create a tree structure of parent-child Business Units. The purpose of using Business Units is mainly for security modelling. As part of configuring security roles, permissions allows you to configure access as follows:

- None Selected
- User
- Business Unit
- Parent: Child Business Units
- Organization

The **Hierarchy Security** area is again a new feature introduced with Dynamics CRM 2015. It provides hierarchical visibility and it is based on the user/manager relationships defined on the user accounts. Using this new structure allows configuration for read, update, append, and append do for a direct manager, as well as read permissions to roles above the direct manager. Using this relationship, we can create views showing activities of all the subordinate roles for presentation on dashboards and reports.

In this section, we can enable or disable using this feature. If enabled, we can define the hierarchical model by selecting either a direct Manager Hierarchy or a Custom Position Hierarchy, as well as the maximum depth for analysis. We can also define entity exclusions so that we only capture the relevant types of records:

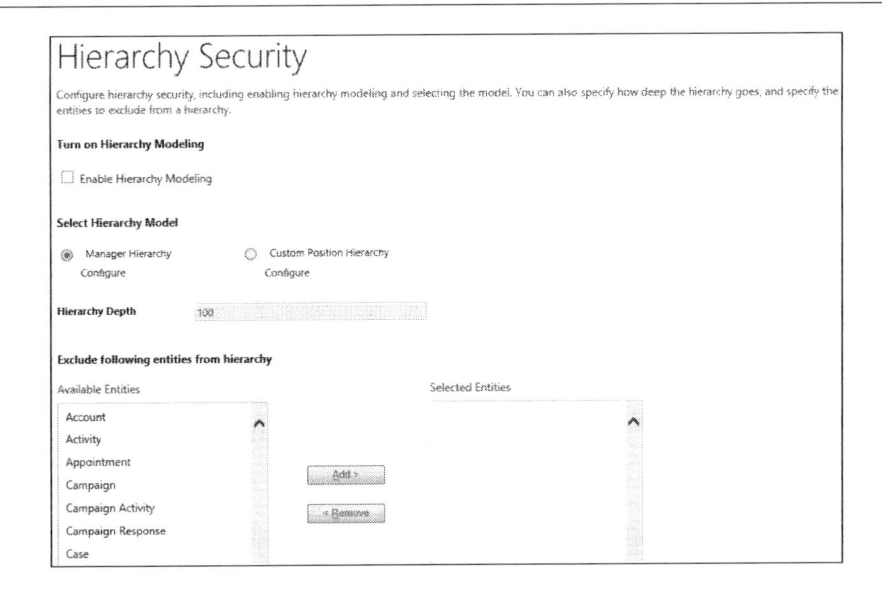

The **Access Team Templates** is where we define and manage templates for **Access Teams**. When creating these templates, we must define the entity related as well as the permissions. You can select one or more access rights to allocate to each template.

Note that once a team template has been added, the associated entity needs to be updated. The entity main form must be customized to include the new **Team Template**.

The access team templates are used in relation to entities enabled for automatic creation of access teams:

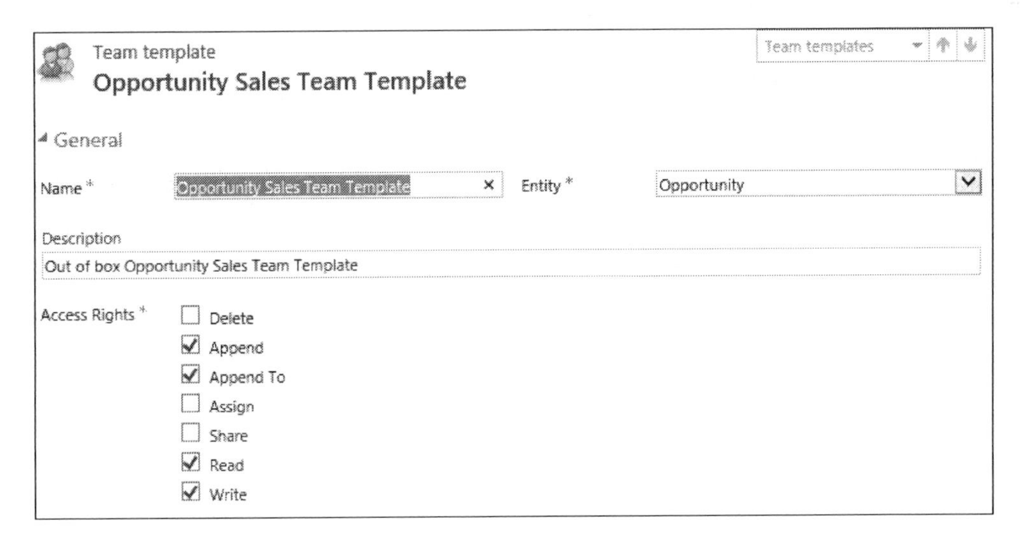

Data Management

The **Data Management** section is found under **Settings | System**. It is here that we configure Duplicate Detection rules and jobs, do bulk record deletion, manage mapping of imported data, as well as manage import jobs. We can also load or remove the sample data for development environments from here:

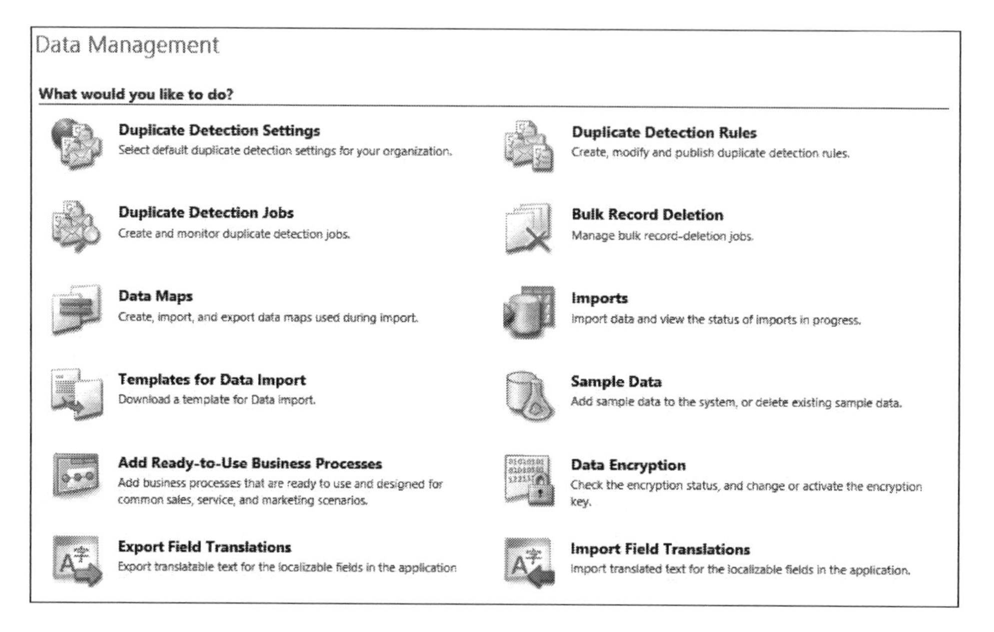

Working with Data

The **Duplicate Detection Settings** area allows us to enable or disable duplicate detection, and has options for some of the most common scenarios when duplicate detection should run. We can check for duplicates on record create and update, on Outlook, going offline and back online, as well as during data import.

In the **Duplicate Detection Rules** area, we have the ability to enable some of the out of the box rules provided, or create new rules and update existing ones. For a rule to be active, it must be published. When editing rules, you must have unpublished the rule first, make the necessary modifications, and then publish the rule again to make it available to all users.

The **Duplicate Detection Jobs** section allows a user to see existing duplicate detection jobs and the status of each job, as well as create new jobs manually. Here we have the option to select various views from a listing of six default system views. We can filter by jobs completed, jobs in progress, jobs not started, and recurring jobs. We can also filter by jobs belonging to the current user.

The **Bulk Record Deletion** section shows a listing of system jobs and the status of each job. You can navigate to a particular job to get more details.

The **Data Maps** area allows us to manage the saved maps for data import. Here we see a listing of existing data maps. We have a choice of views, with filters for active, inactive, and personal data maps.

The **Imports** area is where we can see the current and past import jobs as well as the result status. Various views allow us to select and display the data based on predefined filters, including a listing of all imports, filtered by status or personal imports only.

The **Templates for Data Import** area is where we can extract templates for all the entities in the system. We are presented here with the option to select the entity we need an import template for, and the ability to download it. We can use these templates to create new sets of data for import.

The **Sample Data** section allows us to populate our organization with sample data, or remove this sample data. The sample data provided by Microsoft is just a subset of populated record. We can use this sample data for testing or demonstrating the functionality of the system.

Add Ready-to-Use Business Processes is an addition coming with Dynamics CRM 2015. This will add to the system a set of predefined business processes. These can be used as a starting point for future customizations, or we can use them as such if relevant. Once they are added, we can manage them along with all other custom business processes, as described in *Chapter 4, Building Better Business Functionality*.

All these processes are installed as part of a solution named **Business Processes**. In order to remove these business processes, you can uninstall this managed solution.

The **Data Encryption** section is where we can check, change, or activate the encryption key. This is only available for Organizations configured to use HTTPS.

The **Export Field Translations** and **Import Field Translations** section is where we can manage translatable text for the various languages configured in our Organization. Exporting the translations allows us to download a zipped package containing two XML files:

Name	Type	Size
[Content_Types]	XML File	1 KB
CrmFieldTranslations	XML File	117 KB

The first file, called `[Content_Types].xml`, contains the type definition, while the second file, called `CrmFieldTranslations.xml`, contains the actual field definitions for each locale.

Data Loader Service

The Data Loader Service has been released with Microsoft Dynamics CRM Online 2016 as a preview feature. As such, this functionality is intended for early access, and is not recommended for production use. It is expected that not all functionality is complete. There is no official support provided for preview features. This feature is released only for North America in preview.

As a result of the multiple challenges customers are facing with regards to initial data migration and load scenarios, the Microsoft Dynamics team has taken the task to create a cloud-based Data Loader service. This is targeted to Dynamics CRM Online for now. For the purpose of the preview released at the end of 2015, only the import operation is supported, with export scheduled to follow soon.

This feature support Dynamics CRM 2015 online update 1 and newer versions.

The advantages of this include the ability to quickly configure data import scenarios, no custom code required, and support for bulk data loads, as well as the availability of this tool at no additional cost to the organization owners.

This feature is enabled by default in all new organizations, and is available to users with an Administrator role. It can be accessed through the Lifecycle Services site, available at the following URL:

`https://lcs.dynamics.com/DataLoader/Index`

Configuring the Data Loader Service

In order to configure the Data Loader Service for integration with your Dynamics CRM organization, the following steps must be executed:

- **Deploy the runtime for your Dynamics CRM organization**: This is where you configure your organization.
- **Configure the file format**: As the name states, here you configure the type of file and the specifics. You can choose the delimiter, wrap character, and comment character. You can also configure regional settings here.

With these configurations in place, you are now ready to start importing data. You can now create your field map and start an import. The job execution status is presented in real time, and shows the progress.

The **Data Quality Service** (**DQS**) helps with validating the following two things:

- Metadata
- Look up

Depending on the volume of data, this can take a while. Parallel validation on various entity imports is available.

When validation errors occur, the data can be corrected by exporting to Excel the records that fail, fixing the data and re-importing. This functionality is very much in line with the existing data import features already available on the platform.

Monitoring System Jobs

System jobs, also known as asynchronous operations, are the way to create and manage the execution of asynchronous system operations. These operations include the execution of workflows, plugins running asynchronously, or other background jobs. These operations are managed in the database through records in the **asyncoperation** entity:

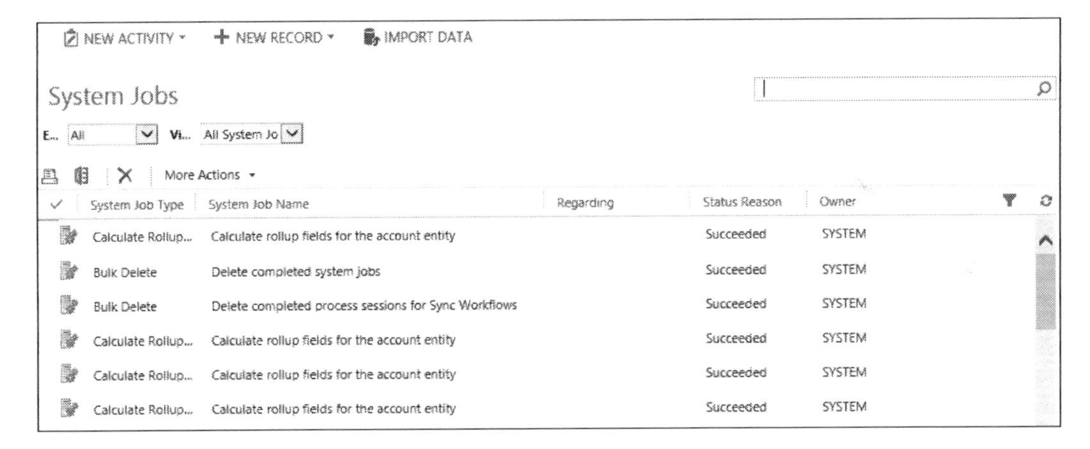

You can filter the view of jobs by entity, and also by using the predefined system jobs views available. These include a listing of all jobs, as well as jobs by status. This makes it easier to find a particular job you are looking for.

Opening a particular job, we can see, besides status details about the owner of the job, the time it was created and completed. For jobs that fail and are set to automatically retry, we have a retry count presented on the job details also:

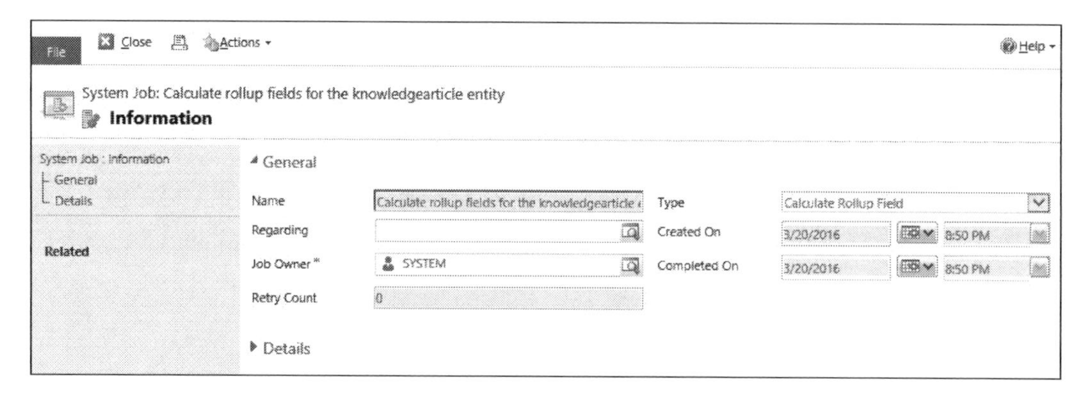

Document Management

The **Document Management** area allows us to configure SharePoint integration. Integrating Dynamics CRM with SharePoint this way provides additional functionality for document management. We can now start to take advantage of all the document versioning features of SharePoint, as well as check-out and check-ins, and auditing:

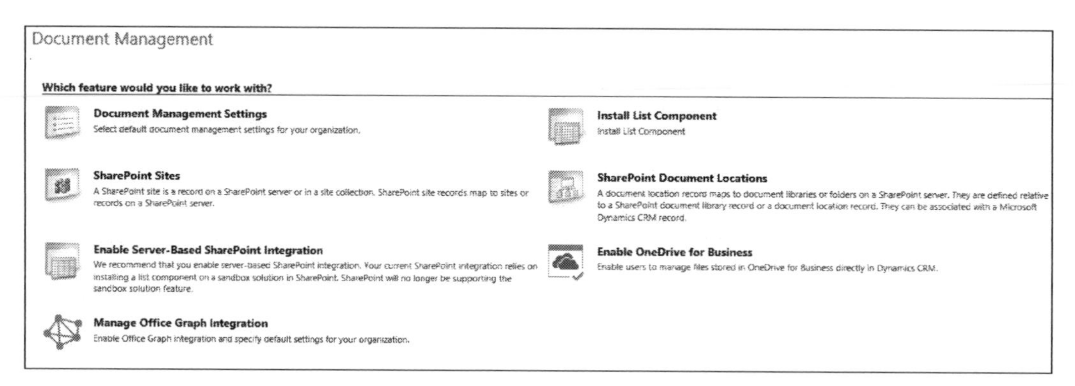

In order to configure the SharePoint integration, the following steps need to be followed.

First off, on the **Document Management** area we have a link to **Install List Component**. This takes us to the **Download Centre** where we can get the **List Component**. This is a SharePoint component that must be installed on the SharePoint server we intend to use for the integration. We select a SharePoint site collection we want to use for integration, and we deploy this component in there. In order to install this, you must be a site collection administrator.

Once this is done, we can go to **Document Management Settings** and follow the wizard to configure the integration. We must provide the URL to our SharePoint site collection, select the entities that will be integrated, and the format is which automatic folder creation will take place on the SharePoint end.

If during the configuration the wizard detects that the site you are pointing to is not a SharePoint site, or the **List Component** is not installed, you will be prompted.

SharePoint Sites allows us to see which integration points are configured. You can have multiple SharePoint sites configured in your environment.

SharePoint Document Locations lists for us all the configured document locations in the system. We can manage from here all locations, add new ones, and modify or remove existing ones.

We can configure SharePoint integration to either automatically let CRM create the structure on SharePoint, we can customize the creation process so that we follow specific business rules around how to create the folder structure on SharePoint, or we can point each record individually to a specific document library and folder on SharePoint.

Added with Dynamics CRM 2016, we now also have the ability to integrate with OneDrive for Business. This allows for private document storage, and is part of the new feature set added for Dynamics CRM Online and Office 365.

Once work is completed on a document in OneDrive and is ready to be released to all system users, the document storage can be changed to SharePoint. At that point the document becomes publicly shared with all users that can access the record, and all the SharePoint editing features are now available.

Another new and notable feature added with this version and based on the Office 365 functionality is the Office Graph integration. This allows for surfacing of relevant documents on a dashboard that can include a stream of tiles generated and ordered through a very complex algorithm that analyzes document relationships and relevance.

The integration of Office Graph is one of the features that has been receiving lots of attention recently. Its integration into Dynamics CRM is a welcome addition. This functionality is targeted at analyzing the entire workplace, by analyzing trends and relevance, and surfacing documents and information based on various complex analysis algorithms.

Machine Learning is at the core of Office Graph. It allows integration with all features wrapped into Office 365, including groups, mail, calendar, events, and documents, as well as information from outside the organization. Content is being analyzed, organized, sorted, and surfaced as needed. This kind of intelligence is expected to drive more features in the future, in order to streamline performance processes and optimize the workplace of tomorrow.

Auditing

Dynamics CRM allows extensive auditing down to the field level. This can be enabled on any organization. Careful attention should be given to how much we need to audit, as this can have a negative impact on both performance and data storage. The more you audit, the more space you will require for the audit logs:

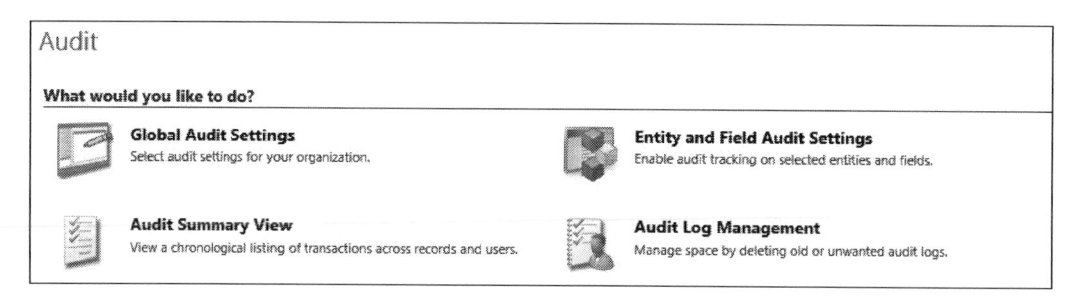

In the **Audit** area we have options to globally enable or disable auditing, configure auditing at the entity and field level, and manage and review the audit logs.

Global Audit Settings is where we can enable or disable auditing and configure auditing for the main modules in the system. This takes us back to System Settings, which we have reviewed earlier in this chapter.

The **Entity and Field Audit Settings** area takes us to the configuration of the Default Solution. Here we can go to each entity and manage auditing settings.

The **Audit Summary View** presents the audit log in a way that allows us to sort and filter in order to easily retrieve the specific records we are looking for. Same-view management functions apply just like any other view in the system.

The last option, the **Audit Log Management**, allows us to present a listing of all the logs, with the start and end dates. For managing space, we can remove older logs from this view.

E-mail configuration

This section of the **Settings** area allows us to configure the type of e-mail integration used, and to manage the various integration points and methods:

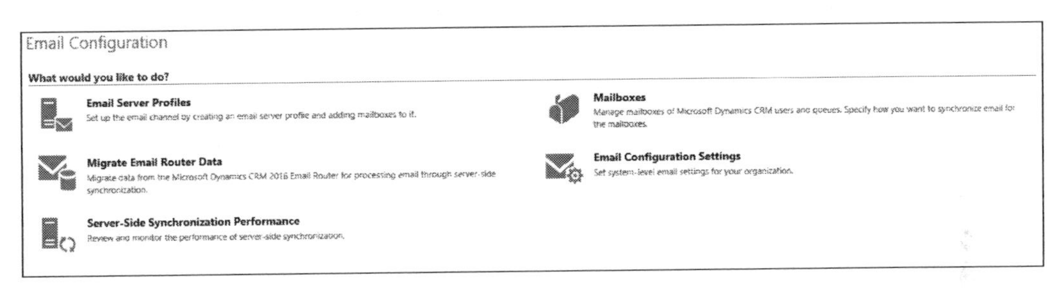

The **Email Configuration Settings** section allows us to configure global settings for e-mail. This leads us back to the System Settings area, which we covered earlier in this chapter.

The **Migrate Email Router Data** area allows us to move our configuration from the E-mail router to the new Server-Side Synchronization available. For this functionality to work, you must have the old E-mail Router available, as well as the new **Server-Side Synchronization** enabled and configured, and the organization must be using HTTPS.

The **Email Server Profiles** section allows us to configure one or more profiles for e-mail handling. We can configure both exchange and POP3-SMTP servers for integration with Dynamics CRM. This allows us to cover configuration for various types of e-mail servers, including public e-mail service from other third-party providers.

For Exchange configuration, as long as the Exchange server is in the same domain as our Dynamics CRM environment, we can use the **Auto Discover Server Location** option, which simplifies the configuration process.

For each profile created, we need to configure the authentication rules, either by using specified credentials, windows integrated authentication, or anonymous, where supported. We can also specify same or separate credentials to be used for incoming and outgoing.

Once a profile is created, we can manage related mailboxes from within the profile or separately.

The **Mailboxes** area allows us to manage individual mailboxes separately. For each mailbox, we can configure the synchronization method as either using an **Email Server Profile** already created, or include specific settings for incoming and outgoing e-mails, as well as appointment, contacts, and tasks. When an **Email Server Profile** is not being used, we can specify to use Microsoft dynamics for Outlook, Server-Side Synchronization, or E-mail Router or a Forward Mailbox as needed. We can do this for both incoming and outgoing messages. For the other items to be synchronized, including Appointment, Contacts, and Tasks, the only available options are Microsoft Dynamics CRM for Outlook or Server-Side Synchronization.

Note that the E-mail Router does not support synchronizing Appointments, Contacts, and Tasks.

Once a mailbox is configured, and the e-mail is approved, we can test and enable the mailbox by clicking on the ribbon on **Test & Enable Mailbox**:

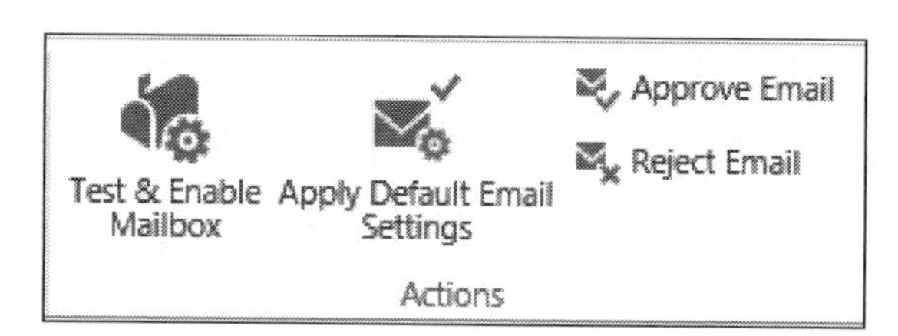

This runs a validation process, and returns status messages regarding the success of your configuration. The process to test the configuration runs asynchronously, which can result in a slight delay before the actual result is displayed. You will first be prompted that the test has been scheduled. Once it's completed, you will get the final results.

Added with Dynamics CRM 2016, the **Server-Side Synchronization Performance** area allows administrators to monitor the performance of this functionality, as well as review various messages. It is a dashboard collecting details on Mailboxes, as well as errors and processing statuses.

Configuring Activity Feeds

The configuration of Activity Feeds is grouped in two separate menus on the **Settings** ribbon. They are as follows:

- **Activity Feeds Configuration**
- **Activity Feeds Rules**

Activity Feeds Configuration

The **Activity Feeds Configuration** is where we get access to all the active and inactive Post Configurations. There are individual records for each entity that has Activity Feeds enabled. Each **Post Configuration** record contains a reference to the entity it applies to, a setting for enabling or disabling the activity feeds wall, and a grid with all the specific rules and their respective status, as they apply to this entity.

Activity Feeds Rules

Using the **Activity Feeds Rules** section, we can get to a listing of all the rules configured in the system. The default view is the **All Activity Feeds Rules**, which presents information about the rule and the entity it references, as well as the status. Each rule must be enabled for it to participate in processing. We can enable or disable rules as needed at different times.

CRM App for Outlook

Newly added with Dynamics CRM 2016 Online, the CRM App for Outlook allows us to surface Dynamics CRM details directly into **Outlook Web Access** (**OWA**). When accessing Outlook directly from the browser, we are now presented with a view into Dynamics CRM if configured as such, and we have the ability to track information and interact with the CRM functionality without the need for the Outlook client and the CRM for Outlook plugin.

This functionality is not meant to completely replace the CRM for Outlook functionality, but provides features that allow online clients to work with Dynamics CRM records and data using a light client.

Details of this functionality have been covered in *Chapter 4, Building Better Business Functionality*.

Process Center

The **Process Center** area allows us to get the configured Business Processes in our Organization. We can filter and sort the view as needed to find the process we need to verify. The status is also presented on this view. A process must be activated to participate in processing, and must be put in **Draft** while modifying it. Options to **Activate** and **Deactivate** are presented on the ribbon.

We can create new processes from here. Processes include **Business Process Flows**, **Workflows**, **Dialogs** or **Actions**. These were all described in detail in *Chapter 4, Building Better Business Functionality*:

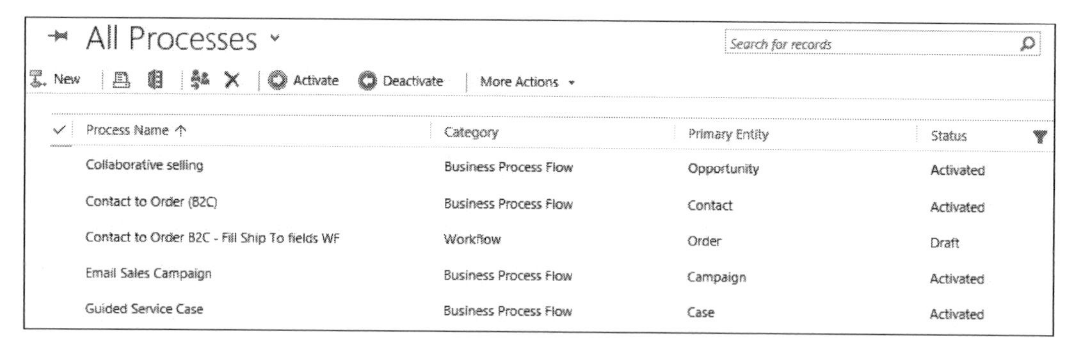

Process Name	Category	Primary Entity	Status
Collaborative selling	Business Process Flow	Opportunity	Activated
Contact to Order (B2C)	Business Process Flow	Contact	Activated
Contact to Order B2C - Fill Ship To fields WF	Workflow	Order	Draft
Email Sales Campaign	Business Process Flow	Campaign	Activated
Guided Service Case	Business Process Flow	Case	Activated

If the set of predefined Business Processes were added from **Data Management** in the **Add Ready-to-Use Business Processes**, they will also be available to activate or deactivate from the **Process Center**. These processes are not editable though. If you want to make modifications, you must disable the original process, save it as a new process, and then you can start modifying it. Once done, re-activate the process:

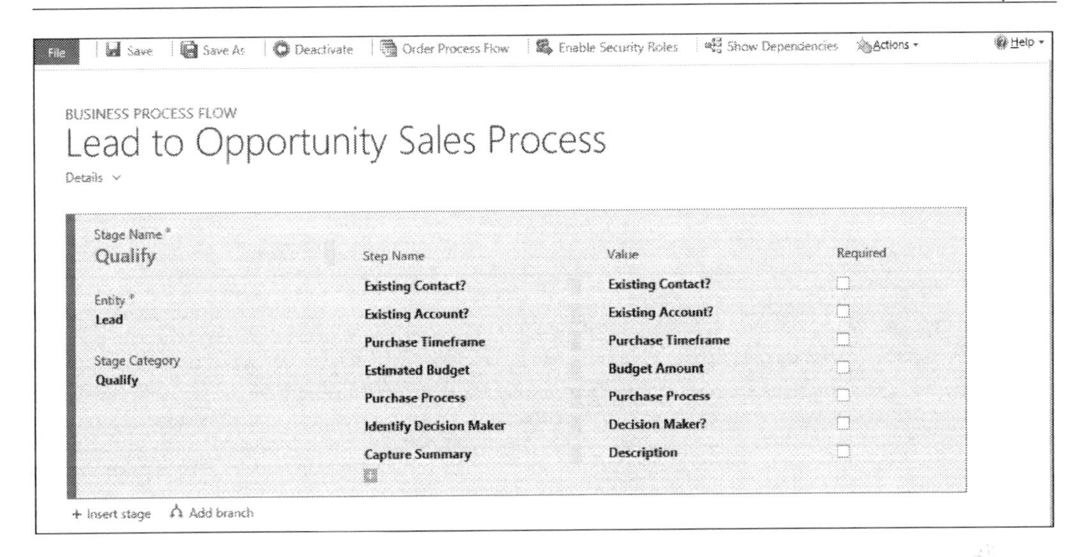

Dynamics Marketplace

The **Dynamics Marketplace** is the App Store for Microsoft Dynamics CRM. Here, partners and **independent software vendors (ISVs)** can commercialize their specific applications and solution extensions. The concept was introduced since Dynamics CRM 2011, and is meant to simplify the process of selling solutions for Dynamics CRM and provide a common area for all solutions to be made available. While this is a good concept, not all ISVs commercialize their solutions through the Dynamics Marketplace.

The **Dynamics Marketplace** is a searchable repository from within your Dynamics CRM Organization. You can filter the results by popularity, by date, or you can navigate to the online repository:

The online repository is powered by **Microsoft Pinpoint**. Navigating to the repository allows us further sorting and filtering capability by business-specific need, by industry, price, version of Dynamics CRM, and by whether the solution is **Certified for Microsoft Dynamics** or not.

Looking at a particular solution in detail, we can see an extensive description of the solution, whether it is available for purchase or free, the business need, and the versions of Dynamics CRM it is compatible with. We can also see the community rating, which should give us pretty good feedback about how successful the solution is with other users:

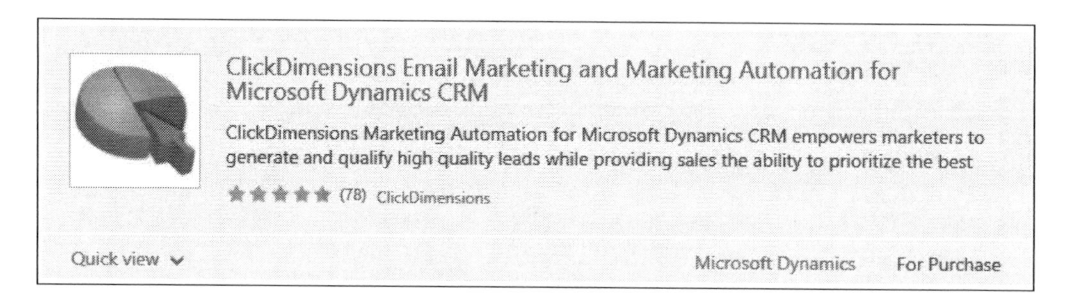

Expand the **Quick view** to get access to the additional details.

Customization Principles

The **Customization** area is where we get access to all the developer options and the management of deployed solutions:

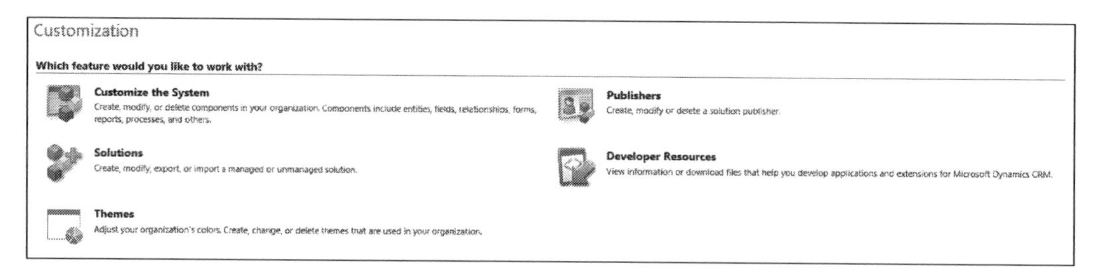

From this area, we can get access to the default solution by selecting **Customize the System**. For customizations that need to be ported to other environments, they should not be done under this section, as they will need to be repackaged later at higher effort and cost. The base solution includes all the components that come standard with the system. Also, when deploying unmanaged solutions, those customizations are merged into the base solution.

The **Publishers** section allows us to manage and configure solution publishers in our organization. All solutions have a publisher associated.

The **Developer Resources** is where we find specific developer information about our organization. Here we have access to the online **Developer Center**, as well as details about the organization-specific endpoints. We can see the **Discovery Service** URL and **Organization Service** URL, as well as the **Organization Data Service**, and the protocols used for each.

The **Solutions** area links us back to the same solution management that is accessible directly from the **Settings | Solutions** ribbon menu.

Finally, the **Themes** area is one of the newer features. This allows some level of branding for the application. Here we can start customizing the core colors, as well as define a corporate logo. The level of branding functionality is reduced. This is not a portal solution, and as such, branding should be kept at minimum, if added at all.

Solutions

The **All Solutions** area is where we manage the various solutions deployed to our organization. We use the ribbon elements to organize the existing solutions, remove solutions or deploy new ones:

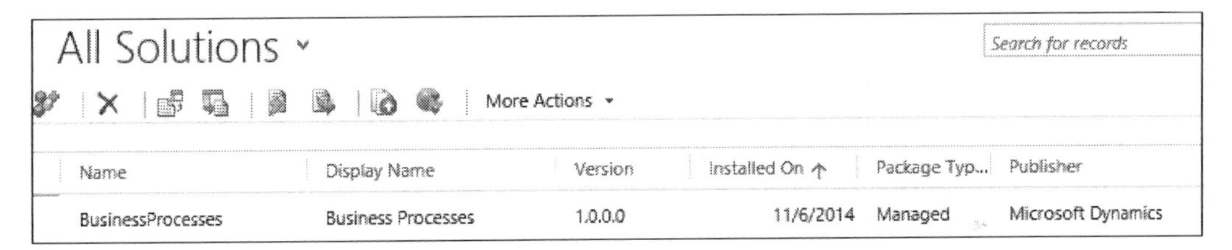

We have covered in **Customizing Entities**, the details of working with solutions in *Chapter 3, Dynamics CRM Customization.*

From the **All Solutions** area, we can also export unmanaged solutions, import new solutions as needed, and export and import translations across the entire organization.

Working with Business Units

The **Business Units** concept is at the core of security model in Microsoft Dynamics CRM. As such, all users will be part of a Business Unit. The structure includes a default Business Unit, created when an Organization is created. From there, child Business Units can be created as needed, resulting in a tree structure as complex as designed. The following screenshot shows a parent Business Unit, with two child ones (**IT** and **Finance**), and **IT** has another three child Business Units (**Cloud**, **Delivery** and **Infrastructure**):

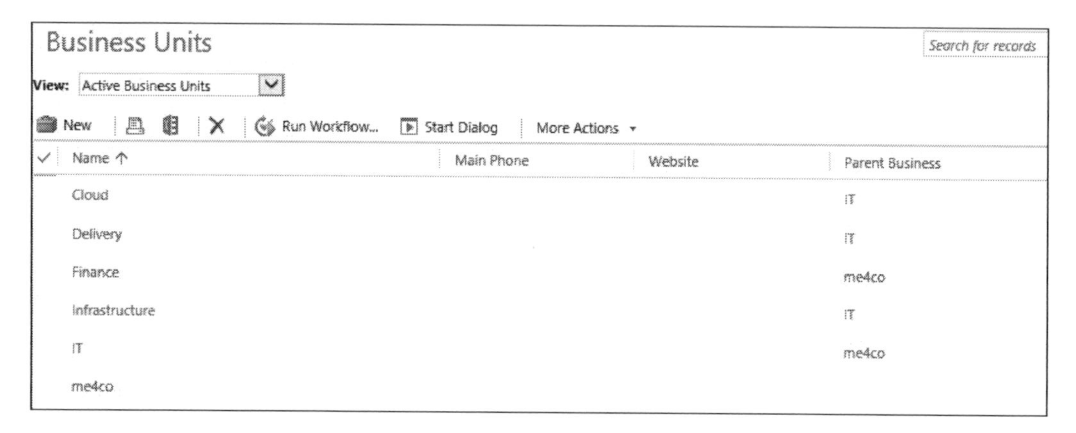

The Root Business Unit is the top-most Business Unit, and it is the one created with the Organization by default. As a rule, there always is a Business Unit in an Organization, and that is the Root Business Unit. This Business Unit cannot be removed or disabled, and is the container that allows transferring security settings with solution packages from one organization to another.

The ribbon depicted in the above screenshot has the necessary commands to create a new Business Unit and remove a Business Unit, as well as a few other options for enable/disable and changing the **Parent Business Unit** under the **More Actions** drop-down.

Defining Security Roles

Once you have the Business Units defined in your organization, the next step is to start configuring the necessary Security Roles. A **Security Role** is a collection of privileges to various components of the organization. Entities and other security elements are grouped in categories, and presented on various tabs. The following screenshot presents the settings for the **Core Records** tab:

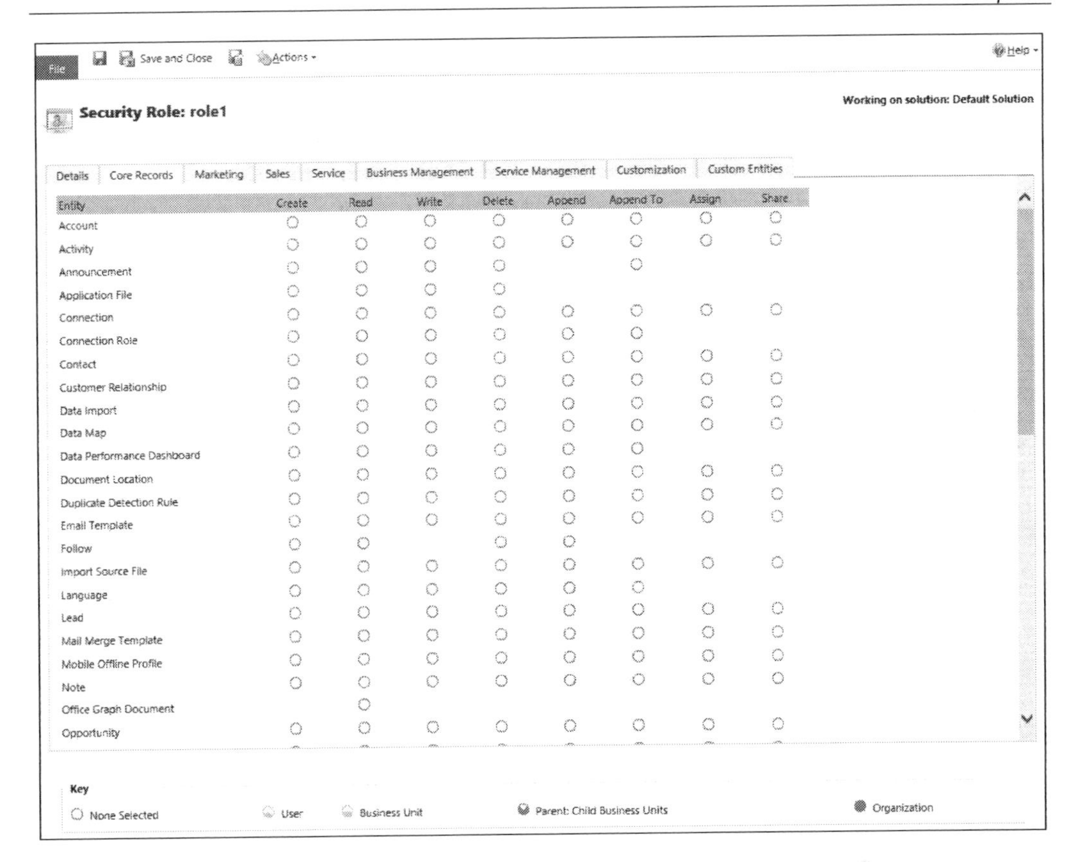

Observe how for each entity we have the various options to configure **Create**, **Read**, **Write**, **Delete**, **Append**, **Append To**, **Assign**, and **Share** permissions. In addition, at the bottom of the screen we can see the representation for the scope. We can give no permissions at all, or permission at the **User** level, **Business Unit**, **Parent: Child Business Unit**, or the entire **Organization**. Each scope is larger than the previous one, and is represented as such through the graphical filling of the circle symbol.

When creating new security roles, always create them within a Solution package, so they can be transferred over to another environment with ease. In addition, in many cases, it is easier to start from one of the existing or default security roles, by saving it as a new role and making modifications to it as needed.

These Security Roles now can be used to assign permissions to users and teams, to configure role-based forms, and so on.

Managing Users and Teams

Once we have the Business Units and Security Roles defined, it's time to start configuring users and teams. The process varies a little bit between an Online deployment versus an On-Premise deployment with regards to the steps to be performed when adding a user to an Organization, but once that's done, assigning roles and permissions is the same.

Creating a new User

In an On-Premise deployment, the process to create a new user is based on the domain account of the user. When adding a user, provide in the user name field the domain\username as configured in **Active Directory** (**AD**). If the user is found, the AD details for the user are brought over and populate the user form.

When adding a user to an Online organization, the process starts from the Office 365 portal:

1. Navigate to **Users** | **Active Users**, and select the user you want to add to your Microsoft Dynamics CRM Organization.
2. Once the user is selected, find the Assigned licenses on the right-hand side, and click on **Edit**.
3. In the tab that slides out, make sure that **Microsoft Dynamics CRM Online Professional** license is checked.
4. You will see a message showing the available number of licenses for the current organization. The following screenshot shows this:

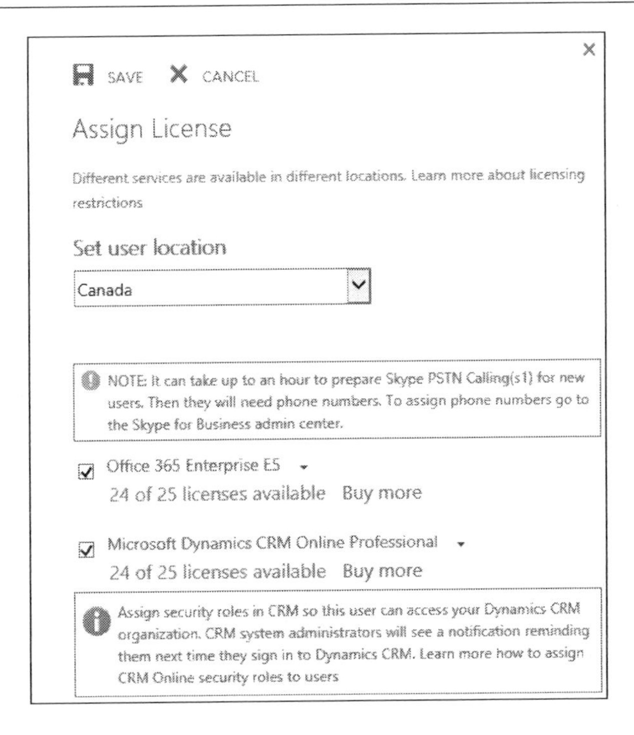

5. Click on **Save** once done. Now the user is assigned a license for the Microsoft Dynamics CRM Online instance.

Alternatively, you can assign a license directly when creating the user on the Office 365 admin portal. You find a section at the bottom of the new user form to select licenses for the user.

Once the user is assigned a license, within the organization's **Settings** area, go to **Security** | **Users**. Make sure the newly added user shows up in this view, if not, refresh the view.

With a user added to the **Enabled Users** list, now we need to assign this user the necessary permissions to access the Organization data. If a user does not have permissions assigned, he/she will not be able to access the Organization, even if he/she does have an account active. Select the user and click the **Manage Roles** ribbon button. In the pop-up window, select the role(s) to assign, and click **OK**, as shown in the following screenshot:

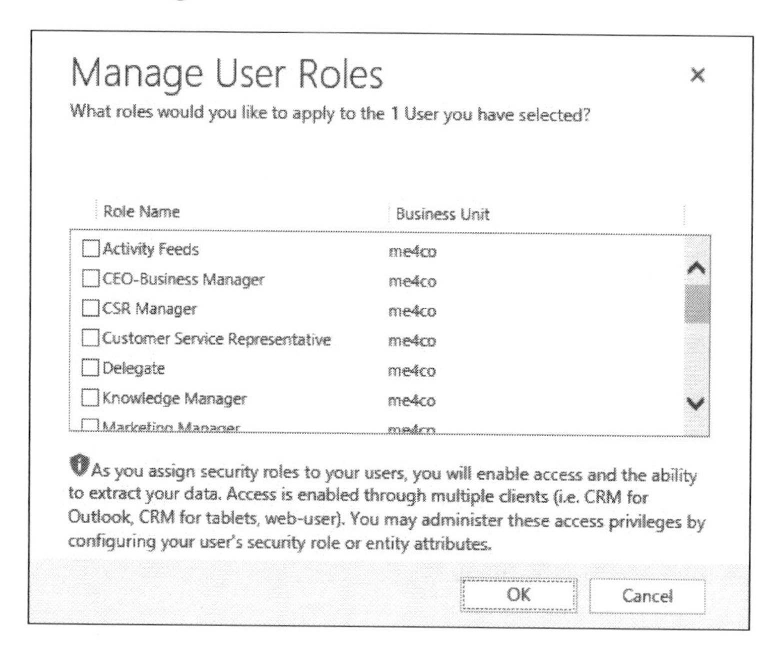

Now we have a user added, a security role assigned, and permissions assigned. By default, the root business unit is assigned to the user, but that can be changed from the user profile page if needed, or by selecting the **Change Business Unit** ribbon button.

Once a user does not need to use the system anymore, the user can be disabled. For Dynamics CRM On-Premise, this is done from the ribbon on the Enabled Users view. In Dynamics CRM Online, you will not have the Disable/Enable button. You can disable a user from the Office 365 portal by removing the license from the user profile.

Mobile Experience

Microsoft Dynamics CRM has been supporting various mobile experiences for a few versions now. Starting with the original mobile page, which was nothing more than a stripped down basic form designed for small screens and presenting reduced functionality, to newer and more robust specific mobile applications that allow us to work not only with various mobile screen sizes, but also provide support for various mobile platforms. We now have applications for the most common platforms, including Windows Phone, IOS, and Android, for both phones and tablets.

This mobile applications interface has been streamlined and standardized, and now it presents a familiar experience across all devices and platforms.

New for Dynamics CRM 2016, this experience has been enhanced again through the addition of the following:

- **Custom Controls**: These controls help create an intuitive experience for users and align with modern standards of visual representation of elements. They are also designed specifically for touch, thus making the experience a more pleasant one.
- **Form Preview for mobile devices**: This feature has been added to assist system customizers and developers in visualizing how their changes and customizations will end up looking on a mobile device.
- **Support for iFrame and web resource**: These are typical customizations that until now have only been available in the desktop browser-rendered application. Now support for these has been added to the mobile applications, thus opening the door to a richer and more elegant experience on mobile platforms.

The following screenshot shows this interface on both a tablet (left) and a mobile device (right):

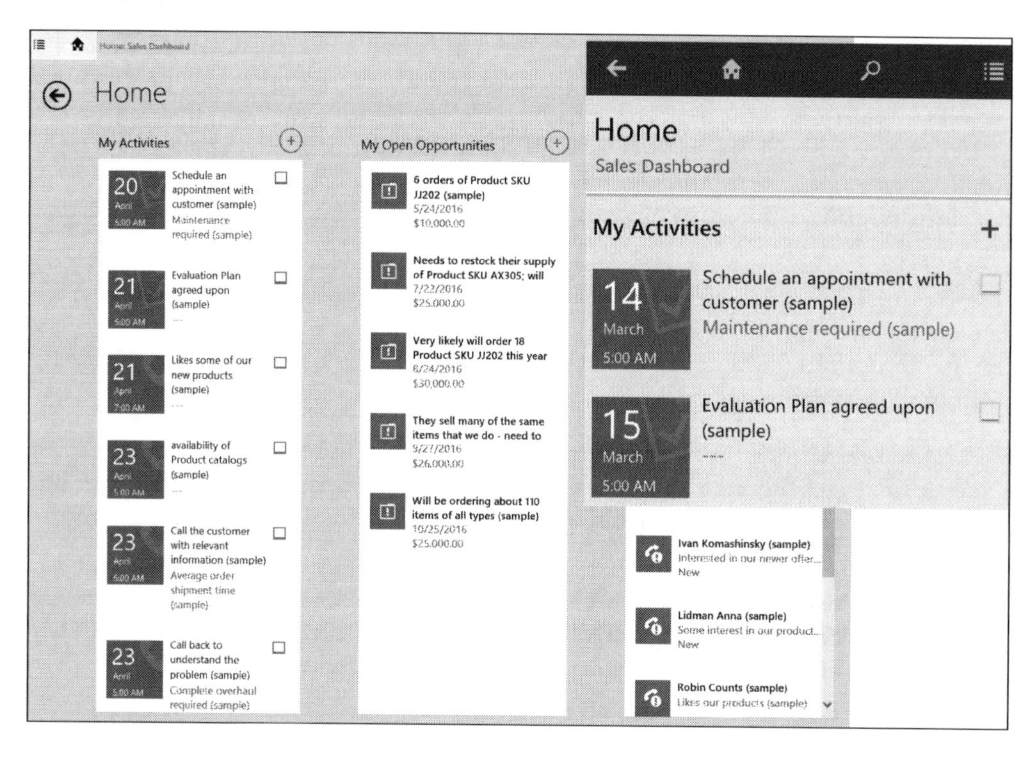

Cortana for CRM

Cortana for CRM is another one of the preview features added with the Microsoft Dynamics CRM online 2016 update. As such, it must be enabled explicitly from **Settings** | **Administration** | **System Settings**. On the **Previews** tab, make sure that the license agreement check box is checked, and then find the Cortana for CRM section and enable it by selecting the **Yes** radio button.

> Note that preview features are not supported by Microsoft support, as they might have incomplete features. Extensive changes can be made to preview features before they are released for production use.

The Cortana for CRM functionality is meant to assist system users in keeping track of various activities in CRM. The following entities are exposed through this integration:

- Activities
- Accounts
- Opportunities

Once the configuration is in place, Cortana will prompt organization users to connect to CRM. The process is simplified to the point where the client-side configuration is simply a matter of following the prompts.

Once configured on a user's device, Dynamics CRM is added to Cortana's notebook, and reminders, prompts, and data are made available for voice interaction.

Summary

Throughout this chapter, we had a high level look at the administration areas of Dynamics CRM. While this is not an in-depth presentation of all the available administration options, because we can dedicate a whole book to this topic, we went through all the available options and looked at what each area is for.

This chapter presented just enough information to get you familiar with the various administration options available with Dynamics CRM, and where to find each option. For in-depth information about each of the particular topics, refer to the SDK available for download for the current version of Dynamics CRM from:

`http://www.microsoft.com/en-us/download/details.aspx?id=44567`

Index

A

B

E

O

P

Q

R

S